# EXPLORING THE OTHER HALF

## CHALLENGES FACED BY WOMEN IN INDIA

SHRADDHA SAROJ & KALPNA GUPTA

*To*

**"HER"**

*Dedicated to all the girls whose voices go unheard*

# Contents

# Contents

# Preface

*The intensity of any issue can be understood either by personally facing it or by trying to understand someone else's perspective. Understanding every aspect of the problem is possible only when there are detailed facts available about it. This book is an attempt to compile the challenges that the Indian women have experienced from centuries and continue to encounter them till date. This book includes real life stories, research papers, review papers, newspaper reports, primary as well as secondary data which tells us the ground reality of the Indian society. This book is written with an aim to draw attention towards these issues and its an attempt to motivate the readers, policy makers and higher authorities to take action to solve these issues at individual and community level and ultimately eradicate them from Indian society.*

*Editor*

# Acknowledgements

***To them that I love and know that I love them!***

*First of all, a heartfelt thanks to all the authors for contributing their time and energy in writing these amazing chapters and patiently cooperating during the whole editing and publishing process. Without you, this mini project of compiling the book would have not been a successful one.*

*Thanks to my guide, Prof. Kalpna Gupta (HOD), Department of Home Science for her unconditional support. She never fails to inspire us, to work hard, to be an honest person and to believe that even sky is not the limit. Her continuance guidance and encouragement acted as a stimulus to compile this book. Thanks to the Home Science Department and Banaras Hindu University, they are the foundation stone behind all the achievements.*

*I would like to thank my darlings, my Mamma and Pappa. You both are my backbone, I will always be grateful to you both for supporting and motivating me to reach greater heights.*

*Thanks to all my teachers who believed in me and moulded me into a confident person. They have always encouraged me to eliminate my weaknesses and work around my strengths.*

*Thank you, all my friends, for holding me up whenever I felt low and making me believe that it was a cakewalk.*

*Thanks to all my lovely students for making my life cheerful and improving my perception of life. Thankyou! for always pushing me to be a better version of myself.*

*I also show my gratitude to all the well-wishers whose names I have missed to mention here, but I would like to remind them that their presence in my life is very important.*

*At last, I would also like to convey my thanks to the Publisher, notion press for making this dream come true.*

*Once again thanks one and all!!!*

# About The Editor

Prof. Kalpna Gupta is currently acting as the Head of the Department of Home Science, Banaras Hindu University, with more than 39 years of experience in teaching and supervision. She has guided several PhD scholars as well as numerous dissertations. She is an energetic Home Scientist and always ready to work for the holistic development of people. Her research interest includes welfare of Girl Child, Parent Education and Divyang Children. She has authored many research papers, review papers and books published at national and international level. Chairperson in International Extention Education Conference on Education Research and Services and National Seminar – "Eco-centric Thought and Action: A Need for Human Existence", sponsored by Department of Higher Education, UP Government. Besides this she had an opportunity to chair the session in 22nd World Congress of Clinical Nutrition.

Shraddha Saroj is presently working as a Senior Research Fellow (SRF) at the Department of Home Science, Banaras Hindu University. Her specialization is in Food Science and Nutrition. She is pursuing her PhD in the field of Clinical Nutrition under the guidance of, Supervisor Prof. Kalpna Gupta, Department of Home Science and Co-Supervisor Dr. D. P. Yadav, Department of Gastroenterology, Institite of Medical Sciences. She has authored 5 research papers and 5 book chapters. She has presented papers at several conferences and seminars.

# Every picture tells a story...

Photo credit: Shraddha

CHAPTER I

# Challenges Faced by Women in Indian Society: An Introduction

*Shraddha Saroj, **Kalpna Gupta, ***Saumya Tiwari, ***Parvati
*Senior Research Fellow, **Professor and Head, ***Research Scholar
Department of Home Science, Banaras Hindu University,
Varanasi, Uttar Pradesh
shradz26@bhu.ac.in

**Bitter but the reality of majority...**

As a girl child, she is dependent on her father,
As an adult, she is dependent on her husband,
During old age, she is dependent on her son,
So, when is she independent?

We continue to live in a male dominated society and India is a perfect example of it. Here, the rule making and decision taking powers lie largely with men. The problem is that in such cases the rules are made in such a way that it favours men.

India claims to be the largest democracy in the world but Indian women are still struggling for their basic rights, ironic isn't? According to oxford dictionary- "Patriarchy is a system of society or government in which men hold the power and women are largely excluded from it".

According to Shraddha, Senior Research Fellow, BHU - Patriarchy is an ideology favouring men, which is conveyed in the form of ideas from generation to generation either verbally, in written form or by practice in the name of culture, tradition etc. and thus end up becoming a way of life followed by both males and females of that particular society.

**PRACTICE OF SATI**

In our country patriarchy has existed from centuries and **Sati Pratha** is an apt example of it. According to Sati Pratha, after the death of the husband, the wife is also burnt alive with the dead body. Many children became orphan losing both the parents due to this practice. **Raja Ram Mohan Roy** and **William Carey** played a significant role in ending Sati Pratha.

Due to some work Raja Ram Mohan Roy had gone abroad and in the meantime his brother died. After which his sister-in-law was burnt alive in the name of Sati. He was deeply hurt by this incident and decided that he will not let this happen again to any other women.

After a persistent battle, finally on **4th December, 1829** Raja Ram Mohan Roy and William Carey persuaded the then governor Lord William Bentick, who declared **Sati as an illegal and criminal offence** in British India. The practice of **polygamy** was also very common in India at that time. William Carey documented, "33 wives of a man were burnt alive at his funeral".

Isn't burning any human being alive inhumane? The practice of Sati was abolished long ago still some of us try to glorify it, as if burning a woman alive is something to be proud of......

**FOETICIDE and INFANTICIDE**

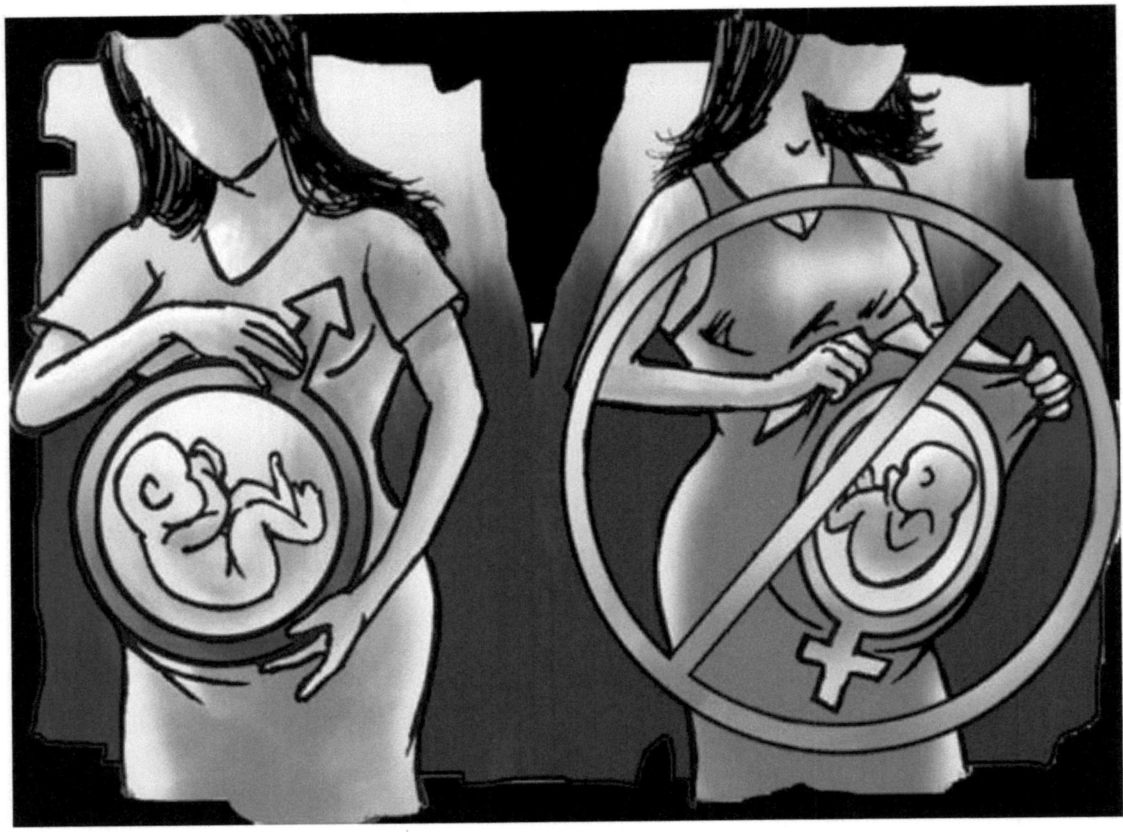

**Fig 1: Depicting female foeticide**

Till date in India people wish to have a son and they continue to give birth until a boy child is born. This practice is more common in middle class and lower socio-economic groups. The way Indians think is reflected in the following statements, "**Ladka hoga to khandan ka naam Roshan karega, Ladki toh paraya dhan hoti hai, Hum ladki se paise nahi le sakte.**" (A boy will take the family's name forward, A girl will get married and leave the family, we can't take money from a girl).

Thirst for a boy child is so strong that it results in determination of sex before the birth of the child which is illegal in India. Laws were made to reduce the practice of foeticide or abortion of the girl child. According to **Pre-conception and Pre-Natal diagnostic technique** (Prohibition of Sex Selection) Act, 1994 commonly called PC-PNDT Act, it is illegal to determine the sex of an unborn child. The law first came into force in 1996 and was amended in 2003, banning practices where medical practitioners try to influence the sex of the child before conception by using techniques such as **sperm sorting** (where a sperm cell is specifically chosen because of its sex chromosome). This act also bans any type of advertisement related to pre-conception and per-determination of sex (Indian Express, 8th June, 2022).

**Under this law till December, 2020 only 617 doctors have been convicted.** Data shows the number of ongoing cases that is 3158. Only 145 medical licences have been suspended or cancelled (Times of India, 25th Dec, 2021). Parliamentary committee on empowerment of women also observed that **18 out of 36 states/UT's have neither got any case registered or have any convictions so far under PC-PNDT Act.**

A report published in economic times on 9th December, 2021 indicates that female foeticide and infanticide are still major issues in India. Omkar Goswami, Chairman, Corporate and Economic Research Group Advisory pointed out that the **global sex ratio at birth (SRB) is 952 girls per 1000 boys** whereas the national censes of 2001 and 2011 indicates that its 915 per 1000 boys which fell to **910 per 1000** boys respectively.

A report was recently registered in Mahoba, Uttar Pradesh against the in-laws of the victim who was **physically assaulted for giving birth to two girl children**. A police case was registered as there was a video recording of physical assault publicly. The victim has been hospitalized (Source: The Indian Express, 8th June 2022).

**MENSTRUATION**

We are living in 2022, but menstruation/menses or periods is still a taboo in our country. Most Indian girls don't know anything about the **menstrual cycle at menarche**. They end up being afraid and confused, unable to discuss about something they themselves don't understand. Many of them have a shameful experience usually in school or at their friends or relatives' home although there is nothing to be shameful about the natural biological process but that how Indian girls are taught to think about it.

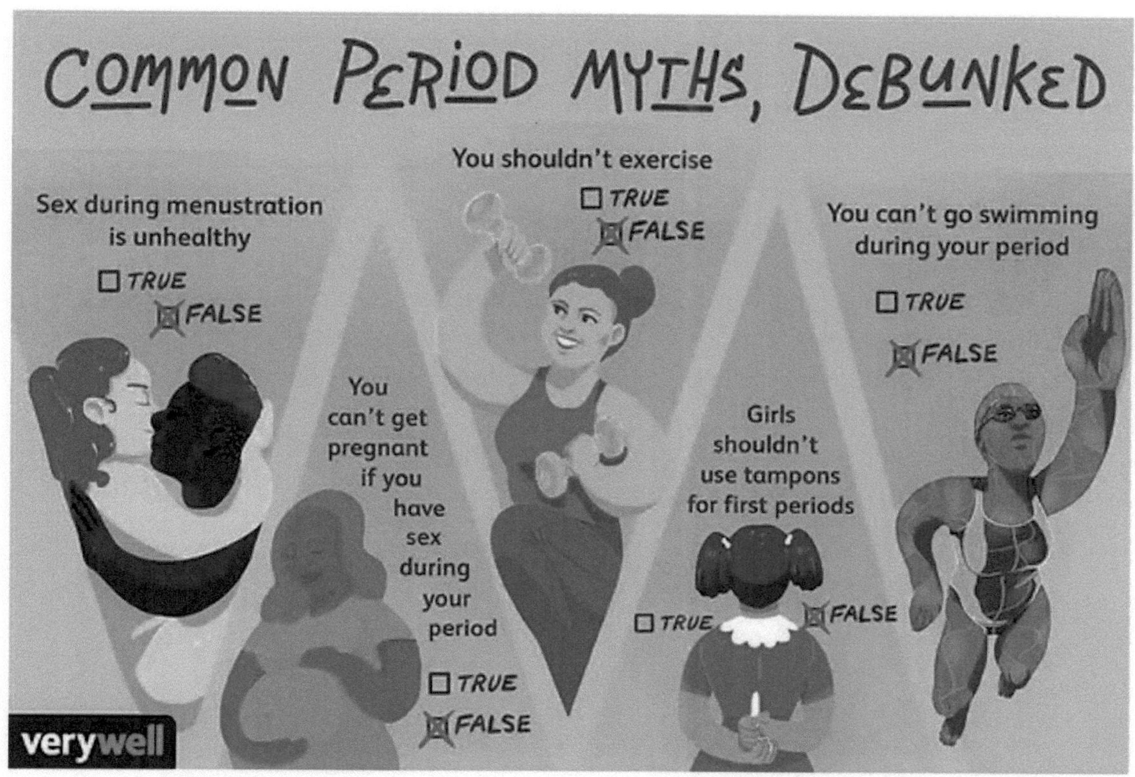


**Fig 2: Depicting common myths associated with menstruation**

**Source:** https://www.verywellhealth.com/period-myths-2721944 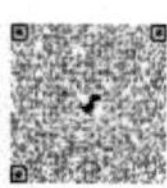

Although there have been mild changes in extreme practices like isolating the person- such as eating and sleeping separately, considering the person impure etc. These practices have reduced (not eradicated) not because of the change in mindset but rather due to urbanization and increase in the number of nuclear families which has made it impossible to isolate if there is a single adult woman in the house who is responsible to take care of every family member. However, such families usually justify their actions by taking the credit of being modern and open minded but in reality, they do it because they don't have a choice.

Till date in majority of Indian families the **males don't have any idea about the menstruation dates of their own wife, sister** etc. They don't have knowledge about the sanitary pads that they should buy in case of an emergency. So far it has remained a forbidden topic to discuss about. Even in the so-called modern families' conditions are horrible, females prefer not to share what they are going through, that's what they are taught to do in this patriarchal society – **'Girl's problem'**. Surprisingly, the famous sanitary pad brand's name **"Whisper" (although an American brand)** means something that has to be spoken softly using one's breath rather than throat as it sharing a secret. Have you ever thought why to – "Whisper"?

**TRAFFICKING**

Human trafficking is another issue severely affecting women and children in India. According to the data obtained from **National Crime Records Bureau (NCRB), 13 persons were victims of human trafficking every day in 2020, out of which 8 were females and 5 were males.**

| Year | Human trafficking cases reported |
|---|---|
| 2018 | 2278 |
| 2019 | 2208 |
| 2020 | 1714 |

**Table 1: Number of human trafficking cases reported under IPC-2020 (NCRB)**

According to Vimal Vidushi, Assistant Prof. College of Education, Ludhiana the major causes of human trafficking include poor socio-economic status, pushing girls into prostitution, annual natural disasters leading to destitution of some families, pressure to collect money for dowry, lack of awareness about the activities of trafficking, domestic violence against women etc.

Promise of better pay and comfortable life, demand for low-wage workers, misconception that physical intimacy with young girls reduces men's chances of contracting HIV/AIDS are some other reasons of trafficking. The increase in the practice of female foeticide in Haryana and Punjab has also fuelled female trafficking cases.

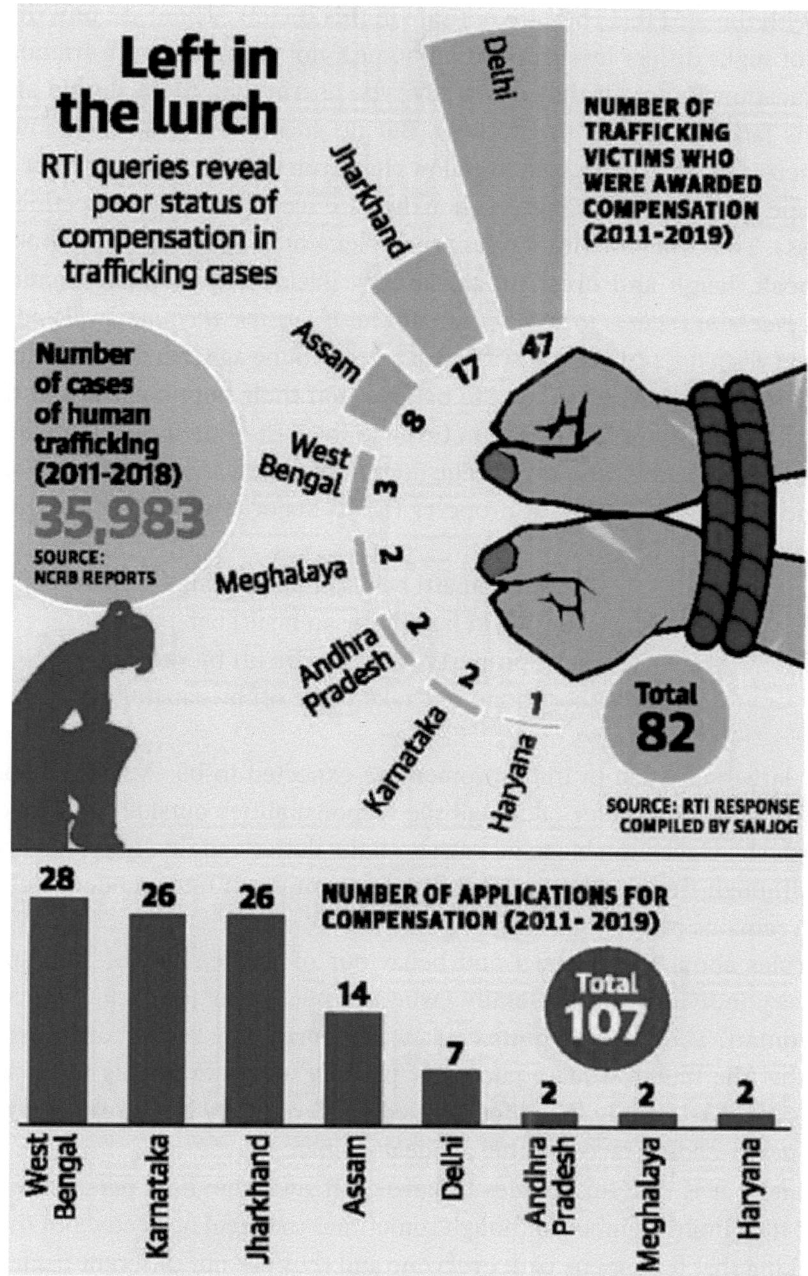


**Fig 3: Shows only 82 human trafficking survivors were awarded relief in the last 8 years.**

**Source: National Crime Records Bureau (NCRB)**

https://www.insightsonindia.com/2020/02/13/insights-into-editorial-only-82-trafficking-survivors-awarded-relief-in-last-8-years/

## UPBRINGING

Girls are brought up with the idea that they are not safe in this society. There are **unwritten rules** like, **not going out at night** (definition of night differs in every Indian home), not going out with friends, on trips, college fests, conferences and even educational tours. If they go on any type of trip then there **should always be a male partner with them** (which means father, husband or brother). But no such rules and regulations are applicable for the dominant half of the society. Girls are motivated to follow these rules by citing example of incidents of kidnapping, sexual assault and even rape. If the girl still disagrees then they are scolded for not respecting their elders and labelled as badtameez (mannerless). Thus, the unwritten rules are implemented by hook or by crook.

How a girl should **speak, laugh and dress** up are already decided in the male dominant part of India. *Male dominance in some of the places in India is to such an extent that if possible then men will end up even making rules for women, when to breathe and when not to.* Girls are trained at a very young age that they should be 'icon of sacrifice and compromise'. **They are subconsciously persuaded to believe that their happiness lies in the happiness of others.** Thus, they are well-trained to adjust in every situation (even at the cost of their own happiness) in order to maintain the family relationships which will otherwise break. The dominating ones are not expected to take this responsibility because they are born and brought up to inherit property rights. Majority of Indian Parents' mindset is reflected in the statements below:

Pita ki sampatti beta sambhalta hai,
Aur pita ki izzat beti sambhalti hai
(Father's property is taken care off by son,
While fathers honour is taken care off by daughters)

## GENDER ROLES

Gender roles are still largely divided in India, women are expected to be expert in household chores and thus labelled as '**housewife**' whereas men prefer taking all the responsibilities outside the house. Even if the woman is economically independent, she is accountable to manage both the duties and finally end up keeping a helper / servant for household chores. Although the females are becoming economically independent but it does not change the mindset of people, which remains patriarchal.

There are some set rules about the conduct and behaviour of women. A girl who speaks less, fulfils all the demands of each and every individual of the family (whether nuclear or joint) and expects nothing in return, is considered as an '**ideal woman**'. Thus, being a **mute** cook, washer man, gate keeper, dishwasher, house cleaner etc...... are just a few activities that the Indian woman performs 'proudly' never expecting to be paid or recognized for it. Their hard work and sincerity are usually taken for granted and even they don't realize it most of the times. Thus, they end up running the never-ending race of being an ideal woman.

Under such circumstances it is rare for females to have their own standing, personality or way of life. Usually, their life revolves around the family members although sometimes they feel neglected but they ultimately accept that as a part of their life thinking that it happens with everyone and they are not different from others.

## MARRIAGE AND DOWRY

Women after reaching the marriageable age must fulfil certain criteria in order to be a suitable choice for becoming bride. Girls who maintain the so-called beauty standards (which are largely decided by men) such as **fair skin** colour and **hour glass figure** are always the first choice for the other party. In order to achieve this, young girls reduce their dietary intake drastically thus, facing vitamins and minerals deficiency (for example: prevalence of Anaemia in India among adult women is 57% as per National Family Health Survey-5).

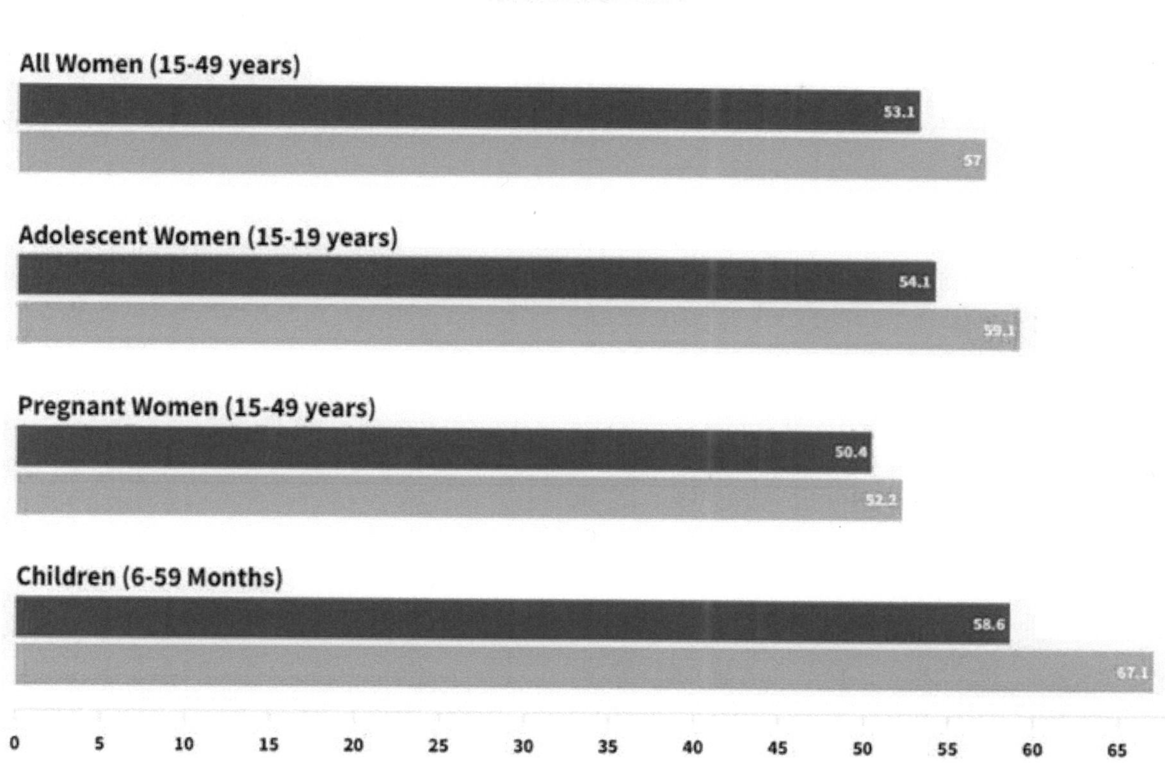


Fig. 4: Prevalence of anaemia among women and children in India

**Source: NFHS 4 & 5**

Young girls admire the film and television stars and always try to follow them so as to look physically attractive. They don't realize that they are professionals and get paid for it, they loose or gain weight in guidance of gym trainers and nutritionists.

Complexion referring to skin tone/colour is another important criterion that has to be kept in mind in general for all the girls but specifically for a bride. Naturally different skin tones are found in India based upon different geographical areas and hereditary factors. Even in the matrimonial advertisement in the newspaper people usually mention the skin colour (wheatish being the most common one). Have you ever found the concept of matrimonial hilarious as if trying to sell something? There is no such bar for body shape or skin colour for boys, in their case their occupation is taken into consideration. The brides should be as fair as possible, the more the skin tone shifts towards darker skin shades, the more will be the increment in dowry.

Girls who are **experts in handling domestic chores** as per Indian Standards and also **well-educated** (literate to be more precise because if she is educated then she is seen as a danger for the existence of patriarchy) are considered as a perfect marriage material.

The number of degrees a girl has, has become an important factor these days, preferably the qualification should be less or equivalent to the boy. If the girl has not done any **professional course**, then again, it's challenging for the family to find a suitable groom. Hence, such families again end up facing the burden of dowry during marriage and even after marriage. If the girl's family is unable to fulfil the demands, then the girl faces emotional blackmail, physical abuse, sometimes divorce and the worse, **dowry deaths**!

**Dowry Prohibition Act** was passed in 1961, which prohibits giving or taking of dowry. Still giving as well as receiving dowry is considered not only normal but something to be proud off, to **show off** in the society. Even in 2022, marriages without dowry are rare to find in India. Additionally, in the central part of north India marriages without dowry are seen with an eye of doubt, as if something is wrong or abnormal. Isn't it chucklesome!

In fact, the whole marriage is full of drama, never missing any emotion. The bride's family usually under debt continuously spends money for fulfilling every valid as well as invalid demands of the barati (Groom's procession), trying their best not to disappoint them in any way. Brides' family members are ever ready to apologize even if its not their mistake just to ensure that everything ends smoothly.

The groom's and his family's chest size increases to 56 inches and their walk reflects the pride of a peacock, indicating the achievement to be born – **"as a boy".**

Data obtained from National Crimes Record Bureau indicates that in 2020, 19 women became the victims of dowry deaths every day in India.

| Year | Dowry Deaths |
|---|---|
| 2018 | 7167 |
| 2019 | 7141 |
| 2020 | 6966 |

**Table 2: Shows number of dowry deaths in India**

Source: National Crime Records Bureau (NCRB)

In 2020 under Dowry Prohibition Act, the highest number of cases were reported in U.P. where the number of victims (2302) exceeded the number of cases (2274). This was followed by Bihar where the number of cases were 1046 with 1047 victims.

**DOMESTIC VIOLENCE**

Domestic violence cases are under-reported in India. The largest under-reporting is in Bihar, Karnataka and Manipur, where the prevalence of domestic violence is around 40% while reporting is less than 8% (The Wire, 12th Feb, 2021).

| Year | Cases registered under cruelty by husband and relatives |
|---|---|
| 2018 | 1,03,272 |
| 2019 | 1,24,934 |
| 2020 | 1,11,549 |

**Table 3: Indicating data about cases reported under cruelty by husband or relatives (Section 498A of the IPC)**

Source: National Crime Records Bureau (NCRB)

The reasons of under-reporting include embarrassment, financial dependency, fear of retaliation, victim-blaming to following a convoluted bureaucratic procedure. Instead of going by civil or criminal lawsuits against the spouse and their relatives (as is captured by NCRB data), the NFHS only captures if the women respondent was subject to domestic violence by her husband, irrespective of reporting that incidence. Thus, comparing the data obtained from NFHS and NCRB helps in determining the extent of under-reporting.

Indian daughters are also trained to believe that, "**Shaadi ke baad pati ka ghar hi larki ka ghar hota hai**" (After marriage the girl should consider the house of the husband as her own). Although it sounds normal but the belief is so rigid that the girl is unable to share in case, they are in any serious problem due to the husband or the in-laws as they don't have anywhere to go. Even if they share most of the times the girl's family try to convince her to solve the issues and go back (even in most cases of domestic violence). They are also trained to believe that – "**Is ghar ki izzat tumhare haath mai hai beta, aur us ghar ki izzat bhi tumhare haath mai hai**" (It is the duty of girls to maintain the honour and prestige of both the families i.e., her parents and her in-laws). The question is, if every person's prestige is in the hands of girls, then, who will take the responsibility of maintaining **Girl's Honour**?

**SOLUTION:**

The solution of all these problems and issues is explained in the following points:

1. **Education** – Educating the females is the first step that should be taken to create awareness among them. It is important to develop their logical reasoning capacity instead of just letting them blindly follow any practice that has continued from many years. They should also be aware about their rights as Indian citizen as well as various laws written in Indian constitution which will protect them from exploitation.
2. **Gender Sensitization** – Sensitizing both the genders is an important step so that both males and females become compassionate and sympathetic towards each other. Thus, after understanding the challenges each gender faces in a patriarchal society, these individuals will ultimately contribute in the development of a better place to live in.
3. **Economic Independence** – Even after being literate most of the females end up being economically dependent on father or husband thus, unable to come out of the circle of patriarchy. Economic independence provides confidence and strength to take their own decision, which is the most important character of a strong personality. Along with earning it is also important to keep in mind where to invest the hard-earned money. Some suggestions include- after fulfilling the basic necessities some part of it can be saved for emergencies, some can be kept for educating girls who can not afford it as well as some of it can be invested for social cause.
4. **Organization** – Instead of waiting for someone to come and solve the problem, it's the duty of those women who are aware and economically independent to form an organization at community level. To fight against the existing social issues and help those who are either unaware of their rights, cannot afford to fight legally or are too afraid to speak. As its well-known – "United we stand, divide we fall", hence it's the responsibility of women leaders to come forward, form a strong organization and eliminate the termites that have been eating the society from centuries.

**CONCLUSION:**

There are many atrocities faced by women like discrimination at work place, child marriage, acid attack, sexual abuse, emotional abuse, rape and the list is very long. It is not possible to cover all the women issues in one chapter. Several new as well as already mentioned challenges are discussed in detail in the following chapters. Hope this introductory chapter is helpful in giving an idea about the belief, ideas and opinion of the Indian society and how it affects the life of the Indian women.

There is a dire need to work for the upliftment of women and that will be possible only when we all join hands and work together. Hoping that, this chapter motivates you to understand the seriousness of the issue and we come together to put efforts for a better future for the coming generation.

**Reference:**

1. NFHS - 4 and 5 (National Family Health Survey), 2015 - 2021. http://rchiips.org/nfhs/
2. NCRB (National Crime Records Bureau), https://ncrb.gov.in/en/crime-in-india-table-addtional-table-and-chapter-contents
3. The Indian Express, 4th Feb, 2016. Sex determination: An old law, a new debate https://indianexpress.com/article/explained/sex-determination-an-old-law-a-new-debate/
4. The Times of India, 25th December, 2021. Just 617 convictions in 25 years under PNDT Act: Parliament. https://timesofindia.indiatimes.com/india/just-617-convictions-in-25-yrs-under-pndt-act-parliament-report/articleshow/88483156.cms
5. Soman, Priya. RAJA RAM MOHAN ROY AND THE ABOLITION OF SATI SYSTEM IN INDIA. *International Journal of Humanities, Art and Social Studies (IJHAS).* 1(2): 75-82.
6. Dibin Samuel, 4th, Dec 2009 https://www.christiantoday.co.in/article/wiliam.carey.played.significant.role.in.abolishing.sati.system/4906.htm
7. NBT, 4th Dec, 2019. Raja Ram Mohan Roy and Sati Pratha https://navbharattimes.indiatimes.com/education/gk-update/sati-pratha-nishedh-adhiniyam-things-you-must-know-about-sati-pratha/articleshow/72362475.cms
8. NEWS 18, 1st Oct, 2020. Rape Every 16 Minutes, Dowry Death Each Hour: NCRB Data Shows How Unsafe India is for Women. https://www.news18.com/news/india/rape-every-16-minutes-dowry-death-each-hour-ncrb-data-shows-how-unsafe-india-is-for-women-2925445.html
9. The dowry prohibition act 1961 (Modified on 3rd December 2018) https://www.indiacode.nic.in/bitstream/123456789/5402/1/a1961-28.pdf
10. CNBCTV18.COM, Sep 16, 2021, 07:57 PM (Published), 19 women were killed for dowry every day in 2020: NCRBhttps://www.cnbctv18.com/india/19-women-were-killed-for-dowry-every-day-in-2020-ncrb-10758421.htm
11. Vidhushy, Vimal. (2016). Human trafficking In India: An analysis. *International Journal of Applied Research* 2016; 2(6): 168-171 https://www.shram.org/uploadFiles/20180319102934.pdf
12. The Economic Times, Dec 09, 2021, Households are better off than ever but female foeticide continues unabated. https://economictimes.indiatimes.com/opinion/et-commentary/households-are-better-off-than-ever-but-female-foeticide-continues-unabated/articleshow/88193488.cms
13. The Indian Express, 8th June 2022 12:34 AM, Bias against girl child: Science must speak *loudly* https://www.newindianexpress.com/opinions/2022/jun/08/bias-against-girl-child-science-must-speak-loudly-2462957.html
14. BBC News, 28 May 2020, Why India must battle the shame of period stain https://www.bbc.com/news/world-asia-india-52830427
15. The Wire, 12th, feb, 2021, https://thewire.in/women/domestic-violence-india-underreported
16. Snehal Kulkarni, 16th April, 2019, Readers blog by The Times of India, Of daughters and sons – Why Indians prefer a son as their first child? https://timesofindia.indiatimes.com/readersblog/loveyourself/of-daughters-and-sons-why-indians-prefer-sons-as-fist-child-3073/
17. Tracee Confort, 11th November, 2021. 7 Facts About Your Period https://www.verywellhealth.com/period-myths-2721944
18. INSIGHTS IAS, 13th Feb, 2020. https://www.insightsonindia.com/2020/02/13/insights-into-editorial-only-82-trafficking-survivors-awarded-relief-in-last-8-years/

CHAPTER II

# Female Foeticide: A Cry Still Unheard

Saumya Tiwari*, Shraddha Saroj*, Parvati*
*Research Scholar
Prof. Kalpna Gupta (HOD)
Department of Home Science, Banaras Hindu University,
Varanasi, Uttar Pradesh
saumya@bhu.ac.in

**Abstract**

India has long been obsessed with boys and views on the birth of a girl as a poor investment in the future. Girls are viewed more as consumers than producers in Indian patriarchal culture, and this restricted perspective has resulted in abhorrent behaviors like female infanticide and female foeticide. Female mothers often feel terrible after having a daughter since there is social pressure on them to produce male offspring. Such women run the danger of getting physically hurt and having their spouses reject them. This may even result in rejection from in-laws and society at large. These underlying reasons, which are covered in this chapter, are ones where large-scale female foeticide is practiced. Every act of violence against women has a history and justification, and proponents of acts like infanticide and foeticide are among those who passionately support these arguments. Therefore, it is crucial to identify those reasons that have long supported these behaviors and still work to marginalize women in society. The legislative branch and the judicial branch should act swiftly and effectively to address these issues since they are the underlying causes of this kind of behavior. Women should feel comfortable in their birth and existence by encouraging the value of women and eradicating all the causes behind female foeticide.

**Key words- Female foeticide, society, girl, violence, culture.**

## INTRODUCTION

### What is female foeticide?

Aborting a female fetus illegally is known as female feticide in India. Any number above the assumed natural sex ratio of 103 to 107 males for every 100 females is regarded as suggestive of female feticide. The sex ratio in India's 0 to 6 age group has increased from 102.4 boys per 100 females in 1961, according to the country's census figures. In all of India's eastern and southern states, the child sex ratio is within the normal natural range but is noticeably higher in some western and particularly northwestern states like Maharashtra, Haryana, Jammu, and Kashmir (118, 120, and 116, as of 2011, respectively). In the 2011 census of the western states of Maharashtra and Rajasthan, the child sex ratio was found to be 113, while it was 112 in Gujarat and 111 in Uttar Pradesh.

According to Indian census data, sex ratios for women who have one or two children are poor, but as they have more children, the ratio improves due to sex-selective "stopping practices" (stopping having children based on the sex of those born). The data from the Indian census also hints at a link between a higher socioeconomic status and literacy and an abnormal sex ratio. This may have something to do with the Indian dowry system, where girls who are seen as a financial burden often die in dowries. Data from the 1991, 2001, and 2011 Census show that there are more children per woman in urban India than in rural India, suggesting that female foeticide is more common in urban India.

The question of whether these high sex ratios are exclusively brought about by female foeticide or if some of the higher ratios can also be attributed to natural causes is still being debated. Pre-Conception and Pre-Natal Diagnostic Techniques Act (PCPNDT) was passed by the Indian government in1994 to outlaw and punish female feticide and prenatal sex screening. Determining or disclosing the sex of the fetus to anyone is currently prohibited in India. The PCPNDT Act has, however, raised questions about how effectively the authorities have been enforcing it.

## CAUSES OF FEMALE FOETICIDE

- **RELIGION CAUSES**

Numerous ideologies and traditional faiths that hold that son is essential for religious formalities that are carried out at various stages of life feel that the influence of religion has a significant impact on them. "Sau Putra Bhava," "Doodho Nahao Pootho Phalo," etc. bless a woman when she gets married. The significance of son choice in contemporary culture is also symbolized by such religious blessings. The most important ceremonial act in India is cremation. It is believed that having a son perform the cremation ensures that the parents will have direct access to paradise. The ancient Vedas and Upanishads stipulate that for these rites and customs to be prominent, only the family's son should carry them out. This privilege is given to the son or any male family member since these ceremonies are seen as a privilege. In India, many different goddesses and their manifestations are worshipped, but in addition to the assassination of a female fetus, other crimes against women like rape, adultery, etc. are also committed. Women are cherished and held in high regard throughout the Rig Veda as a higher and more superior species. The gender ratio in our nation has been severely distorted by religion and culture. The ancient traditional norms, however, place a high level of respect on women because of their great veneration, which is a gift from God and not something that religious texts discount. Even though a daughter is seen as a blessing from Goddess Laxmi, many families choose to murder the female fetus to have a son, who will purge them of all their sins once they pass away.

- **SOCIAL CAUSES**

Female foeticide is a practice that has numerous societal justifications since it is thought that daughters do not provide parents with a social safety net. In traditional Indian society, having a daughter is viewed as a pointless investment that would not pay off because daughters typically marry and live with their husbands and their family after birth. Aside from the costs associated with raising her, educating her, etc., the dower is determined to be an extra expense. Due to the need for parents to uphold their social position, daughters are sometimes viewed as a dishonor in Indian culture. A normal, traditional Indian family wants for the continuation of their family name, which, in their opinion, can only be done only by a son. Since daughters do not retain their maiden names after marriage, they are undesired. In higher caste and among the wealthy, where they must maintain their reputation among higher caste, infanticide and foeticide are extremely common practices. The safeguarding of the girl child, however, is the top priority for the middle class and lower class families. As the number of crimes against women rises in our nation, many families are terrified for the safety and protection of their daughters. Therefore, the parents think that murdering the daughter before she is born is preferable to prevent her from being a victim of several crimes that would ultimately ruin her life and disgrace her parents. A significant factor in the practice of female foeticide is also estimated to be poverty and illiteracy. A son is favored in the family as economic support since a significant portion of the population lives below the poverty line. However, raising daughters ends up costing more for these households. India's rural and remote populations still hold the view that the best way to keep women under control is to minimize their worth. As a result of their lack of knowledge, parents pass on the same ideas to their offspring since they are unaware of the societal changes that have occurred in India's education system and women's standing in recent years. Women are now being degraded and disrespected in a new way—by being killed before they are even born. Numerous factors contribute to the exclusion of female fetuses from households, but economic considerations are frequently one of the main drivers. The practice of female feticide violates a woman's right to be born, get an education, and establish her own means of support in society at large. Many people favor sons over females and support their sons in pursuing higher education and careers. Daughters, on the other hand, are not allowed to receive a rudimentary education since it is thought that they would get married and need to stay home as housewives. While the law mandates that sons and daughters receive an equal portion of the property, in many rural areas of India, parents worry that if their daughter receives any property, the father's lineage would inevitably lose ownership of the land. In a similar vein, inheritance also plays a crucial part in removing the daughter.

- **LEGAL CAUSES**

It has been 18 years since the Pre-Conception and Pre-Natal Diagnostic Technique Act of 1994 was passed in response to an alarming rise in the horrific slaughter of female fetuses using cutting-edge scientific methods. Given that there has been a steady decline in the child sex ratio, the 2011 Census's child sex ratio of 914:1000 makes it clear that questions remain about the Act's effectiveness and implementation. Female feticide is a barbaric practice that has been outlawed by the Pre-Conception and Pre-Natal Diagnostic Technique Act of 1994. However, this law has shown to be insufficient and ineffective. Due to the Indian community's lack of respect for the Act's regulations, the law's poor execution has therefore indirectly contributed to the rising rate of female foeticide. Numerous innocent female lives may have been saved if the rules had been stricter and were put into practice as intended. It is very unfortunate for our nation that, even after 68 years of independence and the mention of the right to equality in Article 14 of the Indian Constitution, foeticide continues to be legal in our nation. The absence of attempts by the government and organizations to create effective legislation is what is causing the genocide in India today. This has led to more crimes against women, which has diminished their dignity both domestically and abroad. Female feticide and sex selection crimes are difficult to identify since they are committed in secret, which eventually results in fewer instances being reported to the courts.

**STRATEGIES TO CURB FEMALE FOETICIDE**

**Changes in Viewpoints and Perspectives**

It is necessary for rural residents to adjust their attitudes toward females since they are in a situation of poverty and backwardness. The birth of girl children should be valued, and they should be viewed as devoted family members. They need to promote positive attitudes about girls and believe that when their growth and development take place in a healthy way, they will not only become useful members of their families and communities but also productive citizens of the nation. As these people's perceptions and worldviews shift, they will effectively make a crucial commitment to reducing the acts of female feticide.

**Advancing Acquisition of Education**

Education is seen as a tool that imparts knowledge and understanding to girls about a variety of topics, not just academic principles, which will help them in one way or the other. The ability to distinguish between suitable and inappropriate behavior, support their daily settings effectively, instill the virtues of diligence, ethics, conscientiousness, and morality, and become productive citizens of the country, all are benefits of educating girls. In order to encourage females to attend school, girls' education centers should be developed in rural regions. These facilities will provide the girls the chance to improve their reading abilities and learn about various academic topics.

**Giving Equal Rights and Opportunities to Boys and Girls**

Equal rights and opportunities for boys and girls should be provided. The pursuit of education is one of the crucial areas in which boys and girls need to be given equal rights and opportunities. A person's ability to increase their own prosperity as well as the prosperity of their families and communities is greatly influenced by education. When they develop their knowledge and skills, they will not only increase the likelihood that they will succeed in their careers but also develop into family support systems. Therefore, it can be concluded that granting females the same freedoms and privileges as men will help people form positive viewpoints, which will lessen the incidence of female infanticide and female feticide.

**Usage of Laws and Policies**

In order to raise community understanding that girls should not be viewed as liabilities but as valuable human beings, the Government of India has implemented a number of initiatives, projects, regulations, and policies. The Government of India launched the Beti Bachao Beti Padhao campaign with the primary goal of raising public awareness about the need of protecting girls' rights and ensuring their access to quality education. With an initial investment of 100 crores of rupees, the program was initiated. Specifically targeted by this campaign are the states of Haryana, Punjab, Delhi, Uttarakhand, Uttar Pradesh, and Bihar. In light of this, it is frequently stated that using legal measures and other strategies will significantly reduce the incidence of female foeticide.

**Advancing Skills Development among Girls**

In order for females to be empowered for greater employment chances, parents must frame their viewpoint. Agriculture is said to be the main form of employment in rural regions. Aside from farming, the locals labor in a variety of other fields, such as the creation of handicrafts and artwork, silk weaving, pottery making, the manufacture of food, and so on. For their daughters to do well in their employment responsibilities, parents must instill effective skills. Girls will assist their parents in the creation and manufacture of the products as well as in the marketing of them, as their skills and capabilities grow. Developing girls' skills in this way will help to value their birth and reduce instances of female foeticide.

**Motivating Girls to Participate in Activities**

The involvement of females in social, cultural, and religious activities should be encouraged by the parents. Girls' parents should foster a passion for and interest in helping their daughters improve their skills in extracurricular and creative activities. Playing musical instruments, singing, creating crafts and artwork, dancing, role-playing, and participating in sports are some of these activities. Girls who are encouraged to participate in activities will help to improve the families' ability to support themselves when they are talented in these areas, motivated to engage in social, cultural, and religious activities, and able to use these skills in a constructive way. The practice of female feticide will decline as a result of this, there will be an encouragement in the development of favorable perspectives toward females.

**Implementing and Executing Measures and Schemes for Women and Child Development**

It is crucial to implement policies and strategies aimed at encouraging the development of women and children. Various government initiatives aimed at enhancing the prosperity and wellbeing of women and children have been put into action. People and society may form positive viewpoints and celebrate the birth of the female child when they raise knowledge about policies and programs and get assistance from them. The idea is then emphasized that if people become aware of the numerous programs and initiatives that are primarily aimed at enhancing the welfare of women and children, they would be able to make a meaningful contribution to ending female feticide.

**CONCLUSION**

An issue that involves social behavior and prejudice at its origins cannot be solved by law alone. If the objective of a balanced sex ratio is to be accomplished, a comprehensive effort incorporating all facets of society is required to alter the dominant societal thinking and eliminate gender-based discrimination. To realize the long-term goal, initiatives are being made to foster a culture where sons and daughters are equally valued. Of course, it is important to acknowledge that feticide is a form of murder and that both parents should be punished. People need to be informed about reforming laws that contain specific deterrent information. There is a lot of pressure on women to be tested and get an abortion if they are found to be female. It needs a new mindset to spread the message that having a female kid is not a curse. She won't be a hassle. She doesn't damage the nation's economy. She cannot serve as a vehicle for the payment of dowry. It's important to have the idea in your head that she's the girl, the mother, and your life partner. However, via a number of initiatives and programs, the Indian government has been working hard to improve the position of girls in the nation and to encourage their educational pursuits. The position of females in society has undoubtedly increased, but much more work has to be done before girls are treated on a par with boys. In conclusion, this may be argued to be more of a social sickness than a legal one. We need to genuinely let go of this son's preoccupation and realize that having females in our family would make our lives just as joyful, if not more so. However, this does not imply that the law has no place in society. For every infant girl to get the respect she deserves, we must all work together.

**Reference**


1. Data Highlights - 2001 Census Census Bureau, Government of India.
2. India at Glance- Population Census 2011 - Final Census of India, Government of India (2013).
3. "Sex ratio worsens in small families, improves with 3 or more children | India News". The Times of India.
4. IMPLEMENTATION OF THE PCPNDT ACT IN INDIA - Perspectives and ChallengesArchived 2019-10-06 at the Wayback Machine Public Health Foundation of India, Supported by United Nations FPA (2010).

5. James W.H. (July 2008). "Hypothesis:Evidence that Mammalian Sex Ratios at birth are partially controlled by parental hormonal levels around the time of conception". Journal of Endocrinology. **198** (1): 3–15. doi:10.1677/JOE-07-0446. PMID18577567.
6. "UNICEF India". UNICEF. Archived from the original on 2014-12-23. Retrieved 2012-05-06.
7. Supinder Kaur, A Frightful Reality, Book on Female Foeticide, 2009 Edition **(2009).**
8. Madhusoodhan Tripathi , Book on Female Foeticide in India: A Harsh Reality by, 2011 Edition **(2011)**
9. Dhruv Dixit and Tara Sharma, Book on Female Foeticide,2012 Edition **(2012)**
10. Sab. P and Radhakrishnan EM., Status and Effectiveness of the Act in Rajasthan, A Research Report, Prayatn, Rajasthan., **(2007)**
11. T.K. Roy, Sunita Kishore and Arnold., Sex Selective Abortion in India, Population and Development Review, **28(4)**, 759-785, **(2002).**

CHAPTER III

# Acid Attack

## *A Major Issue in India*

Sheetal Prajapati
Research Scholar, Department of Education
Central University of Rajasthan, Bandarsindri, Ajmer
sheetaldna@gmail.com
Dr. Narendra Kumar
Assistant Professor, Department of Education
Central University of Rajasthan, Bandarsindri, Ajmer
drnarendra09@gmail.com

**Abstract**

In terms of acid attacks India, Pakistan and Bangladesh are at the top of the list. Every year, India has the highest number of acid assaults in the world. According to the statista research department in 2020, the number of instances registered was 182. Day-by-day the number of cases decreases because of the strict actions taken by the government of India and supreme court of India. But still India is at the top position in this violence. There are several reasons comes under this issue like marriage, dowry system, jealousy, say no to sex, etc. This chapter discusses about the real story of acid attack victims, facts and figures registered under this issue, initiatives of government of India and little-bit about the success story of these women. This research also raises awareness of acid attack survivors and how they are internally motivated to achieve success in their life. Most of the victims think that after this incident their life ends, but this is not true, so these incidents need to be discussed so that every victim becomes motivated to live their life so that the suicide ratio will also decrease.

**Keywords:** Acid attack, India, government, real story.

**Introduction**

Women plays a vital role in our society and culture. In present time, every woman has their own job or duty but unfortunately our society is male dominant society. We must remember that a woman's life is far more complicated than that of a guy. A woman must look after her own personal life, while she is a parent, she must also look after the lives of her children. If she is married, she may be under much more strain. Nonetheless, they will function admirably in the workplace, sometimes even better than their male peers. In the current world, violence against women has become a significant topic of discussion on every platform and generally the victims of acid attacks are only females. "Violence against women is a manifestation of historically unequal power relations between men and women, which have led to domination over and discrimination against women by men and to the prevention of the full advancement of women." Acid assaults are at an all-time high in India, with 250–300 occurrences documented annually, but the "real number could reach 1,000," according to Acid Survivors‘ Trust International. This is one of the gender-based violence because of their lower social, economic, and legal status, women are more vulnerable to violence.

Acid attacks at high rates show a country's failure to safeguard its citizens from this particular danger. However, developing countries such as Colombia, Pakistan, Nepal, Bangladesh, Uganda, and India account for 90% of acid assaults (Atiyeh et al., 2008). Every year, around 1000 of the 1500 total instances reported worldwide are perpetrated in India (Nguyen, 2015).

'Acid assault,‘ as its name implies, is an 'attack of acid or attack with acid.‘ This is another sickness induced by humans, and it describes the inhumanity of those humans who inflict acid attacks by implying that they no longer possess humanity. The motives behind this include vengeance, anger, hatred, and others. As we can see, the majority of the victims in this instance are females. However, this does not rule out the possibility of it occurring in boys; in fact, boys have been known to be victims of it.

In a study conducted by UNICEF reveals, “Acid attack is a serious problem all over the world, even children have become victim of acid attack in many cases. **In an Acid attack, acid is thrown at the face or body of the victim with deliberate intent to burn and disfigure.** Most of the victims are girls, many below the age of 18, who have rejected sexual advances or marriage proposals. Acid attack or vitriolage is defined as the act of throwing acid onto the body of a person with the intention of injuring or disfiguring [them] out of jealousy or revenge”.

Acid attack, also called as vitriolage, is a form of interpersonal terrorism that entails the intentional application of sulfuric, nitric, or hydrochloric acid to another person with the primary goal of disfigurement. Acid attacks have been reported on women, particularly young women/girls, for refusing suitors' overtures, for rejecting marriage proposals/offers, for denying/disputing dowry, domestic fighting, and property disputes, among other things. The attacker cannot bear his refusal, loss of dignity and shame, insecurity, revenge, patriarchy, aggression, and anger; his so-called male ego gets in the way of all of this, and as a result, he exacts revenge by destroying the body, particularly the face, of the women who dared to deny him. Acid attacks are a common occurrence in India. Between January 2002 and October 2010, 153 incidences of acid assault were recorded by Indian press (media), compared to 174 judicial cases in 2000.

| Year | Number of cases reported |
|---|---|
| 2018 | 228 |
| 2019 | 249 |
| 2020 | 182 |

**Fig 1: From 2018 to 2020, the number of acid attacks reported in India**

These data do not reflect the true scale of the problem because 60% of acid assaults in India go unreported. Many victims are hesitant to disclose because they are ashamed and stigmatised, and many rural regions lack the resources to deal with the crime (Acid Survivors Trust International). In India, the annual number of incidences is estimated to be approximately 1000. (Acid Survivors Trust International).

**Effects of acid attack**

The most noticeable impact of an acid assault is long-term physical deformity. As a result, the victim faces both physical and psychological obstacles, which necessitate long-term surgical therapy and in-depth intervention from therapists and counsellors at each step of physical recovery. Their psychological, sociological, and economic vitality in societies are all impacted by these far-reaching repercussions on their life.

***Disfigurement of the face and its impact on body image:*** The most visible impact of acid attack is facial deformity. Victimization had a terrible effect on one's body image and physical attractiveness, as one of the victims in the sample expressed it: "I was gorgeous and I can never be so beautiful again."

***Distress in the mind:*** What happens to you has always been a source of anxiety for you. As a result of the findings, it is obvious that psychological discomfort is an inescapable side effect of acid assault. Suicide attempts can result from such distress. Victims believed that suicide is the best option since they would never be the same again.

***Depression:*** Another major psychological impact of such incidents is depression. Victimization like this can lead to great sadness and depression in the victims. Level of anxiety also enhances due to this.

***Loss of self-identity:*** The majority of women who are victims of such abuse are unable to face people for long periods of time due to a sense of loss of true identity. Victims thought that their ugliness obliterates her identity. They just want to lack their-self in the room so that people can't watch them.

***Social effects*** also affect the victims, such as relationship with family, extended family and peer group. According to the findings, there is both a favourable and unfavourable alteration in relationships with very close family members. In each and every case, the individual witnessed support and encouragement while also having to deal with unfavourable behaviour from family and friends. So, social effects are also observed by the victims itself.

**Real life stories of Acid assaults**

Researchers discusses about the stories of 5 women's those are suffering from this violence.

This is the story of ***Lalita*** and she was only 23 years old in 2012 when she became a victim of acid attack. In 2012, Lalita and her mother visited to her maternal village in Uttar Pradesh, India, to attend a relative's marriage. A family feud erupted after a night of excessive drinking, notably enraging Lalita's 18-year-old cousin. A minor squabble rapidly grew into something far more serious. "I shoved a female who had come to the wedding with my cousin and who was refusing to pay a small auspicious amount at the altar. He saw this as my family's final insult and vowed vengeance," she explains. He threatened to throw acid on her for her pride in her appearance. "I thought it was simply something spoken in the heat of the situation at the time, but man actually followed through on his threat," she adds, her voice heavy with shock. Around November 11, 2012, after five months, Lalita and her mom was walking across to the grounds late at night to refresh themselves, two men who covered their mouth grabbed her, pushed her to the floor, and splashed acid on Lalita's face while her mom looked on in horror.

Once Lalita pointed a torch in his face, she claims she was able to notice her cousin's voice and eyes. She was taken to a local hospital for treatment of her injuries for two months, but her family quickly needed money. "I receive Rs 4,500 ($69) monthly, out of which Rs 1,500 ($22) simply goes on rent". His father Anand, serves as a gas station attendant in Mumbai, she says dejectedly. "How was I able to afford for such a long time to stay in the hospital?"

A cousin persuaded Lalita to travel to Mumbai, there the acid victims NGO- 'Make Love Not Scars' secured finances for additional medical treatment services, after she spent months in despair at her grandma's house without getting any help for her severe injuries.

**According to Dr. Ashok Gupta, who has treated on more than 150 cases of acid assault in his 35 years of experience as a plastic surgeon, a sufferer of a mild assault needs at least 15 to 20 surgeries. Treatments can be excessively expensive, with surgery costs ranging from Rs 2-4 lakhs.** "I've heard from some hospitals that they were charging up to Rs 6 lakhs for a routine surgery," said by Dr. Gupta. In light of these staggering costs, the Supreme Court's direction to the government to offer Rs 3 lakhs in compensation per sufferer is grossly inadequate. Acid attacks are extremely difficult to treat in government hospitals and emergency departments because they are already filled. "I n most emergency facilities and ambulances, and specialised neutralisation chemicals rarely are quick-acting solutions provided to reduce the damage. It all stems from the lack of a basic national advisory council of experts to provide instructions for what to do in the event of an attack, according to Gupta.

**When somebody's face is sprayed with acid, their eyelashes and lips can completely melt away. The ears seize up and the nose melts, sealing the nostrils. The acid burns every inch of skin it comes into contact with when it spills or drips on the neck, chest, back, arms, or legs.** Everything which comes in the contact of acid will dissolve completely. When acid burn wounds heal, they leave behind thick marks that hold the skin taut and create ugliness. The suspect's vision is affected in 90% of instances, resulting in vision loss. There's also the psychological scarring. Acid assaults are rarely taken out with the intent of murder, due to the high survival percentage among victims. They're meant to disfigure and mutilate the victim, condemning them to a life of misery.

Lalita has recently been battling with her family members about getting a job once her surgeries are finished. "They won't be here forever, and I'll have to fend for myself," she says. "Before this, I was quite shy and only spoke to a few people. That is no longer an option for me" she said.

This is the story of ***Aarti Thakur***; she experiences that a man is approaching to her at a railway station in Mumbai i.e., Goregaon station. She sensed something wasn't right away. After already being assaulted twice in two months from a knife-wielding stranger, she had come to recognize the danger signs. She had already been stabbed in the face the very first time and had 16 stitches. However, what happened this time was even worse than she had expected.

"I was gasping for air. Everything became a silvery black colour. The liquid was soaking into my scalp, forcing it to melt away. "I went to a police officer and screaming that I'd been attacked again," Aarti remembers calmly and measuredly. Because she was carrying a scarf on her face, the harm to it was minimal. However, the acid burned her forearms, neck, and portions of her cheekbones and eyebrows.

Three years later, Aarti, is battling the perpetrators of the assault in court while still trying to obtain finances for the operation she needed. She began working again after a year and a half of solitude in her home, and she is regaining confidence in her abilities as well as her appearance. However, she is justifiably enraged at how the acid assault on her may have been avoided.

Her ordeal began in 2011, when her landlady's son confessed his feelings for her. Aarti will be forced to marry him by the landlady. Aarti initially laughed it off as a joke, but then emphasised that she was already engaged and declined his third and final wedding proposal. The first incident occurred soon after, when she was traveling home from work at an IT firm. However, she did not recognise the assailant, and the police dismissed the incident as a normal robbery attempt.

Aarti moved to a different area of Mumbai along her single mother and little sister, who were reliant on her. She was terrified that she had been attacked on purpose. A little more than a month later, a second attempted attack occurred. There was no officer available to take her complaint this time. Aarti became suspicious; just a few people knew wherever she had moved, and one of them was her previous landlady. She was taken aback when she saw her boy standing in front of her office building on January 30, 2012. A man carrying acid valued Rs 5 in a bottle ruined her life forever the next day.

The police finally intervened this time, apprehending the son, his mother, and two others. The son, angered by the perceived insult to his pride and jealous of her imminent marriage, allegedly paid two men to purchase and spray acid on her as a final act of vengeance.

Some men grow outraged by such "unrequited love" because they subscribe to a patriarchal paradigm in which women are supposed to smile demurely and quietly accede to claims of love.

Here researcher discusses the story of ***Laxmi Aggrawal,*** Laxmi Agarwal (1 June, 1990) is an acid attack sufferer from India, as well as a fighter for acid attack victims' welfare and a TV host. She is one of the famous cases of acid assault and also having an inspirational story for every acid attack victim. Laxmi was born into a poor household in New Delhi. In 2005, when Laxmi were 15 years old and in 11$^{th}$ grade, she was contacted by Naeem Khan, a 32-year-old man who worked in her neighbourhood. He made a proposal to Laxmi, but she declined. She didn't tell anyone since her family would have blamed her and put a stop to her education. Ten months ago when she received the identical message from Naeem, telling her that he loves her and wants to get married her. She remained silent. Kamran, Naeem's older brother, and his girlfriend, Rakhi, assaulted her with acid in no time. While riding his bike, Kamran called Laxmi's name from behind. Rakhi flung acid right at Laxmi's face from the backseat as she looked behind in answer to her name. Laxmi passed out and tried to go up and call for aid after regaining consciousness, but she was involved in many car accidents. Arun Singh phoned the cops, but when he took a look at her skin which is dissolving, he realised it because of the acid the skin was melting. Someone else sprinkled water on her face in an attempt to cool her off, but the acid moved down and burned her neck. Then Arun managed to get her into his car's back seat. The seat cushions later developed burn holes as a result of this. He referred Laxmi to Ram Manohar Lohia Hospital (RML Hospital) for treatment. The police arrived at the hospital without delay. Arun then inquired about Laxmi's family and residence. He arrived at her residence, notified her family, and brought them to the hospital. She undergone a number of procedures, including eye surgery. Naeem Khan was detained four days after the attack, but he was freed nearly a month later. He married off right away. He was condemned to life in jail after huge demonstrations and media attention.

In 2006, Laxmi filed a public interest litigation (PIL) after the acid attack that damaged her face and other bodily parts. She declined to engage with Naeem Khan, one of the trios, she was assaulted using acid by 3 men on Tughlaq Road in New Delhi. In addition to requesting for compensation, her PIL requested the creation of a new legislation or amendments to existing criminal statutes such as the IPC, Indian Evidence Act, and CrPC to cope with the offence. She also called for a complete prohibition on the sale of acid, citing an increase in acid attacks on women throughout the country. At a hearing in April, the Centre assured the Supreme Court of India that it will work with state and local governments to prepare a plan before the next hearing on July 9. Unfortunately, it declined to do so, which infuriated the court. Whenever the administration failed to develop a plan, the Supreme Court vowed to intervene and issue orders unless the government developed a policy limiting the sale of acid in order to reduce chemical assaults the court had previously ordered the centre to convene a discussion of Chief Secretaries of all states and union territories in six weeks to discuss enacting legislation to regulate the selling of acids, and also policies for intervention, remuneration, welfare, and rehabilitative services of those who have been affected.

Meanwhile, the Supreme Court found in Laxmi's favour in 2013 to restrict the sale of acids at shops. Acid could no longer be sold to anyone under the age of 18 according to the new restrictions. Before purchasing acid, one must additionally present a photo identification card.

Despite all of the laws, Laxmi argues that little has changed on the ground. "Acid is easily accessible in stores. Our own volunteers went out and bought acid without difficulty. In reality, I've bought acid myself" she stated. "We've started a new project called 'Shoot Acid.' We are attempting to obtain data on the sale of acid in each area via the Right to Information Act. We want to present the material gathered through this project to the Supreme Court in order to educate them of the current situation." Acid attack survivors have begun a hunger strike in order to seek speedy justice and rehabilitation. She penned a poem on the occurrence and her feelings at the time. She started a campaign named as "Stop Acid Sale" for that she was honoured for her fight against acid attack violence by then-US first lady Michelle Obama and many others while she was in the US to accept the "International Women of Courage award". She received the International Women Empowerment Award from the Ministry of Women and Child Development, the Ministry of Drinking Water and Sanitation, and UNICEF in 2019.

This story is one of the motivational stories for every acid attack victim as well as for every girl to become successful in their life.

**Rules of Government for Acid Attack Victims**

Until such guidelines are framed and made functioning properly in the States/Union Territories where regulations to regulate the sale of acid and other toxic materials are not in place, the Chief Secretaries of the concerned States/ Administrators of the Union Territories should also ensure that the following guidelines are followed with immediate effect:

- The sale of acid over the counter is illegal unless the seller keeps a log/register of the sale of acid, which will include the name(s) of the person(s) to whom acid(s) is/are sold, as well as the quantity sold. The location of the person to which the log/register is sold must be included in the log/register.
- Government-issued photo ID that includes the individual's address.
- Describes why and for what purpose acid was obtained.
- The supplier must notify all acid stocks to the relevant Sub-Divisional Magistrate (SDM) within 15 days.
- No acid shall be sold to anyone under the age of eighteen.
- In the event of an undeclared stock of acid, the concerned SDM has the authority to seize the stock and levy a fine of up to Rs. 50,000/- on the vendor.
- Any person who violates any of the above directives may be fined up to Rs.50,000/- by the concerned SDM.

The following guidelines must be followed by educational institutions, research laboratories, hospitals, government departments, and departments of Public Sector Undertakings that are required to preserve and store acid:

- A register of acid usage must be kept and lodged with the appropriate SDM.
- A person will be held responsible for having acid on their premises and keeping it safe.
- The acid must be stored under the person's supervision, and students and staff leaving laboratories or storage facilities where acid is utilised must be checked.
- As compensation for the expense of after-care and rehabilitation, the responsible State Government/Union Territory must pay nearly Rs. 3 lakhs to acid attack victims. Within 15 days of the occurrence of the incident, a sum of Rs 1 lakh shall be paid to the victim to facilitate emergency medical attention. The sum of Rs. 2 lakhs must be paid as soon as feasible, and in any case within two months.

Because this regulation took effect on October 8, 2016, victims who were the victims of an acid attack prior to that date are not eligible for a grant from PMNRF. Obtaining a grant from PMNRF requires sending a copy of the FIR, a medical report, the victim's bank account information, and proof of residence to the Ministry of Home Affairs, Government of India, North Block, New Delhi. In the instance of underage victims or victims who have died as a result of an acid attack, the bank account information of their parents or next of kin may be provided.

**Conclusion**

An acid attack has the long-term effect of ruining the victim, who is subjected to constant torment, irreparable injury, and other problems. Despite their readiness to resume normal life, they have little faith that people will treat them as normal humans in light of their appearance and limitations following the attack. It's possible that they won't be able to work. As a result, they prefer to live in the shadows and keep themselves hidden from the public. In order to prevent attacks on women, offenders should face harsh and severe punishment. In order to save themselves from offenders, women should learn physical defensive measures. There are several things that can be done to prevent acid attacks. Women should take the lead in improving the lives of acid attack sufferers. Another helpful strategy could be increased public awareness and media coverage of these cases that is more compassionate and mature. A value-based education is urgently required; new laws, institutions, and lip service to give reservation will not enough to address this heinous crime. In the offense of acid attack, both the body and the soul are destroyed.

We sincerely hope that the abysmal state of the legal system in relation to acid attacks may be changed, so that the victims' suffering can be alleviated and Indian community can become a safer place for women. 70% of acid assaults are caused by rejection in love, refusal to marry, or other personal reasons. All of the victims showed changes in body appearance, depression, and PTSD symptoms, and they tended to employ avoidant coping at the beginning of their victimisation. Our legislators have enacted a number of laws and schemes, including a ban on the sale of acid, stiffer penalties for criminals, and free treatment for acid attack victims; however, the primary focus should be on prevention. To modify the traditional societal norms that excuse violence against women, a variety of actions should be implemented, including strengthening NGOs, electronic, print, and social media campaigns.

Laws have been enacted to provide financial assistance to victims in the form of compensation. The Uttar Pradesh government went above and beyond to assist these victims by launching the Rani Laxmi Bai Mahila Samman Kosh Yojana, which assists victims by not only providing compensation but also providing free treatment without financial constraints. The dependants of the victims who died are also compensated under this system.

**References:**


1. Atiyeh, B. S., Costagliola, M., & Hayek, S. N. (2009). Burn prevention mechanisms and outcomes: Pitfalls, failures and successes. Burns: Journal of the International Society for Burn Injuries, 35(2), 181–193. https://doi.org/10.1016/j.burns.2008.06.002
2. Acid Survivors Trust International. (n.d.). A worldwide problem. Acid Survivors Trust International. https://www.asti.org.uk/a-worldwide-problem.html
3. "A/RES/48/104 - Declaration on the Elimination of Violence against Women". United Nations General Assembly. Retrieved 6 August 2014.
4. Das, A., Banik, S. (2019). A Study on Acid Attack in India and it's Impact, JETIR, 6(1), ISSN-2349-5162
5. Dhar, Sujoy. "Acid attacks against women in India on the rise; survivors fight back". USA TODAY. *Retrieved 2020-02-15.*
6. Harris, Rob. "Acid Attacks". The New York Times. Archived from the original on 2012-03-31. *Retrieved 2008-12-01.*
7. Kantya, L.A. (2020, September 30). Acid Attack. https://indianlawportal.co.in/acid-attack/
8. Kumar, V., (2021). Acid Attacks in India: A Socio-Legal Report, *Dignity: A Journal of Analysis of Exploitation and Violence,* 6(1) DOI:10.23860/dignity.2021.06.01.05. https://digitalcommons.uri.edu/dignity/vol6/iss1/5
9. Mahapatra, C. K., Nanda, H. (2015). Acid Attack and Women in India: A Critical Analysis. *International Global Journal for Research Analysis,* 4(7), ISSN No 2277 - 8160

10. Nguyen, K. (2015, Sep 16). India's acid attack victims face long wait for justice. Thomson Reuters Foundation. https://in.reuters.com/article/india-acid-attack-victims/indias-acid-attack-victims-face-long-wait-for-justice-idINKCN0RG1FO20150916
11. Singh M, Kumar V, Rupani R, Kumari S, Shiuli, Yadav PK, et al. Acid attack on women: A new face of gender-based violence in India. *Indian J Burns,* 2018;26:83-6
12. Statista Research Department. (2021, Oct 19). Number of acid attack cases in India 2018-2020. https://www.statista.com/statistics/1103056/india-acid-attack-cases/
13. "Women in Modern Society" Victor Tembo MCIPS, CIPP™, MIAPM
14. Yeasmeen, N. (2015). Acid Attack in the Back Drop of India and Criminal Amendment Act, 2013, International Journal of Humanities and Social Science Invention, 4(1), pp. 06-13, ISSN (Online): 2319 – 7722, ISSN (Print): 2319 – 7714, www.ijhssi.org
15. Zalmai, A. S., & Amiri, A. (2021). Acid Attack and its Clinical and Psychological Effect. *International Journal of Academic Research in Progressive Education and Development*, 10(3), 11–19, DOI:10.6007/IJARPED/v10-i3/10708, http://dx.doi.org/10.6007/IJARPED/v10-i3/10708
16. https://en.wikipedia.org/wiki/Acid_attack
17. https://en.wikipedia.org/wiki/Laxmi_Agarwal
18. https://www.aljazeera.com/features/2016/3/10/indian-acid-attack-victims-share-their-stories
19. https://www.mha.gov.in/sites/default/files/AdvisoryAfterSupremeCourtOrderInLaxmCase_Short_1.pdf
20. https://pmnrf.gov.in/en/about/grant-to-acid-attack-victims

CHAPTER IV

# Be the Change You Want to See in the World

## *No one has the right to stop girls' education and ambition*

Dr. Isha Kishnani
King George Medical University
Lucknow
partheesha58@gmail.com

As a child I was naive to believe that my privileges would last forever, until I became mature enough to observe the difference in the mindsets, within the four walls of my home sweet home. When I got introduced to society, I saw the so called 'social moulds'. I saw a subtle difference between men & women. The expectation from a man is be the bread earner whether he likes it or he dislikes it. I'm sure this pressure isn't easy to handle. The expectation from a woman, on the other hand, is manifold. She is the giver of life i.e., a mother, an obedient wife, a secret keeping friend, an understanding sister and a polite daughter. Why have we created such divisions?

As a child, I grew up in a nuclear family. My mother abandoned me and my brother at a very early age. I was raised by my father, a step mother and my grandmother. My father was the only working person in the family, a noble doctor by profession. He always inspired me as a child and would often tell me you will achieve greatness one fine day. These words gave me confidence and inspired me to work a little bit harder, to walk an extra mile and excel in every field, be it studies or sports. I looked up to him for his deep compassion for his patients and his attitude to give whatever he can. He extended his hand to help the needy and never feared to make a tough call to save someone's life. I was mesmerised by the way people looked up to him as if he was some kind of GOD on Earth, who would heal patients by divine grace but in reality, he was able to treat them by his learned knowledge and skills.

One the other hand, my step mother thought differently. She was reluctant to allow me to pursue higher education. She did not allow me to step out of the house to appear in AIPMT (All India Pre Medical Test). My father was appalled by this out and he made sure that I do appear for the upcoming UP CPMT (Combined Pre-Medical Test). I qualified the exam in the first attempt with flying colours and got a superb rank. But that's not all. I paid for this achievement a great deal. My step mother was adamant to not let me study any further and get me married. My father's opinion was a pole apart. He wanted me to become a doctor. The ball was in my court. I had to make a decision really quick and face consequences based on what I'd choose for the rest of my life.

But as they say nothing comes easy in life, to achieve great heights you have to make great sacrifices and face the unknown. Hence, I paid the price of the unwavering faith and courage by eloping from my parental home to my Fufa ji's and Bua ji's home. They helped me to get admission in my dream college "KGMU" (my father's Alma Mater too) and secured my future. Soon after, my passion to study and work diligently paid off and I mixed well with my colleagues and patients. I enjoyed every bit of it. With the sturdy support of my Fufa ji and Bua ji, I worked hard and earned respect in the eyes of the society and I instilled confidence in young girls to choose a course as tough as MBBS and that too with sheer determination in oneself.

My work and empathy for patients gained recognition. I achieved medals and certificates for my academic endeavours, but most importantly I was blessed with peace and happiness within. The pillars of my journey, Fufa ji and Bua ji stood by me throughout and I'm truly grateful to them from the core of my being. Their faith in me gave me assurance that I stood for the right thing. And believe me, till date I have no regrets for leaving my home because doing that served a greater purpose which was beyond my imagination in the beginning. I have received love, countless blessings and affection of unknown persons which truly makes the profession as a doctor worth the effort and time. I'm proud of what I've become.

I strongly believe that be the Change you want to see in the World. Take a leap of faith. Don't get perturbed and quit so easily. Fight for what's worth fighting for.

The journey may seem hard but it is always bearable. Wear the armour of belief in yourself and continue to march forward with your head high & chin up, with fire in your heart, with the flame of light in your eyes, with radiance on your face and a gleaming smile which will make every battle half won.

I'd end by saying that follow your passion with all your heart and you will realize nothing is impossible!

CHAPTER V

# Challenges faced by Women in Indian society

Dr. Komal Makhijani
Former Research Associate at IBSD, Shillong
kml21770@gmail.com

**Prologue**

Many of the prominent World leaders have quoted that the progress of a nation is reflected in the status of the women in that country. But my question is- Are the Women in Independent India still Completely Free?

Do we have equal rights, opportunities and absolute freedom to lead our lives on our own terms? Forget about life, do we even have that much freedom to go out for fresh air alone at 10 PM without giving a second thought about our safety? Do we have the liberty to wear what we want without being judged or getting in-secured about how the outfit will be received publicly? Till today why can't an Indian woman stay single all her life and live life on her terms? Because unfortunately once we are married no matter what position we hold in the outside world, we still are expected to leave our crown in the garage and take over the family responsibilities once we enter the house.

Indian women have no doubt travelled far and wide in breaking age-old shackles and taking full control of their life in terms of career and personal choices but what % of Indian women are we really talking about- 1% maybe.

What about the other 99%?

## 1. Introduction- My story

We are currently living in the age of social media and everything whether it is worth sharing or not has to be posted "ONLINE" to get validation otherwise it does not exist. But is it the actual reality or is it just our Insta Version and why do we really need a fake reality, why We- the highly celebrated Women of India not acceptable in our original form? The biggest challenge faced by Indian women today is that they are always judged and criticized for whatever they do and I still don't understand why, when we are already in 2022 and claiming to be a developed nation, a superpower till 2050. However, before getting into the details of all the challenges we face as women in India, I should start with my introduction.

This is my story, a young girl born and brought up in a small city called 'Ajmer'- highly known for its religious diversity and is marked on the map in Rajasthan. I grew up in a patriarchal family where men were supposed to be the bread winners and women were demanded to be the Perfect Homemakers. But owing to the convent education imparted to me I grew up to be a very ambitious individual who in spite of believing in the family values did not want to be a homemaker, rather wanted to create a niche of my own in the outside world just like my father, brother or any other male counterparts I have grown up watching, do.

Starting with childhood, I was always a short heighted chubby individual and my physical appearance by default gave right to every other individual to fat shame me whether they were related to me or not, but they considered it as their birth right and I have to accept it no matter what influence it had on my growing years or my perception of myself. I really Thank God Instagram was not invented by then otherwise it would have ruined my life forever.

Early Childhood- The good part of being born in the 90's is that I had an amazing childhood because we had summer breaks where we used to go out in the playgrounds and play outdoor games which really helped us to learn how to function in teams where actual humans were involved as compared to the dummies we are dealing with in our Online "Ludo" or "Candy Crush". Another bonus was going to schools regularly where apart from gaining academic knowledge our whole personality was conditioned to be grown up as well-behaved beings. At this point, the statistics which needs to be discussed is the average dropout rate of girls was 17.3% at the secondary level education and

4.74% at the elementary level in 2018-2019. The reason being either the family could not afford their education, the family thinks it's a waste of time and money and the girl should rather learn cooking/stitching in order to train them to become perfect bahus, or mostly because of lack of sanitation facilities in schools, yes this still exists that girls dropout of schools just because there are no toilets in their schools. Post 2020 however Edu-tech has taken over so no exact statistics of what is the current percentage of girls taking their education seriously now. Mostly people are learning from Facebook posts and Instagram reels these days.

Moving on, I grew up around a lot of men, being the only girl child and also in my colony a lot of guys were simultaneously born along with me so even my friends were usually boys. One thing I would like to highlight here is we should always raise our kids- whether it's a girl or a boy in a mixed environment rather than restricting them to their own gender because these early ages of growth lay the foundation of how they perceive and deal with the opposite gender. Girls/boys both should opt for Co-education in schools or at least have brothers/sisters at home or male/female friends so they learn to be comfortable around them and understand how they function differently from their own gender. There is nothing wrong in having a correct set of friends around you who genuinely respect you and treat you as an equal and society should also be less judge-mental while spotting around a mixed gender group of friends. Ladka Ladki sirf dost bhi ho sakte hain- no big deal, the real deal is we have to raise/condition the kids properly at the tender age.

Next comes the deadly teenage, where you don't know what is really happening? And this is difficult for both the genders equally, just they face different issues. Girls have to be introduced with menstruation and associated effects along with how they need to take proper care of their private parts, chest development, acne etc. while boys are also struck with puberty related changes which decides their future baritone, beard growth, raging hormones, peer pressure and on top of that boards.

Both the genders equally face the pressure of scoring good marks and higher ranks in their Intermediate term, however, to fulfill different set of future expectations. Girls are expected to get good marks so that they can be eligible wives to learned men, boys are expected to score high because that eventually decides their dowry range (Although the current generation is barring all these age-old norms, still these issues are prevalent in rural areas and even in highly educated families). Girls at this stage should not even be talked about marriage and should be encouraged to educate themselves. Financial independence should be every girl's first choice not a final resort, when due to a sudden mishappening in future she is left with no choice but to self-sustain. What if a woman in her forties, becomes a widow, has no option of going back to her parental house because her father is not anymore and the brother is not financially strong enough to feed more than his own family, where will the girl go? How will she survive, feed her kids when she has got just secondary education and do not possess any vocational degree? Who will hire her? THINK, before you plan your future.

Next comes Adulthood- when we were kids, we thought adults have their lives sorted and hence wanted to grow fast because we thought we will get rid of the home work and this science le lo, commerce opt kar lo pressure, but who knew once you grow up the level of tests life throws at you also grows exponentially. This stage is particularly challenging for Women because society expects you to finish your formal education, find a suitable groom, settle down have kids because otherwise it would be difficult to conceive at a later age or they will allow you to get work experience for a year or two so that you don't get to complaint later ("Jaa Jee le Apni Zindagi" Theory). And this time bound happiness is applicable to only Women in India, Men do not face such deadlines. I always believe that it is equivalent to hell experience- being an ambitious, independent and on top of that competent women in India because once you realize your worth and do not wish to settle for anything less than what you deserve, you are instantly declared a rebel, by first your close ones and then eventually the Great Indian Judge-mental Society (The "Char Vella Log" who I do not understand why are so jobless to interfere in another person's life choices).

Then it's time for the Big Fat Indian Wedding Phase of an Indian Women's Life- I have now turned into a 32 year old, single, ambitious, financially independent and the scariest of all- an explorer cum wanderer who wants to shift places every now and then to experience different work places, traditions, cuisines and is interested in building in my professional and personal network by meeting likeminded people and has been sadly but honestly being termed as "Awara" by own mother because women my age are supposed to be already married with two kids by now. The irony is boys who were born with me, who are my age and still single are considered mature, eligible, sensible bachelors who decided to first become financially stable and then settle down. And on top of that if a woman has the audacity to point out the discrimination, they are advised to keep their voices low and do not try to compete with men as they are just trying to be responsible sons before they become "the so-called responsible husbands", when the truth is those guys are just commitment phobics who eventually want to try/test/go out with every other girl they meet and settle for the most perfect match. Another issue is the liberty/freedom to choose your own partner. Women in India still do not reserve 100% rights to marry a person of their choice- and for convenience here we are talking about only straight homo sapiens. If I have go into the details of how much the LGBQTIA community faces in-spite of all the laws being passed in their favour, a separate volume of books will be required. Discrimination between a girl and a boy in India starts even before the birth and that is one of the biggest challenges a woman faces when she decides to create a path of her own. The upcoming section discusses a few challenges faced by Indian Women even in 2022 followed by a few modifications which might be considered.

**2. Women Categories in India**

Women in India are divided into three categories currently- The first one is the "Privileged category"- Here we are talking about women belonging to upper class who have either inherited parental properties, have achieved breakthrough in their careers or having potential stake's in Multi-National companies, enjoying premium wine and dine experiences every day or at least every weekend, going out with their girl gangs for Sunday brunches and scrolling through Instagram all through the week to find a new hangout place to chill with their friends or to host a kitty. The second category is the "Ambitious/Progressive category"- these are women who belong to middle class families, have seen bad days in their childhood where it was difficult to afford luxury meals in the last days of the month and thus were determined to work hard, acquire good positions in order to raise the standard of living of their families and also to settle well for themselves. The last one is the "Ignorant/Unprivileged category of women- these either were born back-to-back in the hope of them coming out as a boy, or fall prey to the crutches of early marriages or teenage romances and now being in their early 20's or 30's have no idea what it is to live life on their own terms because they already have given the right to take all important decisions concerning them and their future to the significant men in their lives. Another category of women which is recently ringing bells is the "Experienced/Learnt from their Past/Woke" or we can say the "Second innings" category- this involves women in their 40's who have been excellent homemakers, sacrificed their early life for their kids and family to settle down and have now decided to make a mark in the outside world to create an identity of their own.

**3. Status of Women in Society**

The default settings even in a computer when you start writing an email is Respected Sir why not Madam/Ma'am, why it is always understood that a man is in charge, why not a woman? A recent famous OTT Drama series glorified women by quoting "Common man hota hai because Woman cannot be common, they are always special, is it so? Women in India are given special treatment only for some holy days (Navratri and Durga Puja), otherwise there are a lot of issues this gender is facing on a day-to-day basis namely- body shaming, online trolling, menstruation and PMS jokes and leaves, debates on period and maternity leaves, dowry, child marriage, constant threat of being raped or sexual harassment in public, pressure to always look attractive, womb to tomb discrimination, judgements on their choices, pressure to put up family's reputation and interests over their own happiness, and the list is endless. Women are constantly trapped to make rightful decisions when it comes to Society, Sanskar and marital choices, which might not benefit women personally but will keep up the family reputation as women are born to carry the same in their flesh and blood. Domestic violence is on the rise even in educated middle and upper classes and the laws pretending to protect these still give do not give women the freedom to make reasonable choices nor are they trusted to make moral choices, just expects Women to compromise at every level.

Why compromises must be made only by women?

**3.1 Entry into Restricted/Male Dominant Professions**

The nuclear family culture has given the right to Indian women to go out and work, again this is 90% to sustain the family because of rising inflation, improved standards of living in urban areas and also to some extent the desire to be financially independent has propelled women to become a paid employee, otherwise every woman is a working individual, it's just only who are working professionally are earning. However, opportunities outside the house for women earlier were only restricted to semi professions like nursing, teaching, clerical, etc. It is now they have entered full-fledged, male dominated professions like Medicine, Media, Law, Business, STEM and humanities. Aviation industry is also providing women success stories starting from Gunjan Saxena to the latest Mahasweta Chakraborty, a member of 'Operation Ganga' who flew six evacuation flights to bring back 800 stranded students amidst Russia-Ukraine crisis. These days we can witness women pandits and Imams to carry holy matrimonial processions as well. Railway stations completely operated by women (Matunga, Mumbai), Full women cabin crew staff to even Samsung opening up full female staff outlets to Nirbhaya Squads are all tiny steps towards women entering new horizons. But the roadblocks in this direction are gender pay gaps, motherhood penalties, sexual harassment at the workplace, promotion biasness, working hours flexibility are hindering the women to climb the ladder and rise through the ranks. One modification in this regard can be Women who have achieved a mark and uphold managerial positions need to be supportive of each other rather than standing against or competing against one another just as men do and thus can grow together.

### 3.2 High on EQ's Low on IQ's

A women herself might be going through the lowest phase of her life, but if her family needs her, she will be there rock solid with a smile facing the issue without even hinting the internal battles she is going through and contrast to this men cannot tolerate the same hurt they inflict on women, still the saying goes like "**Mard to Dard nahi hota**", when actually it should be like "**Mard ko Aurat jitna dard kabhi sehna hi nahi padta**", whether its physical, emotional or any other category of pain you can think of or inflict on any living being. But women are perceived as just **wax dolls** whose main aim in life should be to grow as beautiful ladies and become a **trophy wife**. Another side of the story, if a woman is indeed near perfect in looks, she is perceived to be as dumb. A woman mastering both beauty and brain departments is considered a rare species in India and unlike Men we can either be High on Emotional Quotient, Low on Intelligent Quotient or vice versa but never a balance of both. A challenge faced by women in India is they either have to live with this notion all their lives or spend their entire life defying the same.

### 3.3 Women Post Marriage

Why does a married woman have to look like one i.e., to portray all the symbols of marriage while all men have to do is wear a ring that also they take out usually when they are in social gatherings without their better half. Why pregnancy and marriage are termed as a career ender for a woman? WHY are women asked whether they will continue working post marriage? No man has ever been asked that question because they are considered as the default bread owners of the family. Why is an Indian woman always liable to take up the last name of Husband/ father?

What joy people get in getting the Perfect Homemaker tag or being a Multi tasker every time- nothing, it's just a pretentious act women put up just to maintain the so called "**ghar ki shanti**". Vulnerability and Dependence on men, if women are not financially independent were and still are the root cause of unhappy women in Indian households. Plight of single mothers in on another level, because such women not only face financial issues by suddenly taking the responsibility of being the bread earner but also have to face the vultures outside the house who takes her as an easy prey since she is all by herself now. Who gave this quote- "**Akeli ladki khuli tijori ki tarah hoti hai**", from where these ideas are stemming? My guess would definitely be a male writer who is either not raised well or does not really have enough sense what does being a woman really mean.

The simple reason to why smart, educated, financially independent women are choosing to remain single these days is very much clear, they do not want to give up the entire life which they have created for someone who does not even acknowledge their importance and is more interested in unlocking random tijoris every night.

### 3.4 Typical Beauty Standards

Women come in all shapes, sizes, mindsets, aspirations and dreams just like any other living being then why are we stereotyping them? Why is it so difficult to accept them in their original skin? Women are trolled in case their Stretch marks are visible. Till when will women be judged for something which is not even under their control. Stretch marks are something a woman gets usually after giving birth, the most difficult and purest job a human being can do and on top of that people have the courtesy to mock the after effects. Where have we lost the humanity?

Body shaming, eve teasing, judgements on Dressing, Hair and Make-up choices- whether to put or not, which brands you use, which salon you go? are just a few issues to name. A recent ad by Dove propagated as #stop the beauty test campaign featured how an Indian woman goes through a series of tests and interviews before being selected as a daughter-in-law, wife for a male candidate who gets offended even when asked about his current CTC. Men can be anything but women always need to put out their best foot when they are being screened as prospective brides. If a woman who is well aware of her rights, do not wish to participate in this circus and decides to challenge Patriarchy- is again instantly credited as a trouble maker who has the audacity to speak up where in the name of culture her existence is threatened, her parents are embarrassed in front of everyone, her self-esteem is diminished just because she could not match up to the unreal, one sided standards of the prospective groom? Till when will this be continued and who is benefitting from this? The same groom will cry after a year even after finding the most beautiful bride, complaining that she spends too much money and time grooming herself and does not really look after him. Sort out your choices first Dear Men, what exactly do you want from Women?

**3.5 Safety Concerns**

Statistics show that a woman is raped every 16 minutes in India and our country enjoys a higher rank in the list of places being regarded as 'unsafe' for women. In this section my only question is WHY do we need special protection Squads for Women in this Independent India we are talking about? Every year Women's Day is celebrated, not to glorify the beauty and grace of women, but to bring about awareness among the public regarding women's safety. Women are expected and encouraged to increase their moral strength and face the world without fear. Women are taught to be bold and outgoing in these days of modernism. My point is why so much expectation and work are required from a woman's end when she is not even happy being raped/molested or even touched by her own partner without her consent. Do we even need to point out the challenge faced by women in India in this regard?

I will simply conclude this section by vouching that there is not even a single woman in this country who has at least once not being sexually harassed- whether it is at home, office, bus, train, a fare, social gathering or even while walking on a heavily traffic loaded road. Do we still need separate rights to actually fight for our rights? Shouldn't slogans like **"beti bachao and beti padhao" be replaced by "Ladka Padhao and Acha Insaan Banao"**- is it not a basic criterion for every human being.

**4. Break the stereotype**

Today one segment of Online stories focuses on Women empowerment or promoting uploads without filter but the major section is still influenced by near perfect size, always glowing with lustrous hair, party ready Women no matter its day, night or even early morning. A recent campaign which garnered much attention on Online portals was #Breakthebias. My question here is why do we need such campaigns for women every now and then, highlighted particularly in the first week of March (International Women's Day celebration on 8th March) or in the second week of May (Mother's Day Celebration). Is it just these days we should respect and honor The Women in our life along with the eight days of Navratri Festival or will it be fair enough for them to enjoy this status everyday just like men do? Do we need to be treated respectfully just on Women's Day or the eight days of Navratri, what about the other 356 days of the year?

*** Amelioration in the status of women**

Women in India are Reaching Pinnacle of success. They have already crossed horizons and are no more restricted to clerical jobs of being nurses, receptionists (No offense against the people working on these positions, rather huge respect for covering the ground work), have now started holding positions of power like doctors, lawyers, scientists, engineers and even entrepreneurs. India is witnessing a Wave of Women Entrepreneurs- Indra Nooyi-Pepsico, Nykaa- Falguni Nayar, Bharat Biotech- Suchitra Ella, Biocon- Kiran Mazumdar Shaw, Sugar Cosmetics- Vineeta Singh, Mama Earth- Ghazal Alagh, Emcure- Namita Thapar, Chanel-Leena Nair, One Digital- Himani Ahuja, The Kharigars- Aashita Chadha are just a few to name. But not just the urban, even the rural women manage their own finances in terms of land mortgages, tea plantations, ownership in fields, etc. Women in India are no longer meant to be admired just for their looks, they are leading empires now. The other side of the story however is that they are still judged for female health issues, Jokes/ memes about PMS, Maternity leaves and menstruation leaves are still debatable, shared responsibility at the house is still a taboo so a lot of scope of improvement is there. But times are changing for Indian women and that is something which needs to be celebrated as well as the progress should be amplified. Recognition, Appreciation and Acknowledgement of the work they do, the sacrifices they make is the right of every woman and if done at the right time can be a big motivation for them to bloom and prosper. I would like to suggest examples of few movies here which demonstrates the fight of the female protagonists, their endurance, and finally, their overcoming of the old culture or religion, which was responsible for restraining their friendship, love, and life- "Water" by *Deepa Mehta*, "The Phantom Lover" by *Ronny Yu*, and "Rashomon" by *Akira Kurosawa*, "English Vinglish" by *Gauri Shinde* are a treat to watch, to learn and to celebrate womanhood because otherwise being a Woman in India is a hard pill to swallow.

**Conclusion**- Two clan of Modern Women are existing in India- Urban and Rural and then there is another upcoming tribe who wants to stick to their roots but also be financially and emotionally independent- to make their own choices as they are capable enough to decide what works best for them. Women in India are constantly torn between their happiness and responsibilities, they have to make choices between their freedom or family, career or marriage, kids or promotion, it's always ye ya wo, why can't they get both, is it the birth right of only men to get everything according to their wish and women could not even dream big. We are living in 2022, its high time we get excited about career milestones, travel journeys, personal Development rather than pregnancy and engagement announcements. The goal of this gender should no longer be limited to making significant contribution to the perpetuation of the human species. When women are allowed to flourish, they glow differently. However, is it not even their basic right till date, they need to take permission or fight for something which is considered to be a default setting for the opposite gender. Women in India should be given equal access to jobs and education, we should celebrate their promotion, give them equal rights to choose the right time and a partner of their choice to spend their lives with. They should be always told that there is No need for them to sacrifice their life or happiness for anyone, because at the end of the day no one really remembers what good you have done, all they remember are your flaws, shortcomings and failures. There is no lack of policy decisions or initiatives in India regarding empowerment of Women, the problem is it's still not in practice.

As an independent single woman myself, I do not want to walk through fire for anyone to prove my worth or purity, I just want to live a simple peaceful life that too on my own terms, without being judged or expected to take permission even to breath.

Another important message which needs to be conveyed to young girls in India is that social media is lying to you. It is the biggest gimmick of the present century showing you people having the time of their life with luxury vacations, glowing skins, perfect romantic partners and a very sorted professional life which pays for their vacations, but the reality is quite the opposite. So do not get fooled, do not fall under pressure to fulfil unreal expectations of anyone, enjoy the simplicities of life, work hard to become a better version of your own self, do not ever compare your life with anyone else's because you might not be knowing what battles those people must be facing in their real life.

Last but not the least, always work on your timeline. Do not fall crutches of the unreal, age-old societal deadlines of when you should get married, when is the right time to have a kid, when can you start/transition to a new career. Nobody can define this for anyone and there are no set standards. Everyone progresses at their own pace and limits. Do not ever compare your Chapter No. 1 to someone else's Chapter No. 7. Enjoy the chapters in between because every phase, struggle, difficulty or challenge in your life, demands a different version of you and teaches you important lessons. My last piece of advice to every girl would be to Love and accept yourself the way you are, realise your strengths, do not compare or idolize anyone just for what they pretend to be, focus on scholarships rather than relationships in your early years and believe in yourself. If you have put your heart and soul into your dream, payback will be much bigger then what you have anticipated. So, Dream Big, Work Hard and Rule the World because as women we have everything what it takes to be at the Top. If we can bring Life on Earth, we can do anything.

**REFERENCES**

1. **https://www.sentinelassam.com/north-east-india-news/assam-news/status-of-women-in-indian-society/**
2. https://www.sentinelassam.com/north-east-india-news/assam-news/women-empowerment-a-distant-dream-in-india/
3. http://everythingexperiential.businessworld.in/article/Women-of-Today-The-Changemakers-of-Society/08-03-2021-383218/
4. https://www.thehindu.com/news/national/average-dropout-rate-of-girls-recorded-at-173-at-secondary-level-in-2018-19-wcd-ministry/article33761098.ece

CHAPTER VI

# Dowry System and the Dowry Prohibition Act, 1961

Suman Preet Kaur
Assistant Professor, Department of Sociology
Chandigarh Group of Colleges, Jhanjeri
sumanpreetk.19@gmail.com

**ABSTRACT**

Practice of dowry poses great threat to the life of females. Dowry is an age-old practice in Indian society referring to property or valuable security given by one party to another as a consideration for marriage. This custom of dowry was started in the medieval period. Women were gifted with wealth and jewel from their parents during her marriage and this served as a tool of financial independence for the bride even after marriage. This menace is the root cause of almost all violence against a married woman. In most cases after marriage the problem of dowry will arise. If the wife is not able to provide all, which her husband and in laws demand, her life in the groom's house become miserable. She will be treated cruelly, and, in some cases, she may lose her life.

**INTRODUCTION**

The Dowry System in India is linked with the Marriage establishment. But unlike the present time dowry was completely a voluntary gift in the ancient time to the daughter and her husband. The ancient literaturedepict and suggest that marriage ceremony was one of the important rituals in a person's life, almost compulsory and binding for all theHindu men in general and all women in particular, but there is no mention of Dowry Systemin those texts and literature. During the Vedic period, marriage was a holy bond which was blessed by the Gods and Goddesses themselves and this holy bond could not be broken by any sort of human actions. Authors of literature dedicated towards the writing concerned with dowry system growth in India show that in the past the daughters were not having any rights of inheritance and weredenied of this right, only the son's had the right of inheritance andeventually, only the sons inherited their father's property.

In thisscenario, the parents of the daughter during the time of her marriage out of sheer love and affection used to gift some part of their money and jewellery to her, which apparently have started and triggered the Dowry System the country.

According to Webster's New International Dictionary, "Dowry is the money good or estate which a woman brings to her husband in marriage."

Max Radian says, Dowry is the property which a man receives when he marries, either from his wife or her family."

Ram Ahuja has defined 'dowry as gift and valuables received in marriage by the bride, the bridegroom and his relatives'.

According to the definition of dowry under section 2 of the Dowry Prohibition Act 1961 it is clear that dowry is a property which woman brings to her husband at marriage and includes the land, all sorts of properties, valuable securities given or agreed to be given directly or indirectly at the time of marriage. The term dowry does not include repayment of marriage expenses. The term dowry does not include Mahr.

In this Act, "dowry" means any property or valuables security given or agreed to be given either directly or indirectly.

1. By one party to the marriage to the other party to the marriage, or
2. By the parent of either party to a marriage or by any other person, to either party to the marriage or to any other person,

at or before or any time after the marriage in connection with the marriage of the said parties but does not include dower or mehr in the case of persons to whom the Muslim Personal Law shariat applies.

Explanation: For the removal of doubts, it is hereby declared that any presents made at the time of marriage to either party to the marriage in the form of cash, ornaments, clothes or other articles, shall not be deemed to be dowry within the meaning of this section, unless they are made as consideration for the marriage of the said parties.

Dowry system has eaten into the bones of our society. The birth of a daughter is no occasion of joy for the parents. A girl when becomes young is a burden on her parents. They must face great difficulties in finding out a suitable match for their daughter. It is a problem to get her married in a rich and respectable family without a decent dowry. Many girls commit suicide to save their parents from the evil of dowry. This custom is the root cause of many other evils. Parents collect money by fair and foul means to satisfy the greed of the bridegrooms.

Our government has decided to root out this evil from Indian society. Laws are being made toend this evil. Youngsters are also coming forward to raise their voice against this curse.

Religion, customs and age-old practices have put an Indian woman in a exploitable position in many domains of life. The low rates of democracy, lack of economic independence have resulted in the women being dependent on the men folk and other institution in the society. They are usually ignorant of their rights and do not have proper assess to justice.

**Historical Background**

The original purpose of dowry was to provide 'seed money' or property for the establishment of new household, to help the husband feed and protect his family and to provide some support to his family and family if he were to die. Therefore, the wife brings some other valuable things as the marriage property of her own, which did not include in the dowry, and which was, as a result, her alone. This property was "beyond the dowry".

Young boys who have high salaried jobs or promising careers demand huge amount of money from the girl's parents to accept her as their daughter in law. Now dowry in Indian marriages has become the commercial aspect of the marriage.

Since British rule till date efforts are being made to remove this social evil from Indian society, but still, this evil persists almost in every Indian state.

**Causes of Dowry**

**1. Social custom and Tradition**

Customs influence the way people dress, eat, and in general behave; they may take on the force of moral or statute laws. The social custom and tradition are one of the reasons for Dowry. There is a feeling that practicing customs generates and strengthens solidarity and cohesiveness among people. Many people give and take dowry only because their parents and ancestors had been practicing it.

**2. Security**

In materialistic societies, there are constant pressure on the individual and families for having more and more money not only to provide comforts to families and themselves but also to have some future security therefore, the parents of the bride give money to her daughter so that she secures herself in future.

**3. Caste system**

Dowry system is related to the caste system, as it is paid in order to marry a girl to a boy of the same caste. It is mainly practiced among the higher caste of the girl's family. If the girl is married to a boy from another caste, then it is considered as prestige problem (insult in Indian society specifically among Hindu's). In order to prevent that the bride's family will offer dowry as much as they can so that the bride groom of the same caste will marry the bride.

**4. Desire of the girl's parents**

It is the desire of the girl's parent that "she should live happily with her husband and in-laws and so they think of marrying their daughter in a rich family even if they have to give heavy dowry. The aim of the bride's family is that though they are poor, their daughter should not lead the same life.

**5. Greediness of the boy parents**

Greedy means that wanting more money, power, food etc, than one really needs. In some families when they arrange marriage for their son, they will demand dowry to make easy money, because if the bride's family is unable to give the dowry which is demanded by the bridegroom's family, they will leave the bride and try to get another girl.

**Consequences of Dowry**

**1. It causes economic burden to the bride's family:** Dowry has become a great economic burden for some families, specially, the middle-class family. These people try to maintain their social status by providing education to their children, necessities of life and meeting various social obligations. With the limited money they have to fulfil lot of needs. At the time of their daughter's marriage many parents borrow money or sell their property or mortgage to fulfil the dowry demanded by the groom's party. This incurs debt which is passed on from generation to generation which ultimately leads to the total collapse of the family.

**2. Dowry harassment and murders:** Sometimes women are ill-treated, tortured mentally or physically by their husbands and in-laws in the name of dowry. If the bride's family cannot fulfil their expectation, then they start to torture her. We find many cases in the media regarding the suicide or unnatural death of married women because of dowry.

**3. Dowry leading to immorality:** Practice of dowry is not only regarded as unlawful but even as immoral. According to Gandhiji, one who makes dowry a precondition for his marriage, not only shows disrespect to a woman but also humiliates his own nation, education and womanhood. Practice of dowry leads to immoral practices like corruption to earn money.

**4. Psychological Crises and Emotional Disturbances in the Family:** Practice of dowry leads to unhealthy and unwanted competition among the parents. These ultimately hamper the family peace and happiness. Dowry practices create quarrels and conflicts between husband and wife, daughter-in-law with the other members of the family. These may ultimately influence well-being of the children in the family.

**Measures to Solve the Problem of Dowry**

**Legislative Measures**

**THE DOWRY PROHIBITION ACT, 1961**

**Introduction**

This Act was a legislation in 1961 to deal with increasing cases of harassment of women and families for dowry. For the purpose of this Act, dowry includes anything from property, goods or money given in exchange of marriage. While the Act says it applies to both the bride and the groom's family, in India, the practice tends to be that the family of the woman is expected to give the dowry to the groom's family.

**Objectives**

The objective of the Act is two-fold. One to prevent and eradicate the practice of giving or taking dowry, and second, to criminalise the demand of dowry by any party involved in a marriage arrangement.

**Important Provisions**

This is a short and specialised legislation with only 10 sections that aim to directly tackle the issues and criminalise the same.

**Section 1 Short title, extent and commencement.**

This Act may be called the Dowry Prohibition Act, 1961. It extends to the whole of India except the State of Jammu and Kashmir. It shall come into force on such date as the Central Government may, by notification in the official Gazette, appoint.

**Section 2 Definition of 'dowry'**

In this act, `dowry' means any property or valuable security given or agreed to be given either directly or indirectly:

by one party to a marriage to the other party to the marriage; or

by the parents of either party to a marriage or by any other person, to either party to the marriage or to any other person; at or before or any time after the marriage in connection with the marriage of said parties but does not include dower or mahr in the case of persons to whom the Muslim Personal Law (Shariat) applies.

**Section 3 Penalty for giving or taking dowry**

If any person, after the commencement of this Act, gives or takes dowry or attempts to do the same, they will be liable to be punished with an imprisonment term of not less than five years and a fine of rupees 15,000 or the value of the dowry whichever is higher. The court may also decide to give an imprisonment of not less than 5 years based on the circumstances of the case, but the reasons for doing so must be clearly recorded.

**Section 4 Penalty for demanding dowry**

If any person demands directly or indirectly, from the parents or other relatives or guardian of a bride or bridegroom as the case may be, any dowry, he shall be punishable with imprisonment for a term which shall not be less than six months but which may extend to two years and with fine which may extend to 10,000 thousand rupees. Section 4 A which was added through an amendment in 1986 ban the advertising of offers for shares of property in lieu of marriages. The punishment for such advertising is an imprisonment of 6 months extendable up to 5years.

**Section 5 Agreement for giving or taking dowry to be void**

Any agreement for the giving or taking of dowry shall be void and therefore, unenforceable under any law in force.

**Section 6 Dowry to be for the benefit of the wife or her heirs**

Any dowry received must be transferred to the woman and her heirs or future heirs in connection of whose marriage it is received and the failure to transfer the same will be punishable with 6 months imprisonment extending up to 2 years with a fine of rupees 5000.

**Section 7 Cognisance of offences**

The Metropolitan magistrate or a Judicial Magistrate of the first class will be the authority responsible for taking cognisance of Acts prohibited under this Act.

**Section 8 Offences to be cognisable for certain purposes and to be non-bailable and non-compoundable.**

The Code of Criminal Procedure, 1973 (2 of 1974) shall apply to offences under this Act and the investigating officers will have the power to create offences under this act non-bailable and non –compoundable. Therefore, they can arrest a person without a warrant or without an order of magistrate. Section 8 A creates a burden of proof on the person accused of giving and taking a dowry to prove that they have not committed such an Act. Section 8B gives the power to the state government to appoint dowry prohibition officers who will be responsible for the implementation of this Act and to deal with cases of dowry demand.

**Section 9 Power to make rules**

The Central Government may, by notification in the official Gazette, make rules for carrying out the purposes of this Act.

**Section 10 Power of the State Government to make rules**

The State Government may, by notification in the official Gazette, make rules for carrying out the purposes of this Act. This section was added through the 1986 Amendment to allow the state government to make rules to ensure the implementation and enforcement of this act.

**Non-Legislative Measures:**

**1.Public Awareness against Dowry:** It is necessary to develop awareness against the practice of dowry to abolish this problem from the society. Different media including newspaper, internet, television, etc. be effectively used to convince people that the practice of dowry is not only illegal but also unethical.

**2.Educational Development:** Development of education especially among the girl is very important. It can help in reducing this problem. Through education girls can be economically independent which will enable them to improve their status as well as enable them to take their own decision. Besides this, moral education can help to highlight the evils of the practice of dowry.

**3.Encouraging Inter-caste Marriage:** The endogamous nature of the caste is one of the influencing factors of this problem. So, inter caste marriage may also be helpful in reducing this problem from our society.

**4.Role of Voluntary Association:** It is suggested that voluntary associations should take initiative in this regard and make propaganda against the evil of dowry. Such association should take up cases of victims of dowry harassment and get them justice. They can create a wave against the practice of dowry.

**Criticism**

The evil practise of dowry still exists in society, despite the law. Several states in India amended the Dowry Prohibition Act, 1961, with a view to making it more efficient. However, the attempts were not successful in curbing the dowry menace.

The joint parliamentary committee on the dowry of 1982 cited two main reasons for the failure of the Dowry Prohibition Act. Firstly, the definition of dowry according to Section 2 of the Act excludes all presents (whether cash or kind) from being termed as dowry unless they have been given as a consideration of marriage which is almost impossible to prove that the gifts or presents given at, after or before the marriage was given as a consideration of marriage. The undisputed reason is that no giver of dowry will ever come forward to say that he has given the gifts as a consideration of marriage, as giving dowry is as much of an offence as taking dowry.

Secondly, the Act did not have an effective enforcement instrumentality. No court can take the cognizance of a dowry offence except on complaint, made by a person within one year from the date of the commission of a dowry offence. It is unrealistic to expect the bride or bride's parents or other relations to go to lodge a complaint. The parents are usually the victims of dowry. They are unwilling (and certainly reluctant) to come forward because of their apprehension that it may lead to the victimization of their daughter.

**Importance and Impact**

This is an important legislation to prohibit and curb the evil practice of giving or taking of dowry. While it addresses an important issue, it has been criticised for not achieving its purpose as the practice of dowry continues to exist in today's scenario also. While, this legislation creates criminal punishment for the demand and supply of dowry, it has been ineffective because it does not address the deeply rooted cause of social inequality and social practices that make families think such customs are inevitable, if not, actually necessary. On the same line, there is no effective way to enforce the Act as it is almost impossible to regulate all social customs and events related to marriages, hence, despite awareness and education, people refuse to give up their customary practices.

**REFERENCE:**

1. Ahuja, Ram(1992) Social Problems in India. Rawat Publisher, Jaipur
2. George,Alex Andrews(2021), Important Acts that Transformed India, McGraw Hill publisher, Chennai
3. Myneni, S.R(2017), Sociology, Allahabad Law Agency, ISBN-10 9380231466, ISBN-13 978-9380231464
4. https://www.academia.edu/36168706/Dowry_Death_and_Dowry_System_in_India_Resarch_Paper_by_Dev_Raizada
5. International Journal of Scientific and Research Publications, Volume 7, Issue 3, March 2017 263 ISSN 2250-3153 www.ijsrp.org Dowry System in India by Leila Ateffakhr
6. https://en.wikipedia.org/wiki/Dowry_system_in_India

CHAPTER VII

# Stepping Stones: The Story of an Independent Woman

Manasi M
MA Politics and Human Rights
School of International Relations and Politics
Mahatma Gandhi University
manasikukkuz@gmail.com

It is a fact that women in this world 'survive' in one way or another and even I am not special. Mental traumas, physical health problems, and insecurities are not a new story for women. Here, I don't attempt to narrate an inspirational story for the thriving women. I write this as an appeal to every woman that we can survive here and we have to.

Myself Manasi M, a 23-year-old woman from Kerala. To be precise, a Dalit woman. I was born in a remote village in Palakkad district of Kerala. I had no parents, no siblings. I lost my parents when I was one and half years old and I don't even remember their faces. They had a love affair and married against the will of their respective families. I grew up by listening to two different stories of my family's past.

In one version, my father had some health problems which eventually lead to his death. Unfortunately, my mother couldn't help herself from falling into a deep depression. Her physical health also weakened. When I was one and half years old, I lost my mother too. I wasn't breastfed well and struggled to live. According to my grandparents, I was crying all the time and they tried their level best to help me with several medications. Ignorance is not a mistake and they gave me cow milk which made my situation even worse. They feared that they will lose their grant daughter too.

Regarding the second version, I warn you this story has elements of superstition. In India, every village families have these kinds of stories. My mother was educated and she worked as a nurse while my father was a farmer from a rich family. He was the only brother to five sisters and lost his father during his teenage. Even though both of my parents belonged to the same caste, both families did not agree with the marriage citing economic and educational reasons. My mother's family members considered my father a loser as he was not educated. On the other side, my father's family members thought my mother was trying to steal my father's savings or property. However, with a strong desire to live together, they left their families and went to a hilltop. When I started to kick inside my mother's womb, they returned to their families. People say that my father's sister did witchcraft and he fell ill. According to my grandmother's narration, it was her witchcraft that killed my father (Though, I don't believe this now).

My grandparents were getting older and they found it harder to raise a single girl child. They were scared about my future. I was just four years old when they planned to send me to an orphanage. Fortunately, my teacher Ms. Sreekumari intervened and stopped them. I remember her words, "Now she is studying, so let her enjoy her world. Don't worry about her and she is growing. After a few years, she will stand by herself. "

My childhood narration is never complete without addressing the serene beauty of my village. I only had two pairs of dresses. My grandparents treated me well. I don't know if they were sympathetic to me. I also received special consideration between my cousins and relatives.

In my childhood days, I worked in paddy fields. As the children can be employed at low wages, landowners were more interested in employing us. We were unaware of the legal points against child labour and our families were appreciating us as they received an extra income. This is still a reality in certain tribal regions in the Wayanad district. I had seen children plucking coffee beans without attending school. Blind authorities! I feel.

The ninth standard was my turning point in life. I always used to sleep with my grandmother. One day my cousin came to our home. I decided to give her company at night. Suddenly, I heard a noise from my grandmothers' room. I was afraid; I get up from my bed and ran there. When I opened the door, I saw my grandfather running to his bed. As an ignorant child, I was shocked and thought that my grandfather was raping his partner. Today I feel like my innocence was beyond any logic. I failed to understand their sexual relationship. I feared he will rape me also. See, how a single girl child from a marginalised background is raised in India without any orientation of sex education.

The next day, I moved to my aunt's home. They thought that it was just a holiday visit. After one week, they started to enquire about the reason and I replied to them that I am alone at my home and will feel good with the company of my aunt's children. After a few days, my aunt got a call from my village and she stopped questioning me anymore.

I decided to work in a fancy shop to meet my financial needs. The shop owner was a kind person. He asked me open a bank account so that I can keep my money safely. I opened one and gave the ATM card to my aunt. One day, she asked me to withdraw some money from the account so that she can buy me a gold earring. She put my ATM card on the table which I forgot to take. I could only try to take the money the next day. I was startled. I didn't find any money in the account. Afraid of losing the money, I went to the bank and engaged in an argument with the staff. When I started to cry, the bank manager called me into his cabin. He showed me the details of the date, time, and video of that person withdrawing my money from the bank. That was my cousin. I was shocked again. It was better to lose money rather than see her taking that. At home, everyone was behaving normally and I was burning inside with fear. After some time my aunt asked me about the money. Unwillingly, I explained to her about the incident. Aunt started to beat my cousin with anger. My uncle and aunty started to scold each other also. After that incident, my cousin stopped talking with me. Sadly, I realised that I am an odd one in that family.

When I was 14, I worked for a pencil company. It was a big company. I remember them filling my age as 18 to pass any legal hurdles. I had to carry heavy loads there and faced several health issues also. There were agents for recruiting children like us and my aunt insisted me and my cousin to go to work in our teenage. I won't ever criticise her regarding this. Because she was the backbone of that family. Uncle was an alcoholic and seemed very irresponsible towards the family. Due to this, my aunt fell into a debt trap, and sending us to work didn't seem unethical to her.

However, inside of that house, I was not safe. I repeat. I was not safe. My uncle seemed sexually frustrated. I remember him staring at me when there wasn't anyone else in the house. Sometimes, he raised his *dhoti* and underwear and showed his penis while rubbing his knee. A kid like me was freezing and sweating at the same time. I really felt so. I was quite ignorant like any other rural girl in India and feared to share this with others. Molestation inside the family didn't end here. One day, I and my cousin brother were lying down in the afternoon for a nap. After closing my eyes, I felt his hands placing over my body. He slowly started to touch me and quickly pressed my breasts. I was shocked like I wasn't even able to move at least one of my fingers. After a few seconds, I was able to make some sound and he suddenly woke up and went out. I started to cry thinking of my fate. I was thinking about whether this will happen to me if I had my parents alive and looking after me.

Eventually, these incidents made me 'escape from the family' institution. I started dreaming of a peaceful life and future studies. After passing the 10$^{th}$ standard, my aunt asked me to stop studying and carry on with any jobs. While asking me to do so, she also wanted her daughters to continue with academics. Though I felt sad about her hypocrisy, I took a strong decision to leave my village in order to continue with my higher studies. I wasn't such a strong girl to flee all of a sudden. I was afraid of society. But, I slowly made my decision to move. I was of the thought that if anything is going to damage me, it is rape. I realised that if I continue to fear travelling outside my village, I won't reach anywhere. Fear and anxiety killed me every second. I decided to call my tuition sir who sponsored my tuition fees for class ten. He encouraged me to pursue my higher secondary studies and joined a school in Palakkad town. Thus, 2014 marked the beginning of my hostel life. Thankfully, tuition sir sponsored my expenses for the next two years also.

I completed higher secondary education with a first-class. After the course, I had no other option but to go back to my aunt's house. She again tried to lock me there according to their plan. She always scolded me. No one was in favour of me. I was depressed. I even tried to commit suicide several times. There wasn't any hope left to live and I was thinking about how to die all the time. Somehow, I went to meet my first standard teacher who stopped me from going to the orphanage. I told her everything. She gave me a teacher's contact number. Her name was Latha. She was a mother of two boys. So, she loved girls very much. I contacted her and she asked me if she can meet me. I went to her. I will say that she is the best human being I have ever met.

After some time, I got admission to a government college in Chalakkudy, Thrissur district. I went to the college with my old hostel inmate's friend. When the class started I went to Juvana aunt's home. I stayed there for two to three days. They were social workers and treated me well. Fortunately, I could get into the hostel soon. It was during this period that I closely understand contemporary politics and literature. I started to read, started to speak. I earned the energy to survive alone and to understand people.

When I was in the second semester, I was infected with dengue fever. I was admitted in the hospital. I didn't know how to handle that situation. I wasn't even able to stand up. Then, some friends took care of me. Latha teacher supported me mentally and financially. Those three years in college were beautiful for me. I experienced everything. My attitude towards sex began to change. I had a relationship for two and a half years. I learned to express every emotion from how to cry, to love, to be angry, and to be happy.

After graduation, I was a little confused about whether to go for a job or study further. I did some small works like surveys associated with an NGO. Then, I decided to apply for post-graduation in Politics. Entrance exams were conducted during the survey. Even though I was not interested, at a certain point, I decided to join Mahatma Gandhi University. When the Covid19 led to the closure of institutions and hostels, I remember how much insecurity and space lessness was felt by independent women like us. Thankfully, I was with one of my friend's families for several months. Our course was completed in 2021. Now, at this time when I write this, I stand confused about the future. After the introduction of the National Education Policy (2020), M.Phil. was withdrawn. Average students like us cannot pursue a Ph.D. without a research orientation. Though I wasn't interested to leave the academic space, the lack of seats for a Ph.D. and withdrawal of M.Phil. now forces me to choose other ways.

Being an independent woman in India is not that easy. We will face a lot of hurdles from the social and political systems. I don't find any particular policy formulations or schemes that would aid such independent women like us. When I write this, I appeal for a better future and proactive state mechanisms to ensure the welfare of women in India.

# Marriage: Contract based on profit or Relationship based on love ?

CHAPTER VIII

# Acid attack: An Identity Erasure

Sobia Jan
Research Scholar
Department of Applied Sciences
University of Kashmir
Drsobiajan@gmail.com

**Abstract:**

Acid attacks on women have turn out to be the most scorching area and are considered to be the wickedest and the most brutal kind of violence committed mostly on women. Worldwide, India has the utmost number of acid attacks every year, and despite the actions taken by the Indian Government and the Supreme Court of India, the crime is on the rise. This increase can be attributed to the patriarchal ideology that is prevalent in India and to India's inadequate legal system, which does not deliver efficient remedies to the victims. The consequences of an acid attack are the lifelong bodily deformity. The only intention of the lawbreakers is to disfigure the body of the target. Generally acid are thrown at the face of the target so that it would burn and damage skin tissue. At times it makes the person blind, as well as everlasting pocking of the face. Moreover, overall life of victim degrades in the society like social, economic and psychological life. This article will discuss the occurrence of acid attacks in India. The study concludes that majority of acid attacks occur in Uttar Pradesh, most of the which took place in the year 2019 and majority of the acid attacks occurred due to refusal/ rejection of marriage or love.

**Keywords:** Acid Attacks, Violence, Women, India, Bodily Disfigurement.

**Introduction:**

The position of women in India is very weak and feeble. Since ages, she has been made to suffer multitudinous and countless number of violence during her lifetime. Out of these incalculable number of violence, acid attack is considered to be the most horrendous and awful kind of violence where the woman is made to suffer for no blunder and blooper on her part. Violence on women has always been a contentious issue. Some say that it is escalating, while others give credit to the more reporting that is being done. Undoubtedly, usually throughout the orb, women occupy a very frail and portentous status. It has been rightly said that from her cradle to her last breath, she is subjected to everlasting and ceaseless numbers of violence. It is not only predominant in developing and underdeveloped countries, but women in developed countries are also ensnared and entwined in the perils of violence (Goswami and Handa 2020). Acid attack is one of the violence women faced. Acid attack is "any act of throwing acid or using acid in any form on the victim with the intention of or with knowledge that such person is likely to cause to the other person permanent or partial damage or deformity or disfiguration to any part of the body of such person" (National Commission of India). In a layman's language, acid attack is the thoughtful attack where acid is used as a weapon and is thrown on someone to torment, pester and harass that person. The most usually employed chemical in acid attacks is sulphuric acid (oil of vitriol); hence, it is called as vitriol age. Acid attack, also known as acid violence or vitriol age, has appeared as a spiteful and vicious act that shows the gravity and enormity of the enduring atrocities and violation of human rights.

**Review and Literature:**

The severity of bodily injury depends primarily on the concentration or the type of acid used for the attack, and secondarily on the amount of time the body was exposed to the acid. The longer a body is exposed the more damage the victim will endure. Acids are so corrosive they rapidly dissolve skin, fat and muscle, and even reach bones and organs in some cases (Law Commission of India, 2009). Victims endure complete or partial destruction of essential body parts such as eyelids, ears, nose, nostrils, mouth, lips, eyes, cheeks, chin, neck, forehead, skull, breasts (including destruction or cessation of development of breasts in young girls), shoulders, and hair, all of which impair a victim for life (Law Commission of India, 2009).

Menon and Vashistha (2013) conducted a study on 'Vitriol age & India- the Modern Weapon of Revenge'. The author in the article highlights the common reasons of acid violence and the post attack evil consequences that the victims and their families undergo. Two of the most important issues raised by the authors in this article are 'role of police in the investigation of acid attacks' and 'judiciary's role in prosecuting the perpetrators of acid attack'.

Law Commission of India (2009). Victims also suffer severe psychological trauma, primarily due to the pain and terror they undergo during an attack, and secondarily due to the realization that they have a permanently disfigured/ disabled body This destruction of the victim's primary physical/social identity exposes them to severe psychological diseases over the lifespan.

Karmakar (2006) conducted a study on "Forensic Medicine and Toxicology: Theory, Oral & Practical". The author mentioned the permanent disfigurement of head and face and permanent loss of eyesight. The book highlights the motive behind this heinous crime. The author also mentions about the treatment or first aid that should be provided to the victim immediately after the attack.

Patel (2014) conducted a study on "A desire to disfigure: Acid attack in India. International journal of criminology and sociological theory". **The study reveals that Victims report suffering severe depression, insomnia, recurring nightmares, and fear of another attack, headaches, and reluctance to face the world or participate in society. Victims also experience increased anxiety.**

**Research Methodology:** The secondary sources of data has been used to collect the data. The data has been collected mostly from various journals, books, articles, government published annuals reports, website of different government agencies.

**Result and discussion:**

| S.NO | Year | Acid Attacks | Percentage |
|---|---|---|---|
| 1 | 2018 | 228 | 34.7 |
| 2 | 2019 | 249 | 37.8 |
| 3 | 2020 | 182 | 27.7 |
| | **Total** | **657** | **100.0** |

**Table No.1: Year wise Acid Attacks**

*Source: National Crime Records Bureau*

| S.NO | States | Acid Attacks | Percentage |
|---|---|---|---|
| 1 | Uttar Pradesh | 260 | 39.5 |
| 2 | West Bengal | 248 | 37.7 |
| 3 | Delhi | 114 | 17.5 |
| 4 | Gujrat | 35 | 5.3 |
| | **Total** | **657** | **100.0** |

**Table No.2: State wise Acid Attacks**

*Source: National Crime Records Bureau*

| S.No | Reasons for Acid Attacks | Number | Percentage |
|---|---|---|---|
| 1 | Dowry | 30 | 4.5 |
| 2 | Marital dispute | 79 | 12.0 |
| 3 | Property dispute/ Family related dispute | 90 | 13.7 |
| 4 | Refusal/rejection of Marriage/Love | 108 | 16.4 |
| 5 | Unknown | 350 | 53.3 |
| | **Total** | **657** | **100.0** |

**Table No.3: Reasons for Acid Attacks**

*Source: Gathered by investigator*

**Year wise Acid Attacks**

Table.No:1 showed that India faced total 657 acid attack cases in period of 3 years (2018, 2019 and 2020) out of which majority i.e. 37.8 per cent (f=249) acid attacks cases took place in the year 2019, followed by 34.7 per cent (f=228) in the year 2018. However, lowest number of cases i.e. 27.7 per cent (f=182) took place in the year 2020.

**State wise Acid Attacks**

Table.No:2 reveals that out of 657 acid attack cases highest number i.e. 39.5 per cent (f=260) took place in Uttar Pradesh, followed by 37.7 per cent (f=248) in West Bengal, 17.5 per cent (f=114) in Delhi. However lowest number of acid attack cases i.e. 5.3 per cent (f=35) took place in Gujrat.

**Reasons for Acid Attacks**

Table.No:3 highlights that there are different reasons behind acid attack cases. However, highest number i.e. 53.3 per cent (f=350) acid attack cases has unknown reasons. Whereas, 16.4 per cent (f=108) attacks occurred due to refusal/ rejection of marriage or love, followed by 13.7 per cent (f=90) cases has property dispute/family related disputes behind attack, 12.0 per cent (f=79) cases occurred due to marital dispute. However lowest number of attacks i.e.4.5 per cent (f=30) occurred due to dowry.

**Summary and Conclusion:**

Acid attacks are the supreme criminal form of violence that is resorted to and is mostly gender specific. While acid attacks are reported in many parts of the world, the incidents of acid attacks in India have been on the increase. Since acid attacks have such severe consequences, victims need immediate remedies including compensation so that they can protect themselves at least from physical disabilities with the help of corrective surgeries. The study concludes that majority of acid attacks occurred in Uttar Pradesh, most of the attacks took place in the year 2019 and majority of the acid attacks occurred due to refusal/ rejection of marriage or love.

**Reference:**

1. Goswami. S and Handa.R.K (2020).The Peril of Acid Attacks in India and Susceptibility of Women. *Journal of Victimology and Victim Justice*. 3(1). Pp 72–92. www.in.sagepub.com/journals-permissions-india.
2. Karmakar (2007), Forensic Medicine and Toxicology by Hardcover, 1,220 Pages, Published by *Academic Publishers*. ISBN-13: 978-81-89781-40-8, ISBN: 81-89781-40-5
3. Law Commission of India. (2009). 226th Report: The inclusion of acid attacks as specific offences in the Indian penal code and a law for compensation for victims of crime. https://lawcommissionofindia.nic.in/reports/report226.pdf.
4. Minakshi. G (2016). A Review of Literatures on Acid Attacks in India, 1 MSSV J. *Human. Soc. Sci.*, 1, 1, available at https://www.mssv.co.in/Journal/vol1no2/MSSVJHSS010201.pdf

5. Menon and Vashishtha (Oct, 2013) International Journal of Humanities and Social Science Invention ISSN (Online): 2319 – 7722, ISSN (Print): 2319 – 7714.Volume 2(10) PP.01-09. www.ijhssi.org
6. Patel, M. (2014). A desire to disfigure: Acid attack in India. International journal of criminology and sociological theory, 7(2), 1-11 https://ijcst.journals.yorku.ca/index.php/ijcst/article/view/39702

CHAPTER IX

# Women and Human Trafficking

Dr. Loveleen Kaur
Assistant Professor, Post Graduate Studies Department,
Punjabi University Regional Center,
Bathinda, Punjab
loveleenchatha@gmail.com

**Abstract**

The present article traces the history of trafficking in the world. Trafficking of humans like commodities is a crime violating the rights of individual. It also articulates how women are more vulnerable to fall a prey of trafficking and how this shady business of earning money is increasing manifolds. Trafficking is serious violation of human rights by exposing the women and children to physical, emotional and psychological abuse. It also highlights the various types of trafficking prevalent in the society.

The simplest meaning of the term trafficking is an illegal trade of something for profit which is otherwise not allowed openly. The articulations associated with the term are significantly changing. From the illegal trade of commodities, it soon became a trade of human beings especially the vulnerable ones like the children and women. The present paper aims to study the history of human trafficking and the important literary works that speak against this practice of trading bodies across borders. Human trafficking is a crime because it violates human rights by forcing them into an illegal trade especially for economic or commercial exploitation. The term trafficking has acquired a gendered nuance in the contemporary world wherein it comes to be associated with the women and girls.

Tracing the economic incentives associated with trafficking, it is a lucrative industry generating easy money for the traders of bodies. It is one such industry that sans border, race, ethnicity, caste and social status and is prevalent across the globe. It seems to indicate a transnational organized network that operates at several levels. Women and children are bought and sold like cattle in markets for sexual exploitation, to work in porn industry, illegal adoptions, sex tourism, organ trade and even for the trade of wombs. They are forced to work in hostile environments. The advent of the era of information technology has given this industry a new dimension, helping the trade into flourishing at the global level. Internet has led to a greater organization, better management of this business, especially the porn industry that works digitally. Some of the social networking sites are working as its commercial centers where information and services are provided digitally. Recently a famous platform was attacked globally for virtually attacking victims and forcing them into this trade.

The United Nations has banned trafficking and declared it as a punishable crime under its UN convention and protocol. It defines human trafficking as:

**The recruitment, transportation, transfer, harboring or receipt of persons by means of the threat or use of force or other forms of coercion, of abduction, of fraud, of deception, of the abuse of power or of a position of vulnerability or of the giving or receiving of payments or benefits to achieve the consent of a person having control over another person, for the purpose of exploitation.** (qtd. In "United Nations office on Drugs and crime" Article 3, paragraph (a).

Trafficking of women and children is regarded as modern-day slavery by the international community which is rapidly rising at national, international as well as regional level. It is all the more alarming because it is a gender and age sensitive phenomenon. Human trafficking has its origins in the traditional notion of slavery. In the past, it was thought that criminals or prisoners could be put to some use by making them work in place of merely getting rid of them. Slowly this usability came to be associated with the sexual usability. In Tony Morrison's *Beloved*, the central character Sethe takes the dire step of killing Beloved just to save her from experiencing the same physical, mental and spiritual trauma that she herself had experienced as a slave.

**Slavery**

Slavery and trafficking can exist in all forms and situations. Some important characteristics needed to identify it is the existence of complete control of one person over the other, no value or remuneration of someone's services and it is always profit oriented. The most significant element of the slavery and trafficking is the loss of one's conscious and free will over oneself. Slaves are normally considered as half humans who are always at the threshold of the mainstream society. In the past they were either the offspring of erstwhile slaves, some unwanted children of poor families who were compensated for money, or they were prisoners of war. Conventionally they were only made to work inside the domestic spheres which slowly widened and encompassed other spheres of work also.

Slavery had been prevalent in India from the ancient period onwards with the existence of the *daasis* and the courtesans. Even the civilizations as old as the Mediterranean, the Roman and the Middle Eastern has exercised slavery and influenced it in America and the Europe by considering themselves as the masters of their slaves. These slaves were forced to do household work as well as prostitution. African slaves were extensively trafficked for working in the plantations, in mines and at homes. Slavery is defined by the use of force, the profit from the unpaid labor and the use of violence as a means to control the slave. During the ancient times, slaves were captured forcibly and were put for auction but the modern slavery is a well-organized sector that lures its victims for a better future and the use of deceit where poverty is one of the driving forces that makes the victims land into the racket of trafficking and slavery.

**Prostitution**

Prostitution is the modern form of gendered slavery which is the result of the gender inequalities and the assault of society on women. Women's body is used as a site of making profit. In the past also erotic display of the female body has been extensively used in various art forms including painting, sculptor, poetry as well as drama. It was during the sixteenth and the seventeenth century that its status changed tremendously. The Western traders dealt in the trading of the Japanese slave women who were bought for the leisure of their troops in various colonies. Some efforts were made to resolve the problem of prostitution and slavery with the setting up of Advisory Committee on Social and Moral Welfare Board in early 1954. The *Devdasi* system which evolved during the Pallavas and the Cholla dynasty believed in offering women to the deities for appeasing the Gods. The women called the *Devdaasis* were offered for the overall well-being of the society, for the fertility of the land and for a good harvest. However, this practice transformed later into the establishment of prostitution and came to be known as the *Tawaifs* in the North India. The poor and the needy girls were used in the name of social tradition and custom. In the west also, prostitution remained a regulated profession especially in the city of Amsterdam where play houses and brothels were designated for this profession. It was considered as a shameful profession and was always kept out of the civil society. The Catholic Church considered it as a sin which could be only redeemed through the path of nunnery. During the golden age of the Dutch, Amsterdam remained a flourishing center of trafficking of bodies for sexual indulgence because of the extravagant lifestyle of the age. It was also the economic compulsion of the victims which forced them deeper into the never-ending pits.

Slavery and prostitution are the two facets of the modern-day human trafficking where someone else's body is used and exploited for financial and economic gains. Trafficking is the import and export of human being like goods from an economically backward area to an economically developed area. Trafficking is an umbrella term for various crimes against women like child marriage, prostitution, womb trade, organ trade and pornography. A very shocking revelation was made by *The Tribune* of a bride bazaar in Hyderabad wherein agents exploited girls from poor families into marrying rich old age grooms who took the girls abroad and dumped them into prostitution. These girls were forced into flesh trade in the name of marriage, and their families happily married them into these fake wedlock's which were merely a cast for prostitution. The plight of child victims is also evident through the pain of Nujood, the main protagonist of the novel *I am Nujood, Age 10 and Divorced*. It reveals the shocking plight of very young girls who are sold in the market for flesh trade. It is a biopic based on the story of a young Yemenese girl, born into a strongly patriarchal Khardji family. After her first year at school, she was married off to a middle-aged man, barely at an age when she couldn't even understand the meaning of marriage. Her father convinced her elder sister that he was unable to pay off for his family due to which he is going to marry Nujood at a very tender age in return of some money. Nujood is married and is taken to her in laws house where nobody even acknowledges her presence. She finally reclines to her room with the hope of getting a sleep but the very first night, at the age of 10, she is sexually slaughtered by her middle-aged husband. She screams in pain and suffering and her screams fall on the deaf years of her family. She has no escape from her situation, since neither her parent, nor her in-laws give an ear to her woes. She is forced to work at home during the day time and for her husband at night in the bed.

**Organ Trade**

Another type of trafficking which has no gender marked boundaries is the organ trade. It raises a doubt whether science is a boon or a curse for mankind; wherein organs are harvested and traded for money. Here also the most vulnerable ones are the marginalized people especially the women and the kids. Often it comes as the responsibility of a woman to feed her family and in situations where the husband doesn't earn, the woman is forced to do odd jobs to make her both ends meet. So, organ trade is a very lucrative offer left for the poor and vulnerable to fetch some money by selling their vital organs. In a popular show *Human* on the online streaming platform "Hotstar", the dark side of human trafficking is exposed wherein humans are smuggled and kept captive for conducting vaccine and other medical trials. It reveals how large capitalist houses work in an organized way to carry out their shady affairs. Manjula Padmanabhan's play *Harvest* of the same name also portrays the theme of organ harvest which leaves the economical and gendered marginalities exposed to the threat of trafficking. Another important seminal work of a reputed journalist Scott Carney, *The Red Market: On the Trials of World's Organ Brokers, Bone thieves, Blood Farmers and Child Traffickers,* explores the trafficking of vital organs like blood, kidney, bones and even eggs. The book also exposes one such police raid in which it unearthed a "Bloody factory" wherein nearly seventeen captives were rescued whose blood was extracted twice a week to be sold in the local market in return of the money that went into the pockets of their masters. They were again mostly women and children who are the most vulnerable group of a society. He also refers to a bone bazaar and a refugee camp organized for the survivors of the 2004 tsunami in India. The camp was named as kidneyvakkam after its illegal trade of kidney. He also portrays the horrors of red-light areas where young girls are sold for a petty sum of money and are injected with artificial growth hormones to prepare them for flesh trade.

**Surrogacy**

Another type of issue that also falls under the umbrella term of trafficking is surrogacy or the sale of the womb. Surrogacy is a debatable issue which has again exposed women for economically weaker sections of society to various physical and mental health issues. Due to the rise in infertility among the couples, rich people often look out for soft targets who are willing to offer their womb in return of money. In these cases, the poor who are often ignorant and illiterate are at the receiving ends. They deal with their customers through agents who lure them into handsome returns but often the majority of the profit goes into the pockets of these agents who exploit the illiteracy and economic issues of the women offering their wombs. Due to innovations in the field of science and technology, surrogacy has increased manifolds wherein it's social, mental, physical and cultural aspects are often ignored. There is a complete dearth of legislations in India dealing with surrogacy. Carney, in one of his chapter talks about the commercial trade of the female eggs that are harvested and sold as low as one hundred dollars in Cyprus. The women who sold their eggs were mainly poor immigrant women. The place came to be known as the surrogacy capital where wealthy couples from other countries travelled for fertility tourism, an offshoot of globalization. Through his book Carney forces one to contemplate the moral issues raised through this kind of trafficking.

**Bonded Labor**

Another kind of trafficking is bonded labor, which is a much older version of trafficking prevalent in the rural countryside. The marginalized people in the villages often go to local money lenders who gave them a meager amount of loan. However, these people left with nothing else to pay off their loans often signed off their family members, especially kids or women as laborers to pay off their debt. The debt in such cases often used to be much lower than a life span of bonded labor which was free of cost available to the masters. It solely depended on the masters as to what sort of labor was to be extracted from such people. Often, they were moved from one household to the other and were forced to work long hours under inhuman conditions sometimes in the farms, sometimes in the homes and were even exploited sexually. No doubt, the Indian government has abolished bonded labor and child labor through legislation but still a lot has to be done. Sometimes, such legislations are merely present in paper as its execution is a difficult process. Some manufacturing processes which are labor intensive require cheap labor. It is here that women and children are employed who are mainly underpaid with no fixation of working hours. They are employed in carpet making factories, match stick industries, manufacturing of tobacco-based products, cracker making and the handling of other hazardous products. Life is miserable for such people as there is no end to their vicious circle of exploitation. Often the debt of one generation is paid through various generations which never allow them to come out of this cycle.

Siddhartha Kara has extensively researched for nearly eleven years on the system of this labor trafficking in countries like Nepal, Bangladesh, Pakistan and India and authored it in his seminal work *Bonded Labor Tackling the system of Slavery in South Asia.* He exposes how the countries of first world seek to employ cheap labor from the developing South Asian countries to fulfill the demands of their capitalist units that are set up in these areas.

**Pornography**

Another practice that makes women and children more vulnerable in the world of trafficking is pornography. Pornography is the display of human bodies for voyeuristic pleasure in weird modes. The models that are displayed are sometimes either drugged into performing unpleasant acts or are forced into it. Digital pornography, employing minor children especially girls, is an offence, but despite of all checks and bounds it works in abundance. The novel *How to Make Love like a Porn star* is based on the life of a famous porn star Jenna Jameson where she talks about the difficulties she faced and the struggle she did for her de-addiction. She was hooked on drugs to perform in the industry and the ensuing dysfunctional social, emotional and familial relationships. The book therefore articulates the dirty secrets of this business where woman is reduced to a commodity put on sale.

**Beggar**

Another form of trafficking is for the purpose of employing the underprivileged in begging business. Humanity is centered on the emotion of pity out of which people normally donate alms. However, there is well planned nexus that operates in almost major metropolitan cities of India that kidnap young children or mentally deranged woman who are transported to far off placing and made to beg on streets and crossings. It is a form of exploitation where women, the destitute, children and the disabled are violated and exploited. Sometimes children are adopted legally, merely for employing them as help. There are numerous cases reported in the Gulf countries where children are used as camel jockeys to be tied to the back of camels during the course of race due to their light weight. It is a very dangerous practice wherein sometimes children fall to their death.

There are numerous studies and researches undertaking to highlight the plight of trafficked women in books, journals, newspapers and documentaries that are quite helpful in creating awareness to these issues. P.M Nair and Sankar Sen in *Trafficking in Women and Children* gives an analysis of several research findings and the action involved on those findings taken on the Trafficking in Women and Children in India (ARTWAC) where numerous institutes like The United Nations Development Fund for Women (UNIFEM) and The National Human Rights Commission (NHRC) are involved. This book offers some valuable solutions to tackle this menace and it also presents some case specific studies.

In his book *Sex trafficking: Inside the Business and Modern Slavery*, Siddhartha Kara describes the economics and the business involved in this trade. He also explores the dimensions involved and how the pimps operate this business evading penalization and punishment. He also traces the reasons why women are more vulnerable to it. In another seminal work on Trafficking, author Anna M. Troubnikoff in his book *Trafficking in Women and Children: Current Issues and Development* is of the view that trafficking is the third largest crime industry after weapons and drugs. The study includes the increasing magnitude of this industry as well as the measures and anti-trafficking steps taken up by various governmental and non-governmental agencies. Aparna Shrivastava in her joint women's program, a study funded by the United Nations Development Fund for Women, *Human Trafficking: With Special Reference to Delhi,* focuses on the issue of ***Devdasi* in South India**. Through her work she urges the government of Karnataka for the rehabilitation of the *Devdasis*. In *Global Trafficking in Women and Children* Obi N.I Ebbe and Dilip K. Das relates human trafficking to the past experience of slavery and colonialism where human beings were reduced to mere commodities. They trace the joint ventures of various countries undertaken to combat trafficking at both national and international levels. *The World of Prostitutes* written by S.K Ghosh talks about the modern and historical perspectives of sexual exploitation of women especially in the red-light areas with special reference to the effect of industrialization, porn tourism, escort services, prostitution in young children as well.

A Delhi based NGO STOP is in the process of bringing about the grass root changes to curb trafficking among women. In one of its publications by Roma Debabrata, *Analyzing the Dimensions: Trafficking and HIV/AIDS in South Asia* through which she highlights the harmful effects of trafficking on the psyche of the victim. She also highlights the spread of sexually transmitted diseases like HIV AIDS among the trafficked women. Gunjan Kinnu in her book *from Bondage to Freedom* explores the legal aspect for the prevention of trafficking.

There is no dearth of study that articulates the ill-effects of trafficking on the victims especially women. Prostitution and trafficking are inter-related words. Any sort of trafficking is not independent from the sexual exploitation of women be it adult women or young girls. It may be voluntary or involuntary. In some cases, the agents are well known to the families and in some cases, they are even the family members themselves. The match making industry also contributes to the racket of trafficking where fake matrimonial sites are created, and brides are lured for their love of a well settled life and are ultimately trapped to be trafficked to far off places. In such cases, their passports are seized and they are never able to see the faces of their loved ones. The concept of NRI marriages which is quite popular in the North India is also a shady affair where thousands of women are sent abroad and are shunned into the brothels of the west.

Another poignant side of trafficking is that even after the victims have been rescued, they are never accepted into the civil society. They are always pushed into the dark for no fault of their own. The rehabilitation of the trafficked women is all the more difficult. In some cases, the children of the red-light area who are mostly **the kids of prostitutes are never accepted in the society**. They are not accepted in normal schools meant for general public. The government and the NGOs are working tirelessly for their upliftment and rehabilitation, but they are never welcomed by society. They are segregated into special schools meant for them. Throughout their lives they live under the stigma of their identity.

It can be thus be argued that woman has always remained at the threshold of the society always left vulnerable, whether economically, socially, culturally or biologically. She has been the victim of man's greed for power, money and sexuality. Trafficking is not something new that the society is facing these days. It is a phenomenon quite old, but its forms have changed today, it has acquired more dangerous and fatal aspects. **Only a collective effort on the part of government and society, both nationally and internationally can wipe off the demon of trafficking**. This doesn't mean that men are not prone to trafficking; it is that women are an easy prey and it has an enhanced economic value for the perpetrator of the crime of trafficking.

**Reference:**


1. Ali, Nujood. *I am Nujood, Age 10 and Divorced.* California: Crown Publishing Group, 2010. Print
2. Carney, Scott. *The red Market: On the Trials of World's Organ Brokers, Bone thieves, Blood Farmers and Child Traffickers.* New York: Harper Collins Publishers, 201. Print.
3. Jameson, Jenna. Strauss, Neil. *How to make Love like a Porn Star: A Cautionary Tale.* New York: Harper Collins Publisher Inc., 2004. Print.
4. Debabrata, Roma. *Analyzing the Dimensio :Trafficking and HIV/ AIDS in South Asia.* New Delhi: Publication of STOP, 2002. Print.
5. Ebbe, Obi. N. I, Das, Dilip K. *Global Trafficking in Women and Children.* London: CRC Press. Taylor & Francis Group. 2008. Print.
6. Gosh, S.K. *The World of Prostitutes.* New Delhi: APH Publishing House. 1996. Print
7. Kara, Siddhartha. *Sex Trafficking: Inside the Business of Modern Slavery.* New York: Columbia University press, 2009. Print.
8. Morrisson, Toni. *Beloved.* New York: VintagePublishers, 2004. Print.
9. Sen, Sankar. *Trafficking in Women and Children in India.* Andhra Pradesh: Orient Longman. 2005. Print.
10. Troubanikoff, Anna M. *Trafficking in Women and Children: Current Issues and Development.* N.p: Nova Society Publishers. 2003. Print.

11. United Nations Office of Drugs and Crime. *UN Protocol to Prevent, Suppress and Punish Human Trafficking in Persons: Especially Women and Children*. New York: United Nations, 2006. Print.

CHAPTER X

# Upbringing of an Indian women

## *Journey from girl's innocence to womanhood full of responsibilities*

Tamisha
Research Scholar
tamisha120394@gmail.com
Dr Narendra Kumar
Assistant Professor, Department of Education
Central University of Rajasthan, Bandarsindri, Ajmer
drnarendra09@gmail.com

**Abstract**

A girl child has to face lots of discrimination from the day she is conceived to the day she dies in the patriarchal system that we have made. It is very difficult for a girl to survive, from female infanticide to acid attacks, a woman has to suffer all of this. The discrimination starts from the place where a child should get maximum protection and that is the family. In India girl child is discriminated against from the day she is given birth, as there is no celebration, there are no congratulations for girl child, if she is born, she is seen as a burden to the family and to the society. In the world we live today, it is really scary for a woman or a girl even a little child to survive. The rape cases that are increasing today have made the life of a girl child like hell. The family members can't even send their two years old outside to play without the fear that something will happen to her. It is not new to us nor is it a very rare phenomenon to see how male child is treated as something precious and a female child is treated as a burden to the family and all the privileges are given to the male child as compared to the female child.

**Keywords:** Society, Childhood, Discrimination, Unemployment, Malnutrition.

### INTRODUCTION

We live in a world where brains and our social system are all dominated by males. We live in a patriarchal society and follow the patriarchal system of living where the rule makers are men and this is where all the problem lies. Women are not even considered as a part of the society where everything is dominated by the males whether they are decisions or the hierarchical cycle. It is really sad to see that even today in this modern world and modern society where many of the countries are called developed even in India where most of the rich people are living and we are living in a technological advanced world, it is still an unsafe and harsh world for women to live in. Society is becoming more unequalled these days. There are many challenges that women are facing today. It is a difficult world for a woman to live in from the day she is born till the date she dies. Even in the modern world, whether you are an Indian living in the USA or India, even if you are living in an urban setting or a rural setting, still not many people are happy when a girl child is born in their house, and if even the second child is girl, then it is a whole lot worse situation.

### Problems at schools and workplace

Not many girls are able to reach the school and even if they are, puberty is standing in the way as a barrier for them to complete their education due to the sanitation facilities at the school which are totally invisible to be honest. It is a reality in the rural areas where as a woman hits puberty their freedom and rights are taken away from them. Even in the urban areas the education of a girl child is not much focused as compared to the education of a boy. This is a sad reality that I even have in my family and even in the family and friends where we are so called educated and modern as compared to others living in rural setting, it is common to hear for a girl that in the end they have to take care of the household, what will they do with so many degrees or what is the use of going to school. Today it is one of the main issues that women are not given equal pay even in the most highest professions whether they are actors or doctors their performance and capabilities are always judged. At most of the workplaces whether they are a corporate job or whether they are in civil services, in a government sector women have to face harassment. Most of the women don't even complain about that. Slowly the number of women to complain about the arrangements are increasing but still 80 out of hundred women stay quiet when they face harassment.

61% of women start out in the labour market with men but their participation decreases with age. There are traditional norms that women have to follow such as household chores, caring for the children and family. Discrimination can be seen when a woman tries to return to the job after having children which results in men bearing all the pressures of providing to the family. "Me too movement", has proved that sexual exploitation occurs in every area of the society. Even if the woman is progressing faster than her male colleagues, it is presumed that it is not by her potential as she does not have the calibre.

**Problems faced by women due to the society**

The problems occur due to the negative outlook of the people when it comes to a woman. Women can't even step out at night without having the guardian with her. Due to the unsafe environment for the girls, the girls are treated differently than the boys. From when a girl is born her gender role is predetermined by the society that what women should do and what a woman should not do, how she should dress, how she should speak, how she should walk and what are her responsibilities. If a woman speaks up against these rules the consequences are mainly beating, rapes, marital rape, sexual harassment, child marriage and even acid attacks. Honour-killing is a prevalent practice in India and even if there are so many rules made by the government to protect the girls and women, they don't really work when it comes to reality. Women even when she's a little girl she is judged on the basis of colour, height and weight. Lifestyle, what she wears and what she eats. If a woman is dark in colour or overweight, she is told by the society that she is not as competent as others.

According to the reports 75% women are beaten by their husbands and they have to go through domestic violence. This has been seen in real life. My friend, who is highly educated having a government job, was going through domestic violence, filed for divorce against her husband and the case is still going on after two long years. She has to face so much mental abuse by the family and the society of how it was her fault and she should have tried to cope up with that and manage it. That it is quite common and it is not a big deal. She should have kept things at home. According to society and relatives she is a disgrace to the family.

Women who are widows and divorcees are seen as lower class in the society they are deprived of opportunities. They are exploited and when it comes to a social setting or a function or any celebration in the family the abuse can be clearly seen by us.

**Role of women in family**

When a woman is born into a family her status and her image changes according to her age in the family. From childhood to marriage to being parent to the stage where a girl lives a different kind of life each moment. In 1951 the birth expectancy of women was only 32.5 years. A major factor to mortality decline has been due to better healthcare facilities, it has reduced infant mortality significantly.

**Status of a girl child**

There are many disadvantages that girls have to face such as severe discrimination against girl child, female foeticide female infanticide child marriage dowry aspiration for male children it can get as severe as girls getting deprived from getting involved in childhood activities. According to the 2001 census 12 million girls are born in India but unfortunately only one third of them are the survivors. Lack of healthcare facilities and malnutrition is one of the main reasons why so many girls die before reaching adulthood.

In most of the weaker sections of the society the privilege is given to the male children as compared to females.

Parents pay more attention to the needs and requirements and health of their male child as compared to female this kind of gender discrimination is one of the main reasons why most of the girls are malnourished. Survey indicates that 56% of female children suffer from anaemia, 45% from stunted growth as compared to males which are only 20%.

**Discrimination against girls**

Girls face discrimination from major to minor extent of their life. Girls are deprived from basic Human Rights in their life. In the aspect of education, diet, nutrition, health care, childhood activities and other opportunities girls are always discriminated against. Many researches have indicated that girls are not allowed to attend the school but their parents sent male children to school. Even in urban areas, a girl child is sent to a government school as compared to a male child who is sent to a better privileged or private school. Deprivation of rights can be considered as a form of abuse. Even children below the age of 10 are suffering from abuse. Some cases are abusive and lead to violent and criminal activities.

**Women unemployment**

Research has indicated that many women are not able to work after bearing child but living with in laws doesn't mean that they are able to keep their jobs. In fact, woman who are living in joint family are less likely to be having a job. According to National Sample Survey office on unemployment 23.4 percent women are doing jobs. India has the lowest levels of employed females. According to the data given by ILO less than 10% of the males share the burden of housework with their wife. Child care and household work are still thought to be work of a female. The primary reason for women not going for jobs is that there is no one to take care of the household work and the children. Many of my colleagues have dropped from their jobs after having a child and were never able to return due to the duties that they have to take care of home, many women leave their jobs even after marriage because they are unable to handle the stress of both household work and the job so for them it is better to leave the job and take care of only the household work to have a happy marriage life, and it is not only one person who is doing that it is a story of more than 90% of ladies living in India. Schemes such as Mahatma Gandhi National Rural Employment scheme is helping rural women to get outside their home and take up a job.

**Education of women**

India is one of the largest democracy of the world, but it still needs social development, education is necessary for the growth of any country. Woman has been confined to household work and taking care of the family, the main root of it is patriarchy as it is believed that educating women is a waste of time and female child is seen as a burden. One of the major reason for this is dowry given during the marriage, and other reasons are lack of safety and security so the families don't want to send their girl child to school or college. As we have seen the Nirbhaya case in Delhi and there were so many even today that we don't know about.

**Stories of the unknown**

Rape and murder of a 6-year-old in Hyderabad, it is in the Print on 15th March 2022. These kinds of incidents are quite common. The female of this house has not stepped out of the house after this incident happened. These kinds of things are making women more vulnerable and the family is scared to send their daughters and wives out of their houses.

"I am so scared, no one imagined something like this to happen to a child. We all live like a family and this is shocking. Our bathroom is outside the house, but I am not waking up during the night to use it. I am not even allowing my child to do that. I don't let her play outside the house anymore; she has to be inside and I will be with her ... We will continue like this," Prema said, who is the mother of the victim.

An article written by Purnima Nandy in Women's web on 17 June 2016 show that how a girl child is written at the point of killing her and putting her life in danger. The saddest thing is that the story is not uncommon or rare in today's world it's not even talking but just painful that even today these kinds of things are happening in our life. Purnima rights article that when she was staying at her relatives' house, she got to meet the neighbours which were a typical Indian household as she said. The family was blessed with a baby girl but there were no family friends or relatives that were there to congratulate them, no one was happy about the birth of the child, no medical care was given after the birth, she was not even given proper care at home and the mother was even expected to get back to work and take care of the family. If it was not against the law and the family would have found that the sex of the chid to be born in their family then I don't think they could have thought twice before killing the child, the case is not unique in this city or in India but at what rate it is happening we are not aware of that. It is one of the few instances that have been happening we don't know how much more other women are suffering in the family and how much they are living with their shattered dreams or how much long will they be able to take up the burden of the family.

It is quite scary to think of like how this girl child will grow up and in what environment she will grow up how much discrimination she will face knowing that at birth this was happening to her.

**Another Incident**

The story is of Sarla Devi from Sitapur, Uttar Pradesh. Discovered cause of 5th class dropout: she was not even 15 years old and she became a child bride, this article was written by Sana Ali on 31st July 2019 in India spend. Sarla was not even aware that there are laws against child marriage. It is not very shocking to know that nearly half of 700 million of World Population of child bride, 42% of child Bride live in South Asia and one of three are living in India as per the reports of United Nations Children's Fund in 2015. We are aware of all the health issues that can Child Bride faces and even the issue of early pregnancy can lead to many complications as Sarla's mother died of cancer when she was just six or seven she has to drop out of the school and take care of the family as it is a predetermined notion that only a female can take care of the family and none of the males can do any household work. In Sitapur out of 800 thousand households only 2.9% have a family member who is covered by a healthcare program. Sarla's mother was also a victim of child marriage and she was married at the age of 13 this is a cycle that had been going on and I don't think that anyone is going to stop the cycle from happening even in future. According to her after she will get married and go away all the household work will be taken care of by her little sister.

**CONCLUSION**

There is a different vocabulary for males and females: a man does something its strategic and if a woman does that its calculated. **When it comes to males, they react but a woman only overreacts as said by Taylor Swift.** It is one of the **millennium developments goals to achieve gender equality and to empower women**. Numerous efforts have been made to achieve this goal. Little girls require the opportunity to grow in a safe environment and have right to being able to achieve their goals and to live a happy life. The primary problem starts from the families the parents and relatives should try to change their viewpoints and provide better opportunities to promote growth and development of the child. It is really important for or everyone from every category and every background to be a weird that girls are equal to boys and they should be e provided with all the opportunities and rights to improve their life. They should be provided education and ability to be creative and engaged in jobs and employment opportunities should be given to them.

REFERENCE


1. *Case studies archive—Ngo for girl child education india, women education charity | iimpact*. (n.d.). Retrieved 15 March 2022, from https://www.iimpact.org/category/case-studies/
2. Desai, S., & Jain, D. (1994a). Maternal employment and changes in family dynamics: The social context of women's work in rural south india. *Population and Development Review, 20*(1), 115–136. https://doi.org/10.2307/2137632
3. Desai, S., & Jain, D. (1994b). Maternal employment and changes in family dynamics: The social context of women's work in rural south india. *Population and Development Review, 20*(1), 115–136. https://doi.org/10.2307/2137632
4. *India witnesses one of the highest female infanticide incidents in the world: Study*. (n.d.). Retrieved 15 March 2022, from https://www.downtoearth.org.in/news/health/india-witnesses-one-of-the-highest-female-infanticide-incidents-in-the-world-54803
5. Parsekar, S. S., Hoogar, P., Dhyani, V. S., & Yadav, U. N. (2021). The voice of Indian women on family planning: A qualitative systematic review. *Clinical Epidemiology and Global Health, 12*, 100906. https://doi.org/10.1016/j.cegh.2021.100906
6. S, R. (2019, February 19). *Great Indian Family doesn't help working women*. Mint. https://www.livemint.com/news/india/great-indian-family-doesn-t-help-working-women-1550524334031.html
7. The unwanted girl child in india who no one cares about! When will all this change? (2016, June 17). *Women's Web: For Women Who Do*. https://www.womensweb.in/2016/06/unwanted-girl-child-in-india/
8. *Website of ministry of women and child development| national portal of india*. (n.d.). Retrieved 15 March 2022, from https://www.india.gov.in/official-website-ministry-women-and-child-development-0

9. Women Education in India Essay | Essay on Women Education in India for Students and Children in English. (2021, March 8). *A Plus Topper*. https://www.aplustopper.com/women-education-in-india-essay/

CHAPTER XI

# Child Marriage in India and its Impact

Raghubar Prasad Singh
Research Scholar
Neha
Student
University Department of Economics
L. N. Mithila University, Darbhanga
rrajji4@gmail.com

**Abstract**

In this country, marriage is considered one of the most important social institutions through which society perpetuates as it is a means of establishing family relations. This social institution is articulated in many forms of rituals and ceremonies. In India, around 45% of girls are married below 18 years of age. Niger is ranked at the top in the world for child marriages below 18 years of age (74.5%), followed by Chad, Mali, Bangladesh, Guinea, and Central African Republic. Most girls who are married before 18 years of age are from poor families. Most of the girls used to face issues like domestic violence, pregnancy problems, and death cases. Girls who are younger than 15 years old are more vulnerable to dying in childbirth than women who are in their 20s. Child brides often show signs and prodrome of sexual abuse and post-traumatic stress, such as feelings of hopelessness, helplessness and severe depression.

**Keywords:** Marriage, Violence, Child Brides, Post-traumatic Stress etc.

**Introduction**

Child weddings infringe on children's rights and place them at high risk of violence, exploitation, and abuse. India has the highest number of brides in the world – a simple fraction of the world total. An Asian nation has the highest rate of child marriages in Asia (the fourth highest rate in the world). This Asian nation has one of the highest rates of child weddings in Asia for both boys and girls. Child marriages are declining (63% in 1985 to 45% in 2010) in South Asia, with the decline being particularly marked for women under fifteen (32% in 1985 to 17% in 2010). The marriage of women aged 15–18 is still common, and thus additional measures are required to shield older adolescents from weddings.

Child marriage is the result of the interaction of economic and social forces. In some communities, marrying a woman as a baby is a component of social norms and attitudes that mirror the low value accorded to the human rights of women. UNICEF's approach to putting an end to child marriages in South Asia recognises the advanced nature of the matter, therefore pinning the socio-cultural and structural factors.

Child marriage in India, according to Indian law, could be a wedding wherever either the girl or boy is below the age of twenty-one. Most child marriages involve women, several of whom live in poor socio-economic conditions.

**Child Marriage in India by SDRC:**

Child marriages are common in Asian countries. approximate vary widely between sources on the extent and scale of kid marriages. The International Center for Analysis on Women-UNICEF publications has calculated India's kid wedding rate to be forty-seven percent from a sample survey of 1998, whereas the United Nations reports it to be half-hour in 2005. The Census of Asian countries has counted and rumoured married ladies by age, with the proportion of females in kid weddings falling in every 10-year census amount since 1981. In its 2001 census report, the Asian country declared zero married ladies below the age of ten, 1.4 million married ladies out of 59.2 million ladies aged 10–14, and 11.3 million married ladies out of 46.3 million ladies aged 15–19. The Times of Asian countries rumoured that' since 2001, kid wedding rates in Asian countries have fallen by 46 percent between 2005 and 2009. Jharkhand is the state with the highest kid wedding rates in Asian countries (14.1%), whereas Kerala is the sole state where kid wedding rates have inflated in recent years. In 2009, Jammu and Kashmir was thought to be the only state with the lowest rate of child marriages, at 0.4%.[4] Rural rates of kid marriages were thrice beyond urban

Asian countries' rates in 2009.

Child marriage was outlawed in 1929, under Indian law. However, during the British colonial times, the legal minimum age of marriage was set at fourteen for women and eighteen for boys. Under protests from Muslim organisations in the undivided British Asian nation, a private law shariah Act was passed in 1937 that allowed kid marriages with consent from the girl's guardian. After India's independence in 1947, the act underwent two revisions. The minimum legal status for weddings was enlarged to fifteen for women in 1949, and to 18 for females and 21 for males in 1978. The kid wedding hindrance laws are challenged in Indian courts, with some Muslim Indian organisations seeking no minimum age requirement, which the age matter be left to their personal law. Child marriages are a hot political topic as well as a recurring issue in the highest courts of Asian countries.

Several states in India have introduced incentives to delay marriages. For instance, the state of Haryana introduced the supposed, 'Apni Beti, Apna Dhan' programme in 1994, which translates to "My Daughter, My Wealth." It's a conditional money transfer programme dedicated to delaying young marriages by providing a government-paid bond in her name, due to her parents, within the quantity of 25,000 (US $330) once her 18th birthday if she isn't married.

**History**

Before the economic revolution, in several elements of the globe, as well as India, China, and Japan, ladies would marry instantly when reaching a certain age, in their mid-teens. These wedding practises carried over into the nineteenth century in societies with mostly rural populations. Men attended to marry later in societies wherever a man and wife were expected to ascertain a menage of their own. The men remained divorced till they accumulated decent wealth to support a replacement home and were married at their mature age to adolescent women. The United Nations agency contributed a dower to the family finances.

In ancient and mediaeval societies, it was absolutely common for women to be betrothed at or maybe before the age of maturity. In line with Mordechai A. Friedman, "arranging and catching the wedding of a girl were the undisputed prerogatives of her father in ancient Israel." Most women married before the age of fifteen, usually at the start of their careers. the Middle Ages, the age of marriage looks to have been around the time of life throughout the Judaic world.

"The varied references to kid weddings within the 16th-century Responsa literature and different sources show that kid weddings were therefore common; it was nearly the norm." In this context, it's necessary to recollect that in halakha, the term "minor" refers to a woman under twelve years of age and every day. A woman aged twelve years and a half was already thought of as an adult in all respects. "

In ancient Balkan countries, early marriage and immature family relationships for women existed. Boys were conjointly expected to marry in their teens. Within the empire, women might marry from the age of twelve and boys from fourteen. In the Middle Ages, under English civil laws that were derived from Roman laws, marriages before the age of sixteen existed. In Imperial China, kid weddings were the norm.

In contrast to other pre-modern societies, Northwest Europe was characterised by comparatively late marriages for both men and women, with both sexes unsurprisingly delaying weddings until their mid-20s or possibly 30s.The data accessible for European countries suggests this was the case by the 14th century. This pattern was mirrored in English common law, which was the primary in Western Europe to ascertain rape laws and ages of consent for weddings. In 1275, sexual relations with women under the age of twelve or fourteen (depending on the interpretation of the sources) were criminalized; a second law was created with a lot of severe punishments for those under the age of ten in 1576. In the late eighteenth and early nineteenth centuries, a British colonial administration introduced wedding age restrictions for Hindu and Muslim women on the Indian landmass.

A Scottish physician living in an 18th century Asian country reported that locals tried to contract marriages for their youngsters at a young age, but the wedding wasn't consummated till the woman "had come of age". However, evidence from nineteenth-century Palestine suggests that husbands generally initiated sexual relations before their better half reached the age of life; however, this was a rare occurrence that was condemned socially and condemned by shariah law courts.Edward William Lane discovered in December that few Egyptian women remained single by the age of 16. However, socioeconomic transformation, educational reforms, and the influence of Western norms brought significant changes, and by 1920, fewer than 100% of Egyptian ladies married before the age of twenty.In

1923, Egypt's parliament set the minimum age of marriage at sixteen for ladies and eighteen for men.

**Causes:**

According to UNFPA, factors that promote and reinforce kid weddings embody financial condition and economic survival strategies; gender inequality; waterproofing land or property deals or sinking disputes; management over physiological property and protective family honour; tradition and culture; and insecurity, notably during war, famine, or epidemics. Alternative factors embody family ties during which a wedding may be a means of consolidating powerful relations between families.

**Dowry:**

Providing a lady with a gift at her wedding is an ancient tradition that continues in some components of the planet, particularly within the Indian landmass. This needs folks to bestow property on the wedding of a female offspring, which is commonly an economic challenge for several families. The problem of saving lots and preserving wealth for gifts was common, notably in times of economic hardship, or ill-usage, or unpredictable seizure of property and savings. These difficulties induced families to engage their ladies, no matter their age, as soon as they'd the resources to pay the gift. Thus, Goitein notes that European Jews would marry their ladies early, once they'd collected the expected quantity of gifts.

A gift is the quantity paid by the groom to the oldsters of a bride for them to consent to his marrying their female offspring. In some countries, the younger the bride, the higher the gift. This follows creates an economic incentive wherever ladies' area units want and are married early by their families to the very best bidder. The kid marriages of ladies may be a response to desperate economic conditions or just a supply of financial gain to the oldsters. The gift is another reason behind kid weddings and kid trafficking.

**Bride kidnapping:**

Bride snatching, conjointly called bride snatching, wedding by abduction, or wedding by capture, may be a practise in which a male abducts the female he needs to marry. Bride snatching has been practised round the world and throughout history. It continues to occur in countries in Central Asia, the Caucasus region, and components of Africa and among peoples as diverse as the Hmong in their geographic region, the Tzeltal in the United Mexican States, and also the Romani in Europe.

In most nations, bride snatching is taken into account against the law instead of a legitimate style of wedding. Some styles of it should even be seen as falling in the time between forced weddings and organised weddings. However, even once the act is against the law, judicial social control remains lax in some areas. Bride snatching happens in numerous components of the planet, but it's most typical in the Caucasus and Central Asia. A bride snatch is commonly (but not always) a style of wedding for kids. It should be connected to the amount of the gift and also the inability or disposition to pay it.

**Persecution, forced migration, and slavery:**

Social upheavals like wars, major military campaigns, forced spiritual conversion, taking natives as prisoners of war and changing them into slaves, arrests, and forced and compelled migrations of individuals usually made an appropriate groom a rare trade good. The bride's families would hunt down any of their bachelors and marry them to their daughters, before events on the far side of their management emotional the boy away. The ill-treatment and displacement of Roma and human folks in Europe; colonial campaigns to induce slaves from numerous ethnic groups in geographic regions across the Atlantic for plantations; monotheistic campaigns to induce Hindu slaves from the Republic of India across Afghanistan's chain of mountains as property and for work; were a number of the historical events that exaggerated the spread of kid marriages before the nineteenth century.

Among Sephardic Jewish human communities, kid marriages became frequent from the tenth to thirteenth centuries, particularly in Muslim European nations. This followed closely once the human community was expelled from European nations and settled within the empire. Kid marriages among the Japanese Sephardic Jews continued through the eighteenth century in monotheism majority regions.

**Poverty, social pressure, and a sense of protection:**

A sense of social insecurity has been a reason behind child marriages across the planet. For instance, in Nepal, oldsters are concerned about social stigma if adult daughters (past eighteen years) lodge in their home. crime like rape, which is not solely traumatic, but could cause less acceptance of the woman if she becomes the victim of a criminal offense. For instance, women might not be seen as eligible for a wedding if they're not virgins. In different cultures, the concern is that an unwed woman could have interaction in illicit relationships, or flee, inflicting a permanent social blemish on her siblings, or that an impoverished family could also be unable to search out bachelors for grown-up women in their economic group. Such fears and social pressures are projected as the causes that cause kid marriages. So far as kid weddings could be a social norm in active communities, the elimination of kid weddings should return through the dynamics of these social norms. The mentality of the communities, and what's believed to be the correct outcome for a baby bride, should be shifted to bring on an amendment to the prevalence of kid weddings.

Extreme economic conditions could create daughters' associated economic burden on the family, which can be eased by their early wedding, to the advantage of the family and also the woman herself. Poor oldsters could have few alternatives they'll afford for the ladies within the family; they typically read the wedding as a method to confirm their daughter's monetary security and to scale back the economic burden of a growing adult on the family. A kid wedding can even be seen as suggesting that of guaranteeing a girl's economic security, particularly if she lacks relations to produce for her. In reviews of Jewish community history, students claim economic conditions, shortages of grooms, and unsure social and economic conditions were the causes of frequent child marriages.

An additional issue inflicting kid weddings is the parental belief that an early wedding offers protection. Parents believe that marriage protects their daughters from sexual promiscuity and sexually transmitted infections. However, in reality, young women tend to marry older men, putting them at an accumulated risk of getting a sexually transmitted infection.

Protection through marriage could play a selected role in conflict settings. Families could have their young daughters marry members of an associated armed cluster or military in hopes that they're going to be better protected. Women can also be taken by armed teams and compelled into marriages.

**Religion, culture, and civil law:**

Although the final mature age is eighteen within the majority of nations, most jurisdictions afford exceptions for underage youth with parental and/or judicial consent. Such laws are not limited to developing countries or to religious beliefs. In some countries, a spiritual wedding by itself has legal validity, whereas in others it doesn't, as the marriage ceremony is obligatory. For Catholics incorporated into the Latin Church, the 1983 Code of ecclesiastical law sets the minimum age for a valid marriage at sixteen for males and fourteen for females. In 2015, Spain raised its minimum mature age to 18 (or 16 with court consent) from the previous fourteen. Marriages under the age of eighteen are permitted in Mexico with parental consent, beginning at fourteen for ladies and sixteen for boys. In Ukraine, in 2012, the Family Code was amended to equalise the mature age for ladies and boys to eighteen, with courts being allowed to grant permission to marry at age sixteen years if it's established that the wedding is in the best interest of the youth.

Many states within the U.S.A. allow kid marriages with a court's permission. Since 2015, the minimum mature age throughout Canada is sixteen. The age of majority in Canada is set by province/territory at eighteen or nineteen; therefore, minors under this age face additional restrictions (i.e., parental and court consent). the Criminal Code, Art. 293.2, "Everyone UN agency celebrates, aids or participates prodigiously in a very wedding ceremony or ceremony knowing that one among the persons being married is under the age of sixteen years is guilty of a chargeable offence and vulnerable to imprisonment for a term not exceeding 5 years." The marriage ceremony Act additionally states: "2.2 not everybody UN agency is under the age of sixteen years can contract a wedding." In European countries and Wales, as well as Northern Ireland, and even without parental consent in Scotland, However, a wedding of someone under sixteen is void under the married Causes Act 1973. The international organization, Population Fund, expressed the following:

In 2010, 158 countries reported that eighteen years was the minimum age for weddings for ladies without parental consent or approval by a pertinent authority. However, in 146 countries, state or customary law permits women younger than eighteen to marry with the consent of their parents or alternative authorities; in fifty-two countries, women under age fifteen will marry with parental consent. In distinction, eighteen is the eldest for marriage while not consenting among males in a hundred and eighty countries. To boot, in one hundred and five countries, boys will marry with the consent of a parent or a pertinent authority, and in twenty-three countries, boys under age fifteen will marry with parental consent.

Lowering the wrongfully allowed wedding age doesn't essentially cause high rates of kid marriages. However, there's a correlation between restrictions placed by law and also the average age of the initial wedding. In the US, per 1960 Census information, 3.5% of ladies married before the age of sixteen, whereas a further eleven.9% married between sixteen and eighteen. States with lower wedding age limits saw higher percentages of kid marriages. This correlation between the higher age of marriage in civil law and the ascertained frequency of kid marriages breaks down in countries with Islam as the state faith. In Islamic nations, several countries don't permit the kid marriage of ladies under their civil code of laws. However, the state recognised Islamic law, non-secular laws and courts all tell us that these nations have the ability to override the civil code, and sometimes do. The United Nations Children's Fund reports that the eight nations in the world with the highest ascertained kid wedding rates are Niger (75%), Chad (72%), Mali (71%), Bangladesh (64%), Guinea (63%), Central African Republic (61%), Republic of Mozambique (56%), and Asian countries (51%).

**Political and financial relationships**

Child marriages may depend upon socio-economic status. The aristocracy in some cultures, as in the European feudal era, tended to use child marriage as a method to secure political ties. Families were able to cement political and/or financial ties by having their children marry. The betrothal is regarded as a legally binding agreement between the families and the children. The breaking of a betrothal can have serious consequences both for the families and for the betrothed individuals themselves.

**Laws against child marriage:**

**The Child Marriage Restraint Act of 1929:**

The Child Marriage Restraint Act, also called the Sarda Act, was a law to restrict the practise of child marriage. It was enacted on April 1, 1930, and extended across the whole nation, with the exceptions of some princely states like Hyderabad and Jammu and Kashmir. This Act defined the age of marriage to be 18 for males and 14 for females. In 1949, after India's independence, the minimum age was increased to 15 for females, and in 1978, it was increased again for both females and males, to 18 and 21 years, respectively. The punishment for a male between 18 and 21 years of age marrying a child is imprisonment of up to 15 days, a fine of 1,000 rupees, or both. The punishment for a male above 21 years of age is imprisonment of up to three months and a possible fine. The punishment for anyone who performed or directed a child marriage ceremony became imprisonment of up to three months and a possible fine, unless he could prove the marriage, he performed was not a child marriage. The punishment for a parent or guardian of a child taking place in a marriage is imprisonment of up to three months or a possible fine. It was amended in 1940 and 1978 to continue raising the ages of male and female children.

**The Prohibition of Child Marriage Act, 2006:**

In response to the plea (Write Petition (C) 212/2003) of the Forum for Fact-finding Documentation and Advocacy at the Supreme Court, the Government of India brought the Prohibition of Child Marriage Act (PCMA) in 2006, and it came into effect on 1 November 2007 to address and fix the shortcomings of the Child Marriage Restraint Act. The change in name was meant to reflect the prevention and prohibition of child marriage rather than restraining it. The previous Act also made it difficult and time-consuming to act against child marriages and did not focus on authorities as possible figures for preventing the marriages. This Act kept the ages of adult males and females the same but made some significant changes to further protect the children. Boys and girls forced into child marriages as minors have the option of voiding their marriage up to two years after reaching adulthood, and in certain circumstances, marriages of minors can be null and void before they reach adulthood. All valuables, money, and gifts must be returned if the marriage is nullified, and the girl must be provided with a place of residency until she marries or becomes an adult. Children born from child marriages are considered legitimate, and the courts are expected to grant parental custody with the children's best interests in mind. Any male over 18 years of age who enters into a marriage with a minor or anyone who directs or conducts a child marriage ceremony can be punished with up to two years of imprisonment or a fine.

**Applicability:**

Muslim organisations in the Republic of India have long argued that Indian laws, passed by its parliament, like the 2006 kid wedding law, don't apply to Muslims, as a result of marriage may be a personal law subject. The city state supreme court, as well as alternative state high courts of India, have disagreed. The City Court, for instance, dominated that the Prohibition of Kid Wedding Act, 2006 overrides all personal laws and governs each and every subject in the Republic of India. The ruling explicitly states that an under-age wedding, wherever either the person or lady is over sixteen years old, wouldn't be a void wedding, however rescindable, which might become valid if no steps are taken by such court as has the option [s] to order otherwise. In the event that either of the parties is younger than eighteen years, the wedding is void. Given the age of consent is eighteen in the Republic of India, sex with minors under the age of eighteen may be a statutory crime under Section 376 of the Indian legal code.

Various alternative high courts in the Republic of India—as well as the Gujarat state supreme court, the state supreme court and therefore the Madras state supreme court—have dominated that the act prevails over any personal law (including Muslim personal law).

**Legal Action on Legal Confusion:**

In Asian country, there is a long-standing legal ambiguity regarding marital rape within prohibited child marriages. Status rape intrinsically isn't against the law in India; however, the position with regard to kids is confusing, whereas the exception underneath the legal code (section 375, Indian Legal Code, 1860) applicable to adults puts an associate degree exception and permits the marital status rape of a lady kid between the ages of 15–18 years by her husband. However, this exception provision was scanned down by the Supreme Court of Asian nation in the case of Free Thought V. Union of Asian nation in October, 2017 and it declares that sexuality with any wife under the age of eighteen shall be considered rape; another new and progressive legislation. The Protection of Children from Sexual Offenses Act of 2012 prohibits such sexual relationships and makes such crimes with marriages an aggravated offense.

**CEDAW:**

The Convention on the Elimination of All Varieties of Discrimination Against Women (CEDAW) is a world bill trying to end discrimination against women. Article 16, Wedding and Family Life, states that both men and women have the right to decide on their relationship, to have ongoing responsibilities, and to decide on the number of children to have and the spacing between them. This convention states that a kid's wedding shouldn't have a legal result. All action should be taken to enforce a minimum age, after which all marriages should be placed into an officer's register. Asian countries signed the convention on Gregorian calendar month 1980, however, created the declaration that, due to the nation's size and population, it's impractical to possess a register of marriages.

**Child marriage's consequences**

**Early Maternal Deaths**

Girls who marry earlier in life are less likely to be told about generative problems, and as a result, pregnancy-related deaths are the leading cause of death among married women aged fifteen to nineteen. These women are twice as likely to die in childbearing than women between twenty and twenty-four years old. Women under the age of fifteen are five times more likely to die during childbearing.

**Infant Health**

Infants born to mothers below the age of eighteen are more likely to die in their first year than those born to mothers over the age of nineteen. If the kids survive, they're more than likely to suffer from low birth weight, deficiency disease, and late physical and psychological feature development.

**Fertility outcomes**

A study conducted in the Republic of India by the International Institute for Population Sciences and Macro International in 2005 and 2006 showed high fertility, low fertility management, and poor fertility outcomes information among child marriages. 90.8% of young married women say they did not use a contraceptive before having their first child.23.9% reported having a baby in the primary year of marriage. 17.3% reported having three or additional youngsters over the course of the wedding. A fast repeat accouchement was reported by one-third of those polled, and an unwanted physiological condition was reported by 15.2%.15.3% reported a termination due to a physiological condition (stillbirths, miscarriages, or abortions). Fertility rates are higher in slums than in urban areas.

**Violence**

Young women in a very young wedding are more likely to experience force in their marriages as opposed to older girls. A study conducted in Bharat by the International Centre for Analysis on Girls showed that women married before eighteen years of age are doubly vulnerable to being overwhelmed, slapped, or vulnerable by their husbands and thrice more susceptible to sexual violence. Young brides typically show symptoms of statutory offence and post-traumatic stress.

**Prevention programmes in India:**

Apni Beti, Apna Dhan (ABAD), which translates to "My daughter, my wealth," is one of India's initial conditional money transfer programmes dedicated to delaying young marriages across the state. In 1994, the Indian government enforced this programme within the state of Haryana. On the birth of a mother's initial, second, or third kid, they're set to receive 500, or US $11 during the first fifteen days to cover their post-delivery desires. In conjunction with this, the government gave the government 2,500, or US $35, to take a position on a long-run government bond in the daughter's name, which might be later paid for with 25,000, or US $355, once she turns eighteen. She will solely receive the cash if she isn't married. Anju Malhotra, associate degree professional on kid wedding and adolescent women, said of this programme, "No alternative conditional money transfer has this focus of delaying wedding... It's an associate's degree incentive to encourage oldsters to value their daughters. "

The International Centre for Analysis on Ladies can evaluate Apni Beti, Apna Dhan over the course of the year 2012, once the program's initial participants turn eighteen, to ascertain if the programme, notably the money incentive, has actuated oldsters to delay their daughters' marriages. "We have proof that conditional money transfer programmes are terribly effective for keeping women at school and obtaining them vaccinated, but we tend to don't have proof that this strategy works for preventing weddings," said Pranita Achyut, the programme manager for Apni Beti and Apna Dhan. "If Haryana state's approach proves to be valuable, it may probably be scaled up to create a big distinction in more girls' lives—and not solely in India."

**Suggestions:**

**EDUCATING GIRLS**

Education plays an important role in keeping ladies safe from kid weddings. In fact, the longer a woman stays at school, the less likely she is to be married before age eighteen and have kids throughout her teen years.

Furthermore, education ensures that women acquire the skills and knowledge needed to find work and support their families. will facilitate breaking the cycle of poverty and forestall child marriages that occur as a result of extreme poorness and/or gain.

**EMPOWERING GIRLS**

Every lady has the right to determine her own future, but not every lady is aware of this—that's why empowering women is thus crucial to ending child marriage.

When women are confident in their skills, armed with information about their rights and supported by peer teams of alternative authorised women, they're ready to get on their feet and say "NO" to injustices like child marriage.

Empowered women are ready to re-shape views and challenge standard norms of what it means to be a woman.

**RALLYING THE WIDER COMMUNITY TO STAND UP FOR GIRLS' RIGHTS**

Parents and community leaders are usually in charge of deciding when and with whom a woman marries. In several ancient communities, it's believed that marriage keeps women safe, protected, and economically provided for by their husbands.

However, the alternative is true – weddings endanger girls' physical and mental state. In fact, women who were married before eighteen are more likely to experience domestic abuse and to report that their first sexual experience was forced. Furthermore, child brides are at a higher risk of HIV infection and are more likely to experience fatal complications during pregnancy and vaginal birth.

When oldsters and community leaders are educated concerning the various negative consequences of kid weddings, it will inspire them to alter their views, speak up for girls' rights, and encourage others to try and do the same.

**PROVIDING INCOME OPPROTUNITIES FOR GIRLS AND THEIR FAMILY**

Providing families with bread-and-butter opportunities like microfinance loans is an efficient way to forestall child marriages that occur as a result of monetary hardship.

When families have inflated economic opportunities, they're less likely to understand their daughters as economic burdens. This can be very true if a woman is in a class gaining valuable skills that may help generate financial gain in the future.

**ENCOURAGING SUPPORTIVE LAWS AND GOVERNMENT**

Petitioning the government to raise the minimum marriage age to eighteen years old in countries where child marriages are common may be a critical first step toward positive change. Once the minimum age is increased, it's imperative to continue raising awareness of those laws among brass and community leaders to make sure the laws are being implemented.

Other legal policies, like registering birth certificates and marriages, are powerful tools for preventing kid weddings. Time is running out for ladies in danger. Within the time it took to browse this story, 80 girls were forced into kid weddings. With every passing moment, the progress that has been created for girls' rights to mention NO to kid wedding is being undone thanks to the impact of the COVID-19 crisis. We are currently two-faced in light of the fact that more ladies may become child brides as a result of the pandemic. We have a tendency to stop the clock and the event so that the ladies can decide their own futures.

**Conclusion**

Child marriages are thought of as one of the social menaces that can't be checked simply without the support of society. Since a long time, there have been calls to make child marriages illegal, initially under the Prohibition of Child Marriages Act; however, Indian society is sophisticated, and making child marriages illegal can only jeopardise the rights of women who are victims of child marriage. Elders of the family forcibly marry their daughters to some elderly man in order that he will offer some cash to the girl's family and, from that money, their economic condition will improve.

Also, from the above discussion, it is often the case that in early marriages, the mothers and child's health is affected. Young brides have a higher risk of obstetrical complications, physiological conditions, iatrogenic high blood pressure, higher mortality rates, premature delivery, and a higher rate of miscarriages and stillbirths. The risks of an early wedding don't seem to be simply restricted to the mother's kid alone, but additionally to the kid that's born out of that wedding as a result of an early physiological condition. The morbidity rates are also high, aside from incidences of premature delivery and low birth weight of the new-born child.

There is tremendous pressure on young wives to have a baby. Early sexual activities additionally expose adolescents to a larger risk of acquiring sexually transmitted diseases (STDs) as well as HIV/AIDS. One of the leading causes of maternal mortality in India is early marriage and physiological condition.

**References**


1. Agarwal, Deepti & Mehra, Sunil. (2004). Adolescent Health Determinants for Pregnancy and Child Health Outcomes among the Urban Poor, Indian Paediatrics – Environmental Health Project, Special Article Services, Volume 41, New Delhi.
2. Bhatt, A. Sen and U. Pradhan (2005) "Child Marriage & the Law in India", Human Rights Law Network, New Delhi. p.259
3. Biswajit Ghosh, (2006): Trafficking in Women & Children, Child Marriage and Dowry: A Study for Action Plan in West Bengal, Dept of Women & Child Development & Social Welfare, Govt. of West Bengal & UNICEF.
4. Child and Law, Indian Council for Child Welfare, Chennai, Tamil Nadu, India, 1998, page 210.
5. Child and Law, Indian Council for Child Welfare, Chennai, Tamil Nadu, India, 1998, page 218.
6. Haberland, N. & E. Chong. (2004). „A world apart: The disadvantage and social isolation of married adolescent girls", Population Council, New York
7. Implementation Hand Book for the Convention on the Rights of the Child, UNICEF.

8. Lal B. Suresh and G. Kavitha, (2013): Economic Impact of Inadequate Sanitation on Women's Health: A Study in Warangal District, International Journal of Environment & Development, Vol.10, No-2, July-December: ISN: 0973-3574.
9. Lal B. Suresh, (2010): Economic and Health Status of Women Ragpickers: An Empirical Study in Andhra Pradesh, India, paper Presented at International Conference held at Beijing, China on Economic and Business, on 7-11 September, Organized by European-Asian Economics, Finance, Econometrics & Accounting Science Association (EAEFEASA).
10. Lal B. Suresh, (2010): The Economic Impact Of HIV/AIDS: A Study in Tribal Areas in Andhra Pradesh, Indian Journal of Millennium Development Studies: An International Journal, Volume 5 • Numbers 1-2 • January & June, 2010; pp. 139-146, ISSN: 0973-3981.
11. Lal B. Suresh, (2012); Current Health Scenario of Subaltern Communities: A Review in Rural India, in Dimensions of Female Sex- Ratio Inter State Variations in India Issues and Challenges, Serial Publications, New Delhi.
12. Lal B. Suresh, (2012): Combating the Child Labour In Andhra Pradesh- India: An Investigation, paper presented at 3rd European Asian Economics, Finance, Econometrics and Accounting conference held on 5-8 September, Taipei, Taiwan.
13. Lal B. Suresh, (2006): Health Status and Health Practices among the Tribals: A Case Study in AP, Journal of Social Anthropology, vol-3, No.2 Dec, Serials, New Delhi. P.no.233-239, ISSN: 0973-3582.
14. Lal B. Suresh, T. Joga Chary, (2006): An Empirical Study on Child Ragpickers in Warangal City, Indian Journal of Human Rights & Justice Vol-2, No. 1-2, p.no. 39-48, Serials, New Delhi.pp.39-48, ISSN:0973-3418.
15. M.E. Khan (1996) „Sexual Violence within Marriage".
16. Miller S. & F. Lester (2003) „Improving the health and well-being of married young first time mothers", W.H.O
17. NIPC, (2000): National Institute for Public Cooperation and Child Development, GOI, Note No. NI/PC/SAP/132/ 2000/908, dated July 31, 2000, page 4.
18. NTK Naik and Lal B. Suresh, (2013): Impact of Alcohol Consumption on Health and Economy (A Focus on Mc Dowellization of World); IOSR Journal of Nursing and Health Science (IOSR-JNHS), Volume-1, Issue-5, Jul-Aug, e-ISSN: 2320–1959, ISSN: 2320–1940, PP 18-23.
19. Saraswat, Ritu. (2006). „Child Marriage: A Social Evil", Social Welfare, April, 2006.
20. Savitri Goonesekere, (1998): Children, Law and Justice: A South Asian Perspective, SAGE, page 141.
21. Srivastava, K. (1983), „Socio-economic Determinants of Child Marriage in Uttar Pradesh", Demography India, New Delhi.
22. The National Institute of Public Cooperation and Child Development (NIPCCD),
23. UNICEF (2005) Early Marriage: A Harmful Traditional Practice: A Statistical Exploration.
24. Verma, A. (2004). Factors Influencing Anaemia among Girls of School Going Age (6-28 Years) from the slums of Ahmedabad City, Indian Journal of Community Medicine Jan-March, XXIX (1).
25. Yadav, K.P. (2006). „Child Marriage in India", Adhyayan Publishers & Distributors, New Delhi. p.303

CHAPTER XII

# Women and Men

## GENDER-WISE PARTICIPATION IN HOUSEHOLD WORK

Dr. Bhawana Asnani
Assistant Professor
Office of Director Students' Welfare, Junagadh Agricultural University
Junagadh (Gujarat)
bhawana_asnani@yahoo.com

**Abstract:**

A woman has been given a role where she just has to be obedient and look after her husband, children and home and in-laws at cost of her own life. Women play a dynamic role in their home activities, as wife, as mother who is responsible for development of the children and as homemaker, in charge of the operation of their homes. It is not only the functions of the family that changed with general social change, but the role of various members within the family also changed. The whole pattern of men-women relationship particularly in urban areas seems to be undergoing a considerable change. The changes in the social conditions and pattern of living have been responsible in the shift towards greater involvement of man in the household task performance.

**Traditional Picture of Gender Roles:**

Traditionally, a woman has been given a role where she just has to be obedient and look after her husband, children and home and in-laws at cost of her own life. But gradually the society realized the importance of a woman in educating, her children, even herself and helping her husband in earning money as well. Traditional societies structured their culture institutions based on the mythical religious conception (Kaila, 2001).

The daughter in-law entered her husband's family as a stranger, because the other members had already imbibed the traditions and customs of the family. The bride's major duty was to make efforts to merge her husband in matters both mundane and spiritual also to adopt herself to the traditions and sentiments of the family of which she had become a full-fledged member. Her position was one of honourable subordinate. She had to adjust herself to her mother-in-law, her husband's sister and the wives of her husband's brothers. It was expected of her to show respect to and obey all the elder members of the family. She had to help the mother-in-law in household duties such as cleaning, washing, drawing water, cooking, rearing children, tending cattle and nursing the sick and the aged. (Benerjee, 1945)

The wife was always supposed to participate in religious ceremonies along with her husband. In fact, no religious rite was complete without her presence. She was called "Ardhangni" his other half. The Mahabharat declared that in truth or reality a house holder's home, even if crowded with sons, grandsons and daughter-in-law and servant is virtually a lonely place for life; if there is no housewife one's home is not the house made of bricks and mortar, it is the wife who make the home. "A home without the wife is like a wilderness". (Prabhu, 1958)

Through the ages, the woman has been the subject of study from the ancient to the modern times. Comments on the nature of women their ambitions and aspirations, desires and wishes, birth and upbringing, relations with husband, paramour, children and after relatives have been the subject of discussions, comments, conversations and investigations throughout the history of mankind. The woman has been branded as a mysterious creature as well as devoted mother and self-sacrificing wife during various periods of the time through which the human civilization has evolved out from its primitive roots to an advanced scientific and technical culture.

Ironically, very little information is available about the civilization in pre-Aryan India. However, opinion of some, archaeologists is that the non-Aryans had originated in India as early as around 2500 B.C. and were of mixed origin and diverse ethnic composition. Later, their intellectual bent of mind influenced the Aryan throughout process.

The law of Karma, reincarnation, animal veneration, female or earth-mother goddesses, deity worship and male and female fertility symbols might have been imbibed by the Aryans from them.

The society was founded on the institutions of home and family. The Rig-vedic expression "The wife is the home" – shows now domestic life was woven around the woman. The Aryan society was patriarchal but the worship of the goddess prevailed. Earlier the mother goddess was worshipped in the form of icons but the Aryans almost replaced the icons with matronly women real mothers who were human and humane. The mother was given a high status in all spheres of life still, they had a desire for a male child. In the Rig-Vedic period the son was to take to the profession of the father, while the daughter was expected to follow her mother.

A description of status, position and education of the women of ancient India is incomplete without the mention of Manu's views. Manusmriti (about 200 B.C.) prescribes duties and obligations of a woman. For Manu, woman is perpetual minor and has to lead whole of her life under the guardianship of the father, the husband or the son. Manu prescribes that the wife must always worship her husband as God even if he is debauch, immoral and lacks character still she has to follow the dictates of her husband. The woman's salvation lies only in the devoted service to her husband. He refers to her duties in the following words: "She must always be cheerful, clever in the management of her household affairs, careful in cleaning her utensils, and economical in expenditure." Manu favoured only the domestic and religious education for women. He also favoured the giving of training in music and dance to the woman in order that she may be able to please her man.

In society the epic period was completely patriarchal and patrilineal, so the husband was considered the senior partner in the home. But the wife was also given the dignity in the household because of her vocation of motherhood. The epic Ramayana and Mahabharata contain description of women who presented ideal conduct and models for the womanhood. But these models also have ingrained in themselves the subordination of the women. Thus, the epics trace the story of the rise and fall of the status of women in Hindu society. (Lal, 2005)

**Changing Scenario:**

Women have a great responsibility to play as a home maker. Technical and industrial advancement on one side have made life easy, while on the other side, the role of woman has also changed considerably. It is not only that the functions of the family that changed with general social change, but the role of various members within the family also changed. Family life today is no more the same as it used to be; home maker's responsibilities have changed considerably. Today the efficient management and running of the home needs specialized knowledge, wide experience and new types of skills. The homemaker also needs knowledge to use new kinds of materials and equipment advantageously.

Women play a dynamic role in their home activities, as wife, as mother who is responsible for development of the children and as homemaker, in charge of the operation of their homes. In recent times, with the increase in educational facilities and wide spread change in resource available, women have gradually started taking employment outside the home. They have now an added major role that of as a wage earner. Traditional societies prevented women from entering the public domain and were given a subordinate position in the society. The life of an Indian woman was like a well-defined predicated master plan.

When the women liberation movement started the scenario of women work changed. Since the mid 1970's sociological interest in women's employment issues expanded rapidly. Women's status had undergone profound changes. As a result, significant change had been noticed in attitude of men and women towards women's education and employment. Women have played a key, unrecognized role in the rapid economic and social development worldwide. Women have been entering work force in record numbers, over the last four decades. Although, women are not a minority, the world of work they have faced many handicaps. In fact, majority of women who wish to pursue a career face the problem. Domestic and outside work often caused imbalance. Gender discrimination is a common phenomenon (Kaila, 2001).

Educated women then started getting jobs in many Government offices and schools but still women were prevented from entering the public domain and were given a subordinate position in society. In the modern era, mythical conception was rejected in favours of scientific world views. However, the prejudices of mythical world survived in the subconscious of modern societies. Some women were allowed to enter the public sphere but those who participated were low in density. Those who were successful in entering the public sphere encountered an invisible 'glass roof' over their heads allowing them to see where they may go, but stopping them from arriving there. Women were low viewed as treating and therefore be restrained.

Through educational reforms, women have demonstrated immense talent in academics and professions and now seek to fulfill their potential in the public sphere. In the case of women, the opportunity to work has too often created a double burden of work within and outside home. Recently, the International Centre for Research on Women (ICRW) attributed the reason for increased homes violence to the gender specific responsibilities such as preparing meals, caring for children and managing the household. And, if any, woman is holding an executive position she has to take care of the office meeting, specially, seminars and other routine office work as well.

**Women, Men and Household Tasks:**

The increase in the participation of women in the labour force of most industrialized societies has drawn the attention of scholars to house work, which is evident in these studies, that changes in marital roles are asymmetrical, wives have become co-providers, regardless of their motivations and personal aspirations while husbands who benefit from their wives' income have not equally shared house work. By their choice to work outside the home and by their inability to effectively use their economic resources to bargain for domestic equality with her husbands, they handle doubles burden of work within and outside home. Middle class working wives have contributed to their reinforcement and continuity of the patriarchal character of the contemporary family. Consequently, a change in the husband's domestic role is a critical indicator of the emergence of marital equality and an acid test for the liberation of women with in the domestic sphere.

The search on house work in dual earner families in western societies have mainly concentrated on time budgets i.e., the amount of time each spouse spends on domestic work, calculated either on a daily or weekly basis. There is a slight change in the amount of time that husbands in dual earner families spend on house work. Most of the other studies have concluded that there is little change over the years in the amount of time husbands in dual earner families spend on domestic tasks. Dual earner families have examined house work in the context of role conflict and the fatigue experienced by employed wives. Their husbands do not assist their wives in childcare. Paid domestic help is sought only by couples and it is usually unreliable. Most Indian wives continue to engage in longer hours of domestic work in addition to time spent on the job. Few researchers have provided qualified evidence comparing the patterns of house work among wives in the single and dual earner household in order to establish the magnitude of role overload experienced by wives among the dual earner wives. However, with the entry of middle-class wives in to the labour force, the supposition that the home is the centre of a women's life is no longer as universally accepted as the belief that raising children is part of becoming and being a woman. The sheer burden of two jobs has persuaded many working wives to express their dissatisfaction and yet adhere to the notion that women are primarily responsible for house work, while others express their discontent by totally rejecting the notion that domestic chores are women's duties. Consequently, there exist diverse attitudes and approaches to house work convergence (Banerjee, 1945).

**Sharing Marital Responsibilities:**

Marriage partners are sharing marital responsibilities to a greater degree today than in the past. As a result, the respective role expectations between husbands and wives are becoming more flexible and functional. More wives are sharing the provider role by working outside the home. Husband is expected to provide greater emotional support in the marriage, including help with child rearing. Decision making has become more democratic, especially among dual-income couples. Their tendency for the person with the greatest competency, interest or time is to perform a given task.

A major area of marital adjustment for many couples concerns the wife's employment outside the home. Most married women would like the option of working outside the home and feel it would help their marriage. Although many husbands agree with this idea, only substantial minority do not. In one survey, three-fourth of the wives either strongly favoured the wife working outside the home or felt neutral about it: only 25 percent of the women opposed the idea. However, only two-third of the husbands favoured their wives working or felt neutral about it while 34 percent of them objecting to the idea. There was greater agreement on this issue among cohabiting couples however once again women felt more strongly than men that they should work outside the home. Couples tend to share power more equally and are more satisfied with their marriages (Blumstein & Schwartz, 1983).

One difficulty that comes with the increased sharing of martial responsibilities is the issue of fairness. More specifically, this is a tendency for each partner to want greater rewards at no additional costs. For example, a husband may want his wife to work to help pay the bills but will still expect her to continue doing all the things she did around the house before taking the job. In turn, a working wife may want to keep most of her earning but expect her husband to help out more around the house. Talk the matter of house work among married couples. Although working wife do less house work than fulltime home makers do, they still do most of the house hold chores. Even though husbands of working wives help out around the house more than husbands of full-time homemakers, their contribution is not impressive (Blumstein & Schwartz, 1983).

**Impact of the Division of Domestic and Outside Work:**

The cultural assumption that the women's place in her home and her feelings to serve the interests of her family plays a decisive role in binding women to house work. The division of household labour has come to two basic conclusions. Women perform approximately twice as much labour as men and women perform qualitatively different types of labou. Blair and Lichter (1991) have reported that among the cohabiting and married couples surveyed in national survey of families and household, women performed on an average of 33 hours of housework per week (Exclusive of childcare activities) as compared to men's average of 14 hours!!!

The need for gainful employment by women has answer for better management of the family and fulfilling its need more and more women are entering the working class to satisfy needs. Though the employment of women outside family is accepted by our society, there is no clarity about their role within family circumstance. Working wives face a crisis of adjustment. As they have to perform a dual role; one at home, mother and wife role and the other outside to achieve gainful employment. Thus, they face a conflict situation.

**Change in Attitudes of Society:**

In Indian society, women's traditional role has been childbearing and home making while men perform roles related to instrument function outside the home. This arrangement served our society admirable for centuries. Thus, there was demarcation between the occupational and domestic roles. The traditional pattern of home maker as the main worker seems to be shifting in the recent years. The educational, political, economic and social changes have necessitated a change in women's status and her role.

The whole pattern of men-women relationship particularly in urban areas seems to be undergoing a considerable change. The present trend is towards an equalitarian ideology or companionship and comradeship family rather than towards traditional institutional pattern. So, the home making roles of men and women tend to converge. This had affected the test performance of both men and women of home and away from home.

The changes in the social conditions and pattern of living have been responsible in the shift towards greater involvement of man in the household task performance. Women working outside homes, changing attitudes towards men's and women's roles, reduced outside help and technical changes in the home have led to sharing, including both physical care and intellectual guidance of child in the recent years.

Men and women have to share equally in the rewarding experiences of life, the family roles of each should be examined and mixture of work role best suited to the individual families should be worked out.

This emphasis is more about the participation of husband in the household activities which may vary with the geographical location depending upon the living habits of people, age of the husband, and size of the family. Education of couple, occupation, duration of marriage, stage of family life cycle, employment of the home makers, hired help in the family and free time available to the husbands and their attitudes towards the participation in household activities in or to reduce homes makers work load as most of them carry the dual role of managing a home as well as paid job outside the home.

**Conclusion:**

In households the activities that take place in homes require labor. Gender is often used to divide labor; however, there is no universal set of tasks defined as "women's" work or "men's" work.

Nature, biological and religious arguments suggest that women are physically or spiritually predisposed to take care of children and husbands; housework is assumed to follow naturally from the nurturance of family members. However, feminist critiques claim that these theories have flawed logic and methods, and cite historical and cross-cultural variation to show that divisions of labor are socially constructed (Thorne and Yalom 1992); only women can bear and nurse children, but the gender of the people who cook or clean is neither fixed nor preordained.

**References:**

1. Benerjee, M. N. 1945. Hindu family and Freudian Theory. Indian Journal of Social Work. V(1944 – 45): 180-186.
2. Blair, S. L. and Licther, D. T. 1992. Measuring the division of household Labour: Gender Segregation of House work among American Couples. Journal of Family Issues. 12, pp. 91-113.
3. Blumstein, P. and Schwartz , P. 1983. American couples: money, work, sex. New York Publication.
4. Kaila, H.L. 2001. Women, Work and Family. Rawat Publications, Jaipur P.P. 21.
5. Lal, S. 2005. Social Status of Women. ABD Publishers, Jaipur, P.P. 63-68.
6. Prabhu, P.H. 1958. Hindu Social Organization. Popular Books, Bombay.
7. Thorne, B. and Yalom, M. 1992. Rethinking the Family: Some FeministFamily: Some Feminist Questions. Longman Publications, New York.
8. Vyas, J.N. 2011. A Comparative Study of Extent of Participation in Household Activities and Attitude about Performing Activities by Young and Old Couples of Mehsana District. Unpublished Ph.D. Thesis, Hemchandracharya North Gujarat University, Patan, Gujarat.

CHAPTER XIII

# Women and Reproductive Health, during COVID-19 Pandemic

## A Case Study in Kolkata

Nabamita De
Assistant professor
Adamas University, Kolkata
nabamita.pompy@gmail.com

**ABSTRACT**

The present study investigates the disruption of prevalence of reproductive health morbidities, treatment seeking behavior, and its association with impact of covid 19 pandemic, among unmarried and married pavement dwellers poor women of Sealdah area Kolkata. The study sample includes 12 women randomly selected from the roadside pavement dwellers of the city. Information on socioeconomic and demographic characteristics, prevalence of reproductive health morbidities, and treatment seeking behavior was collected using narratives through unstructured questionnaire schedule. Results of the study indicate that the prevalence of reproductive health morbidities among both married and unmarried women during pandemic is quite high due to plenty of rigid restrictions of lockdown laid by government, and above all nonavailability of both medical services and medicines have added to the worries of unplanned pregnancies along with risky abortions. Age, stigmas, ignorance, media exposure, and economic status emerged as significant factors of treatment-seeking practices among both married and unmarried women. High prevalence of reproductive health morbidity in this vulnerable group, particularly pavement dwellers settings, requires urgent intervention of health planners. This study reinforces an indirect and mediatory role of socioeconomic and demographic factors in the prevalence of impact on reproductive health morbidities of poor women during covid 19 pandemic along with the impact of two devastating cyclones named AMPHAN in 2020 and YAAS in 2021, associated treatment seeking behaviors and evaluating how much they have been benefited from government and NGOs.

**Keywords** - contraception, COVID 19 pandemic, role of government and NGOs, women reproductive health.

**INTRODUCTION**

The novel coronavirus (SARS-CoV-2) which caused COVID-19 has spread immensely in late 2019, leading the World Health Organization (WHO) to declare the disease as global pandemic on March 11, 2020 onwards. Both the 1st and 2nd wave of the pandemic have swept away innumerable lives worldwide, especially in developing and 3rd world countries. Governments around the world had to quickly adapt and act to curb transmission of the virus and to provide care for the infected. The strain that the outbreak imposes on health systems will undoubtedly impact the sexual and reproductive health of individuals living in low- and middle-income countries (LMICs); however, sexual and reproductive health will also be affected by societal responses to the pandemic, such as local or national lockdowns that force health services to shut down if they are not supposed to be essential, as well as the consequences of physical distancing, travel restrictions and economic slowdowns.

Previous public health emergencies have proved that the impact of epidemic on sexual and reproductive health often goes unrecognized or underestimated, because the effects are often not the direct result of the infection, but instead the indirect consequences of strained health care systems, disruptions in care and redirected resources causes the havoc. In ideal terms of reproductive health, it is defined to include reproductive choice, healthy reproduction, avoidance of gynecological and associated problems, and dignity. The reality of the situation of women in the developing world are far behind this. It is understood that working towards this ideal requires more than a medical approach and is focused on the supply side of service delivery. Special approach is required, in addition, to the demand side including active agents' women, men, families and communities. Yet this multidimensional lookout for reproductive health has unfortunately created a concern for some over the cost-of-service programs, in view of limited resources, and of competition with more narrowly defined goals that have received priority in the past, paramount among them being control of fertility through family planning programs in the developing world.

As we know that during lockdowns due to restricted mobility domestic violence has risen a lot. Which eventually has resulted in injuries and serious physical, mental, sexual and reproductive health problems, including sexually transmitted infections, HIV, and unplanned pregnancies. Thus, here comes one of the objectives of the study, as the pandemic continues, what can we do to ensure the availability of timely and quality maternal health, family planning, and abortion services for the down trodden women?

**METHOD AND RESEARCH SET-UP**

The research was done on the women pavement dwellers both married and unmarried. As it was a case study thus 12 respondents were randomly selected and interviewed with audio recording, for narrative transcriptions. The location of study was Sealdah, a very busy and overcrowded place in central Kolkata in ward no 49 under Kolkata municipality.

The study was divided into 2 sections depending upon the various objectives under a broad heading of "Factors affecting uses of essential health services during pandemic".

The objectives are the following-

**A) DEMAND FOR SERVICES**, under which it was again divided into 3 sections viz:

1. Movement restrictions,
2. Lost income and
3. Concerns about COVID-19 transmission

**B) SUPPLY OF SERVICES**, which was again subdivided into 3 sections viz:

1. Supply chain disruptions,
2. Redeployment/ Morbidity/ Mortality of healthcare workers and lastly
3. Health facility capacity taken up by COVID-19 care.

**FACTORS AFFECTING USES OF ESSENTIAL HEALTH SERVICES DURING PANDEMIC**

The pandemic and both the waves and strict lockdown in India have affected reproductive services such as maternal health, family planning, and abortion services tremendously. While medical facilities and retail chemists were exempted from the lockdown, the curbs on movement, fear of infection among patients and health care providers, resulted in low or no availability of services. Though the Government of India envisioned RMNCAH+N (Reproductive, Maternal, New-born, Child, Adolescent Health and Nutrition) services as essential in mid-April 2020, access and availability continued, and continues, to be challenging.

The COVID-19 pandemic is having bothersome effects on the supply chain for contraceptive commodities by disrupting the manufacture of key pharmaceutical components of contraceptive methods or the manufacture of the methods themselves (e.g., condoms), and by delayed transportation of contraceptive commodities. In addition, equipment and staff involved in provision of sexual and reproductive health services all are diverted to fulfil other covid 19 needs, clinics are all closed and people are reluctant to go to health facilities for sexual and reproductive health services. Many governments are restricting people movements to check the spread of the virus, and providers are being forced to suspend some sexual and reproductive health services that are not classified as essential, such as abortion care, thus denying people this time-sensitive and potentially life-saving service.

## 1. DEMAND FOR SERVICES

This is the first of the two main objectives of the study where it was intended to find how and why women were suffering from reproductive health. Abnormal decreases in maternal and new-born care due to disrupted services and fear of seeking treatment during the outbreak proves that government actions and provision of resources during the COVID-19 pandemic do not ensure essential sexual and reproductive health care services has had continued properly or not. Threats to contraceptive autonomy have also emerged as a result of the COVID-19 pandemic. As hospitals, clinics and providers postpone elective medical procedures, sometimes indefinitely and many have restricted contraceptive services too. As international borders were closed raw materials from foreign couldn't reach India and above that innumerable medicine producing companies were also under lockdown mode, thus there was no production, hence medicines were also not available in market or hospitals. At times it was found stock clearing, i.e., near to expiry dated medicines were also sold to meet the unending demand. On the other hand, there is still a lack of information on status of available services, as well as increased worries and concerns of being exposed or vulnerable exacerbated by the fact that RMNCH facilities are not stand-alone (as they are generally available in hospitals).

## A. MOVEMENT RESTRICTIONS

India documented considerable reductions in attended births, as well as increases in adverse maternal and neonatal outcomes during both the waves of covid 19. Disruptions to ANC can be especially problematic to address iron deficiency and undernutrition in pregnant women, as well as for HIV diagnosis and prevention of mother-to-child transmission. These all were not possible due movement restriction and lockdown.

As local trains and all state-run vehicles were at stake for lockdown and maximum of hospitals and maternity homes were taken over as covid ward and hospitals, thus the women neither travelled to these places for treatment nor these places were serviceable. Police also were very active in checking unnecessary movements except emergencies or having special passes for travelling outside on roads.

## A. LOST INCOME

We all know how the daily wage labourers and the low-income people with meagre salary are suffering unthinkably although out. As Kolkata is a very old city and a business hub, lots of people from suburbs and interiors come and earn their bread here. All hopes crashed when both transport and business stood still. Except for the emergency things like groceries, vegetables, medicines etc, all shops were closed. The poor seemed to be becoming poorer and reaching out for reproductive problems seemed to be luxury in these gloomy days.

## C. CONCERNS ABOUT COVID-19 TRANSMISSION

During both the 1st and the 2nd wave of the pandemic, concerns of transmission were high, but it was during the 2nd phase that the loss of lives and problems seemed to be more. As the days were passing, the strains of the virus were getting stronger and more dangerous. In the 1st phase it was only the senior citizens who were affected mostly, but in the second wave the middle aged and the young adults were affected more. Thus by keeping all these in mind the women in general and specially the low income group women didn't take any risk or chance of seeking reproductive health care issues. More over the health care were disrupted, thus risky abortions and even unwanted pregnancy etc were the unexpected results.

**2. SUPPLY OF SERVICES**

Now we have come to the other important section of the study, that is after demand what else is required on the supply side, there are concerns of fear of being vulnerable and getting affected, inadequate or shortage of PPE, staffs being infected or under quarantine and going to isolation for getting affected, redeployment and shortage of trained staff, overstretched health infrastructure and personals, and above all lack of beds in both private and public hospitals. So many died un attended. There are newspaper reports and news of health facilities being overlooked by large numbers of COVID-19 patients needing management and treatment, especially in the hotspots and even in urban setups.

## A. SUPPLY CHAIN DISRUPTIONS

We can assume that COVID-19 is here to stay for longer than originally seemed to be. As the pandemic continues, what can we do to ensure the availability of timely and quality maternal health, family planning, and abortion services? We also by now know that access to vital sexual and reproductive health services, including for women subjected to violence, will likely become more limited and other services, such as hotlines, crisis centres, shelters, legal aid, and protection services have also been measurably low.

The lockdown has meant that access to and use of contraception has been compromised to a large extent. In line with the Ministry of Health and Family Welfare, Government of India's advisory, public facilities suspended provision of sterilisations and intra-uterine contraceptive devices (IUCDs) during the lockdown. Curbs on movement in urban areas and for ASHA workers in rural areas made access to over-the-counter contraceptives (OTC), condoms, oral contraceptive pills (OCPs), and emergency contraceptive pills (ECPs) difficult. Additionally, in West Bengal prior to the pandemic, abortion was already being done in secrecy, and in these trying times with lack of access, women, in desperation, have been resorting to unsafe abortions which have unmeasurable outcomes.

On another note, organisations such as Family Planning Association of India (FPA India) and Foundation for Reproductive Health Services India (FRHS India) have continued to provide family planning and safe abortion services as much as possible, and others, NGOs such as CEHAT, have helped women to access services.

**B. REDEPLOYMENT/MORBIDITY/MORTALITY OF HEALTHCARE WORKERS**

It was slowly getting proved that gains made in the country to address preventable maternal, new-born, and child mortality and morbidity in the last two decades will be reversed by impact of COVID-19. According to the understanding of health experts, lakhs of couples have lost access to family planning services, and there is an anticipation of an increase in unintended pregnancies, child births, and maternal deaths.

youth are more likely to experience morbidities than other age groups. Increasing the load of morbidities with age, in spite of better treatment-seeking practices among higher age groups, creates a gap between morbidity rate and health care use among them. It shows that this phase of transition from adolescence to adulthood needs special care, both from social institutions, like family and school, and health care institutions to increase awareness about reproductive health aspects to promote a youth-friendly health care system. At places, multipurpose health workers and teachers can be of great help to enhance awareness and motivate both married and unmarried women to seek treatment for various issues related to reproductive health matters. It would be worthwhile to establish a special youth clinic at the local club level to provide both counselling and care for reproductive health problems faced by youth.

This study gave a unique scenario of the heavy burden of gynaecological and related problems that women bear in silence. It also highlighted constraints within the social context, low awareness level of women and quality of care are also under considerations, as affecting women's health and health- seeking behaviour. Few views have come up from the study they are-

1. A health services component that involves selective upgrading of the current Family Planning and Maternal Child Health services being provided at the health centres, as well as introduction of elements of gynaecological services that address gynaecological and related morbidity conditions revealed by pavement dwelling women in the Study. The physical set-up at the clinic also needs to be upgraded and necessary medical equipment and supplies, and in cleanliness and privacy concerns.

2. Officials involved in training to enhance providers‘ awareness and technical skills to enable them to better understand reproductive health problems in prevention and for treatment. Providers also need to be sensitized to women's perceptions of health and illness and to the socio-economic constraints imposed on them, in order to make communication with women and treatment regimens more suitable for the realities of women's lives. A proper health education component which is aimed at raising awareness in women and men of how to avoid reproductive health problems, of symptoms of these problems and of when to seek medical help for their treatment and management also needs to be understood through proper training.

**C. HEALTH FACILITY CAPACITY TAKEN UP BY COVID 19 CARE**

Global Financing Facility (GFF) states that large service disruptions in India have the potential to leave more than 4 million women without access to facility-based deliveries. Therefore, for disruptions in essential services, child mortality in India could increase by 40 percent and maternal mortality by 52 percent over the next year.

There have been reports in newspapers of pregnant women dying as they were denied access to care. According to one such report, "A woman in the eighth month of pregnancy died in an ambulance after eight hospitals either referred her to another facility as she showed symptoms of COVID-19, or cited lack of beds."

Media reports citing data from West Bengal highlight that the number of institutional deliveries may have fallen by as much as 40 percent during the lockdown, with many women giving birth at home. That's a significant reduction, given that a rise in institutional deliveries is believed to be one of the prime reasons India had reduced maternal and infant mortality in recent decades.

There is both confusion and lack of information among pregnant women and their families on where to go and what to do for health services, as hospitals are now dedicated to COVID-19 patient services.

Additionally, according to Sujoy Roy from CINI and White Ribbon Alliance for Safe Motherhood in West Bengal, suffering due to COVID-19 has been exacerbated by the devastation caused by Cyclone Amphan in first wave and YAAS in second wave to homes and livelihoods. There is confusion and lack of information among pregnant women and their families on where to go for health services, as hospitals are now dedicated to COVID-19.

**FINDINGS**

To avoid this potential sexual and reproductive health crisis, governments and their partners (i.e., donors and nongovernmental organizations) should take fast and strong action.

First, they should define, train and promote sexual and reproductive health care, including safe abortion, contraceptive services, and maternal and new-born care as essential and foremost important. This will allow people to move for sexual and reproductive health services even in areas under stay at-home orders or with travel protocols—without fear of legal consequences.

Second, alongside private-sector, governments and their partners should strengthen national and regional supply chains—by taking such steps as prepositioning commodities and identifying alternative suppliers—to make sexual and reproductive health medications and supplies more available to both providers and patients.

Third, to improve access to sexual and reproductive health services, they should make contraceptives available without a prescription; decentralize and mobilize distribution of contraceptives, drugs and other supplies from the national to regional level without much hurdles; deliver services at people's home when possible; and facilitate dispensing of sexual and reproductive health products.

Fourth, they should extensively initiate innovative models of outreach care, such as telehealth, and restricting diversion of resources and staff away from sexual and reproductive services.

Fifth, it would be helpful if women get extensive and flexible health education and counselling on topics such as hygienic behaviour and understanding and identifying signs and symptoms for early treatment. A strategy involving simple perspectives of care would also rely on clinical services to the extent possible providing adequate training to health care providers. These trainings will also have to include sensitization to women's perspectives on social realities so that a provider can draw the required information for a diagnosis well-informed by a woman's complaint, when there is no accessibility of advanced technology. All strategies relying on clinical diagnosis would have to be complemented by an appropriate system of follow-up and by implementation of adequate referral procedures to take care of persistent and serious cases.

Sixth, women need more representation in leadership and decision-making roles throughout the health sector because women constitute over 70 percent of the global health workers but they hold only 25 percent of leadership roles. Moreover, women health workers on the front line need greater safety, support, and appropriate compensation. This is particularly true for community health workers who are frequently underpaid or unpaid, and sent into communities without proper personal protective equipment. Governments and donors should create space for civil society input too, because working toward a positive legacy of the COVID-19 crisis with regard to open and accountable global health governance which includes the requirements and perspectives of women and girls.

Finally, governments and their partners should address the unique needs of vulnerable and marginalized populations, who often face pre-existing barriers to care that are profound during a crisis.

**CONCLUSION**

Outbreaks are inevitable, but unnatural losses for sexual and reproductive health are not. By learning from prior epidemics, putting in place critical resources and systems, and ensuring the provision of essential sexual and reproductive health care services, we can prevent health system disruptions that would have devastating, lasting effects on individuals, families and the global communities.

All communities need accessibility to best-quality, noncoercive services that offer an extensive range of contraceptive and reproductive options. We can estimate the urgency and importance of this phase not only to resist rolling back pre-COVID reproductive rights, but to seize the opportunity to demand greater reproductive autonomy for all individuals everywhere. These efforts could include increasing access to clinic-based and self-managed abortion, as well as to a wide contraceptive method mix. In this uncertain time, we appreciate the need for short term, emergency measures to prevent the spread of coronavirus infection. Yet we must be alert and energetic advocates for a rights-based, person-centred approach to reproductive health around the world. The basic right to control an individual's reproductive destiny is non-negotiable, regardless of COVID-19 or any emergencies.

**REFERENCES**


1. Agrawal, Sutapa. 2008. "Determinants of Induced Abortion and Its Consequences on Women's Reproductive Health: Findings from India's National Family Health Surveys/' DHS Working Paper No. 53. Calverton, MD: Macro International.
2. Bearinger LH et al., Global perspectives on the sexual and reproductive health of adolescents: patterns, prevention, and potential, Lancet, 369(9568): 1220-12
3. Dixon-Mueller R, Starting young: sexual initiation and HIV prevention in early adolescence, AIDS and Behavior, 2009, 13(1): 10
4. Gupta N and Mahy M, Sexual initiation among adolescent girls and boys: trends and differentials in Sub-Saharan Africa, Archives of Sexual Behavior, 2003, 32(l):41-5
5. Hall KS et al., Centring sexual and reproductive health and justice in the global COVID-19 response, Lancet, 2020, 395(10231):1175–1177, http://dx.doi.org/10.1016/S0140-6736(20)30801-1.
6. Senderowicz L, Contraceptive autonomy: conceptions and measurement of a novel family planning indicator, Studies in Family Planning, 2020, 51(2):161–176, https://doi.org/10.1111/sifp.12114.
7. Upadhyay UD et al., Development and validation of a reproductive autonomy scale, Studies in Family Planning, 2014, 45(1):19–41, https://doi.org/10.1111/j.1728-4465.2014.00374.x.
8. UNFPA, COVID-19: a gender lens, 2020, https://www.unfpa.org/resources/covid-19-gender-lens. Purdy C, Opinion: How will COVID-19 affect global access to contraceptives—and what can we do about it? Devex, Mar. 11, 2020, https://www.devex.com/news/sponsored/opinion-how-will-covid19-affect-global-access-to-contraceptives-and-what-can-we-do-aboutit-96745.
9. World Health Organization, COVID-19: operational guidance for maintaining essential health services during an outbreak, 2020, https://www.who.int/publications-detail/covid-19-operationalguidance-for-maintaining-essential-health-services-during-anoutbreak.

CHAPTER XIV

# Poverty and Subordinate Social Status of Women

## Cause of Poor Health and Nutrition of Women in India

Indresh Kumar
All Indian Institute of Medical Science, Bhopal
Kumar.indresh@hotmail.com
Deepa Srivastava
Army Public School, Lucknow

**Abstract**

In research done about the status of women in some of the rich countries of the world, India has stood last, compared the status of women on many topics such as education, health, employment, and violence. If a woman is healthy then the whole family will be healthy and if the family is healthy then the society, state and country will also be healthy. Although the Government of India does not respect the health of women, various steps have been taken in the areas of status, poverty, education, violence against women, gender differences, etc. Along with effort, it is also necessary to have a meaningful implementation on it. In the present research article, these problems of women in their context have been elaborated. Literature on the topic shows that poverty and low level in society are major factors for the poor health and nutrition status of women. Poverty, *low* rates of *female* literacy, and *poor* access to or use of *health* services are some of the underlying factors.

**Introduction**

One-fourth of women of childbearing age in India are malnourished and have a Body Mass Index (BMI) of less than 18.5 kg/m [1]. Malnourished girls are more likely to become malnourished mothers, giving birth to low birth weight babies, and thus the cycle of malnutrition continues for generations [2]. This cycle is being carried forward by young mothers, especially by adolescents, who begin having children before they are fully physically developed [3]. When mothers keep very short intervals between pregnancies and give birth to many children, it increases the nutritional deficiency in the body which continues in the children as well. The failure of the fetus to develop properly is mostly due to the mother not receiving adequate nutrition before conception and during the first trimester of pregnancy [3]. The main reason for the persistence of malnutrition levels among Indian children is the so far achieved failure to correct malnourished women before and during pregnancy. As a result, women's nutrition before-during-after pregnancy - is now included as a special focus area in UNICEF India's nutrition program-building [4].

The result of negligence towards women's health is that the maternal mortality rate in India is higher than in less developed countries like Nepal, Sri Lanka [5]. According to the 2021 Global Nutrition Report, India has the highest number of anemic women in the age group of 15 to 49 years in the world. The situation in India is being considered more worrying because instead of moving forward in the direction of the goal, we are going backward [6]. According to the report of the year 2020, the percentage of anemic women here was 48, which has increased to 51 this time [7].

A joint study by researchers from the All India Institute of Medical Sciences (AIIMS), the Indian Statistical Institute, the Prime Minister's Economic Advisory Council, and Harvard University has found that gender discrimination in India is taking a toll on women's health. . Researchers studied the records of 23,77,028 patients who came to AIIMS for treatment from January to December 2016 [8]. The study found that only 33 percent of women get access to health care. At the same time, this rate in men is 67 percent. The research revealed that a woman's reproductive age plays a big role in determining whether she can reach a doctor for treatment. Women in the age group of 31 to 44 faceless gender discrimination. The figure of 1.5 male patients per female patient has been found in this age range. At the same time, the rate of gender discrimination among women 45 to 59 years old is 1.4 male patients per female patient. Gender discrimination against women up to the age of 18 increases to 1.9 male patients per female and increases to 2.02 male patients per female with females aged 19 to 30 years [9]. Talking about the age of above 60 years in 2016, this rate was 1.7 male patients as compared to one female patient.

Ranjana Kumari, who works for women's rights and is director of the Center for Social Research in New Delhi, feels that a low sex ratio is one such social factor due to which women do not get proper health care [10]. She says, "Due to the mood of Indian society, women are very patient and silent inside the house. In our country, women's health is not given priority. No one wants to spend money on women's treatment. It works both ways. One is that most of the time women are silent about their health. Second, they are brought up in such a way that they become shy and because of shyness or low self-esteem, they go for treatment. Can't say it openly."

**Causes for poor health and nutrition**

It is quite easy to pin down the specific causes of women's health problems. Like we can say that sexually transmitted diseases are caused by different germs; Malnutrition is caused by not eating good food in proper quantity and the problems in pregnancy are often due to lack of proper care in pregnancy [11], but under these direct reasons there are two basic reasons- poverty and low status of women in society - whose due to which health problems of women arise.

**Poverty:**

In India, one-third of the population still lives below the poverty line. In these too, women and girls have to bear the maximum of the ill effects of poverty [12]. Millions and crores of women are trapped in the web of poverty, which starts even before they are born. Babies born from the womb of a woman who did not get enough food during pregnancy are often of low birth weight and small in size and their physical growth is also slow. In poor families, girls are less likely to get enough food than boys, due to which their intelligence becomes frustrated. Generally, girls and women remain neglected in the fields of health and education. Even in the work field, they have to do unskilled work and get fewer wages than men [13]. They also have to work at home (without wages!) As a result, women and their children are at increased risk of ill health due to exhaustion, malnutrition, and lack of care during pregnancy.

Due to poverty, he is forced to live in such conditions which can cause many physical and mental problems for him. For example, poor women often live in very poor housing where there is no trace of cleanliness or clean water. These, and lack of solitude, are more harmful to women than to men. They are deprived of adequate and good food and they have to spend a lot of precious time and energy in finding food that they can afford [14]. She is forced to do such work which is dangerous or in which work has to be done for a long time. There may also be a possibility of sexual harassment. They are employed as daily wage earners to do heavy work but they do not get much power required to do such kind of work [15].

Despite the availability of health services, they are not able to reach them. The reason for this is that they cannot go to household chores or leave wages [16]. They become so engrossed in the struggle to survive that they neither get the time nor the energy to pay attention to the fulfillment of their own needs. Plan your future, learn new skills, or take better care of your children. They are often forced to make arrangements for the survival of the family such as fuel, fodder, and water and also to work on the farms for which they receive neither money nor credit [17].

Poverty compels them to form relationships in which they have to depend on men for survival. which may be harmful to their health [13]. For example, she may outright suffer family violence or say no to unprotected sex because she fears losing financial support and social acceptance.

**The low status of women in society:**

Level refers to the importance of a person in society or family. The level affects the behavior of women; How a woman evaluates herself and accepts herself, what kind of activities, what kind of decisions she is free to take. In most of the communities in India, the status of women is lower than that of men [18]. Social and cultural practices reinforce this low status. Low social status of women encourages discrimination i.e. they are treated badly or they are denied something because they are women. This discrimination may take different forms in different communities, but it always harms the health of the woman [19].

**(I) Boys want not girls:** Many families give more importance to boys than girls because they think that boys can contribute more to the wealth/wealth of the household, can be a support to the parents in old age, can perform the functions after the death of the parents [20]. And can carry forward the name of the lineage. As a result, the birth of girls is not celebrated, as dowry will have to be arranged for them and, after marriage, they will leave the house and are considered a burden on the house [21]. That's why investment in her is limited to making her a good bride and housewife. Because of this, girls are often breastfed for short periods, given less food and medical care, and less education.

**(II) Lack of legal powers and decision-making power:** In many communities, women do not have the right to own property, inherit, earn money or borrow money. If she gets divorced she is not even allowed to keep her belongings or with her children. Even if he has legal rights, the traditions of his community do not allow him to control his own life. Often a woman cannot decide how to spend family money or when to get medical care [22]. She cannot go out of the house or participate in the decisions of society without the permission of her husband or mother-in-law.

When women are denied power in these ways, they have to depend on men to survive. Because of this, they cannot easily demand all that is necessary for good health, such as good and adequate food, family planning, safe sex, and freedom from violence. Due to dependence on husband and family for basic things like bread, cloth, house, and permission, she becomes a slave and is unable to fulfill her inherent potential [24]

**(III) Having more children or fewer children:** Discrimination against women can often lead to early pregnancy because only childbearing becomes the only way to earn respect for herself and her husband [21]. Under all these circumstances women lead a life of poor health and they have less access to health services. They accept this low status as their destiny because they are taught from the very beginning to be inferior to men. They accept their poor health as luck and seek medical help only when health problems become serious or life-threatening.

**(IV) Insensitivity of the healthcare system to the needs of women:** Particularly in rural areas (and in some urban slums), due to inadequate healthcare systems, medical services are either less available or favored by women who are already sidelined by poverty and discrimination. Is. Since government health services are generally inadequate, about 80% of health services are obtained privately for money [25]. Due to poverty and discrimination in the family and society, the health problems of women are not only increased, but due to this, the healthcare system is also unable to provide such health services to women which women need. Government policies and the economic conditions of the world make the problem even deeper [23.

Many people in poor countries do not have access to any kind of health services and even the little money available due to discrimination against women will probably never be spent on their health needs, so if a woman spends money on good services Even if he is in a position to do so, he may not be able to get those services. There may be some reproductive health services being provided but to meet all his health needs, he will have to accompany him to a district hospital or a major city hospital at his own expense [26]. It is therefore important that in the absence of trained doctors, nurses, medics, or health workers are adequately trained so that they can provide women's health services.

**(V) Credit and Structural Cohesion: Keeping the Poor Poor:**

In the 1970s and 1980s, many poorer countries were forced to take loans from the banks of wealthier countries. Though many big projects were taken up these were not as per the needs of the people [27]. In fact, due to these they were displaced from their land and were forced to become economic refugees. But now these banks started asking for their money back and due to this these countries were forced to change their economic policies or bring 'reconciliation' in them. They not only have to return the principal amount but also have to pay huge interest on it. About 30-40 of many countries: Earnings are spent only in paying interest [28]. Poor nations suffer the most because their welfare budgets are already low and inadequate. They cannot spend that much money on welfare programs that benefit the poor such as building schools, health centers, hospitals or providing people with food and fuel at reasonable prices. The governments of poor countries are often asked by international organizations not to make any concessions in food or health services and are instructed to charge for these and to privatize them [29]. However, it is seen that the welfare sector has been affected the most due to a lack of resources.

**Conclusion**

Although men's health is also affected by these factors, women are treated differently, as a group. They generally have less power, lack resources, and their status in the family and community is due to this inequality. More women than men are affected by poverty. Compared to men, more women are denied education and the ability to stand on their own feet. Women have access to important health information and services. Compared to men, there are significantly more women who have no control over their basic health and other life decisions, no recognition or importance is given to the significant contribution of more women to the domestic economy. This contribution includes tasks such as household work, child care, and farm labor, which take a lot of effort and time. Taking such a broader view helps us to understand the root causes responsible for the low health of women. To improve the health of women, it is necessary to treat their health problems. Along with this, it is necessary to bring changes in their life circumstances so that they can get more control and power over their health and life.

**References**


1. Sethi V, Dinachandra K, Murira Z, et al. Nutrition status of nulliparous married Indian women 15-24 years: Decadal trends, predictors and program implications. *PLoS One*. 2019;14(8):e0221125. Published 2019 Aug 27. doi:10.1371/journal.pone.0221125
2. Fall CH. Fetal malnutrition and long-term outcomes. *Nestle Nutr Inst Workshop Ser*. 2013;74:11-25. doi:10.1159/000348384
3. National Academies of Sciences, Engineering, and Medicine; Health and Medicine Division; Division of Behavioral and Social Sciences and Education; Board on Children, Youth, and Families; Committee on the Neurobiological and Socio-behavioral Science of Adolescent Development and Its Applications; Backes EP, Bonnie RJ, editors. The Promise of Adolescence: Realizing Opportunity for All Youth. Washington (DC): National Academies Press (US); 2019 May 16. 2, Adolescent Development. Available from: https://www.ncbi.nlm.nih.gov/books/NBK545476/
4. Fox EL, Davis C, Downs SM, Schultink W, Fanzo J. Who is the Woman in Women's Nutrition? A Narrative Review of Evidence and Actions to Support Women's Nutrition throughout Life. *Curr Dev Nutr*. 2018;3(1):nzy076. Published 2018 Sep 21. doi:10.1093/CDN/nzy076
5. Girum T, Wasie A. Correlates of maternal mortality in developing countries: an ecological study in 82 countries. *Matern Health Neonatol Perinatol*. 2017;3:19. Published 2017 Nov 7. doi:10.1186/s40748-017-0059-8
6. Wells JCK, Marphatia AA, Amable G, Siervo M, Friis H, Miranda JJ, et al. . The future of human malnutrition: rebalancing agency for better nutritional health. *Glob Health*. (2021) 17:119. 10.1186/s12992-021-00767-4
7. Miller JL. Iron deficiency anemia: a common and curable disease. *Cold Spring Harb Perspect Med*. 2013;3(7):a011866. Published 2013 Jul 1. doi:10.1101/Csh Perspect.a011866
8. Banerjee, Joyita et al. "Methodological considerations in designing and implementing the harmonized diagnostic assessment of dementia for longitudinal aging study in India (LASI-DAD)." *Biodemography and social biology* vol. 65,3 (2020): 189-213. doi:10.1080/19485565.2020.1730156
9. Unequal, Unfair, Ineffective and Inefficient Gender Inequity in Health: Why it exists and how we can change it https://www.who.int/social_determinants/resources/csdh_media/wgekn_final_report_07.pdf
10. Buvinić, Mayra, and Geeta Rao Gupta. "Female-Headed Households and Female-Maintained Families: Are They Worth Targeting to Reduce Poverty in Developing Countries?" *Economic Development and Cultural Change*, vol. 45, no. 2, University of Chicago Press, 1997, pp. 259–80, http://www.jstor.org/stable/1154535.
11. Danielewicz H, Myszczyszyn G, Dębińska A, Myszkal A, Boznański A, Hirnle L. Diet in pregnancy-more than food. *Eur J Pediatr*. 2017;176(12):1573-1579. doi:10.1007/s00431-017-3026-5
12. Women in Poverty: A New Global Underclass Mayra Buvinic Washington, D.C. July 1998—N° WID-101 https://publications.iadb.org/publications/english/document/Women-in-Poverty-A-New-Global-Underclass.pdf
13. Thorat A, Vanneman R, Desai S, Dubey A. Escaping and Falling into Poverty in India Today. *World Dev*. 2017;93:413-426. doi:10.1016/j.worlddev.2017.01.004
14. Hawkley LC, Cacioppo JT. Loneliness matters a theoretical and empirical review of consequences and mechanisms. *Ann Behav Med*. 2010;40(2):218-227. doi:10.1007/s12160-010-9210-8

15. McLaughlin H, Uggen C, Blackstone A. THE ECONOMIC AND CAREER EFFECTS OF SEXUAL HARASSMENT ON WORKING WOMEN. *Gend Soc.* 2017;31(3):333-358. doi:10.1177/0891243217704631
16. Gale S, Mordukhovich I, Newlan S, McNeely E. The Impact of Workplace Harassment on Health in a Working Cohort. *Front Psychol.* 2019;10:1181. Published 2019 May 24. doi:10.3389/fpsyg.2019.01181
17. Visaria L, Joshi H. Seasonal sugarcane harvesters of Gujarat: trapped in a cycle of poverty [published online ahead of print, 2021 Feb 10]. *J Soc Econ Dev.* 2021;23(Suppl 1):1-18. doi:10.1007/s40847-020-00120-2
18. Umberson D, Montez JK. Social relationships and health: a flashpoint for health policy. *J Health Soc Behav.* 2010;51 Suppl(Suppl): S54-S66. doi:10.1177/0022146510383501
19. Sharma R. The Family and Family Structure Classification Redefined for the Current Times. *J Family Med Prim Care.* 2013;2(4):306-310. doi:10.4103/2249-4863.123774
20. Vlassoff C. Gender differences in determinants and consequences of health and illness. *J Health Popul Nutr.* 2007;25(1):47-61.
21. National Academies of Sciences, Engineering, and Medicine; Division of Behavioral and Social Sciences and Education; Board on Children, Youth, and Families; Committee on Supporting the Parents of Young Children; Breiner H, Ford M, Gadsden VL, editors. Parenting Matters: Supporting Parents of Children Ages 0-8. Washington (DC): National Academies Press (US); 2016 Nov 21. 2, Parenting Knowledge, Attitudes, and Practices. Available from: https://www.ncbi.nlm.nih.gov/books/NBK402020/
22. Allendorf K. Do Women's Land Rights Promote Empowerment and Child Health in Nepal?. *World Dev.* 2007;35(11):1975-1988. doi:10.1016/j.worlddev.2006.12.005
23. Munkejord MC, Ness TM, Silan W. 'We are All Interdependent'. A Study of Relationships Between Migrant Live-In Carers and Employers in Taiwan. *Glob Qual Nurs Res.* 2021;8:23333936211043504. Published 2021 Oct 31. doi:10.1177/23333936211043504
24. Then C, Chuang E, Washington DL, et al. Understanding Gender Sensitivity of the Health Care Workforce at the Veterans Health Administration. *Women's Health Issues.* 2020;30(2):120-127. doi:10.1016/j.whi.2020.01.001
25. Doyal L. Sex, gender, and health: the need for a new approach. *BMJ.* 2001;323(7320):1061-1063. doi:10.1136/bmj.323.7320.1061
26. Stover J, Hardee K, Ganatra B, et al. Interventions to Improve Reproductive Health. In: Black RE, Laxminarayan R, Temmerman M, et al., editors. Reproductive, Maternal, Newborn, and Child Health: Disease Control Priorities, Third Edition (Volume 2). Washington (DC): The International Bank for Reconstruction and Development / The World Bank; 2016 Apr 5. Chapter 6. Available from: https://www.ncbi.nlm.nih.gov/books/NBK361913/ DOI:10.1596/978-1-4648-0348-2_ch6
27. Abbasi K. The World Bank on world health: under fire. *BMJ.* 2020;318(7189):1003-1006. doi:10.1136/bmj.318.7189.1003
28. Banerjee AV, Duflo E. The Economic Lives of the Poor. *J Econ Perspect.* 2007;21(1):141-167. doi:10.1257/jep.21.1.141
29. Russell S. The Economic Burden of Illness for Households in Developing Countries: A Review of Studies Focusing on Malaria, Tuberculosis, and Human Immunodeficiency Virus/Acquired Immunodeficiency Syndrome. In: Breman JG, Alilio MS, Mills A, editors. The Intolerable Burden of Malaria II: What's New, What's Needed: Supplement to Volume 71(2) of the American Journal of Tropical Medicine and Hygiene. Northbrook (IL): American Society of Tropical Medicine and Hygiene; 2004 Aug. Available from: https://www.ncbi.nlm.nih.gov/books/NBK3768/

# Living or surviving ?

Photo credit: Shraddha

CHAPTER XV

# Challenges Faced by Indian Women due to Urinary Incontinence

Mohini Sen Chowdhury
Research Scholar
Department of Sociology
University of Science and Technology
Meghalaya
mohini.basumajumdar@gmail.com

## Abstract

Urinary Incontinence is a kind of health issue that is quite common among women of all ages. Interestingly, by conducting this study it has been observed that urinary incontinence is somewhere linked with that of stroke. It occurs when a person is not able to control their need of urination. In this regard, women are more likely to get affected in comparison to men. The underlying reasons include pregnancy, childbirth, and menopause which generally seem to impact the urinary tract and its surrounding muscles. Therefore, putting much stress upon the bladder and urethra leads to create problems like urinary incontinence respectively. The proposed research paper would be discussing about the problems faced by women on urinary incontinence.

## Chapter 1: Introduction

### *Research Background*

Continence and Stroke are related to each other. Problems relating to the bladder are quite common after stroke. However, there are varied reasons for which the problems of continence might occur after a stroke. For instance, if a person is not conscious about her surroundings, the person might wet the place without even giving a thought (Brogan *et al.,* 2015).

Urinary Incontinence is a health condition that is caused due to involuntary leakage of urine from the bladder. It has been common among every age group and the number has been increasing day by day. A lot number of women who are suffering from this problem are subject to a feeling of embarrassment, isolation, and depression respectively. The inability to control the need of urinating is quite an unpleasant one. A significant portion of women are not comfortable in speaking out about this problem and hence it remains unresolved.

In addition to this, it has been observed that women in developing countries are susceptible to urinary incontinence due to poor standard of living, low education, anemia, and physical labor respectively. Due to the negligence of this problem, it leads to the medical and psychological morbidity of women. A significant section of women assumes it to be a normal process of aging and do not seek any medical help in further time. As per a report, a close link has been found between depression and stroke survivors effectively (Cai *et al.,* 2015).

### *Aims*

The research aim is to study the impact of incontinence in Stroke patients and the barriers which might take place simultaneously.

## *Objectives*

The objective of the research is a systematic technique that helps in solving a problem. It generates a structure in the proper planning of research. In this case, the objective of the research is to evaluate the impact of incontinence in Stroke patients and its barriers.

- To critically and systematically review the literature on the subject of continence in stroke patients.
- To carry out evidence-based research in barriers to promoting continence in stroke patients.
- To recognize the strategies that might be implemented to overcome these barriers in promoting continence in stroke patients.
- To promote the qualitative research and add evidence base to support the concept surrounding the barriers to promote continence in stroke patients.

## *Research Questions*

Research Questions are a kind of inquiry that is addressed in the process of research. The Research Question here deals with the issue of the impact of incontinence in Stroke patients and the barriers which might take place simultaneously.

- How the stroke does give rise to urinary incontinence?
- Whether incontinence is a permanent result after stroke?
- Are women uncomfortable discussing the health issue of urinary incontinence?
- Do women consider the problem of urinary incontinence as a sign of aging?

# Chapter 2: Literature Review

Stroke is defined to be a medical condition where the brain cells do not receive a proper blood flow, thereby resulting in death. People who are prone to stroke include high blood pressure, high cholesterol, diabetes, and one who smokes. Ischemia and hemorrhage are the two essential causes that lead a person to stroke.

## *The reason behind the continence occurring among patients with a Stroke History*

The brain is regarded to be a complex organ of the body which influences different body functions (Casaubon *et al.*, 2016). There are several urinary inconsistencies in the health unit. Stress Incontinence, Urge incontinence, Functional incontinence, Mixed incontinence and Overflow incontinence are the different kinds of urinary incontinence. Out of all, Urge Incontinence is the most common among stroke patients. It generally occurs when a person experiences an unexpected lea of urine to clear its bladder as it fills up at a faster level.

Urinary incontinence is a situation when a person cannot prevent their urine from being leaked. Factors like coughing, post-pregnancy, obesity are the conditions that lead to urinary incontinence.

After experiencing a stroke, certain medicines are provided to the patients. Such medicines might have side effects and can hinder the controlling process of the bladder. A medicine like diuretics allows reducing the blood pressure which may initially impact the control of the bladder.

Less mobile patients develop the tendency of having constipation. Constipation occurs when a person faces difficulty in clearing the bowels. This is another factor that might lead to continuous problems. The desired person would be restricted in having an adequate amount of food. This would make the person dehydrated and prone to problems like Constipation.

Urinary incontinence is commonly faced by women. Quite a several women limit themselves for not making a physical presence. Incontinence might also hinder the relationships among people, thereby leading to depression. The majority of the women do not find comfort in speaking about the problem in public and remain silent about it.

In according to a recent study which had been conducted wide across the world revealed a close association between stroke and incontinence.

## *Prevalence of Urinary Incontinence among women*

The women in India suffering from urinary problems prefer to remain silent about the problem. On reviewing the matter, it has been found that factors like ***lack of awareness about the condition, psychosocial embarrassment, fear of getting treated, the financial problem*** leads women to seek a poor quality of lifestyle. As per a study conducted by Norwegian Eppincott, it was found that tea drinkers are more likely at a higher risk of developing urinary incontinence. Tea is regarded as a caffeinated drink. Similarly, Arya *et al* (2018) revealed that a high take of caffeine is related to the symptoms of frequent wetting and recurrent urinary tract infection. Whereas Burgio (2016) found that tobacco chewing has a close connection with urinary incontinence.

As per the researchers, the problem of urinary incontinence needs further qualitative studies on the experience of women over the same problem. Certainly, there are minimal studies on the perspective of how women manage their situation in a social realm (Ganapathy, 2018).

## *The active role of Nurses in promoting continence in Stroke Patients*

Appropriate nursing and medical care are being promoted to cure the stroke. It is equally important to be conscious about the effects of stroke on continence which might guide in building a holistic plan for re-gaining continence (Kim *et al.*, 2016).

The process of Catheterisation should not be practiced in any circumstances. In a scenario where the person is not able to pass urine, a sporadic catheterization might be applied to clear the bladder. However, such a practice might bring a reduction in the capacity of a bladder. The most complicated part of catheterization lies in developing infection and it might exist even after the removal of the catheter.

Balancing the intake of fluid is another practice that might improve the urinary incontinence of a patient (Panicker *et al.*, 2015). An individual on average should be drinking about 1.5 liters of fluid in a day. However, a patient is advised to drink about two to three liters of fluid. Immobility is one of a factor that commonly takes place after a stroke. Such a factor might lead a person to develop a higher risk of the urinary tract. Hence, to prevent infection in the urinary tract, one should consume an adequate amount of water. Monitoring of urinary output is very much essential to identify the problems about emptying of the bladder.

The continence could be re-gained if a patient establishes the ability to walk on their own. It would allow them to enhance mobility. The nurse makes an effort in improving the health of a patient. They make sure that the mobility of the patient could be regained. Nurses make the patients sit on a chair, thereby helping him/her on and off a commode in the initial stages. Later, the patient is assisted by the nurse in going to a toilet.

The bedpans are avoided as a majority of the women find it difficult in passing their urine. Similarly, older men with enlarged prostates do not find comfort in passing their urine through bedpans. Mobility of patients thereby ameliorates the morale, appetite, functioning of the bladder. This is regarded to be a vital part of rehabilitation.

As per the evidence, it has been found that Constipation aggravates the problems of continence. To prevent constipation, patients are advised to maintain a diet that is rich in fiber and consume a minimum of 1.5 liters of water per day. This would help in preventing constipation. If the patients are found to be having problems swallowing food, the nurses would offer them pureed fruits and vegetables. The nursing management takes the responsibility of curing the patient in the best possible way.

Presently, a majority number of stroke patients are assessed such as Urine Testing within 24 hours of patients being admitted (Boornema et al.,2018). They are assessed very minutely to check the existence of Urine

Incontinence. To minimize incontinence, a nurse's bell, handheld urinals, and diapers are being facilitated to the patients for reducing the rate of mobility. Assessments like Frequent and Volume Chartings are carried out over 5 days from the time of being admitted. Such assessments help to examine the urinary incontinence among people.

Incontinence results from physical and cognitive disability. This might happen before and after a stroke. To reduce incontinence, toileting assessments should be maintained. This would help to keep a check on the patients. Further, this kind of assessment provides the patient with an idea about the correct posture maintained while toileting.

The Cognitive tests are evaluated in the form of Mini-Mental State Examinations and Abbreviated Test Mental Score. Such a test helps to acquire knowledge about the cognitive development of patients.

### *Strategies about the treatment of Urinary Incontinence*

In hospitals, there are several ways through which urinary incontinence could be cured. However, it depends on the efficiency of the staff members of nursing. Bowel Problems are particularly related to functional disability. Mood Swings, Dysphasia are common problems that are witnessed in stroke patients, but these are not related directly to bowel problems. Immobile patients should be aided by providing wheelchairs, and –held rails (Meyer *et al.*, 2015). These instruments would help the patient is going to toilets and therefore can manage it independently.

Difficulty in communication is another problem that is mostly found in Stroke Patients. Here, the therapist of Speech and Language plays a vital role in improving their condition. A multidisciplinary team should have appropriate knowledge in identifying the potential difficulties occurring in communication. However, it could be expected that with enhanced knowledge and healthcare staff members, the barrier could be eliminated to a greater extent.

The nursing staff members set a toileting schedule for the patients. The patients should be provided with adult diapers, which should be weighed to compute the amount of urine.

The patients should be advised to do pelvic floor exercises. Such an exercise helps in strengthening the muscles for providing support. This helps in improving the control of a bladder, thereby minimizing the leakage of urine (Perna *et al.*, 2015).

Bladder Stimulation is said to be a vibrating device that seems to be effective when a patient faces difficulty in clearing the bladder. Doctors often provide medications to patients that would help in reducing urine production, urgency, and frequency. Weight should be kept in check to improve the control of the bladder in the long run.

Physical Therapy is one of the initial stages in treating urinary incontinence. Effective training of Pelvic Floor Muscle is quite helpful in enhancing the strength of pelvic muscle thereby reducing the severity of urinary incontinence in adults and children respectively.

The hospital to a great extent uses a kind of incontinence pad. Such pads are placed beneath the patients which are supposedly high absorbent in nature. The sheet in turn soaks the unforeseen discharges of bodily fluid (Pradhan et al.,2012). These kinds of pads are extremely useful when the patients do not have the potential to wear a diaper.

Hence, it is equally important to monitor urinary retention with routine measurement. This would help to keep the problem in check and deal with the problem effectively.

Following a report, it has been found that 44% of stroke patients suffer from incontinence. A medical team investigates this matter in treating the continence problems.

## Chapter 3: Methodology

### *Introduction of this chapter*

In this chapter, the methods of research and techniques have been addressed. The method along with the approach plays a vital role in executing the activities which have been carried out in the entire research process. Research Methodologies allow the audience to assess the reliability and validity of the research. A list of methodologies has been listed below which would be developed based on a defined research project.

## Research Design

Research Design is one of the first steps which helps in formulating research. It entails several procedures which guide in collecting the variables of a study. One of the research studies which is commonly used is known as Research Onion. The concept of Research Onion is famously established by Saunders. The research work would not be carried further if found to be inaccurate.

However, in this case, ***Descriptive research design*** has been taken into consideration. Descriptive Research has been effectively applied because it correctly measures the precision level in describing a population, situation, and phenomenon.

## Research Philosophy

Presently there are four kinds of research philosophies. It is with which the aims and targets of the research work would be attained. The four types of philosophy are Pragmatism, Positivism, Realism, and Interpretive respectively. In this case, ***interpretive philosophy*** would be taken into consideration. The reasons for choosing this kind of research philosophy have been primarily because of generating assistance in collecting information about secondary data. The information has been gathered from different kinds of journals and online authentic web portals which has thereby helped in achieving the desired result.

## Research Approach

As per the needs of a defined project, an appropriate type of research project would be implemented. It is for this reason ***deductive research approach*** has been applied in this context. It is based on existing facts and knowledge the data would be further analyzed. In this case, the research is based on the secondary data type.

## Search Strategy

### a. Inclusion Criteria

Inclusion Criteria are defined to be a kind of character that a subject should possess if they are included in the process of study.

- Articles & Journals containing subjects like women aged more than 35 years of age who have been diagnosed with suffering from urinary incontinence.
- Articles and journals were published between the year 2012-2020.
- Articles which is published exclusively in the English language

### b. Exclusion Criteria

Exclusion Criteria are defined to be a kind of character which disqualifies the potential subject from being included in the study.

- Articles & Journals containing subjects like Diabetic Neuropathy, Catheterisation, Incapable of providing informed consent.
- Articles published before 2011.
- Articles not published in the English language.

Research Strategy is a vital aspect in predicting the precision level of a research project. Depending on the aims and objectives of the research project, a case study has been taken into account. Reliability and Validity are the two essential aspects that help in maintaining the accuracy level of a project.

### *Data Collection Method*

Two types of data collection are existent in the process of conducting research. One is the primary data, followed by secondary data effectively. Each of the types entails two kinds of data which are known as quantitative and qualitative respectively. The data has been acquired from various sources. The sources from which the information has been gathered from various databases like CINHL, MEDLINE, Intenurse.com, Science direct, Health Sources, and Cochrane Library respectively. Other sources include the ***Indian Journal of Community Medicine, Journal of Medical Sciences and Research, Journal of Surgical Science, and many others.*** It is through which the disciplinary approach would be attained in this project.

Journals catering to Health care, Department of Health, Institute for Excellence, and many others from which the data have been collected.

## Chapter 4: Data Analysis and Discussion

### *Introduction of the chapter*

This is the fourth chapter of a research project. It is so because an effective analysis and discussion of the accumulated data would be made. It is through which a potential outcome would be deduced. To attain the correct data and particulars, secondary data has been selected. The secondary data has been gathered from different articles and journals.

### *Secondary Findings Analysis*

### *Urinary Incontinence in Older People*

According to the observations of this article (2020), incontinence marks a severe psychological impact on individuals. In a group of a community, the older people had been worst affected with urinary incontinence. Hence, the psychological impacts should be assessed as fast as possible (de Mattos Lourenco *et al.*, 2018). Women are heavily affected by night time incontinence, coital incontinence, co-morbid fecal incontinence. It has been found that people having urgency and urge incontinence are subject to problems like anxiety and depression.

Paying a regular visit to the doctors has not lessened the issue of urinary incontinence among older people. They are quite hesitant in disclosing their problem. A majority of people think that urinary incontinence is an underlying problem of aging. However, other reason for not disclosing the problem lies in embarrassment, fear of consuming medicines, expensive affair, having a belief that there is no effective treatment, the fright of surgery.

Women having continuous symptoms of incontinence, sexual malfunction impact the psychological, economic, and social characteristics of daily lives. All these can put a negative image on the self-image, identity, and control of a woman (Dumoulin *et al.*, 2018).

Similarly, a person must have the capability of understanding and negotiating cultural skills. It is because urinary incontinence might lead to social isolation and health care issues. People belonging to varied cultural backgrounds are not open enough in sharing the issues of incontinence with a health professional of the opposite sex.

It is by using a focus group, it has been found that overactive bladder symptoms might develop a concern and a feeling of frustration among the family members. Husbands and other close members were likely to have sleepless nights as their partners tended to urinate excessively at night.

People suffering from incontinence have been leading a poor quality of life. It has been witnessed that feelings like worthlessness, helplessness, avoiding social interaction and many others have influenced the overall health of a person. A survey was conducted in which 142,000 people had participated (Ramakrishnan et al.,2019). However, it has been found that people suffering from urinary incontinence were twice as likely to be depressed as compared to people not having urinary incontinence.

## *The Role of Physiotherapy in the Rehabilitation of Stroke Patients with Lower Urinary Tract Symptoms*

The above-stated online article has discussed the symptoms of lower urinary tract symptoms which are highly existent in both men and ***women*** after stroke. Physiotherapy is a kind of treatment that has been involved in treating the symptoms of lower urinary tract symptoms. It is with the aid of physiotherapy, an appropriate measure has been taken to prevent, diagnose and treat the patients (Radadia *et al.,* 2018).

The Lower Urinary Tract Symptom could be assessed by scanning the bladder through ultrasound radiations. This is a kind of test that helps in detecting urine retention. Certain tests of urine are assessed for leucocytes, nitrites, glucose, and protein which is finished within a time frame of 24 hours from the time of admission.

A Nurse targeted education program is much beneficial in ameliorating the continence among patients. A standardized rehabilitation centre would help to improve the health condition of patients.

In the caring units, a web-based toileting behavior instrument had been established in understanding the behavior of toileting among women. Such an instrument is posed to be an essential aspect in screening the patients who had experienced a stroke previously.

Following the findings of this article, it has been observed that the stroke patients who had been going through acute rehabilitation were recovering at a rapid level. They gradually developed an ability to control their bowel. Further, it was followed by the proper functioning of their bladder.

## *Strategies for self-management support by patients with stroke*

In the above article, appropriate strategies have been analyzed for self-management support by patients with stroke. Stroke patients have special kinds of needs which often require different care. Such an onset disease requires the help of professional care without whom essential care would not be taken. The task of self-management has a list of actions. The first one is to "**ask**". *(*Deng *et al.,* 2015*)*.

Ask is a set of actions that helps in acquiring an idea about the beliefs, values, knowledge, and behaviours of people in areas of sanitation. People must possess an understanding of their health condition within a community. Self-Monitoring is a kind of personality trait which is used in keeping a track and record of one's own action and performance.

The second set of actions is "**Advise**". With the help of such an action, certain information about risks and benefits of changes are being educated to the people by validating the health education and skills training. In the section on Advice, health education is particularly highlighted. Such education is especially linked with better clinical outcomes at a lower price. Several studies have effectively implemented an intervention program which thereby helps in ameliorating the knowledge about the ill condition of patients. Self-Management helps a lot in managing such a situation (Gurol-Urganci *et al.,* 2018).

The third A which has been addressed in Self Management is about "**Assess**". Such activity should be made use of between professionals, patients, and family members. Assess aids in increasing the determination of the patient's self-efficacy. It is through which the patient might develop a chance to reach their proposed goal (Blaganje *et al.,* 2018).

The fourth A which has been discussed is the "**Assist**". In this section, the importance of the Nursing Process in rehabilitation has been stressed. It is another way through which the self-management of individuals could be enhanced. The Assist allowed the patient to identify their own set of abilities. Availability of multi-professional caring unit, intensive physical rehabilitation plans having professional guidance is the essential steps through which they could be provided with assistance. Technologies to a greater extent were employed in assisting the individuals at rehabilitation centers. Resources like telemedicine, telerehabilitation, virtual reality, and computer programs were engaged in helping the patients stay at the caring unit.

The support strategy of Self-Management is not meant to be short-term, especially the patients who had been suffering from strokes. Hence, health care professionals must monitor the patients regularly and systematically for a longer period. To track their health status, the patients should be regularly visiting the health services, doctors paying a visit at their homes, communicating via telephone calls, e-mails, peer groups, and resources of the community.

Regular Monitoring is an effective tool that could not only be conducted by the health professionals but also by the patients and their family members. However, monitoring could be beneficial if performed within the peer group members (Boornema et al.,2018).

## *Interventions for treating urinary incontinence after stroke in Adult Women*

In the above article (2019), the effects of interventions about urinary incontinence post-stroke among adults have been determined.

The issue of urinary incontinence might influence 40% to 60% of people who are being admitted to the hospital after experiencing a stroke. Out of which 25% have been facing the problem from the hospital. After a stroke, certain physical changes relating to communication and vision changes might lead to incontinence. An alteration in one's thinking, memory, and judgment might even lead to incontinence. Even changes in one's diet, medications might lead to incontinence (Abrams *et al.*, 2018).

Physical Therapy with the help of transcutaneous electrical nerve stimulation might minimize the occurrence of incontinence within 24 hours. Such a kind of intervention has effectively helped in improving the functional ability of patients. On experimentation, about 44% of women were observed to have been suffering from urinary dysfunction. ***Out of which 26% of them had been suffering from Urinary Incontinence, 19% had frequency problems and the remaining 54% were subject to urinary tract infection*** (Shah et al.,2015***)***

It has been estimated that about half of the patients admitted to a hospital due to stroke have no control over their bladder and one-third of the ***women patients*** have a problem with bowels. Unable to control toilets is one of the sensitive issues which they think discussing in public is a shameful act. However, here comes the role of physiotherapists. It is the role of the physiotherapist who would be providing training and a few set of exercises to improve their mobility. They are the ones who would best serve the patients in moving out of bed or chair. The right technique to strengthen one's pelvic floor muscle is made by physiotherapists. The proper functioning of the bladder and bowel is enhanced by them. To see the best result, one needs to practice for several months. After a few months of rigorous training, the patient would be able to witness the best result.

Occupational therapists are kind professionals who help in regaining a sense of independence by performing certain activities. To enhance the mobility of a patient, the occupational therapists might bring certain tools and equipment at home to enhance the rate of their mobility. Such mobility helps the patient in using the toilet. A Set of the instrument which helps in easy mobility includes walking aids and wheelchairs respectively.

## *Improving nurse engagement incontinence care*

Urinary and Fecal Incontinence is the aspects that are creating problems in the lives of people. In the present scenario, Urinary Incontinence has affected about 400 million people across the globe. The health condition of incontinence is a stigmatized condition. However, a large number of women feel that incontinence is an unavoidable feature of childbirth and aging. People, ***mainly women*** experiencing incontinence face hindrances to care.

In the view of *Hunter,* the nurses play a pivotal role in assisting the patients who are affected by Urinary Incontinence. They have the required amount of skill to recognize the people who are suffering from incontinence.

To cure the problem, they make sure that specific interventions are initiated. Such an educational program helps the patients to instil a sense of awareness among them. The nurses who do not have appropriate knowledge on incontinence are not engaged with other nurses in promoting continence care.

It has been evident that the educational programs have been effective in making a positive impact on the staff and patients as well.

## Chapter 5: Conclusion and Recommendation

From this entire chapter, it has been analyzed that the occurrence of depression and incontinence are associated with one another. The patients, ***especially women*** who are affected with urinary incontinence are psychologically influenced. While conducting the research, it has been found that several people had been reluctant in disclosing their problem of urinary incontinence with the health professional. There has been a myth that urinary incontinence is an outcome of aging. As per evidence, it has been evaluated that less than 50% of people report their urinary leakage to their health professional.

Next comes the role of physiotherapy, which has helped in making people recover from the problem of urinary incontinence. An educational program relating to nurses is much beneficial in ameliorating the continence among patients. A standardized rehabilitation center has helped improve the health condition of patients. The patients gradually developed an ability to control their bowel. Further, it was followed by the proper functioning of their bladder. Along with the care taken by the rehabilitation centers, they even maintained a balanced diet. Acute rehabilitation has helped stroke patients to recover at a rapid level.

Next, strategies for self-management support by patients with stroke have been discussed effectively. Following a report, it has been found that the matter of urinary incontinence might influence 40% to 60% of people who are being admitted to hospital after experiencing a stroke. Out of which 25% have been facing the problem from the hospital itself.

Coming to the next point, valid reason has been determined in the occurrence of incontinence among stroke patients. However, about 59% of the strokes are found to be occurring in the older generation. Following the Nation's Report, about 65% of stroke survivors are disabled. The kind of incontinence which is seemed to be the most common is urge incontinence. It generally occurs when a person experiences an unexpected leak of urine to empty its bladder as it fills up at a faster level.

The health care unit has invented a new drug that is catered to patients suffering from urinary incontinence. The name of the drug is Myrbetriq. This medicine works by energizing the receptors present in the bladder's detrusor muscle.

It is highly recommended that an appropriate medication might help to calm the muscles and nerves. This in turn would reduce the spasms of the bladder. In case, if medications are found to be not functioning, Botox should be injected. Consuming plenty of fluids is recommended. Bringing lifestyle change might help to combat urinary incontinence. One should be restricted to consuming alcohol, carbonated drinks, coffee, tea, and spicy foods. Maintaining a food diary would help in understanding which kind of foods might play a role in incontinence.

## References

1. Boornema, A. R., Kalyani, P., & Felix A., W. J. (2018). Prevalence of urinary incontinence and its severity among women in urban Chidambaram- a cross sectional study. *International Journal of Community Medicine and Public Health*, 4543-4547.
2. Casaubon, L.K., Boulanger, J.M., Glasser, E., Blacquiere, D., Boucher, S., Brown, K., Goddard, T., Gordon, J., Horton, M., Lalonde, J. and LaRivière, C., 2016. Canadian stroke best practice recommendations: acute inpatient

stroke care guidelines, update 2015. *International Journal of Stroke, 11*(2), pp.239-252.

3. de Mattos Lourenco, T.R., Matsuoka, P.K., Baracat, E.C. and Haddad, J.M., 2018. Urinary incontinence in female athletes: a systematic review. *International urogynecology journal*, *29*(12), pp.1757-1763.
4. Deng, K., Lin, D.L., Hanzlicek, B., Balog, B., Penn, M.S., Kiedrowski, M.J., Hu, Z., Ye, Z., Zhu, H. and Damaser, M.S., 2015. Mesenchymal stem cells and their secretome partially restore nerve and urethral function in a dual muscle and nerve injury stress urinary incontinence model. *American Journal of Physiology-Renal Physiology, 308*(2), pp.F92-F100.
5. Ding, D., 2015. Endovascular mechanical thrombectomy for acute ischemic stroke: a new standard of care. *Journal of stroke, 17*(2), p.123.
6. Dumoulin, C., Cacciari, L.P. and Hay-Smith, E.J.C., 2018. Pelvic floor muscle training versus no treatment, or inactive control treatments, for urinary incontinence in women. *Cochrane database of systematic reviews*, (10).
7. Ganapathy, T. (2018). Impact of urinary incontinence on quality of life among rural women. *Journal of Medical Sciences and Research*, 71-77.
8. Gurol-Urganci, I., Geary, R.S., Mamza, J.B., Duckett, J., El-Hamamsy, D., Dolan, L., Tincello, D.G. and van der Meulen, J., 2018. Long-term rate of mesh sling removal following midurethral mesh sling insertion among women with stress urinary incontinence. *Jama, 320*(16), pp.1659-1669.
9. Kim, J.S., 2016. Post-stroke mood and emotional disturbances: pharmacological therapy based on mechanisms. *Journal of stroke, 18*(3), p.244.
10. Meyer, M.J., Pereira, S., McClure, A., Teasell, R., Thind, A., Koval, J., Richardson, M. and Speechley, M., 2015. A systematic review of studies reporting multivariable models to predict functional outcomes after post-stroke inpatient rehabilitation. *Disability and rehabilitation, 37*(15), pp.1316-1323.
11. Panicker, J.N., Fowler, C.J. and Kessler, T.M., 2015. Lower urinary tract dysfunction in the neurological patient: clinical assessment and management. *The Lancet Neurology, 14*(7), pp.720-732.
12. Perna, R. and Temple, J., 2015. Rehabilitation outcomes: ischemic versus hemorrhagic
13. Pradhan, R., Mathur, K. R., Mathur, P., Khan, F., Gupta, A., & Chowhan, M. (2012). Study of Common Urinary Problems of Females at a Government Hospital in Central India. *Journal of Surgical Science*, 339-343.
14. Ramakrishnan, D., Krishnapillai, V., Rekha, A., Duttagupta, S., Murali, V., & Ajith, A. (2019). Prevalence and Factors of Urinary Incontinence among Postmenopausal Women Attending the Obstetrics and Gynecology Outpatient Service in a Tertiary Health Care Center in Kochi, Kerala. *Indian Journal of Community Medicine*, 30-33.
15. Shah, R. Z., Sheth, S. M., Talapalli, R., & Vyas, J. N. (2015). Perception of Females about Urinary Incontinence. *International Journal of Therapies and Rehabilitation Research*, 256-259.

CHAPTER XVI

# Impact of Education and Employment on the Household Decision Making of Women

Kajal
Assistant Professor
Department of Economics
Sri Guru Granth Sahib World University,
Fatehgarh sahib
kajalgupta2512@gmail.com

## *Abstract*

Women, being an important part of the society have to keep up with all the responsibilities of children and other members of the family. A woman plays significant role in all the sections of the society whether it is level of household, social, economic or political. Among all these sectors, household decision making is an important element to understand the concept of women empowerment. The present study "Impact of Education and Employment on the household Decision Making of Women" has focused on the various decisions taken at household level such as decisions related to own health care, making major household purchases, visit to her family or relatives and making purchases for daily household needs. The study enlightens the area of women household decision making and find out the extent and change happened during the time span. It has been used the secondary data which has been extracted from the National Family Health Survey and is a comparative study as it used the data of two time periods (i.e., 2005-2006 and 2015-16). Result shows that household decision making is positively associated with education and employment. Government should make some schemes for the empowerment of females at household as well as outside world and also to widen the area of the existing schemes for women empowerment.

Introduction

In democratic countries people have equal rights and opportunities and India is one of those countries. Even after being a democratic country, the Indian society is still under the influence of patriarchal approach, inequality can be seen regarding the rights and the autonomy of women in India. They are having low status in the family as well as in the society (Bharti et.al, 2007). If we

take a look on the history of women, then we can see that gender inequality exists from that very period. This was the time when, Draupadi was put on the dice as an object by her husbands. Also, women dance in private and public places to please men. Women had to depend on their husbands to fulfill all their needs and wants and had to take their permission before making any decision. They were not allowed to speak in higher tone in front of their elders (Hazarika, 2011). But women, who are an important part of the society, should be given all the rights and autonomy within the households as well as in the society. Being a mother, she is the only one in the family who is in the closest relation with her children. The decisions she makes will always be children-centric viz, the decisions related to their clothes and food (Dutta, 2002).

Understanding the dire need to empower the women, several initiatives have been taken at national and international level in the various time periods. Ministry of Human Resource Development (MHRD) and National Commission for Women take many initiatives to give the legal entitlement and rights for women. In India, 'National Policy for the empowerment of Women' has been made in the year 2001, which is popularly known as the 'Year of Women empowerment'. To uplift the women in every corner of country, Self-help groups (SHGs) are made with an objective to empower females by providing them financial assistance and generate income through self-employment so that they can get independence economically (Kapila et.al, 2016). Millennium Development Goals (MDGs) came in September 2000 by the United Nations General Assembly. The IIIrd goal under the MDGs made to promote the gender equality and women empowerment. This includes target on education, employment and political representation of women. Both the IInd and IIIrd goals of MDGs are made to remove the disparities among men and women in primary education. This is essential for the girls to attain free and compulsory primary education as per the International human rights law (UNDG, 2010). After this, Sustainable Development Goals (SDGs) are made to replace the MDGs at the United Nations Conference on Sustainable Development in Rio de Janeiro in 2012. The SDG IV aims to ensure the quality education and to promote the lifelong learning opportunities for all.

According to the Census of India, the term 'household' is defined as a group of those people who live together, eat together under a same shelter. People living in the household may be related or unrelated with each other. The unrelated people are not counted under the household who do not take their meals from the same kitchen. Common kitchen is the defining term for it to be

household or not. But, if a husband and wife living together under a same roof but are not making their food, also includes as a normal household.

There are two well distinguished approaches i.e. social and economic approach, in the literature which are explaining the household behaviour. Under these two approaches, further theories are categorised to well explain the present study. Resource theory and Social theory are under the sociological approach whereas exploitation, altruism and bargaining theories comes under economic approach.

Resource theory is first formulated by Wolfe and then it was elaborated by Blood and Wolfe. Resources are considered as the basis of autonomy in household. As per the definition, resources are that in which one member of the family can offer or give anything to the others for the sake of help or to fulfill their needs. There are some factors which are important in the resource theory viz, money, education and occupational status. These resources are influenced by these factors and explain the women position at household level (Hesse-Biber and Williamson, 1984). As compared to the previous times, the education level of women has increased a lot and alongwith this they are good relative earners in the family, equal decision making starts at household level. Social theory which is based upon the conjugal power of the family. Expertise is the basis for the autonomy in the household decision making (Centers, Raven and Rodrigues, 1971). Exploitation theory is based on dominance. One member of the family, whether this is head of the family or a husband takes all the decision and gives direction to other family members. (McCrate, 1987 and Green, 1994). According to the Stanford Encyclopedia of Philosophy, altruism is that behaviour in a person where he does work or something for the benefit of others. Not only had those persons included who do for the benefit for others, but also those who prevent their close-knit or near ones from any kind of harm. This is also known as unitary model. In this theory, the head of the family is interested in the welfare of the other family members. There is no coercion for any single member of the family (Becker, 1976; Sen, 1987 and Pollak, 2003). According to the Cambridge dictionary, Bargaining is defined as the discussions or negotiations happens among people to reach an agreement on various things such as wages, prices and working conditions. By criticizing the altruism theory, bargaining theory doesn't deal with the homogeneous units of the household. (Blumberg and Colemn, 1989; Seiz,

1995). Economic position of women and their education affects their decision-making power at household level (Agarwal, 1997).

## Significance of the study

The importance of the present study is to find out the household decision making in India during 2005-06 to 2015-16. The study enlightens the area of women household decision making and find out the extent and change happened during the time span. This research finds out the reasons behind the change happened in the decision making at household level. This provides the suggestions to improve the decision making at household level. The study has done some addition in the previous researches and is useful in providing awareness to society regarding the role of women.

## *Objectives*

• To find out the changing structure of decision making at household level during the period from 2005-06 to 2015-16.
• To check the impact of education and employment on the household decision making power of women in India.
• To identify the reasons behind the changes happened from 2005-06 to 2015-16.

## *Review of Literature*

The liberty of women can be expected in the modern and gender- equitable society, where educational and work opportunities are higher and gender equality is present. On the other hand, in the traditional and masculine society, individual decisions and actions of a woman were not accepted. The diversity in the roles of different genders, social ethics and change in the relation between the genders affects the perception of the society.
Bharti (2007) explained that only one-third of women can make their own health decisions and most women are not allowed to visit their relatives without permission. In the same way, Dutta (2002) said that although the paid jobs seem to have slightly increased the influence of women in family decision-making, but the last word was still the husband's ownership regarding the big

decisions of the house. On the other side, Davis (1970) has pointed out that the husband was more dominant when purchasing a vehicle than the wife, who was more dominant when purchasing furniture.
Roy and Niranjan (2005) pinpointed that in the comparison of Uttar Pradesh, women of Tamil Nadu have more freedom to make decisions about health care, freedom of promotion and access to money. In Uttar Pradesh, on the other side, women showed greater self-esteem as they were more critical about that. Kaur et.al (2018) said that women in Hoshiarpur have more freedom in decision-making which may be due to higher literacy rate. Women have more say in social and economic activities in the absence of their husbands. Compared to women living in urban areas, rural women are deprived in almost all areas. It has been seen that there is a dire need for women empowerment in Punjab, but this cannot be achieved unless the women of Punjab understand the reasons for their development and understand that the essence of their true empowerment is in their unity.
Khan et.al (2013) and Dalal (2011) asserted that violence is declining with the increase in the level of education. Education was an effective element in protecting women's rights against partner violence as disclosure rates ranged from 2 to 11 per cent for low education and 5 to 29 per cent for secondary education. Higher educated workers face more participatory violence than non- working workers.
Methodology
In the present times, a big change, i.e. a change in the decision-making pattern related to various activities in the different areas, happens in the lives of every individual due to change in the education pattern, employment level, wealth and, family structures, etc. But, specifically the decision-making pattern of women at household level has changed a lot. The present study is to know that at what level these changes happen and also to identify the reasons behind these changes.
In the present study, we have used the secondary data which has been extracted from the two rounds of National Family Health Survey conducted by International Institute for Population Sciences (IIPS). This is a comparative study of India where the third (2005-06) and fourth (2015-
16) round of NFHS, has been chosen for the study. The NFHS-3 collected the data from a total of 515,507 individuals of 109,041 households, in which the 93,089 women of age group 15-49 has been chosen. This data covers the 99 per cent of the population living in all the 29 states of India. The NFHS-4 gathered the data from 628,900 households, in which the 616,346 households were

occupied. Out of the occupied households, 601,509 households were interviewed. A total of 723,875 women of age group 15-49 were identified, out of which, 88,021 were successfully interviewed.

| Background Characteristics (Education) | Own Health Care | | Making major household purchases | | Visit to her family or Relatives | | Making purchases for daily household needs | | Percentage who participates in all four decisions | | Percentage who participates in none of the four decisions | | Number of Women | |
|---|---|---|---|---|---|---|---|---|---|---|---|---|---|---|
| | 2005-06 | 2015-16 | 2005-06 | 2015-16 | 2005-06 | 2015-16 | 2005-06 | 2015-16 | 2005-06 | 2015-16 | 2005-06 | 2015-16 | 2005-06 | 2015-16 |
| No education | 59.4 | 72.1 | 51.5 | 71.4 | 57.5 | 70.9 | 59.5 | NA | 34.9 | 60.2 | 22.7 | 18.4 | 43931 (47.19%) | 27895 (31.69%) |
| <5 years complete | 61.2 | 75 | 51.4 | 74.8 | 60.4 | 76.1 | 60.1 | NA | 35.2 | 63.8 | 20.3 | 14.9 | 7776 (8.35%) | 5761 (6.54%) |
| 5-7 years complete | 61.0 | 72.5 | 50.6 | 72.2 | 59.8 | 73.8 | 58.4 | NA | 35.7 | 61.3 | 21.7 | 17.3 | 14018 (15.06%) | 14181 (16.11%) |
| 8-9 years complete | 63.6 | 75.3 | 52.2 | 72.7 | 60.7 | 75.4 | 58.3 | NA | 36.2 | 63.2 | 19.7 | 15.5 | 10735 (11.53%) | 13183 (14.98%) |
| 10-11 years complete | 67.2 | 74.9 | 56.3 | 73.6 | 65.9 | 75.8 | 61.6 | NA | 40.5 | 63.5 | 16.8 | 15.9 | 7704 (8.28%) | 10656 (12.11%) |
| 12 or more years complete | 73.1 | 79.4 | 62.6 | 77.6 | 71.6 | 79.6 | 66.3 | NA | 46.1 | 68.5 | 12.1 | 11.9 | 8921 (9.59%) | 16346 (18.57%) |
| **Total** | | | | | | | | | | | | | **92936 (100%)** | **88022 (100%)** |

TABLE NO. 1 EDUCATION WISE CLASSIFICATION OF HOUSEHOLD DECISION MAKING

(Source: National Family Health Survey, 2005-06 and 2015-16)

| Education | % Of difference |
|---|---|
| No education | 9.53 |
| < 5 years complete | 34.55 |
| 5-7 years complete | 73.72 |
| 8-9 years complete | 114.4 |
| 10-11 years complete | 116.89 |
| 12 or more years complete | 172.23 |

TABLE NO. 1.1 REPRESENTING THE CHANGE OF FEMALE PARTICIPATION IN DECISION MAKING WITH EDUCATION CHARACTERISTIC FROM 2005-06 TO 2015-16

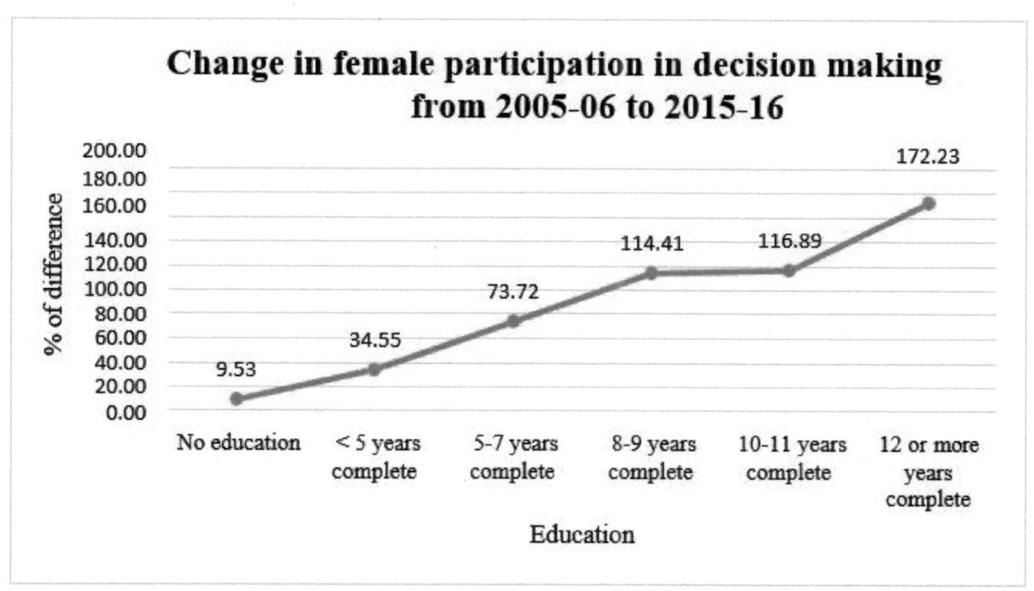


Figure no. 1.1 Education specific change of female participation in decision-making from 2005-06 to 2015-16

Education is the most important element for the development of all the areas, particularly, for the development of women in the household and society. It is a key which opens the door for knowledge, skills, positive attitudes and, values, etc. It gives a boost to the women in the attainment of knowledge in specific area of study and also to experience the lessons of life. The table no. 1 represents that in 2005-06, those women who have no education or illiterate are taking less (i.e.
34.9 per cent) participation in the decision making whereas those who completed the 12 or more years of education, takes 46.1 per cent of the decisions. In 2015-16, this percentage rises from 60.2 per cent to 68.5 per cent. In 2005-06, there are 22.7 per cent of the illiterate women who are not participating in any of the decisions as compared to 12.1 per cent of those who completed 12 or more years of education and in 2015-16, this percentage changed from 18.4 per cent to 11.9 per cent. Role of women in particular decision making is not changing a lot with their education level, but those women who have higher education have shown more participating behaviour in the decision making. The table and figure no 1.1 showed that the highest change (i.e. 172.23 per cent) from 2005- 06 to 2015-16 happens among those females who completed 12 or more years of education. The basic reason behind this is that with the enhancement of education, there is more decision making among females at household level (Soharwadi, 2014; Baliyan, 2014; Pal and Haldar, 2016; Javed and Mughal, 2019).

Employment is an important factor through which people sustain their livelihood. The table no. 2 represents the decision making of women with their employment status which divided into four categories viz, those who are employed, are employed for cash, are not employed for cash and, are unemployed or not employed. In 2005-06, 38.8 per cent of the employed women are taking decisions and 35.1 per cent of the unemployed women. Those women who are employed for cash are largely participate (i.e. 44.3 per cent) in the decision making whereas those who are not employed for cash are less (i.e. 29 per cent) participating. Same situation is in the 2015-16, where the participation level increased upto an extent. The highest role in decision making is played by those women who are employed for cash i.e. 70.4 per cent. This is because women's autonomy in decision making increases with their employment level which leads them towards the economic empowerment (Acharya, 2010; Rosa, 2010).

| Background Characteristics (Employment past 12 months) | Own Health Care | | Making major household purchases | | Visit to her family or Relatives | | Making purchases for daily household needs | | Percentage who participates in all four decisions | | Percentage who participates in none of the four decisions | | Number of Women | |
|---|---|---|---|---|---|---|---|---|---|---|---|---|---|---|
| | 2005-06 | 2015-16 | 2005-06 | 2015-16 | 2005-06 | 2015-16 | 2005-06 | 2015-16 | 2005-06 | 2015-16 | 2005-06 | 2015-16 | 2005-06 | 2015-16 |
| Employed | 63 | 79.6 | 55.3 | 78.3 | 62.9 | 79.2 | 63.7 | NA | 38.8 | 67.9 | 19 | 11.5 | 39,835 | 21132 (19.36%) |
| Employed, for cash | 67.7 | 81.1 | 61 | 80.7 | 68 | 81.4 | 69.5 | NA | 44.3 | 70.4 | 15 | 10.2 | 25,601 | 17236 (15.80%) |
| Employed, not for cash | 54.6 | 72.7 | 45.1 | 68 | 53.7 | 69.8 | 53.2 | NA | 29 | 56.8 | 26.1 | 17.6 | 14,234 | 3896 (3.57%) |
| Not employed | 61.7 | 72.9 | 51.1 | 71.8 | 58.7 | 73.1 | 57.4 | NA | 35.1 | 61.5 | 21.6 | 17.5 | 53,225 | 66890 (61.28%) |
| **Total** | | | | | | | | | | | | | **1,32,895 (100%)** | **109154 (100%)** |

Table.no. 2 Employment wise classification of household decision making

| Employment (past 12 months) | % Of difference |
|---|---|
| Employed | -7.16 |
| Employed, for cash | 6.99 |
| Employed, not for cash | -46.39 |
| Not employed | 120.20 |

TABLE NO. 2.2 REPRESENTING THE CHANGE OF FEMALE PARTICIPATION IN DECISION MAKING WITH EDUCATION CHARACTERISTIC FROM 2005-06 TO 2015-16

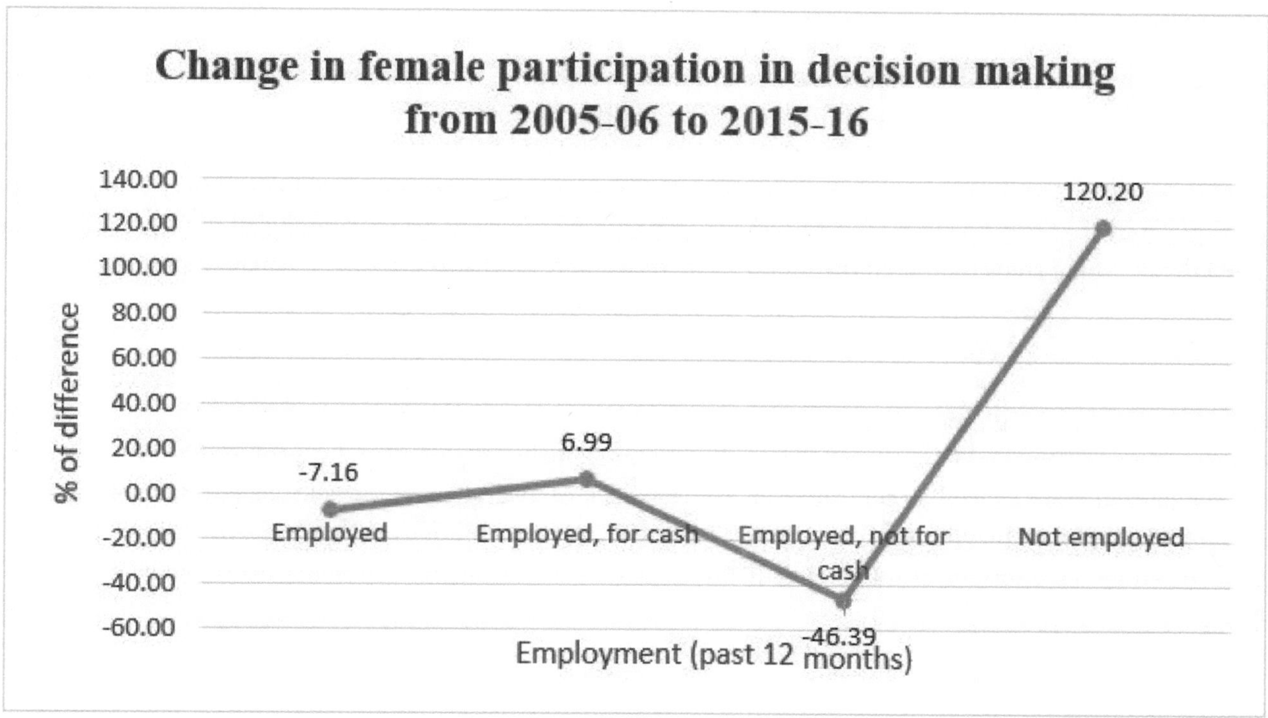


Figure no. 2.2 Employment specific change of female participation in decision-making from 2005-06 to 2015-16

The table and figure no. 2.2 showed that the change in the participation of decision making from 2005-06 to 2015-16 is highest among those females who are not employed. This is due to the reason that although they don't have employment or they are not employed but their autonomy

depends upon the household income as well as upon social factors. There is positive association between household income and females' decision making (Banerjee and Roy, 2015). 8Another factor is the literacy among females. There is a huge increment in the education facilities for women from 2005-06 to 2015-16. As there are more initiatives and policies made to empower them. SDG IV aims to ensure the quality education and to promote lifelong learning opportunities for all and SDG V to empower and give equal status to females. The gross enrolment ratio for tertiary education has been increased to 24.5 per cent in 2015-16 (GOP, 2020). There is also an important point to be consider here that paid employment seems to have slightly increased women's influence in decision-making in the household (Dutta, 2002).

## *Results*

To attain the privileges that should be already available for the empowerment of women such as education, health facilities, job opportunities, decision making and better standard of living, women have to encounter a lot of barriers in the society. On the basis of the involvement of a woman in the decision making process of her household, one can apprehend her status and sovereignty. In this modern and gender-equitable society, where educational and work opportunities are higher, the liberty of women is expected. It has been resulted out that with the enhancement of education, the autonomy of women in household decision making is increasing. Women, who have completed 12 or more years of education, are more participating in the household decision making. Another is that women's autonomy in decision making increases with their employment level. Another thing to be noted is that, paid employment seems to have slightly increased women's influence in household decision-making.

## Conclusion

Women empowerment is a multidimensional phenomenon which gives a realization to women about their power and autonomy in the development process. It enhances the abilities of women in various fields such as social, economic and political activities, etc. There is a huge change in the household decision making of India from 2005-06 to 2015-16. Out of total, 36.7 per cent of the women, who participates in the household decision-making in 2005-06 whereas this increased to 63 per cent in 2015-16. To improve the decision making among all the age groups, there is dire need to take some steps to uphold the literacy rate of women. So that there can be equality among

all age groups. The study suggested that to improve the household decision making power among the rural females, government should focus more on education and employment sectors as these two are highly correlated with household decision making especially in the rural areas of India. Employment is a major factor related to household decision making of females. Government should promote female employment by promoting quota system and several schemes at state as well as central level. There is lack of awareness about various government schemes on education and employment opportunities, family planning, etc. which affected the decision making at household level. There should be a dire need for the positive change and advancement of thought in the society. Government should make some schemes for the empowerment of females at household as well as outside world and also to widen the area of the existing schemes for women empowerment.

## Reference:

1. Acharya, D. R., Bell, J. S., Simkhada, P. V., Teijlingen, E. R., & Regmi, P. R. (2010). Women's autonomy in household decision-making: A demographic study in Nepal. Reproductive health, 7(1), 15-26.
2. Agarwal, B. (1997). Bargaining and gender relations: Within and beyond the household. Feminist economics, 3(1), 1-51.
3. Baliyan, K., & Kumar, S. (2014). Participation of farm household women in agricultural activities and its determinants: A study in western Uttar Pradesh. The Indian Journal of Labour Economics, 57(3), 327-341.
4. Banerjee, S., & Roy, A. (2015). Determinants of female autonomy across Indian states. Journal of Economics, Business and Management, 3(11), 1037-1040.
5. Becker, G. S. (1976). Altruism, egoism, and genetic fitness: Economics and sociobiology. Journal of economic Literature, 14(3), 817-826.
6. Bharati, S., Pal, M., Som, S., & Bharati, P. (2007). Empowerment of women through household decision making power in India: A state wise analysis. In Seminar on Gender Issues and Empowerment of Women, 109-128.
7. Blumberg, R. L., & Coleman, M. T. (1989). A theoretical look at the gender balance of power in the American couple. Journal of family issues, 10(2), 225-250.
8. Centers, R., Raven, B. H., & Rodrigues, A. (1971). Conjugal power structure: A re- examination. American Sociological Review, 36(2), 264-278.
9. Dalal, K. (2011). Does economic empowerment protect women from intimate partner violence?. Journal of Injury and Violence Research, 3(1), 35-44.
10. Davis, H. L. (1970). Dimensions of marital roles in consumer decision making. Journal of Marketing Research, 7(2), 168-177.
11. Dutta, M. (2002). Women's power and authority within middle-class households in Kolkata. Contemporary South Asia, 11(1), 7-18.
12. Government of Punjab. (2020). Economic Survey of Punjab, 2019-20. Economic Advisor, Punjab Retrieved from
13. https://www.esopb.gov.in/static/PDF/EconomicSurvey-2019-20.pdf.

14. Green, K. (1994). Unbearable weight; Feminism, western culture, and the body by Susan Bordo.
15. Wayne State University Press. 17(1), 176-178.
16. Hazarika, D. (2011). Women empowerment in India: A brief discussion. International Journal of Educational Planning and Administration, 1(3), 199-202.
17. Hesse-Biber, S., & Williamson, J. (1984). Resource theory and power in families: Life cycle considerations. The Family Process, 23(2), 261-278.
18. Javed, R., & Mughal, M. (2019). Have a son, gain a voice: Son preference and female participation in household decision making. The Journal of Development Studies, 55(12), 2526-2548.
19. Kapila, M., Singla, A., & Gupta, M. L. (2016). Impact of microcredit on women empowerment in India: An empirical study of Punjab state. In Proceedings of the World Congress on Engineering, 2.
20. Kaur, R., Singh, B., Sandhu, L. K., & Kaur, G. (2018). Dimensions of women autonomy in household decision making in rural Punjab. International Journal of Sustainable Development, 11(01), 11-40.
21. Khan, H. M. A., Sindher, R. H. K., & Hussain, I. (2013). Studying the role of education in eliminating violence against women. Pakistan Journal of Commerce and Social Science, 7(2), 405-416
22. McCrate, E. (1987). Trade, merger and employment: Economic theory on marriage. Review of Radical Political Economics, 19(1), 73-89.
23. Ministry of Health and Family Welfare. (2005). National Family Health Survey of India, 2005-06. Retrieved from
24. https://dhsprogram.com/pubs/pdf/FR339/FR339.pdf
25. Ministry of Health and Family Welfare. (2015). National Family Health Survey of India, 2015-16. Retrieved from
26. https://dhsprogram.com/pubs/pdf/FR339/FR339.pdf
27. Pal, S., & Haldar, S. (2016). Participation and role of rural women in decision making related to farm activities: A study in Burdwan district of West Bengal. Economic affairs, 61(1), 55- 63.
28. Pollak, R. A. (2003). Gary Becker's contributions to family and household economics. Review of Economics of the Household, 1(1), 111-141.
29. Rosa, K.D. (2010). Empowerment of Women: The Impact of Employement. Delhi: Abhijeet publications.
30. Roy, T. K., & Niranjan, S. (2005). Indicators of women's empowerment in India. Asia-Pacific Population Journal, 19(3), 23-38.
31. Seiz, J. A. (1995). Bargaining models, feminism, and institutionalism. Journal of Economic Issues, 29(2), 609-618.
32. Sen, A. (1987). Gender and cooperative conflicts. World Institute for Development Economics Research, 47-58.
33. Soharwardi, M. A., Khan, A. S., & Khalid, M. (2014). Socio-economic determinants of women empowerment: A case study of Cholistan Desert, Pakistan. International Journal of Scientific & Engineering Research, 5(11), 1200-1213.
34. United Nations Development Group. (2010). Thematic paper on MDG 3-Promote Gender Equality and Empower Women. Retrieved from
35. https://www.unwomen.org/media/headquarters/media/publications/unifem/undgmdg3paperen.pd f?la=en&vs=1024

CHAPTER XVII

# Women Leadership: Raising Nation at New Height

Dr. Niharika Singh
Assistant Professor
Department of English
Dr. Rammanaohar Lohia Avadh University, Ayodhya
Singh16niharika@gmail.com

## *Abstract*

Women are natural born leaders, and they excel in any leadership role they are assigned. Women serve effectively in any managerial role since they possess various attributes such as empathy, strong communication, and listening skills. Women in leadership positions tend to be more collaborative in institutions and organizations. It is found in a study that women's bend toward collaboration has an altruistic side as well: "Specifically, we find that women are much more likely to pick the 'team' option when doing so would have a position impact on their partner's incomes, and show that this pattern is consistent with a higher level of 'advantageous' inequity aversion among women than men." This indicates that women have an innate desire for the organisation to prosper as a whole. There are numerous misconceptions about whether or not women should lead organisations, but gender should not be a factor in determining a person is capable of being a great leader. Individual qualities and personality features should determine a person's leadership ability.

**Keywords:** Leadership, Gender, Inequality, Organization.

When we talk about a leader then the first question that comes in our mind is, what is leadership and what are their traits?

A common definition of Leadership is 'the art of motivating a group of people to act toward achieving a common goal.' And a leader should have different traits like empathy, honesty, integrity, confidence, commitment, passion, a good communicator, have decision making capabilities etc. Thus, if we think of a woman with these qualities she can be a good leader than men. According to a new nationwide Pew Research Centre Social and Demographic Trends survey that when it comes to leadership traits then public rates women superior to men.

But, however, in many cases, women are not encouraged to take on leadership roles as often as their male counterparts. There are always debates on Male vs Female leadership. When employees are asked to characterise a good leader, the majority of them think of a man. According to some statistics, women have more developed skills associated with encouraging and supporting, while men are considered at decision-making and problem-solving.

Bengaluru-based Preethi is a talented and ambitious young lady who relocated to the city with her husband and mother-in-law following her marriage. Preethi, who is now the happy mother of a nine-month-old, participated in a three-month sales training course in the city after her relocation. She had landed a job at a high-end fashion brand 10 km from her home as a result of the course. Unfortunately, Preethi's mother-in-law became sick soon after, and with no alternative means of support, she was unable to continue working. As a result, Preethi was forced to make the unavoidable decision to leave the workforce in order to care for her child and mother-in-law. When we asked Preethi's husband about the idea of her going back to work, his only question was, "Who would look after our baby?"...... Preethi's situation is strikingly close to that of the vast majority of Indian women nowadays.

Despite the fact that we are now in the twenty-first century, and women all over the world are breaking new ground in every aspect of life and work. In fact, the poor position of women's participation in the Indian workforce generates headlines every few months, only to be rapidly overshadowed by the avalanche of other news and information available in the market today. The World Bank's India Development Report puts India 120$^{th}$ out of 131 nations in the world in terms of female labor-force participation. Women's participation in the formal workforce, particularly in senior positions, has remained low around the world. Out of 1,500 large public companies listed across 27 countries analysed by Quartz, 95 percent of companies are led by a significantly male-dominated management.

Another instance of gender inequality can be found. The percentage of men and women at each academic career stage in the School of Natural Sciences is depicted in the graph below. At the Assistant Professor level, there is a noticeable fall in the number of women, and the gender gap continues from there. This is especially pronounced at the highest levels, indicating a troubling tendency in the School's retention and advancement of women.

As a result, those are some examples of male dominated leadership. Why is this case? Why is it that a woman, who possesses all of the qualities of a good leader, is so far behind men? That is because, in traditional childhood game play, women are trained to be cooperative, collaborative, and relationship-driven, whereas men are socialised to be competitive in their play, and they live in a dualistic state of winning and losing. Because women are more hesitant to speak up about their professional objectives, a 2015 Harris Poll study of Saba Software revealed that 60 percent of male employees want their firms to have an active part in their individual career prospects, compared to 49 percent of female employees. Women perceive work more holistically as a component of their whole life plan than males, who tend to be career-centric and desire to maximise their financial return from work.

Apart from that, for a long time, women's career success has been defined by their ability to adapt to their field's male-dominated culture and business procedure. In the words of Deborah L. Rhode, "Some highly male dominated settings invite a top-down style, and women who were firsts in those settings, such as Margaret Thatcher, Golda Meir and Indira Gandhi, led in ways that were as commanding as those of men." (Deborah L. Rhode, 2017) At the regional, national, and global levels, women are increasingly establishing themselves as leaders in entrepreneurship, administration, education, engineering, and health care, among other fields. However, the dispute over whether a man or a woman is better has raged on for centuries. Women have traditionally had superior management skills and a number of unique abilities that are only found in women. Women are always looked down upon, and society does not believe that women make better leaders, which is why women are denied equality on many social platforms. Despite the fact that women put in the same amount of effort and are equally committed. Women are frequently undervalued in management positions, although there are numerous characteristics that demonstrate that women can be better leaders than males. At the regional, national, and global levels, women are increasingly establishing themselves as leaders in entrepreneurship, administration, education, engineering, and health care, among other fields. However, the dispute over whether a man or a woman is better has raged on for centuries. Women have traditionally had superior management skills and a number of unique abilities that are only found in women. Women are always looked down upon, and society does not believe that women make better leaders, which is why women are denied equality on many social platforms. Despite the fact that women put in the same amount of effort and are equally committed. Women are frequently undervalued in management positions, although there are numerous characteristics that demonstrate that women can be better leaders than males.

The first and foremost trait for a leader is managerial skill and women have been managing households for ages. Even when money is scarce, they know how to spend and conserve it. It's because they understand how to effectively manage resources, assign them, and maintain a balance. The majority of women use the 'to-do list approach,' which makes them experts at planning and scheduling. Most men, on the other hand, choose the "cross the bridge when it comes" attitude, which rarely works in their favour. According to a study conducted by the Peterson Institute for International Economics, there is a connection between the number of women in the C-Suite and company earnings. When comparing organisations with and without female executives, companies with at least 30% of women in leadership positions have a net profit margin that is at least 1% higher. A Fortune ranking of the most admired firms, which includes such titans as Amazon, JPMorgan, Starbucks, and Microsoft, demonstrates that diverse companies develop more creative and profitable solutions and implement innovations faster. It turns out that the most profitable businesses have more female executives than the less profitable ones. Furthermore, Apple is ranked first on this list because it has the highest percentage of women in senior management roles – 29 percent, which is still an alarmingly uneven ratio. Gender diversity, like racial diversity, increases a company's overall performance because people with diverse abilities and perspectives can collaborate in the decision-making process, resulting in more creative ideas and the implementation of new inventive ways. Here is the report of Gallup who says women's higher engagement levels likely result in more engaged, higher-performing teams.

Women are strong communicator, which is a very important trait of leadership. Female leaders know how to employ communication, which is regarded to be one of a woman's strongest skills. An open communication stream enables for the creation of roles and duties while talking with employers, co-workers, or partners. Women have the ability to communicate with others properly and sensitively in order to secure a commercial agreement. Their soft talents enable them to effectively apply items in the corporate environment. Better communication allows for a more efficient flow of information, which is essential in running a business. Men favour action over words, but women prefer to talk it out over a discussion before getting down to work. They also have excellent listening skills, which helps them relate better to staff and customer concerns. Communication is essential for the development and maintenance of strong relationships, whether in the workplace or in one's personal life.

According to Regan & Brooks, "Leaders who build among relationships are described as collaborative and caring as well as courageous and visionary." (Regan & Brooks, 1995) Women aren't necessarily better at making relationships and forming teams than their male counterparts. They can, on the other hand, use their intuitive natures to detect and resolve disagreement within a team, as well as follow their instincts to prefer a team approach over asking an individual to take on too huge a challenge. Strong female leaders frequently feel compelled to question "how things have traditionally been done." They may be more inclined than some male leaders to defy convention when it comes to finding a more effective solution because they don't necessarily accept a standard approach to strategy.

Empathy is typically seen to be a feminine trait. However, it is the single most critical leadership trait that helps ensure overall success, according to a study by Development Dimensions International, a worldwide leadership consulting business. Empathy in a leader encourages both co-operation and commitment in the business, while being a soft talent or interpersonal people skill. Empathy has become such an important trait for leaders and businesses that many companies now provide empathy training.

Leadership is difficult and uncertain, regardless of gender. It only gets tougher when you add in the additional home and family duties that many women have, not to mention the career momentum stall that commonly comes with childbirth and raising infants. Despite this, millions of women persevere and develop successful enterprises as a result of their tenacity and determination.

Women who are successful often able to inspire other women leaders and bring about organisational transformation. Leaders deal with complex challenges with limited data and are more impacted by market forces and other external entities. Women who are successful have learnt to predict what will happen next and to urge their colleagues to do the same. As Mary Lou Decosterd stated, "Women approach leadership and life through a learning lens. It isn't that men don't learn and value learning, but women view learning differently than men do." (Mary Lou Decosterd, 2013) First and foremost, successful female leaders are trustworthy. Your team will commit to goals, communications will improve, and ideas will flow more freely if you create a trusting environment. Most significantly, your staffs are more accepting of change and willing to embrace a new vision.

The following four specific claims about women's leadership skills were found in the Caliper study: 1. Female leaders have a higher level of persuasion than male leaders. 2. When faced with rejection, women leaders learn from their mistakes and persevere with a "I'll show you" attitude. 3. Women leaders display a problem-solving and decision-making style that is inclusive and team-building. 4. Women in positions of leadership are more prone to break norms and take risks.

Success at work should never be biased; it should be completely based on their merit or the excellence of their work performance. Thus, in a nutshell, some common traits of successful women possess; a clear vision for the future, self-confidence, they put their heart and soul in what they believe, they are wise in choosing their battles, good at prioritizing things, working hard and staying persistent, being grateful, take failure and success the same way, possessing a strong support system, never stop learning, always stay optimistic, have an ambition and choose their strengths and what they love.

Now we'll look at some modern role models who are trend-setters and successful female leaders. Despite being underrepresented in most aspects of professional and business life, women around the world are rapidly catching up to men. According to the Fortune India 2019 survey, India's top female leaders are Zia Mody, Kiran Mazumdar

Shaw, Suneeta Reddy, Alice G. Vaidyan, Zarin Daruwala, Mallika Srinivasam, Arundhati Bhattacharya, Kaku Nahate, Shobhna Bhartia, and Renuka Ramnath, who have led some high-profile companies to profitability.

The noble profession of law cannot stay noble simply by calling it that unless there is a strong presence of legal consultants who have the grace, dignity, and prestige associated with it, as well as deep proficiency and experience. An excellent legal consultant examines the case with perfect objectivity, integrity, and accessibility, as well as tenacious courtroom skills and endurance. The central focus of such consultants is always to serve their clients in a timely and efficient manner. And they believe in defending the actual rights of their clients as their main commitment. In an interview with Shenomics Zia Mody Stated, “As women leaders we have the opportunity and, therefore, the duty to ensure that we retain our women in the workplace, at all costs. We cannot let them leave without us having done our best to make them stay.” She possesses a vast store of legal knowledge, which she has acquired over the course of more than 30 years of dedicated practice. She is currently the Managing Partner and Founder of AZB & Partner. Zia has successfully catered to a variety of Multinational clients for corporate merger and acquisition, securities, private equity, and finance-related projects, making her the perfect person to approach for these services whenever they are needed.

Kiran Mazumdar Shaw has long been regarded as one of India’s most powerful female figures, and with good reason. She was a trailblazer for women in India’s biotech industry, which has traditionally been dominated by men. She experienced hurdles when establishing Biocon and later growing it into a global brand, and she was rewarded for her efforts. Kiran Mazumdar Shaw is a pioneer of India’s biotechnology industry and the founder of Biocon, the country’s largest biotechnology company. Mazumdar Shaw is a thought leader who has made her country proud by building a globally recognised biopharmaceutical enterprise that is committed to innovation and affordability in delivering best-in-class therapeutics to patients around the world. She was named one of TIME magazine’s 100 most influential people in the world.

Suneeta Reddy, managing director and a member of the founding family, joined the Apollo Hospitals Group in 1989. Her financial skills have been a crucial role in the group’s spectacular development and profitability, since she leads the finance section. Reddy is currently concentrating on corporate strategy, corporate finance, capital, and investments, as well as leveraging mergers and acquisitions to fulfil the company’s goals of quicker growth and increased profitability. “The healthcare industry has played an important role in increasing life expectancy across the board, and in improving all WHO indicators such as the infant mortality rate in India. This has been done by people, who are committed to improving the life of every Indian. Women have always been great nurturers – their capacity to nurture is infinite – whether it be their patient, their family at home or their business. The success of women around the world is testimony to this,” says Reddy in an interview with Business World.

Alice G Vaidyan has been named Chairman-Managing Director of the state-owned General Insurance Corporation of India for the first time in the country’s insurance industry’s history (GIC Re). Vaidyan has firsthand experience working at all levels during her career. She began her career at the branch level, then advanced to the divisional level, then to the regional office, and eventually to the corporate headquarters. GIC re-entered the top 10 global reinsurers’ league under her leadership, stepping up two positions, a goal she set for herself when she was appointed CMD. GIC Re’s market share has climbed from 55 percent to 65 percent in her two years as CEO, and its premium business has expanded from Rs.18, 436 crore to Rs. 41,799 crore.

Zarin Daruwala, the chief executive officer (CEO) of Standard Chartered Bank (SCB) India, is a woman who got a gold medal when she qualified as a company secretary and received a rank in her chartered accounting examination. She worked for the ICICI Group before joining Standard Chartered Bank, where she had positions in human resources, corporate planning, investment banking, and credit. She’s held positions of leadership in a variety of sectors, including corporate finance and agribusiness. Standard Chartered Bank India’s retail banking (RB) division seemed to be in trouble when Daruwala took over as CEO in 2016. Daruwala determined that the company needed to change course and continue to invest in technology. She was personally responsible for the transformation strategy, which resulted in the bank’s retail banking business returning to profitability in the first half of 2019. In her interview with Business World she says “As a leader, I feel it is important to have a couple of attributes. One is all about building a team which shares your vision while the other revolves around the never-say-die attitude.”

A effective leader, it is claimed, is someone who not only ensures that his or her organisation makes a profit, but also considers the welfare of society. One of them is Mallika Srinivasan. Despite her hectic schedule, she makes it a point to give back to the community. Mallika Srinivasan, the current Chairperson and CEO of Tractors and Farm Equipment Limited (TAFE), is well-known for her commercial acumen and contributions to the Indian agriculture machinery industry and academia. TAFE is now the world's third largest tractor producer and India's second largest in terms of volume, with operations in 82 countries. When she joined TAFE, the leadership abilities and commercial acumen she obtained at Madras University and the Wharton School of Business came in help, and she was able to improve the firm's competitiveness. Mallika Srinivasan is now one of the country's most successful female CEOs.

In the fourth edition of Fortune's 'World 50 Greatest Leaders' list, Arundhati Bhattacharya, Chairman of State Bank of India (SBI) is rated 26$^{th}$. Arundhati Bhattacharya has now joined the list as the lone Indian corporate leader. Fortune said that Bhattacharya, the first woman to lead India's largest bank, had guided SBI through turbulent waters while revealing the people that have made the list. Bhattacharya has assisted in bringing the 211-year-old organisation into the digital era, as well as overhauling the human resources department for over 2,00,000 people. Bhattacharya is even claimed to be overseeing a complicated six-bank merger that will propel the SBI into the top 50 banks in the world.

Shobhna Bhartia is a prominent statesperson and the first and youngest woman to become the chief executive of a national newspaper. She is the Chairperson and Editorial Director of HT Media Limited, India's largest publicly traded media firm and a member of the prestigious Birla group. She led the cultural makeover of HT Media throughout the course of her three-decade career, transforming it into a high-quality, forward-thinking professional media firm. She was the driving force behind the company's quick expansion and entry into education. Her efforts have helped the company win international awards, including the Best Media Company to Work For in India in 2012. Shobana has earned numerous honours and medals, including the Padma Shri for Excellence in Journalism, a National Award from the Government of India. From 2006 to 2012, she was the Presidential nominee to the Rajya Sabha, India's Upper House of Parliament. She was also a member of the Parliamentary Energy, Women's Empowerment, and Human Resource Development Committees. She has also served as the chairperson of the Audit Bureau of Circulation and the Press Trust of India. She has served on the boards of Indian Airlines and educational institutions in India. She is also serving as the Pro Chancellor of Birla Institute of Technology and Science, Pilani (founded by her grandfather).

Renuka Ramnath is the Founder, Managing Director, and CEO of Multiples Alternate Asset Management, a private equity manager and advisor to funds with a market capitalization of over one billion dollars. She has worked in the Indian financial sector for over 30 years, in private equity, investment banking, and structured finance. Renuka began her career with the ICICI Group, where she held positions of leadership in investment banking, structured finance, and e-commerce. As the MD and CEO of ICICI Venture, she helped it grow to become one of India's largest private equity funds. Renuka has a complete cycle track record of investing cash acquired from worldwide institutions, making her one of India's most experienced private equity fund managers. Renuka is a Board member of EMPEA, the global industry association for private capital in emerging markets.

As a result, encouraging women's leadership is just as vital as establishing an atmosphere that allows women to develop their leadership skills. Despite several efforts to empower women and place them in positions of leadership, the global representation of women in such roles remains disturbing. Women account for only 4% of CEOs in the world's 500 largest corporations, even a smaller percentage of national heads of government, and the smallest percentage of international leadership positions in the world today.

Gender inequality in leadership roles not only inhibits progress in many areas, but it also costs the global economy a lot of money. As a result, there is a strong need to foster female leadership. As in the words of Selena Rezvani, "As more doors open for women my belief is that the leadership landscape will continue to progress from a gender perspective. One major reason is that women's natural leadership style- which differs from that of men- is a perfect complement to the talent needs of the new economic era we are entering. Economic, global, generational and technological changes require a leader with a mix of hard and soft skills, and women's natural propensity in these areas makes them ideal business leaders. More and more research substantiates that contrary to outmoded, archaic thinking, women are well prepared to lead in the twenty-first century." (Selena Rezvani, 2010)

At the conclusion of this paper, I'd want to state that the days when males were deemed superior and ruled the entire world are long gone. Women are increasingly being recognised for their hard work, intelligence, and leadership qualities. Let us reaffirm that all women in the world are equal to and powerful as all males. Women are currently achieving extraordinary success in a variety of professions, including politics, business, journalism, sports, and governance. With a rising number of working women, we have finally demonstrated that our job is more than just fetching coffee, cooking lunch, and caring for our families and surroundings. We women are excellent multi-taskers, and no one can argue that our approach differs from that of men. Women have demonstrated outstanding leadership qualities to the rest of the globe.

## *Reference:*


1. Decosterd, L. M. *How Women Are Transforming Leadership.* PRAEGER, 2013.
2. Rezvani, S. *The Next Generation Women leaders: What You Need To Lead But Won't Learn In Business School.* ABC-CLIO, LLC, Santa Barbara, 2010.
3. Regan and Brooks. *Out of Women's Experience: Creating Relational Leadership.* Corwin Press, 1995.
4. Rhode, L. [Deborah]. *Women and Leadership.* Oxford University Press, 2017.
5. www.yourstory.com/journal/women-in-workforce-what-it-would-take-to-achieve-g-pre59syolk/ October 9. 2018
6. www.pewsocialtrends.org/2008/08/25/men-or-women-whos-the-better-leader/ August 25. 2008
7. www.naturalscience.tcd.ie/equality/genderbias.php/ March 21. 2018
8. www.news.gallup.com/businessjournal/183026/female-bosses-engaging-male-bosses.aspx/ May 7. 2015
9. www.fortuneindia.com/mpw?year=2019

CHAPTER XVIII

# Marital Adjustment of the Indian Married Working Women

Mahwish Fatima & Das Ambika Bharti*
Department of Psychological Sciences
Central University of South Bihar, Gaya
ambika@cub.ac.in

**ABSTRACT**

As per social and technological changes taking place, it has been observed that people's perception towards marriage and the role of women in society is changing. In the post-independent era, it has been seen that in the urban set-up, working women taking the dual responsibility of work and home are appreciated. Marital adjustment refers to a state of accommodation which is achieved in different areas where conflict may exist. Marital quality is a dynamic concept as the nature and quality of relationships can change over time. Now more number of women prefers to be engaged in some kind of employment, but the attitude towards women especially married women and their role in family has remained the same, as even today taking care of the family and children is considered as their primary responsibility. A working woman bearing dual responsibility with family and at job thus often fail to discharge her duties equally efficiently; feels tense and continuous tension creates stress which in turn may affect her mental health status. This study intended to study the influence of work status on the marital adjustment of the Indian married women. Sixty (N=60) Indian married women (30 working and 30 non-working) were drawn from the population using the purposive sampling technique. The finding suggests that the working and non-working women have equal levels of marital adjustment and no significant difference exists between the two groups. The findings have implications in understanding the present generation's Indian working women and their marital adjustment.

**Keywords:** Indian married women, work status, marital adjustment

**INTRODUCTION**

The status of women in India has been subjected to many great changes over the past few millennia. With a decline in their status from the ancient to medieval times, to the promotion of equal rights by many reformers, the **history of women in India has been eventful**. (Jayapalan, 2001). The status of Indian women has radically changed since independence (National Resource Center for Women, 2009). The celebration of **International Women's Year in 1975** and the activities of **UNESCO** also created awareness of the problems of women. But the attitude towards women especially married women and their role in family has remained the same.

**Working women in Private Sector and Public Sector**

Women workforce constitutes an integral part of total workforce in India. On 31st March 2004, women constituted 19 per cent of the total workforce. The participation of women in the labor force has always been lower than that of men, in the rural as well as urban areas. The work participation rate for women has increased significantly. In 1981, work participation rate for women was only 19.67 per cent which increased up to 22.73 per cent in 1991 and 26.68 per cent in 2001. In the women workforce, women from rural areas are greater in number as compared to the urban women. Amongst rural women workers, a majority is employed in agriculture and some are employed in cottage industries. In the urban areas, women workers are primarily employed in the unorganized sectors. As on the 31st March, 2005 a total number of 50.16 Lacs women employees were engaged in the organized sector, out of which 29.21 lacs (58per cent) in the public sector and 20.95 lacs (42per cent) in the Private Sector. Employment of women in public sector increased by 1.1 percent and by 2.5 percent in the private sector during 2004-2005. The zone wise analysis showed an increase of 8% in North-Eastern zone, followed by Western zone (3%) and Central zone (1.3%) and Northern zone (1.2%). Only Southern zone registered a marginal dip of 0.8 %. Gender wise employment in organized sector as surveyed on 31st march 2004, reported, male population constituted 81% while female population constituted 19% employment. (naukrihub.com, 2004).

**Marital Adjustment**

Success in marriage is much more than finding the right person; it is a matter of being the right person. Simple as it seems the notion of marital adjustment is difficult to conceptualize and difficult to measure through empirical research. For both husbands and wives relationship and conflict resolution style impact the satisfaction couples experience over the course of their marriage for the first five years, with conflict resolution style becoming more influential in predicting satisfaction as years pass. The various factors that impact marital adjustment for men and women can be filtered into eight major domains: communication, sexual relationship, own leisure, division of household tasks, time together, external network and finances (Vangelisti & Huston, 1994). How couples negotiate these various issues impacts the level of marital adjustment for both. Marital quality is a dynamic concept as the nature and quality of relationships can change over time (Larson & Holman, 2002). There are number of ways to conceptualize the notion of quality of relationship. Glenn (1998) identifies two major approaches to the measurement of relationship quality; looking at individual feelings of the people in a relationship and looking at the relationship itself. Ernest and Leonard (1939) defined marital adjustment as "the integration of the couple in a union in which the two personalities are not merely merged, or submerged, but interact to complement each other for mutual satisfaction and the achievement of common objectives". Marital adjustment refers to a state of accommodation which is achieved in different areas where conflict may exist (Srivastav, Singh, & Nigam 1988). Marital happiness, marital conflict, marital commitment, social support, marital interaction, marital discord, forgiveness, and domestic violence have each been conceptualized as dimensions of marital quality and are sometimes combined as a single indicator of marital quality (Stanley, 2007). Marital happiness has also been found to correlate with the presence of children in the household, household income, welfare use, egalitarian attitudes, traditional marital attitudes, religiosity (Amato et al., 2007), and the interdependence of familial and friendship networks (Kearns & Leonard, 2004). Cherlin (2005) says that as marriage has evolved over the decades, being married has become less about securing one's role as an adult and more about a milestone representing successful self-development. Renne (1970) established that marital satisfaction was an essential and influential component of emotional and psychological well-being, and it had a positive association with general happiness and perception of overall individual health.

Depression was negatively correlated with marital adjustment (Manju, 2016) which was affected by marital duration. Younger women (less than five years of marriage) are more adjusted in comparison to the older women (more than 5 years of marriage). Rao (2017) conducted a study aiming at exploring the relationship between marital adjustment and depression among couples. Results indicated highly significant relationship between marital adjustment and depression. The findings of the results also show that both, women and men have to face more problems in their married life. Working married women have to face more problems in their married life as compared to non-working married women (Hashmi et al. 2006). The results further show that highly educated working and non-working married women can perform well in their married life and they are free from depression as compared to educated working and non-working married women. A study was conducted by Amirthagowri, (2008) showed that working women above 30 years had more familial problems than their counterparts. Working women of SC community grappled with familial problems significantly. Working women with only school level education were affected significantly with more familial problems relating to income and status, and family support, than their counterparts. Hashmi, Khurshid and Hassan (2007) found that working married women face more problems in their marital life when compared to non-working married women. In another study, (Singh et al. 2006) families with employed and non-employed women across different educational levels from Ludhiana city were compared on their existing level of marital adjustment. The findings revealed that sexual dimension of marital adjustment among husbands and wives was unaffected by wives' education level and employment status. Husbands showed no variation on the emotional dimension of marital adjustment with wives' educational level and employment status, whereas, wives were seem to be more emotionally dependent on their husbands when they were educated up to Level III or were nonemployees. Malhotra and Sachdeva (2005)conducted a research to study the effect of different professions and multiplicity of social (familial) roles on the role conflict amongst working women. For this purpose, a 3x3 factorial design was used. Results revealed significant main effects of women's professions and social roles as well as an interaction effect on the role conflict.

**STATEMENT OF PROBLEM**

To explore marital adjustment of Indian married working women

**OBJECTIVES**

1. To explore the marital adjustment of Indian working women with respect to see the influence of Indian couple's work status on their marital adjustment.

**METHODS**

**HYPOTHESIS**

**Hypothesis 1:** Marital adjustment of working women would be significantly low compared to their non-employed counterparts among Indian married women.

**DESIGN**

The design that is used for the study is Quasi-Experimental Design since the participants are chosen in view of their characteristics.

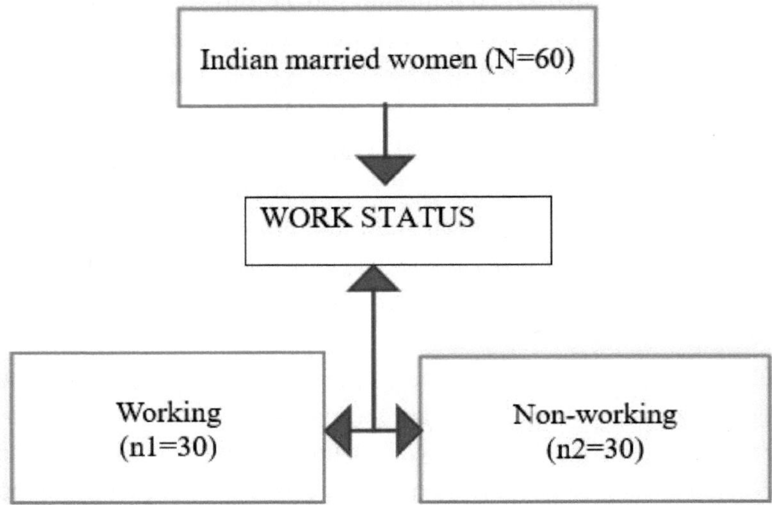


**SAMPLE**

The sample for the present study comprised of 60 Indian married women (N=60). Where, 30 ($n_1$=30) married women were working while the rest 30 ($n_1$=30) were non-working married women. Sample of working women was proportionately collected from three areas of occupation:

1. Medical profession
2. Teaching profession
3. Bank employees

**Inclusion Criteria:**

- The duration of the marriage for the married women must not be less than 10 years.
- The age range must be between 30-45 years.
- Must not suffer from any chronic disease, head injury or any major clinical history.

**Exclusion Criteria:**

- Indian women who have been married for more than 10 years
- Below 30 and above 45 years of age.
- People suffering from intellectual dysfunction.
- Suffering from any chronic disease, head injury or with any major clinical history.

**TOOLS**

1. **Socio demographic sheet**- Was developed for the current study purpose. With the help of this relevant Socio demographic information about sample was collected. Such as age, gender, education, marital status, residential area, work status, years of married life, work/organization type, annual income.
2. **Marital Adjustment Questionnaire** Pramod Kumar and Kanchana Rohtatgi (1976): This questionnaire consists of 25 Yes/No type items. The split half reliability of the test was found to be .70 while the test – retest reliability was found to be .84. The validity of the test was around .71.

**PROCEDURE**

The researcher approached Indian married women, who meet the inclusion criteria mentioned above, The purpose of the study was explained. After getting informed consent from the subjects, the required tools were administered to gather the data. The researcher also followed all the ethical guidelines set by the APA. The three areas which were used to collect the data from working women were 1: Bank employees 2: Medical Profession 3: Teaching Profession

**RESULTS**

Independent t-test was done to compare the scores of married working women and married non-working women. Further, scores of married working women and married non-working women were compared using Independent t-test. All the analysis was done using Statistical Package in Social Sciences (SPSS) Version-20.

| Marital adjustment and its domains | Sample type | N | Mean | SD | t-value | Significance |
|---|---|---|---|---|---|---|
| Social | Working women | 30 | 10.07 | 1.112 | .964 | .199 |
| | Non-working women | 30 | 10.33 | 1.028 | | |
| Emotional | Working women | 30 | 13.43 | .898 | 2.000 | .339 |
| | Non-working women | 30 | 14.03 | 1.377 | | |
| Sexual | Working women | 30 | 4.07 | .365 | 1.000 | .050 |
| | Non-working women | 30 | 4.00 | .001 | | |
| Marital adjustment Total | Working women | 30 | 27.57 | 1.775 | 1.912 | .060 |
| | Non-working women | 30 | 28.37 | 1.450 | | |

**Table: Descriptive statistics and t-value for marital adjustment of the working women and non-working women**

Result table shows that the non-working women scored higher (Mean=10.33, SD=1.028) on the social dimension of marital adjustment as compared to their working women (Mean=10.07, SD=1.112) counterparts. But, the group mean difference was statistically non-significant. It can be seen that both the working and non-working women have the same level of adjustment on the social front too.

The non-working women scored higher (Mean=14.003, SD=1.377) when compared to their working women (Mean=13.43, SD=.898) counterparts on the emotional dimension of marital adjustment. However, t-test was not found to be statistically significant. Hence, both the groups are able to adjust equally on the emotional aspect of marital adjustment.

The working women recorded a higher score (Mean=4.07, SD=.365) on the sexual dimension of marital adjustment as compared to non-working women (Mean=4.00, SD=.001) counterparts and this difference was found to be statistically significant. (t=1.000, p<0.05). Thus, the working women differ significantly from the non-working women on the sexual dimension of marital adjustment.

The non-working women had a higher score (Mean=28.37, SD=1.450) on the overall marital adjustment as compared to non-working women (Mean=27.57, SD=1.775) The t-test was not found to be statistically significant. Therefore, the working and non-working women have equal levels of marital adjustment and no significant difference exists between the two groups.

Hence, the findings reject the hypothesis 1 stating "Marital adjustment of working women would be significantly low compared to their non-employed counterparts among Indian married women."

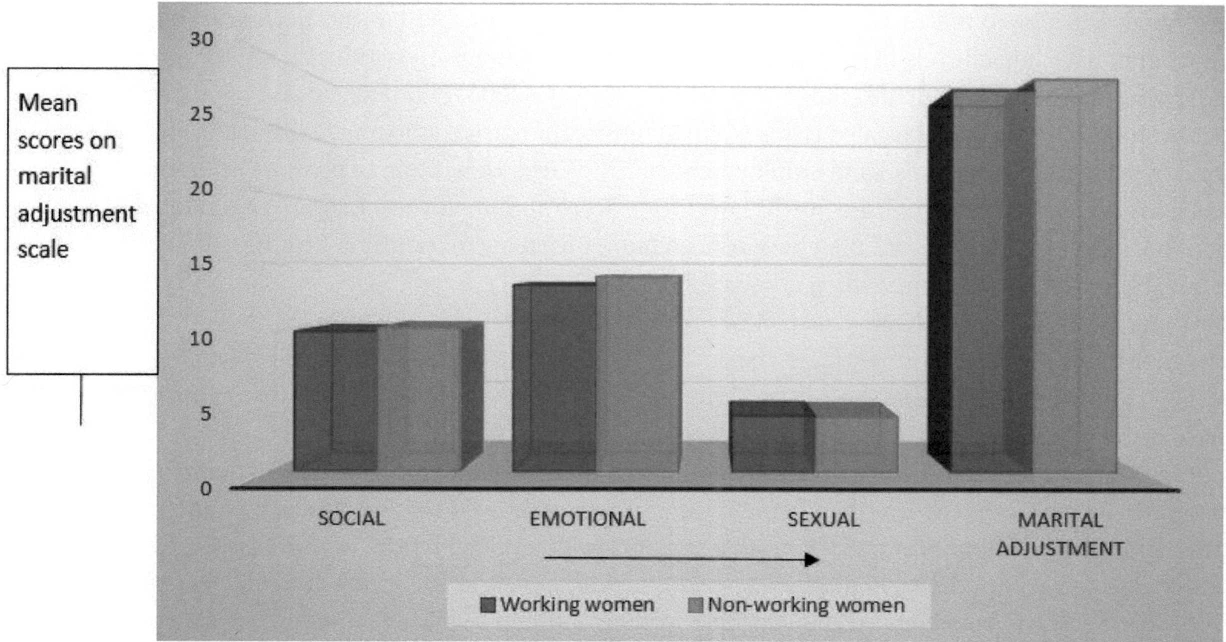


**Figure 1: Comparative bar diagram of mean scores of married working women and Non-working women on the marital adjustment scale**

Figure 1 represents a comparative bar diagram depicting almost same levels of marital adjustment and along all of its three dimensions which are, social dimension, emotional dimension and sexual dimension. It can be clearly seen in the figure that not much difference exists between the two groups compared. The level of adjustment for both the working and non-working women is seen to be comparatively equal. Thus, the findings rejects the hypothesis stating "Marital adjustment of working women would be significantly low compared to their non-employed counterparts among Indian married couples."

**DISCUSSION**

The meaning, implication of the study, results, and the congruence or the lack of congruence with the results of other studies, were all explored. The primary variables of marital setting in accordance to their work status was examined.

The present study was undertaken to study the influence of work status of the married Indian couples on their marital adjustment.

The non-working women scored higher on marital adjustment as compared to working women. However, this difference was not found statistically significant. Results suggest that married working women and married non-working women are experiencing equal levels of marital adjustment. Both types of married women are able to be well adjusted in a wedlock. On the sexual dimension of marital adjustment, the working women scored higher and this difference was found to be statistically significant, indicating that working women are better adjusted when it comes to their sexual needs. Another study by Hashmi, Khurshid and Hassan (2006) aimed to explore the relationship between marital adjustment, stress and depression. Results indicated highly significant relationship between marital adjustment, depression and stress. The findings of the results also show that working married women have to face more problems in their married life as compared to non-working married women. Hashmi, Khurshid and Hassan (2007) found that working married women face more problems in their marital life when compared to non-working married women. Another study conducted by Beegam, Muqthar, Wani and Singh (2017) demonstrated that single working couples have better marital adjustment than dual working couples. Findings also shows significant mean difference between marital adjustment scores of single and dual working couples. Findings of the above-mentioned studies indicate that married non-working women are better adjusted in a marriage.

The working women scored higher on marital adjustment when compared to their non-working counterparts. This difference was not found to be statistically significant, thus concluding that both working women and non-working women have equal levels of marital adjustment. Working and non-working women are comparatively same when adjusting in their marital life. Singh, Thind and Jaswal (2006) studied families with employed and non-employed women. The findings revealed that sexual dimension of marital adjustment among husbands and wives was unaffected by wives' education level and employment status. Wives were seem to be more emotionally dependent on their husbands when they were educated up to Level III or were nonemployees. Rao (2017) conducted a study whose findings show that both, women and men have to face more problems in their married life. The findings suggest that women are able to adjust superiorly when compared to men.

**SUMMARY AND CONCLUSION**

The present study aimed to investigate the marital adjustment of married working women and non-working women. The prior findings encouraged the present study to see the effect of work status on married Indian women and their marital adjustment.

Psychometrically sound tools were used as per the need of the study which included a demographic data sheet to classify the participants into two groups of employed and non-employed single employed women.

Further appropriate and inferential descriptive statistics were applied on the data to test the hypotheses framed.

An extensive and comprehensive discussion of the result has led to the following conclusions: No difference in marital adjustment exists between married working women and non- working women.

**Limitations and Future Suggestions**

Following are some points which worked as limitations to the study and more confidence might be gained if it is checked in further studies:

1. Owing to small sample size of the present study generalization of its findings has its own limitations.
2. Sample consisted only of urban participants and no rural participants were a part of the study which might have biased our results.
3. The couples were assessed only on three spheres of a marital setting. Other dimensions like emotional intelligence, cognitive development, etc. could have been used to see their impact on marital adjustment.
4. Participants comprised of only the Bihar region and hence generalisations are difficult to be drawn.

Based on the findings and conclusion of the present study following points are suggested for future implications:

1. Marital adjustment profile of couples identified in the current study may help in early identification of couples who may have lower levels of adjustment in a marital setting.
2. Interventions for couples with low level of adjustment and poor psychological well-being can be held.

**REFERENCES:**

1. Jayapalan, N. (2001), "Status of women in Hindu society", in Jayapalan, N., *Indian society and social institutions*, New Delhi, India: Atlantic Publishers and Distributors, p. 145

2. Women in history" *nrcw.nic.in*. National Resource Center for Women. Archived from the original on 19 June 2009.Retrieved 24 December 2006.
3. http://www.naukrihub.com/industrialrelations/women-employment.html (2004)
4. Vangelisti, A. L., & Huston, T. L. (1994). "Maintaining marital satisfaction and love." In D. J. Canary & L. Stafford (Eds.), *Communication and relational maintenance* (pp. 165–186).
5. Manju. Marital Adjustment and Depression (2016) *The International Journal of Indian Psychology* Volume 3, Issue 4, No. 59
6. Rao S. Marital Adjustment and Depression among Couples (2017)*The International Journal of Indian Psychology* Volume 4, Issue 2, No. 87
7. Hashmi H., Khurshid M., Hassan I. Marital Adjustment, Stress and Depression among `Working and Non-Working Married Women (2006).*Pakistan Journal of Psychological Research,* 2015, Vol. 30, No. 1, 65-79
8. Rajakumari Amirthagowri, A.J.A. &Ponnambala Thiyagarajan, A. (2008), "Status of Working Women in Family", *Journal of Community Guidance & Research*, 25, 2, p. 152-158.
9. Ritu Singh et al. (2006), "Assessment of Marital Adjustment among Couples with Respect to Women's Educational Level and Employment Status", *The Anthropologist, the International Journal of Contemporary and Applied Studies of Man*, 8, 4, 259-266.
10. Sunita Malhotra and Sapna Sachdeva, (2005), "Social Roles and Role Conflict: An Interprofessional Study among Women", *Journal of the Indian Academy of Applied Psychology*, 31, 1-2, 37-42, January – July. Available at http://www.scribd.com/doc/7781153/ jakt05i1p37

CHAPTER XIX

# The Role of Women in Upbringing the Society – A Prelude

**Varsha Chopade**
Library Assistant, Rajagiri College of Social Sciences,
**Vijesh P V**
Librarian, Rajagiri College of Social Science
**Francis A J**
Librarian, School of Management,
Rajagiri College of Social Sciences, Rajagiri Valley,
Kochi, Kerala
varshakisanc@gmail.com

**Abstract:**

Violence against women has reached its peak in the modern world. In a country where **women are worshiped as goddesses, atrocities against women and family disputes are increasing day by day**. In a country where the Buddha preached the message of peace, in such a nation, it is very sad to see atrocities are committed on women. It was heart-breaking to see such violence. In fact, women should get support and respect from both parties i.e., parents and in-laws. The persecution of many married girls for dowry must stop. We have a lot of cultural values and traditions. Women and children are being abused in the name of tradition and customs and this is true. It is unfortunate for the country that girls are not safe even in their families. Many crimes can be reduced if the law is strict, punishment is provided and justice is given fast. Women are beaten in many homes. Domestic violence must stop. Women must learn to fight for their rights. And the main thing is that women should support each other without insulting other women. The next generation needs to be nurtured and respected by paying more attention to upbringing. It is a matter of pride that women are working in the big positions, but they also sometimes face sexual violence in offices and institutions. Although abusing and commenting on women is a crime by law, this type of thing we read in the newspaper every day. If you nurture your children well and take good care of them, this proportion of crime will not be vanished but will definitely help to reduce it.

**Introduction:**

Indian understanding is bound up with many norms and cultures. There are a lot of rules for women. The struggle of Rani Lakshmi Bai of Jhansi and India's first teacher Savitribai Phule has always given mental strength to Indian women. Women drive airplanes, trucks, and autos. They are not behind in any way. Women only need the support of their families. If they get, they will surely leap into the sky. In a country that had women like Devi Ahilya Bai Holkar, we have to think about how crime has increased and why it has increased? The reason may be due to a lack of upbringing, values, and good manners. If the future generation gets the right culture, many negative things in the country will be reduced. Many crimes are being committed due to a lack of law and order. Therefore, children's upbringing should be done properly.

**What should be done to enable a mother or a woman to give upbringing to the future generation of the country?**

The rights and entitlements given to women by the Indian Constitution should be exercised or they should be informed. The government has enacted many laws, policies, and provisions for the protection of women but due to illiteracy and lack of knowledge of the law, women are facing many difficulties. Without education women will not understand their rights. Someone said that, if the girl is educated then progress is sure to come, education is very important in the modern world. Following are the reasons for the increase in the crime rate:

- Influence of old stereotypes
- Illiteracy

- Poverty
- Unemployment
- Patriarchal culture
- Rising Population
- Inflation
- Natural Disasters
- Misuse of social media and internet

The country has many problems. How can a woman who is so upset with herself rare her children properly? If we think that the future generation of the country should be intelligent and virtuous then women should be respected. Only a happy person can create a happy world. Many women are working shoulder to shoulder with men, running big businesses, and taking care of their families. The truth is that the woman who faces many difficulties is the mother of eternity. There are many government initiatives and schemes to address the issues of women. Women should be aware of these initiatives and move forward in life. If we think positively about the progress of the country by considering women, men, and youth in a positive way, then of course some changes are likely to take place. See how crime has increased in all areas of India.

**Crime rate:**

Crime against women has increased in India, cybercrime and harassment are on the rise in every state. Delhi and Uttar Pradesh have the highest crime rates in the country (figure 1) (figure 2) and (figure 3). These figure shows how crime has increased in the year 2020.

Several measures are being taken to prevent these crimes but the police are not succeeding as they should. The cooperation of the people is invaluable, only our unity and alertness can reduce these huge multi-crimes.

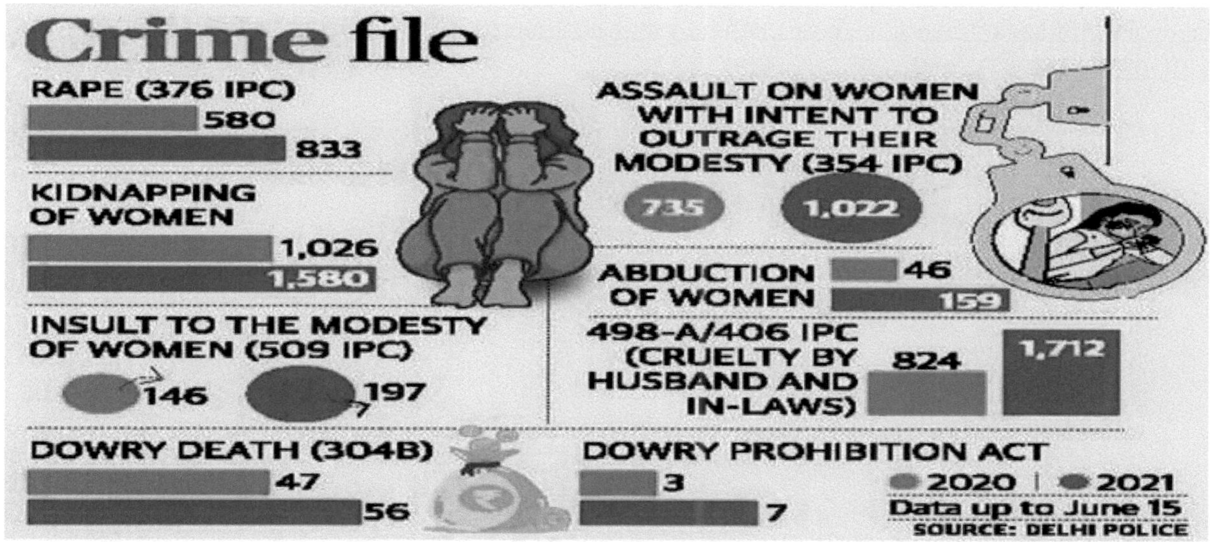


**Crimes against women saw over 63% rise in 2021 so far City: Delhi**

Source: https://www.thehindu.com/news/cities/Delhi/crimes-against-women-saw-over-63-rise-in-2021-so-far/article35181148.ece

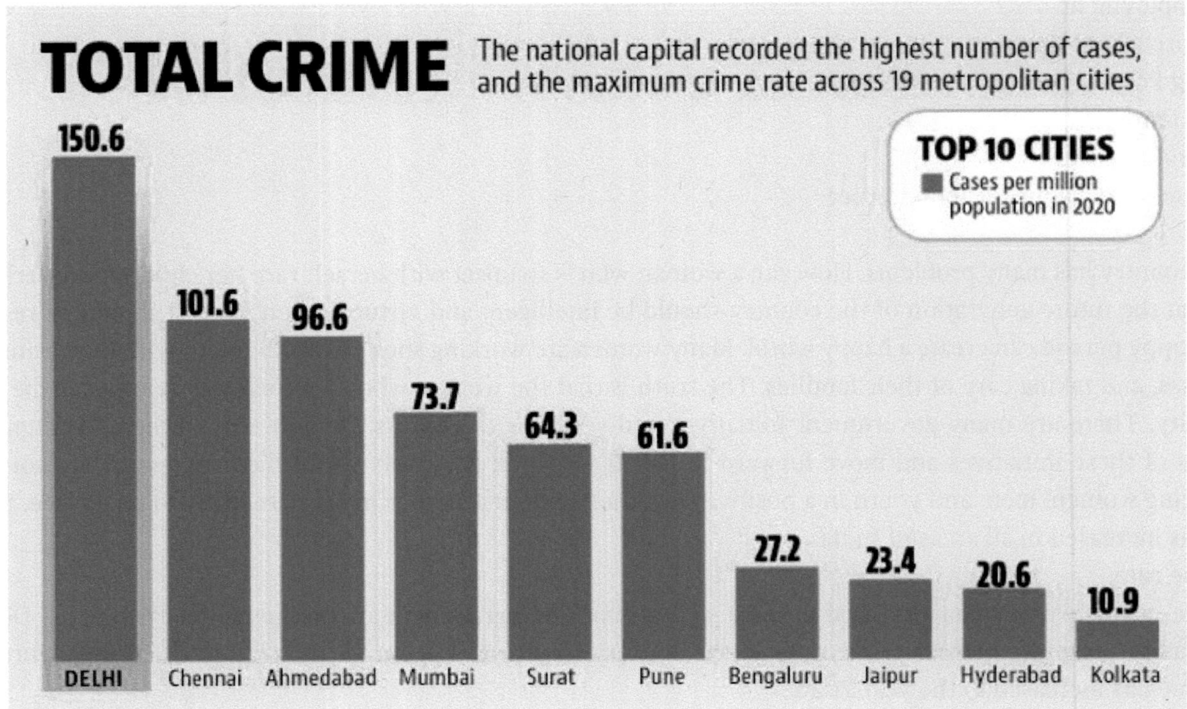


**Among 19 metro cities, the crime rate in Delhi highest in 2020**

https://www.hindustantimes.com/cities/others/among-19-metro-cities-crime-rate-in-delhi-highest-in-2020-101631728619971.html

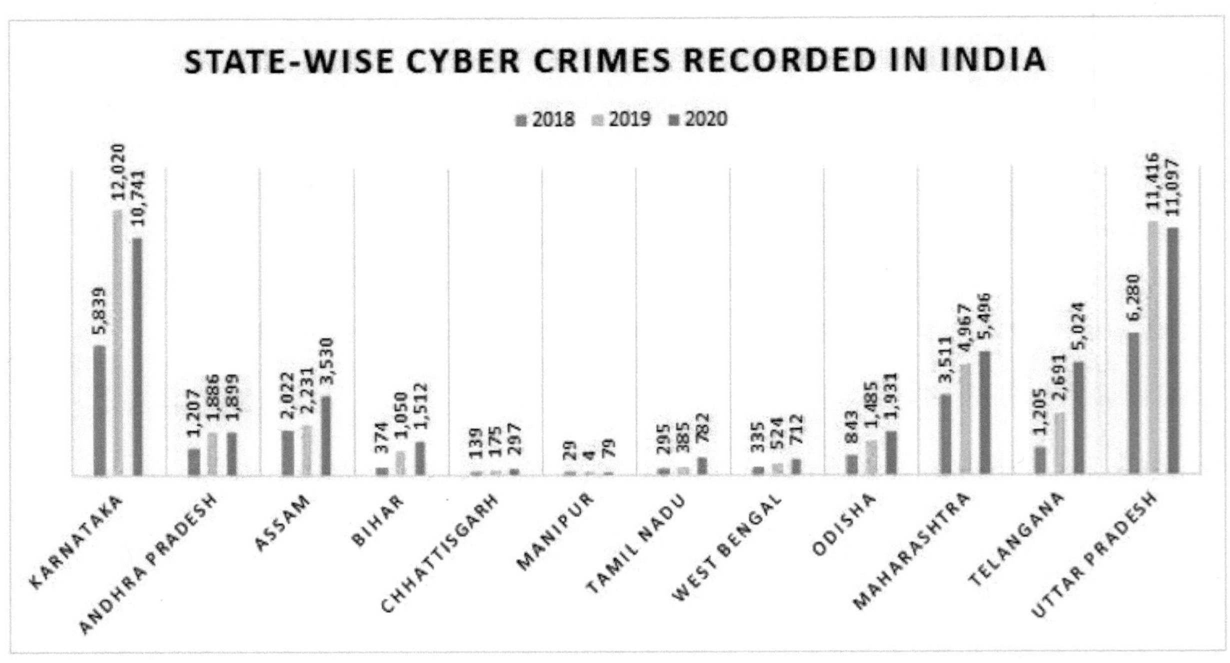


**Crime in India (National Crime Records Bureau)**

https://www.nextias.com/current-affairs/17-09-2021/crime-in-india-2020-ncrb

This increase in crime is a matter of great concern. If we want to reduce crime and criminals, then we need to cultivate and nurture. Also, many measures are needed.

**What is Upbringing?**

Upbringing and caring are rites taken from parents and society. Upbringing is essential for the mental and physical growth of children. The future of children and their behaviour depends on upbringing. It is said that small children are like clay balls and only a woman can take care of a child in a good way because only a mother can understand her child.

Mother knows well what her kids need without asking another person. Only a mother can nurture her child and make him a better person. In fact, women's anatomy is delicate. But women are very strong and accept any challenge easily and try to accomplish their commitments.

Five points are necessary for the growth of a child.

- High Parental Nutrition
- Food Nutrition
- Outdoor Sports or game
- Education (School).
- Books (Moral values and great persons biography)

Education is more important but the ethical value of education is most important to all children. Every child gets child cultural education from his family. Parent's behaviour is most important because everyday children observe their them, relatives, friends, and neighbours. Children behave according to the behaviour of their parents and this is also true. They behave as you would shape them.

**Why proper upbringing of children is necessary?**

The holistic development of children is essential not only for the benefit of the nation but also for the happiness of the family. Many social organizations, many social reformers and the government are working for this. Every citizen is important to the country. Therefore, it is important for everyone to follow the rules for denial.

Every citizen has the right to equality. **We teach children that we are all one. India is everyone's country but we see many disputes and bloodshed over religion and caste.** If anyone in the country, be it of any caste or religion, is doing something good and positive for the society, then definitely support them. Because if the country wants positive changes, then children must be brought up in a positive and impartial manner. Fostering is not just about a healthy diet but also about influencing children with positive thinking.

There were many great personalities in the country like Swami Vivekananda, Bhagat Singh, Dr. Babasaheb Ambedkar, Dr. APJ Abdul Kalam, Dr. Sudha Murty and Mother Teresa. We can learn a lot from our national heroes and great personalities. How we follow someone and how we use our time is very important. Yoga and physical exercise also play a vital role and are very important for the mental and physical growth of everyone. Every child physically develops through exercise and can get a healthy body. If the body is healthy then the mind also stays healthy and happy. If we sincerely want to create a happy and joyful society, then everyone with children, need to correct their mistakes.

Child trafficking and prostitution are common problems in our country, many children are killed and their organs are sold. Our country is in a horrible situation. It is also true that **poverty, along with unemployment**, is causing many problems in the world. In fact, there is fierce competition in many areas. Everyone needs education and a job. A well-paying job brings family stability. So many jobs need to be created. Only when the family is happy, we can nurture the next generation and it can curb crime. For a healthy, happy family; understanding and upbringing with great values are important factors.

**The heritage of the great men of the country and the extraordinary examples of upbringing:**

I have already said that the country has many traditions. We can learn from many types of literature. But what matters is the quality of the books and the topics. Books help children to develop a love of literature, writing, various arts, crafts, and science. For that, development of school libraries should be done. I guess a lot of people help to the new social initiative but every work should be done honestly. Family culture and upbringing are important for that.

Rabindranath Tagore was a master of many subjects and many arts. When someone asked him about this, Rabindranath said, "When I was young, my mother used to work a lot, sometimes I used to spend time with my father. Our family was religious. I used to love the chirping of birds. My father used to tell me that it was a beautiful chirping. I used to see the beautiful sun every day. I used to see its various shades. It made me love art. The sound of cows and cattle came to mind. Nature is so beautiful. My father taught me to experience all these things. I fell in love with these things unknowingly. All those things have bought many changes in my life". We can learn a lot from this small beautiful story.

This example shows how good manners and upbringing change our life. The most important thing is that children should follow good manners and good things.

Former President of India and Missile man Dr. A. P. J. Abdul Kalam was a great personality, Dr. Kalam is a highly renowned researcher, and he is highly respected in the country. There is no doubt that he became a good man because of his parent's right upbringing. He was great by nature but he was a highly cultured man and the country will never forget the great work he did for the country. Dedication and sacrifice for the country will remain in the hearts of Indians. His books are very inspiring. We have a lot to learn from them and their speeches. Many of their beautiful things will inspire you and they are definitely useful for raising and upbringing children.

**Role of mother in child's upbringing:**

**Jijabai Bhosale (Mother of Chatrapati Shivaji Maharaj)**

The mother plays a key role in raising the children. Shivaji Maharaj is known as a very charismatic and powerful king. Shivaji Maharaj's mother took good care of him. Taught to respect, not just adults but everyone. Jijau Maa Saheb (Mother of Shivaji Maharaj) had taught Shivaji Raje that women should be protected and respected by everyone. He won many battles. There is a beautiful short story, I have not forgotten this beautiful inspirational story told by Thakur Sir from our college. Once when Maharaj went to the battle of Jalna, he saw a page of the Quran (the Muslim scripture). They must have been flying. Shivaji Maharaj picked it up and placed it on his head. He greeted the page and respectfully sent it from his man to the mosque. It shows how much respect they had for other religions. This was the result of the mother's upbringing. Jijau imparted martial arts and politics lessons to Shivaji Raje. She nurtured courage and encouragement in Shivba and made him a great person. He is referred to as the shining sun and his credit goes to his mother's upbringing.

**Role of family and friends in children's upbringing:**

I am a mother of two kids and also a library teacher. I daily meet so many people like students, parents and teachers at school or college. At every stage of life, we are learning something from known and unknown persons.

Every parent wants their children to behave well. But do we ever observe how we behave? Of course not.

We always listen and read that child follow their parent's behaviour. But this seems to be very wrong sometimes...please read the following short story carefully.

A poor couple is living in our village with two children. The boys' names were Rakesh and Rajesh. They had no complaints about their parents. Due to lack of money, they didn't know about education and school. Going to the farm every day and earning money was a routine. The father of these children was addicted to alcohol. So, it was customary to drink alcohol and beat his wife. The money earned during the day was wasted on alcohol. When Rakesh and Rajesh get angry, the father says that drinking alcohol is great fun, it feels like going to heaven.

Rakesh was an understanding boy, but Rajesh used to behave like his father. The day was passing. Their mother used to tell them that drinking alcohol or other bad habits are injurious to their health. If you love your mother a little, never drink alcohol in your life. Alcohol does not bring happiness to the house but it brings misery to the house. The children would listen and both help their mother, but Rajesh used to ignore her a little and started behaving like his father.

Once a time came when both of them started working for the carpenters in the village. Rakesh began to work hard; he was listening to his mother. He also had many good friends. Rajesh was working but he started spending the money with his friends without giving it to his mother. His friends were addicted. Rajesh thinks that drinking alcohol is a very good thing. He started drinking alcohol with his friends. His father joined him. Rakesh didn't like it at all so he started living separate along with his mother. After a year they both got married. Rajesh did not improve, he started drinking more. And on the other hand, Rakesh was making progress. Rajesh's life was ruined. There was no peace in his house. Rakesh was happy with his mother and family.

When I met both of them and their mother, I asked them one question. You were born in the womb of the same mother and both of you were given the same learning by your mother. The two grew up together in the same house but how is there such a difference between conduct and thought?

Both were silent. Their mother said, "I gave them both the same culture and same value education, but seeing the situation, Rakesh decided to work hard, to get rid of poverty. He is happy with his family. What you sow is what you reap. On the other hand, Rajesh imitated his father, his friends were not good and he was not listening to what I was saying. So, their lives went in two directions. No matter how good the teaching of parents, friends should be very good. This proves that our friends play a very important role in your life. Our progress valuation or devaluation depends on who we make friends with within society. From this, it is understood that upbringing includes family as well as your friends and neighbours. But it also matters what we learn from someone.

**Contribution of teachers and the vital role of books in children's upbringing:**

Sometimes teachers and books are more involved in the upbringing of children than parents. The right enlightening books can change a person's life. Books are our best and true friends. A quality and enlightening book can change a person's thinking and behaviour.

Apart from schooling, it is important for children to read about national heroes, heroic female characters, children's magazines, various scientific topics. Reading newspapers daily will help in general knowledge. Cultures are created not only by education but also by reading good literature.

Of course, in the past, there were no computers and facilities like today but still, there was a lot of quality writing. Now kids love games on mobiles and other gadgets more than reading. Due to this the children's stubbornness has also increased.

In Indore, I was in charge of the library of the D-Ed College and the school of an organization. I used to pay attention to school children personally. One day, a seventh-grader brought his mobile phone to the library and started playing games on his mobile phone without reading books.

I asked about the mobile phones, then he told me, "I do not know anything. I love mobile games. My mother has given me this mobile. Why don't you just ask her?" he said nervously. He again smiled and said to me, "Teacher, look at my friend Raja he is sincerely reading the book, he is wearing spectacles because he loves books and read lots of books. I know very well that books are good than mobile, light of the mobile is very dangerous. Very danger"

I laughed softly and said, "You have a lot of knowledge. So why did you bring a mobile? Is mobile dangerous or think one more time and tell me".

He calmed down again.

The other kids stopped reading and started watching what we were talking about.

I do not want to bother the other kids; I asked the library assistant to take care of the library and took the boy out. I called his mother and immediately called her to school.

I didn't know why the boy was smiling. In time, the boy's mother arrived. I told her what had happened.

She laughed a lot and said, "He does use mobile in the class, right? I am so fed up telling him not to use the mobile, he doesn't listen even after saying a lot. He is crazy about mobile; he even takes mobile in the toilet. Hmmm, that's the way it is in every home these days. What can I do? At last, I told him to use his mobile wherever you want. Live your life now. (Ab Ji le apni Zindagi). If he is using mobile. I have no problem. Otherwise, what will he learn? We have a big business. He should be able to read and write that is enough. Otherwise, what is the use of degrees?

I didn't like her at all. She was talking because she thought she was right; she was fed up with the boy's bad habits and she was saying this because she thought there was no solution.

I said quietly, "You may think this is appropriate, but you can't break school rules. You can't bring a mobile phone. He should get rid of this dangerous habit."

The boy looked at his mother and quietly handed the mobile to his mother.

I complimented the boy as he returned the mobile to his mother.

Well done "I said to that boy and went back to work".

The next day I began to explain the merits and demerits of mobile and how dangerous mobile is? I told all the students the advantages and disadvantages of mobile. Some students agreed with me. There was also a student who would bring a mobile to the school library. He began to realize that the use of mobile phones is dangerous, so he started looking at books. He started reading. I was happy.

I used to go to him and give him new books. He read a book called "Eklavya" and said to me, "Teacher, I made a mistake... I should not bring a mobile phone to school. I want to become a doctor. I will try to change my bad habits". Along with the other children, the boy now became interested in reading books. Maybe he agreed with me. He started to love reading. I told him and my other students how important books are for mental health. I used to try to inculcate its positive effects in their minds. I used to tell them to use mobile for urgent work. Because it is true that anything that goes too far is harmful. So, I used to pay attention to every student's mental health personally. I used to try to inculcate in the children the habit of coming to the library.

The day was passing. As it was a transfer job, the host was transferred back to Kerala. We settled in Kerala. A few years passed.

Yesterday I got a call from that boy.

I was not surprised. Because some students are still in touch with me today.

I said, "Son, how are you?"

He happily said, "Teacher, I will be a doctor. I got admission to MBBS. You gave me valuable guidance. I fulfilled my wish. I still have to learn a lot. You say do something for the country, I will give unmatched service to the people of our country at reasonable fees ".

His happiness was priceless. He was talking full length. Tears of joy came to my eyes. I blessed her and said, "Will your mother be happy now? Live your life now. (Ab Ji le apni jindagi). Be very happy. Aayushman Bhava "

He said," Yes! Thank you, teacher ".

We laughed a lot at this.

This is an example of how books change one's life. Every teacher, librarian is working hard for this. But it is also true that student participation is very important.

**Great social workers and their work-related to upbringing and child development:**

Padma Shree awardee Sindhutai Sapkal whose upbringing shaped the future of many orphans' children. Sindhutais's upbringing changed the future of millions of orphan children. Sindhutai nurtured the children as mothers. She tried her best to bring a change in the lives of these poor, homeless children. These children of Sindhutai are working in many reputed positions. Sindhutai or Mai spent her life for these orphans with utmost honesty and sincerity. She used to say that, God may have chosen me as a mother for these beautiful children. Proper upbringing, care and education have changed the lives of many children. The life story of Sindhutai Sapkal is about perseverance and determination. Even after being born in independent India, she fell victim to the social oppression that was present in Indian society.

Taking lessons from her life: she built six orphanages for orphans in Maharashtra, providing them with food, education, and shelter. Organizations run by them helped helpless children and homeless women. She gave inspirational speeches in public forums and sought public support to help the underprivileged and neglected sections of society. In one of her incomparable speeches, Sindhutai expressed her desire to spread her story everywhere to inspire others. She became popular when one famous actor made movie on her life. She has written her autobiography **"Mi Vanvasi"**, that book became very popular, translated into many languages. Her happiness lies in living with her children, making their dreams come true, and settling them into life. Sindhutai spent her whole life-giving orphan girls' and boys' roofs, food, cloth, quality education, and rites. Sindhutai has received 750 national and international awards for her great work for orphans. A high jump taken by an uneducated, destitute woman teaches us a lot of good learning about upbringing.

**Conclusion:**

The good upbringing of children gives good citizens to the country and it helps to strengthen the country. In fact, sexism needs to be eradicated. Gender equality will play a vital role in the progress of the country. While it is not possible to stop many atrocities against women, it is imperative to curb them. It is certain that the government will consider providing psychiatric treatment to mentally ill women, rather than village remedies and witchcraft. Women should be given priority in politics, sports, culture, and jobs. Women should create respectable citizens for the country by creating their own identities. A woman deserves respect and love because she is the wife of the moment but the mother of eternity. It is a fact that she has a lion's share in children's upbringing.

**References:**


1. https://www.csmonitor.com/World/Making-a-difference/2015/1210/Sindhutai-Sapkal-was-begging-at-train-stations-when-she-found-her-calling-helping-street-children
2. https://dmerharyana.org/sindhu-tai-sapkal-biography/
3. https://www.unwomen.org/en/digital-library/publications/2019/05/respect-women-preventing-violence-against-women
4. https://www.thehindu.com/news/cities/Delhi/crimes-against-women-saw-over-63-rise-in-2021-so-far/article35181148.ece
5. https://www.hindustantimes.com/cities/others/among-19-metro-cities-crime-rate-in-delhi-highest-in-2020-101631728619971.html
6. https://en.wikipedia.org/wiki/A._P._J._Abdul_Kalam
7. https://www.nextias.com/current-affairs/17-09-2021/crime-in-india-2020-ncrb

CHAPTER XX

# Political Empowerment of Women in Jammu and Kashmir

Jan Mohammad Dar
Research Scholar
Department of Political Science
Jiwaji University, Gwalior (M.P.)
Janmohd2014@gmail.com

**"You can tell the conditions of the nation by looking at the status of its women" - Jawaharlal Nehru**

Political empowerment is, therefore, a "progress as well as goals; which means redistribution of powers", "between states, sections, castes, creeds, gender or individuals". "Women's can become empower through organized mass movement, which can change the basic power relations". Women had to implement a proper strategy and planning for the development.

Empowerment means to control over material resources, intellectual resources and ideology. It involves power to, power with and power within. Some define empowerment as awareness, building leading to greater participation in effective decision-making power and control over the transformation of action. It means one should liberal in our decision making which he/she wants and to influence others on our work.

In the political arena, the position of women was not satisfactory. They remained on the periphery of the political arena like other Indian states. The presence of women in political process of J&K was very low.

## 2.1 Pre-1947 period

The first step to give a representative character to governance was taken in the pre-1947 period. The praja sabha which was formed in 1934 through a regulation of Maharaja Hari Singh, the Dogra ruler, was to be the first legislative body to have an electoral component.

Electoral process was quite restricted for two reasons: firstly, as stated above, the official members outnumbered the elected members and secondly, the franchise right, like in the rest of the Indian subcontinent, was very limited. A number of qualifications were attached to the right to vote. These qualifications related to education, holding of property, professional occupation and the like. Ordinary masses were excluded from the electoral process. Poor, illiterates and the women were not enfranchised.

The state of Jammu and Kashmir had its first electoral experience, in the year 1934, which was a landmark in the development of parliamentary institutions in the state. It was the first ever election in the state in 1934, in this election 130,994 person was enfranchised to elect 33 members to assembly named as the Praja Sabha. The members elected in this election, majority of them were from Muslim Conference. In the election of 1938, the total number of voters turnout was 2, 20,370 out of 33 seats Muslim Conference won 10 seats without contest, because of freedom movement. In 1938 Muslim Conference converts into National Conference. In 1939, however, the balance between the electoral and official members within the Praja sabha was changed. The number of elected members was now increased to 40 and they formed the majority. The number of official members was reduced to 35. In third election of Jammu and Kashmir 1946 National Conference could not participate, it was the easy walk for other parties, Muslim Conference and Hindu Rajya Sabha the predecessor of the Praja Parishad.

## 2.2 Post-1947 period

In 1948, the constitution-making process was initiated through a proclamation of Maharaja. With the help of this proclamation, the right of the people to make their own constitution was recognized. By this proclamation, the constituent assembly was convened in 1951. As per the proclamation every person who is a state subject of any class is not less than 21 years of age, has been a resident in the constituency for such period as may be prescribed by the rules was to be entitled vote. On May 1951, the state government issued an order which introduced the principle of Universal Adult Franchise.

However, the distinction was still maintained as the jurisdiction of the Election Commission for this state continued to be regulated by the laws of the state and not by the Union laws. Against the representation of the People's Act, 1950, the state was regulated by its own people's Representation Act, 1957. The issue related to delimitation of Constituencies for the purpose of election to Legislative Assembly and Legislative Council, qualification of voters, conduct of elections, etc., were to be governed by this Act.

### 2.3 The Constitution of Jammu and Kashmir and the electoral provisions

After independence of India, the women have been visible in every demonstration of state; even they showed their anger against the cruel rule of Maharaja. They also protested against the arrest of Sheikh Abdullah in 1953 and the Hazratbal holy episode in 1963. The women were restricted from these movements and were kept under their homes. During the elections of 1951 National conference won all seats except two, the Praja Parishad boycotted the election.

Electoral Process of the State is governed by the Constitution of Jammu and Kashmir Section 139 to 142 deals with the elections. Section 139 and 140 provide the basis of universal adult suffrage and bar exclusion from electoral rolls on the grounds only of religion, race, castes or sex. Every Person who is of 18 years has entitled the right to vote in the Legislative Assembly. However, Section 140 makes it very clear that the right to vote in the Legislative Assembly is given only to a 'Permanent resident of the state'.

The Electoral Politics of the State right from the very beginning was noncompetitive. The mainstream political space was dominated by the ruling Party and there was no space for the oppositional Politics. There were two trends that dominated the electoral Politics –the Phenomenon of uncontested returns and the tendency for massive majority in favor of the ruling party. It was during the 1951 assembly (Constituent Cum legislative Assembly) election that the unique trend of uncontested returns was initiated in this state. As many as 73 out of the 75 Assembly seats were returned uncontested during this election. The 1951 election also set the trend for massive majority in favour of the ruling party. The National Conference returned all the Seventy-five seats of the Assembly at that time. The trend continued even in the latter period.91% of the seats of the Legislative Assembly in 1957, 93% in 1962 and 81% in 1967 was captured by the ruling party (NC till 1962 and Congress 1967).

| Year of Assembly Election | The ruling Party | The Percentage of Seats in Legislative Assembly |
|---|---|---|
| 1951 | J&K National Conference | 100.00% |
| 1957 | J&K National Conference | 90.66% |
| 1962 | J&K National Conference | 93.33% |
| 1967 | Indian National Congress | 81.33% |

**Table 2.1 Massive Majority of Ruling Party (1951 to 1967)**

Source Department of Information and Public Relations JK Govt.

### 2.3.1 Assembly Election, 1951

During the 1951 elections, the National Conference did not face any competition for as many as 73 seats. It had to contest only two seats as the rest were returned by this party without any contest. Election had to be conducted only for two Constituencies in Jammu region. Hence most of the voters in the Jammu region and all the people of Kashmir and Ladakh region did not get an opportunity to exercise their Right to Franchise. However, without Contest, The NC could win all the Seats of the legislative cum Constituent Assembly.

| S.No. | Name of the party | Seats Contested | Seat Won | Percentage of Votes Polled |
|---|---|---|---|---|
| 1 | National Conference | 73 | 73 | 98% |
| 2 | Praja Parishad Party | - | - | - |
| 3 | Harijan Mandal | 2 | - | 2% |
| 4 | Yuvak Sabha | - | - | - |
| 5 | Independents | - | - | - |

**Table 2.2 Show Number of Seats Won by different parties in 1951 elections**

Source: Election Report of 1951, Government of Jammu and Kashmir.

**2.3.2 Assembly Elections, 1957**

The elections held in 1957were maiden elections after the Jammu and Kashmir state adopted its own constitution. In this election some minor political parties came out to be the winners of few seats. However, election the National Conference once again emerged as a largest party which got majority in 68 out of 75 seats. The opposition Party Praja Parishad managed to win 5 seats, and one bagged by Harijan Mandel. Though 44.28% votes were casted in favour of opposition parties but only managed to get 9.30% of seats in total.

| S.No. | Name of the party | Seats Contested | Seat Won | Percentage of Votes Polled |
|---|---|---|---|---|
| 1 | National Conference | 75 | 68 | 56.21% |
| 2 | Praja Parishad Party | 12 | 5 | 26.09% |
| 3 | Harijan Mandal | 6 | 1 | 5.82%% |
| 4 | Praja Socialist Party | 8 | - | 2.36% |
| 5 | Independents | 21 | 1 | 8.91% |

**Table 2.3 Show Number of Seats Won by Different Parties in 1957 Elections**

Source: Election Report of 1957, Government of Jammu and Kashmir

**2.3.3 Assembly Election 1962**

During the 1962 Assembly elections, the National Conference once again came out to be the single largest party. It won 70 out of 75 seats. out of these 75 seats, there were 32 seats in which candidates who were in fray did not faced of these seventy seats, the party did not faced any sort of competition. Thus, these candidates were declared unopposed winners. Praja Parishad Party won 3 seats and the remaining 2 won by independent candidates. This election was important as it witnessed the breaking the shackles of social stigma of women taking part in elections. However, only one woman took part and that was her unsuccessful attempt as she failed to win the seat.

| S.No. | Name of the party | Seats Contested | Seat Won | Percentage of Votes Polled |
|---|---|---|---|---|
| 1 | National Conference | 75 | 7o | 66.96% |
| 2 | Praja Parishad Party | 25 | 3 | 14.47% |
| 3 | Harijan Mandal | 10 | - | 1.89% |
| 4 | Democratic National Conference | 20 | - | 1.89% |
| 5 | Praja Socialist Party | 6 | - | 0.94% |
| 6 | Independents | 38 | 2 | 7.43% |

**Table 2.4 Show Number of Seats Won by Different Parties in 1962 Elections**

Source: Election Report of 1962, Government of Jammu and Kashmir

**2.3.4 Assembly Elections, 1967**

In this election Congress won by 61 seats, the opposition could manage to get only 14 seats, with Bakshi National Conference got majority of votes over 8 seats, 3 won by Jana Singh, one by Rebel Front and two won by independent candidates. In this election there were 75 candidates contesting the election including a woman who contested election but could not get a seat in the state legislature.

| S.No. | Name of the party | Seats Contested | Seat Won | Percentage of Votes Polled |
|---|---|---|---|---|
| 1 | National Conference | 37 | 8 | 21.47% |
| 2 | Congress | 75 | 61 | 53.2% |
| 3 | Jana Sangh | 29 | 3 | 16.45% |
| 4 | Democratic National Conference | 18 | - | 3.15% |
| 5 | Praja Socialist Party | 4 | - | 1.00% |
| 6 | Plebiscite Front | 38 | 1 | 1.65% |
| 7 | Communist Party of India | 3 | - | 0.54% |
| 8 | Independent | 39 | 2 | 7.22% |

**Table 2.5 Show Number of Seats Won by Different Parties in 1967 Elections**

Source: Election Report of 1967, Government of Jammu and Kashmir

**2.3.5Assembly Election, 1972**

In this election there were 75 seats on which elections were held; out of which six contestants were women, which represents 8% of total candidates. In pertinent to this, out of six, 4 women got majority in the election and become members of the assembly for the first time. These members were Zainab Begum from National conference, Hajra Begum, Nirmal Devi and Shanta Bharti were associated with Indian National Congress.

In total there were 342 candidates who contested this election, out of which 8 were women. Thus the total percentage of women containing this election was just 2.33%.

| Constituency | Rank | Candidate | Party | Votes polled | Percentage of voters |
|---|---|---|---|---|---|
| AMIRAKADAL | 1 | Zainab Begum | INC | 7446 | 38.12 |
| HABBAKADAL | 5 | Khemlata Wakhloo | IND | 894 | 6.22 |
| ZADIBAL | 10 | Misra Bano | IND | 287 | 1.54 |
| DODA | 4 | Amina Begum | IND | 979 | 8.08 |
| BANIHAL | 1 | Hajra Begum | INC | uncontested | |
| TIKRI | 1 | Nirmal Devi | INC | 11929 | 63.37 |
| JANDRANGHA ROTA | 1 | Shanta Bharti | INC | 10172 | 62.90 |
| JAMMU SOUTH | 3 | Hussan Ara | IND | 534 | 2.52 |

**Table 2.6 Show Women Contestants 1972 Assembly Elections**

Source: Election commission of India

**2.3.6Assembly Elections, 1977**

In the 1977 legislative assembly elections, Congress was ousted from power at the center. As a result of Accord with the center in 1975, Sheikh was brought back to the power by the center. National Conference under the great leadership of Mirza Mohd and Sheikh Mohammad Abdullah won 47 seats, and other oppositional parties get only 29 seats. Janta Party won 14, Congress (I) 11, Jana Sangh 3, one each by Jamait-i-Islami and Independent candidate. Four women candidates also contested the election but only one could manage to win the seat.

| Constituency | Rank | Candidate | Party | Votes polled | Percentage of voters |
|---|---|---|---|---|---|
| BARI BRAHMINAN | 1 | Gurbachan Kumari | JNP | 8124 | 39.21 |
| HABBAKADAL | 2 | Jag Mohini | JNP | 14084 | 40.92 |
| JAMMU EAST | 6 | Shanta Bharti | IND | 348 | 1.63 |
| BASOHLI | 4 | Parkash Rani | JPN | 2167 | 13.44 |

**Table 2.7 Show Women Contestants 1977 Assembly Elections**

**Source: Election commission of India**

**2.3.7 Assembly Election, 1983**

In 1983 elections of Jammu and Kashmir Assembly turned out one of the most bitterly contested since 1951. It was the very crucial test for the Farooq Abdullah to contest election. In this election national Conference won 43 seats, Congress (I) win 26 seats, peoples Conference and Panther Party 1 and an independent candidate won only one seat each. In the 1983 assembly elections of Jammu and Kashmir, 7 women contested elections, but none of them achieved the success in winning the seat thus all the 76 seats were won by men.

| Constituency | Rank | Candidate | Party | Votes polled | Percentage of voters |
|---|---|---|---|---|---|
| UDHAMPUR | 3 | Jay Mala | IND | 3768 | 13.75 |
| BARI BRAHMANAN | 2 | Gurnbachan kumri | JKN | 10131 | 34.10 |
| RANBIR SINGH PORA | 10 | Vimla Sharma | IND | 44 | 0.14 |
| JAMMU CONTONMENT | 5 | Jaya Mala | IND | 606 | 1.91 |
| MARH (SC) | 11 | Sandal Devi | IND | 133 | 0.53 |
| BASOLI | 3 | Parkash Rani | BJP | 1958 | 7.46 |
| NOWSHERA | 13 | Jaswanti | IND | 47 | 0.14 |

**Table 2.8 Show Women Contestants 1983 Assembly Elections**

Source: Election commission of India

### 2.3.8 Assembly Elections, 1987

In this election there were 76 seats in the assembly, but single women candidate was elected as member of the assembly, other 12 women members could not win any seat in the assembly. The total number of women contestants were 13. Swaran Lata from the Indian National Congress won the seat in the assembly and become member in the state legislature.

| Constituency | Rank | Candidate | Party | Votes polled | % of Voters |
|---|---|---|---|---|---|
| SAMBA | 8 | Sudarshan Sambyal | JPP | 601 | 1.59 |
| BARI BRAHMANAN (SC) | 1 | Swaran Lata | INC | 14539 | 45.51 |
| BARI BRAHMANAN | 2 | Gurnbachan Kumari | IND | 8466 | 26.50 |
| BISHNA (SC) | 8 | Gurnbachan Kumari | IND | 190 | 0.62 |
| BISHNA (SC) | 9 | Suman Dogra | IND | 132 | 0.43 |
| JAMMU WEST (SC) | 13 | Pushplata | IND | 42 | 0.13 |
| JAMMU EAST | 3 | Shanti Devi | IND | 1398 | 4.97 |
| JAMMU EAST | 4 | Jai Mala | JPP | 634 | 2.25 |
| JAMMU EAST | 12 | Ram Piyari Khajuria | IND | 88 | 0.31 |
| JAMMU EAST | 17 | Vidya Devi | IND | 13 | 0.05 |
| CHHAMB | 7 | Sunita Devi | JPP | 172 | 0.58 |
| NOWSHERA | 8 | Jaswnati Devi | IND | 186 | 0.47 |
| RAJOURI | 5 | Saire Begum | IND | 285 | 0.61 |

**Table 2.9 Show Women Contestants 1987 Assembly Elections**

Source: Election commission of India

### 2.3.9Assembly Elections, 1996

In the 1996 assembly elections of Jammu and Kashmir, the number of seats had increased up to 87. In this election 15 women participate in the election for their empowerment and only two of them were elected for legislative assembly. The two women members, who made their entry in the state legislature as ministers of the state were Sakina Itoo who was given the mandate by national conference and Mehbooba Mufti by Indian national congress. In this election National Conference emerged first time single largest party in all regions of the state, 43 out of 46in Kashmir.11 out of 37 in Jammu and 3 out of 4 seats won in Ladakh. The other opposition parties won only few seats.

| Constituency | Rank | Candidate | Party | Votes polled | % of Voters |
|---|---|---|---|---|---|
| HANDWARA | 4 | Taja Begum | JPP | 973 | 5.94 |
| HABBAKADAL | 2 | Sarla Taploo | BJP | 1969 | 19.69 |
| SONAWAR | 5 | Hafiz Begum | IND | 307 | 1.83 |
| BATAMALOO | 4 | Mehbooba | JD | 725 | 5.22 |
| NOORABAD | 1 | Sakina Akther | JKN | 12553 | 53.12 |
| BIJBEHARA | 1 | Mehbooba Mufti | INC | 10051 | 45.28 |
| PAHALGAM | 2 | Gulshan Akther | INC | 4078 | 18.33 |
| LEH | 4 | Spalzes Angmo | BJP | 2474 | 7.63 |
| DODA | 8 | Amrita Bhat | IND | 26 | 0.09 |
| RAMBAN (SC) | 4 | Amrit Barsha | INC | 1197 | 4.53 |
| SAMBA (SC) | 2 | Swaran Lata | INC | 8090 | 24.13 |
| VIJAYPUR | 3 | Rani Gargi Blowria | INC | 5484 | 11.18 |
| VIJAPUR | 4 | Suresh Jamwal | BJP | 4221 | 8.61 |
| VIJAPUR | 5 | Gurbachan Kumari Rana | JD | 2069 | 4.22 |
| GANDHINAGAR | 9 | Kanta Devi Sharma | IND | 194 | 0.37 |

**Table 2.10 Show Women Contestants 1996 Assembly Elections**

Source: Election commission of India

### 2.3.10 Assembly Elections, 2002

In 2002 Assembly elections of the state, the polling was held on the basis of adult franchise for 87 seats. The women contestants were 30 but only two women got elected for the state legislature. Out of 30 total women candidates, 21 candidates were mandate by political parties and 9 contested as independent. It was a positive indication as women took initiative as independent candidates in this way attempted to make a space for themselves. In this Election for the first time National Conference did not rule. The Mufti Mohammad Seyed becomes the Chief Minister of the state for three years and after that Ghulam Nabi Azad succeeded him in the remaining time to complete the term of six years.

| Constituency | Rank | Candidate | Party | Votes polled | % of Voters |
|---|---|---|---|---|---|
| MARH | 10 | Usha Rani | SJP (R) | 157 | 0.33 |
| SUCHETGARH | 13 | Balvinder Kour | JD (S) | 153 | 0.37 |
| SUCHETGARH | 11 | Vijay Chib | IND | 298 | 0.72 |
| R.S.PURA (SC) | 1 | Suman Lata Bhagat | INC | 19669 | 41.40 |
| DEVSAR | 7 | Khalid Mushtaq | NCP | 299 | 1.32 |
| NOORABAD | 2 | Sakeena Akther | JKN | 3301 | 27.15 |
| WACHI | 4 | Nishat Akther | JKN | 2058 | 14.53 |
| PAMPORE | 6 | Hafeeza Begum | IND | 157 | 1.58 |
| BADGAM | 5 | Amreen Badar | INC | 766 | 3.40 |
| CHADOORA | 8 | Shamima | BJP | 178 | 0.65 |
| BATAMALOO | 4 | Shameema Begum | JKNPP | 110 | 2.64 |
| AMIRAKADAL | 5 | Afroza Qadir | JD (U) | 65 | 2.85 |
| AMIRAKADAL | 8 | Khalid Tabasum | IND | 10 | 0.44 |
| SONAWAR | 3 | Khem Lata Wakhloo | INC | 680 | 10.79 |
| SONAWAR | 5 | Hafiza Bagum | IND | 206 | 3.27 |
| HABBAKADAL | 4 | Shameema | JKN | 286 | 13.87 |

**Table 2.11 Show Women Contestants 2002Assembly Elections**

Source: Election commission of India

**2.3.11 Assembly Elections, 2008**

The 2008 assembly elections in the state will be remembered for a host of reasons. The separatist call for boycott elections, but the voter turnout particularly in the conflict-ridden valley of Kashmir was much higher than expected. In this election, there were 1354 candidates, including 468 independent members and 67 women contestants, were in the fray for the 87-member assembly. Out of 67 women contestants only three women were declared successful. The 2008 assembly election had also witnessed unprecedented participation by women- as voters and as candidates, it witnessed double participation of women as compared to the 2002 election in which women were only 30.

Table 2.12 Women representatives in Jammu and Kashmir Assembly from 1967 to 2008.

| S.No. | Elections | Total contestants | Total number of women contestants | Percentage of women contestants | Total number of elected women | Percentage of total women elected |
|---|---|---|---|---|---|---|
| 1 | 1967 | 206 | 1 | 0.49 | 0 | 0 |
| 2 | 1972 | 337 | 6 | 1.78 | 4 | 5.33 |
| 3 | 1977 | 409 | 4 | 0.98 | 1 | 1.32 |
| 4 | 1983 | 512 | 7 | 1.37 | 0 | 0 |
| 5 | 1987 | 528 | 13 | 2.46 | 1 | 1.32 |
| 6 | 1996 | 547 | 15 | 2.74 | 2 | 2.30 |
| 7 | 2002 | 709 | 30 | 4.23 | 2 | 2.30 |
| 8 | 2008 | 1354 | 67 | 4.94 | 3 | 3.44 |

**Table 2.12 Women representatives in Jammu and Kashmir Assembly from 1967 to 2008**

Source: Statistical Data on Election, 1967 to 2014, Election Department, J&K Government, Jammu and data culled from press clippings.

2.3.12 Assembly Elections, 2014

The last Jammu and Kashmir legislative assembly election was held in the 25 Nov to 20 December 2014. Out of 87 seats PDP won 28 seats, BJP won 25 seats, JKNC won 15 seats and INC won 12 seats in the state. 26 women candidates also contest the elections, though the number was for more less than previous election held in 2008. The main reasons behind this were the continuous mass upsurge and human rights violation out of 26 only 2 women got majority in the said election and became members of the legislature.

| Year | Total seats | Women candidate | Elected women | Runner up |
|---|---|---|---|---|
| 1962 | 75 | 01 | 00 | 00 |
| 1967 | 75 | 01 | 00 | 00 |
| 1972 | 75 | 06 | 04 | 00 |
| 1977 | 76 | 04 | 01 | 01 |
| 1983 | 76 | 07 | 00 | 01 |
| 1987 | 76 | 13 | 01 | 01 |
| 1996 | 87 | 15 | 02 | 03 |
| 2002 | 87 | 30 | 02 | 02 |
| 2008 | 87 | 67 | 03 | 04 |
| 2014 | 87 | 26 | 02 | 01 |
| | Total | 117 | 16 | 13 |

Table 2.13 shows Women's Representation in Jammu and Kashmir assembly from 1962 to 2014

Source: http :// eci. nic .in / eci -main 1/Election statistics .aspx.

In the above-mentioned data about the women representation in the state of Jammu and Kashmir very low as compared to other states of India. From 1962 to 2014 only 171 women candidates have electorally tried and tested their fate, out of which only 16 have emerged as successors and other 101 women became losers. It means there is need and necessity, to develop political consciousness among the women and empower them in all aspects of life especially in political fields, so that they can become decision makers in the state and will improve their conditions.

Women do not form a political constituency anywhere in India, much less so in Jammu and Kashmir. Here women have never been seen as a factor to change the electoral outcome. No specific appeal is made to women as voters and political parties do not encourage their participation as voters or contestants.

The only activity where women parties in large numbers is that of voting. But even here there remains a gap between male and female voters. The gap may be narrowing at certain periods, but remains nevertheless. During 1972 general elections there was a huge gap of 15.35 % between men and women voters. The percentage of women voters during this election was merely 53.92 % while it was 69.27 % for men. The gap was reduced in 1977 to 12.75 %. This situation, however, was much more encouraging during 1983 and 1987 elections when the women's participation as voters was as high as 70.48 % and 70.36 % respectively (as compared to 75.56 % and 78.65 % of men respectively.) however, the participation of women as voters was affected severely in the period of militancy. In 1996 elections, only 46.08 % women cast their votes in comparison to 60.57 % of men. The percentage of women voters was further reduced during 2002 elections. Though the overall voter participation was affected and even among men only 48.26 % men cast their votes, but the number of women who cast their votes was still lower. Only 38.27 % of women voters exercised their right to franchise in this election.

There are various reasons behind the low participation of women in legislative assembly, illiteracy, patriarchal families, less exposure, conflict area, a huge contingent of forces and less interest of political parties for the mandate of women and boycott call by separatists.

| Constituency | Women MLA | Party | Year |
|---|---|---|---|
| Hazratbal | Asiea | PDP | 2014 |
| | Shameema Firdouse | NC | 2014 |
| Amirakadal | Zainab Begum | NC | 1972 |
| Wachi | Mehbooba Mufti | PDP | 2008 |
| Noorabad | Sakina Itoo | NC | 2008 |
| | Sakina Itoo | NC | 1996 |
| Bijbehara | Mehbooba Mufti | INC | 1996 |
| Phalgam | Mehbooba Mufti | PDP | 2002 |
| Banihal | Hajra Begum | INC | 1972 |
| Basohli | Kanta Andotra | INC | 2004 |
| Tikri | Normal Devi | INC | 1972 |
| Jandrah Gharota | Shanta Bharti | INC | 1972 |

Table 2.14 Shows General constituency: winning women candidates

Source: http :// eci .nic .in / eci -main 1/Election statistics .aspx.

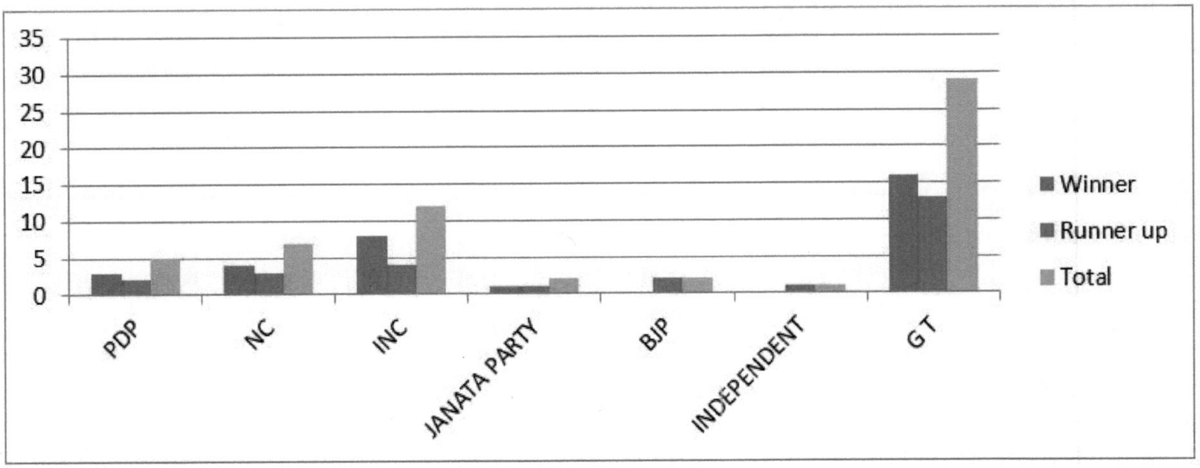


Fig. 2.1Status of women in various parties in Jammu and Kashmir Assembly

2.4 Women Representation in panchayat

The local self-government is the ideal concept in the country of India. The name and structure of these local bodies may change from state to state but its goal remains always the same as to involve the common people to formulate their local plans, implement and monitor them. Panchayati Raj Institutions make villages self –sufficient to solve their day-to-day needs and determine their new goals. During the medieval period, in spite of many political changes in the cities and towns, the system of local institutions or panchayats in the village never altered. The Panchayat Raj in Jammu and Kashmir has its own ideal history.

Three-Tier Model

The three-tier system provides by this act consisting of Halqa Panchayat, Block Development Council and Development Board. In addition, there is Panchayati Adalat for every Halqa.

In 2001 Panchayati elections were both male and female participates. In the below table shows women representation in this election.

| District/ State | Total no. of Sarpanch's elected | Women Sarpanch's Elected | Total no. of Panchs elected | Women Panchs elected |
|---|---|---|---|---|
| Srinagar | 67 | - | 247 | 1 |
| Kupwara | 168 | - | 915 | 2 |
| Baramulla | 162 | - | 902 | 4 |
| Leh | 68 | - | 448 | 36 |
| Kargil | 65 | - | 453 | 2 |
| Budgam | 61 | - | 3 15 | 2 |
| Anantnag | 251 | 02 | 1190 | 24 |
| Pulwama | 202 | | 684 | 24 |
| Total Kashmir division | 1044 | 02 | 5155 | 71 |
| Jammu | 294 | 1 | 2443 | 42 |
| Kathua | 182 | 1 | 1389 | 23 |
| Poonch | 115 | 1 | 1026 | 13 |
| Udhampur | 212 | 3 | 1792 | 38 |
| Doda | 216 | 1 | 1698 | 26 |
| Rajouri | 160 | 1 | 1364 | 24 |
| Total (Jammu division) | 1 179 | 7 | 9714 | 166 |
| Total (J&K) | 2,223 | 9 | 14,888 | 237 |

Table 2.15 shows Women's representation in 2001 Panchayati Raj Elections

Source: Rural development department of Jammu and Kashmir

The provision was changed by Jammu and Kashmir Panchayati Raj Act in 2003 which granted 33 percent reservation to women in Halqa Panchayats. After analyzing, the above-cited information in table 2.15, it becomes clear that Jammu division is ranging from 0.5% in respect of Sarpanches 1.70% in respect of panches and Kashmir division is ranging from 0.19% in respect of Sarpanches to 1.37% in respect of panches. During the period of these five years many developmental works took place and woman was seen, active participants. But, the conditions in Kashmir remained intense due to which many panches and Sarpanches resigned on the basis of threats. On 17th December 2003, the Jammu and Kashmir Panchayat Raj (Second Amendment Bill) was passed to ensure effective participation of woman and other weaker sections of society in the functioning of local- self-government. On 18th June 2004 as SRO 181, a notification came and provided reservation for panch seats to woman and other backward classes in every Halqa Panchayat, with rotation after every general election.

This Act provided a base to woman of Jammu and Kashmir to represent them in local self-government. Conditions in 2006 were not good enough for contesting elections, so elections were suspended. In 2011, the Government could conduct Panchayati Raj elections in 16 phases from 13 April to 18 June for 4130 Sarpanches and 20559 panches on nonparty basis with great transparency. As per the Rural development records woman succeeded in gaining one-third of panch seats but a female Sarpanches is still rare, as only 28 women managed to win.

| Districts | No. of Sarpanch's elected | Women Sarpanch's Elected | No of Panchs elected | Women Panch's elected |
|---|---|---|---|---|
| Kupwara | 355 | 0 | 2694 | 937 |
| Baramulla | 350 | 2 | 2352 | 714 |
| Bandipora | 114 | 0 | 865 | 288 |
| Ganderbal | 103 | 0 | 719 | 227 |
| Srinagar | 10 | 0 | 78 | 25 |
| Budgam | 282 | 0 | 2108 | 686 |
| Pulwama | 166 | 0 | 841 | 218 |
| Shopian | 103 | 1 | 620 | 177 |
| Kulgam | 158 | 0 | 1040 | 324 |
| Anantnag | 296 | 0 | 2037 | 673 |
| Leh | 93 | 0 | 588 | 199 |
| Kargil | 95 | 0 | 656 | 204 |
| Kashmir Province | 2125 | 3 | 14,598 | 4672 |
| Doda | 231 | 1 | 1420 | 489 |
| Ramban | 124 | 1 | 831 | 292 |
| Reasi | 146 | 2 | 992 | 354 |
| Udhampur | 204 | 5 | 1543 | 548 |
| Kathua | 244 | 4 | 1642 | 562 |
| Samba | 100 | 1 | 724 | 260 |
| Jammu | 295 | 2 | 2153 | 746 |
| Rajour | 289 | 3 | 1972 | 690 |
| Poonch | 189 | 4 | 1537 | 524 |
| Kishtwar | 134 | 0 | 836 | 287 |
| Jammu province | 1956 | 23 | 13,650 | 4752 |
| Total | 4082 | 26 | 28248 | 9424 |

**Table 2.16 shows Total number of women elected as Sarpanch's and Panch's in J&K, 2011**

Source: Rural development department of Jammu and Kashmir

Analysis of above table shows that out of 4082 sarpanch posts in 22 districts only 26 women could manage to win success rate of less than one percent (0.70%) However 9071 woman Panches managed to win out of 20559 posts success rate of more than forty-four percent (44.12).

After a gap of seven years the panchayat elections were held in 2018 which were held in 2016. In this election women representation decrease as participants because due to various reasons like continues conflict in the state, boycott call etc.

| Serial No | Districts | Selected Sarpanch's | Women Sarpanch's | Selected Panch's | Women Panch's |
|---|---|---|---|---|---|
| 1 | Kupwara | 356 | 125 | 3161 | 586 |
| 2 | Baramulla | 365 | 60 | 3330 | 323 |
| 3 | Bandipora | 108 | 31 | 514 | 123 |
| 4 | Ganderbal | 70 | 21 | 297 | 68 |
| 5 | Srinagar | 10 | 4 | 39 | 3 |
| 6 | Budgam | 122 | 32 | 516 | 138 |
| 7 | Pulwama | 24 | 5 | 73 | 6 |
| 8 | Shopian | 20 | 4 | 68 | 12 |
| 9 | Kulgam | 35 | 13 | 121 | 24 |
| 10 | Anantnag | 166 | 50 | 634 | 120 |
| Total of Kashmir Division | | 1276 | 345 | 8753 | 1403 |
| 11 | Leh | 93 | 31 | 687 | 117 |
| 12 | Kargil | 98 | 21 | 775 | 196 |
| Total of Ladakh Division | | 191 | 52 | 1462 | 313 |
| 13 | Doda | 237 | 91 | 1683 | 488 |
| 14 | Ramban | 140 | 49 | 901 | 287 |
| 15 | Reasi | 153 | 58 | 1191 | 375 |
| 16 | Udhampur | 236 | 78 | 1848 | 592 |
| 17 | Kathua | 257 | 92 | 1943 | 583 |
| 18 | Samba | 100 | 31 | 788 | 251 |
| 19 | Jammu | 306 | 104 | 2407 | 771 |
| 20 | Rajour | 312 | 108 | 2415 | 745 |
| 21 | Poonch | 228 | 81 | 1856 | 596 |
| 22 | Kishtwar | 136 | 42 | 892 | 271 |
| Total of Jammu Division | | 2105 | 734 | 15924 | 4959 |
| Total of Jammu and Kashmir | | 3572 | 1131 | 26139 | 6675 |

Table 2.17 shows Women's representation in 2018 Panchayati Raj Elections

Source: Rural development department of Jammu and Kashmir

The total number of women Sarpanch representatives in the 2018 Jammu and Kashmir panchayat elections were1131out of 3572 with a percentage 31.66 %.The total number of women panch representatives in the 2018 Jammu and Kashmir panchayat elections, were 6675 out of 26139 with a percentage 31.66 %.The representation of women in 2018 panchayat elections is low as compared to 2011. In 2011 elections, there was 29.22% women representation and in 2018 it was 26.72%. There are various reasons behind the low participation of women.

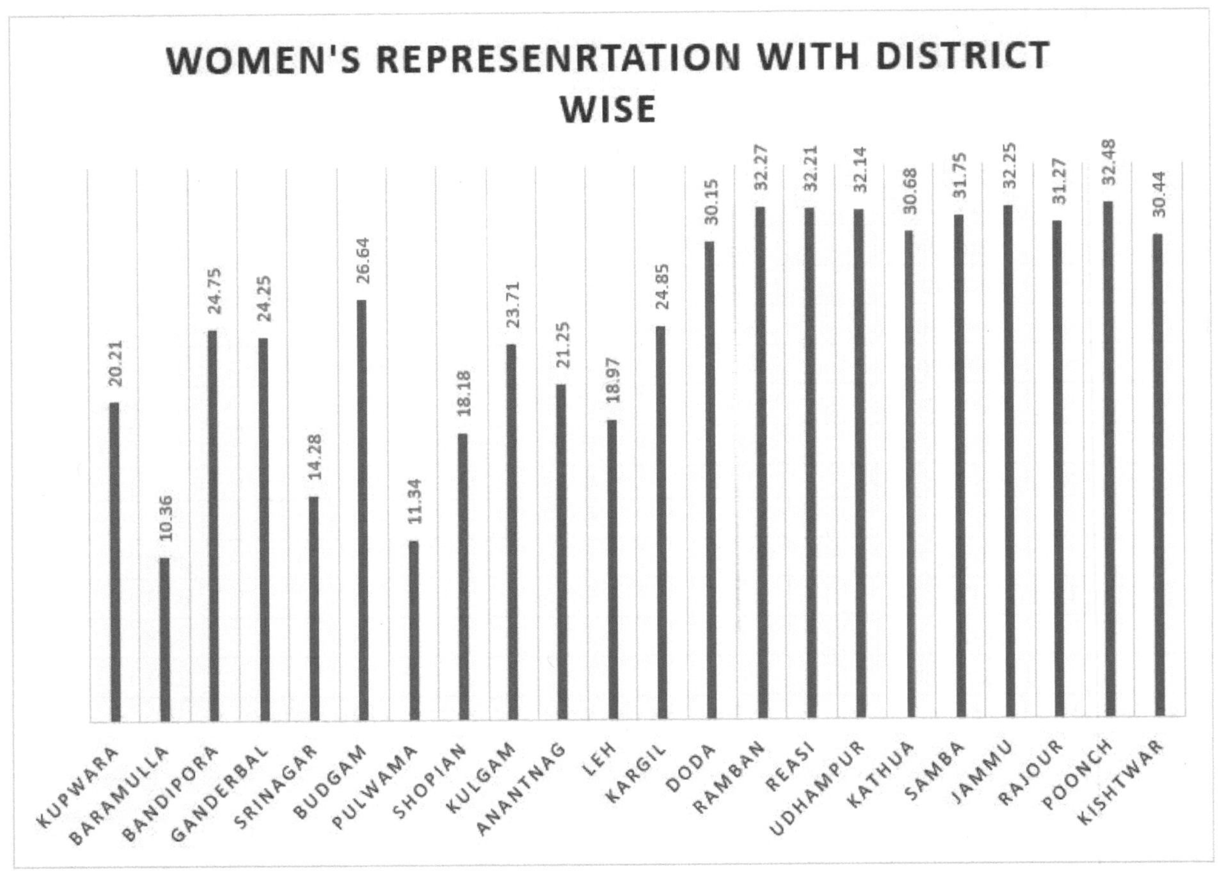


Fig. 2.2 women representation in panchayat elections of 2018

2.5 Urban Local Governance in J&K

The municipal elections of 2018 in the state of Jammu and Kashmir were held in four phases 8, 10, 13 and 16 October. The number of wards (electoral constituencies) was 1145 out of which 244 wards (4.7) were uncontested. Out of a total of around17 lakh electors, the final state voter turnout was 35.1% that is 5.97 lakh electors voted. Major political parties in the state boycotted the elections NC and PDP.

In Srinagar Municipal Corporation getting a poll percentage 1.8% and in Jammu Municipal Corporation where percentage of voter turnout was 66.2% that is higher than Kashmir.

| Districts | Total No. of Wards | Total No. of elected members | Elected women |
|---|---|---|---|
| Kupwara | 39 | 36 | 13 |
| Baramulla | 88 | 68 | 17 |
| Bandipora | 43 | 40 | 13 |
| Ganderbal | 17 | 17 | 6 |
| Srinagar corporation | 278 | 74 | 30 |
| Budgam | 72 | 44 | 16 |
| Pulwama | 69 | 12 | 2 |
| Shopian | 17 | 13 | 4 |
| Kulgam | 40 | 16 | 5 |
| Anantnag | 137 | 92 | 30 |
| Leh | 13 | 13 | 4 |
| Kargil | 13 | 13 | 4 |
| Kashmir division Total | 826 | 438 | 144 |
| Doda | 37 | 37 | 12 |
| Ramban | 20 | 20 | 6 |
| Reasi | 26 | 26 | 9 |
| Udhampur | 41 | 41 | 14 |
| Kathua | 80 | 80 | 25 |
| Samba | 37 | 37 | 16 |
| Jammu | 79 | 79 | 23 |
| Rajouri | 62 | 62 | 10 |
| Poonch | 30 | 30 | 10 |
| Kishtwar | 13 | 13 | 4 |
| Jammu corporation | 449 | 75 | 22 |
| Jammu division total | 874 | 450 | 151 |
| Grand total | 1700 | 888 | 295 |

Table 2.18 shows Elected women representatives in the Urban Elections in 2018

Source: ceojammukashmir.nic.in

In 2018 Municipal elections the percentage of women was seen low as in the panchayat elections. In this election in Jammu Division total elected persons are 888 out of which only 295 were women members. In Kashmir division including Leh and Kargil 438 out of which only 144 are women candidates. In Jammu, the women percentage in municipal elections is 33.22% and in Kashmir, it is lower than Jammu 32.87%. The government of Jammu and Kashmir has taken steps to make the women participation more and more in the grass root level.

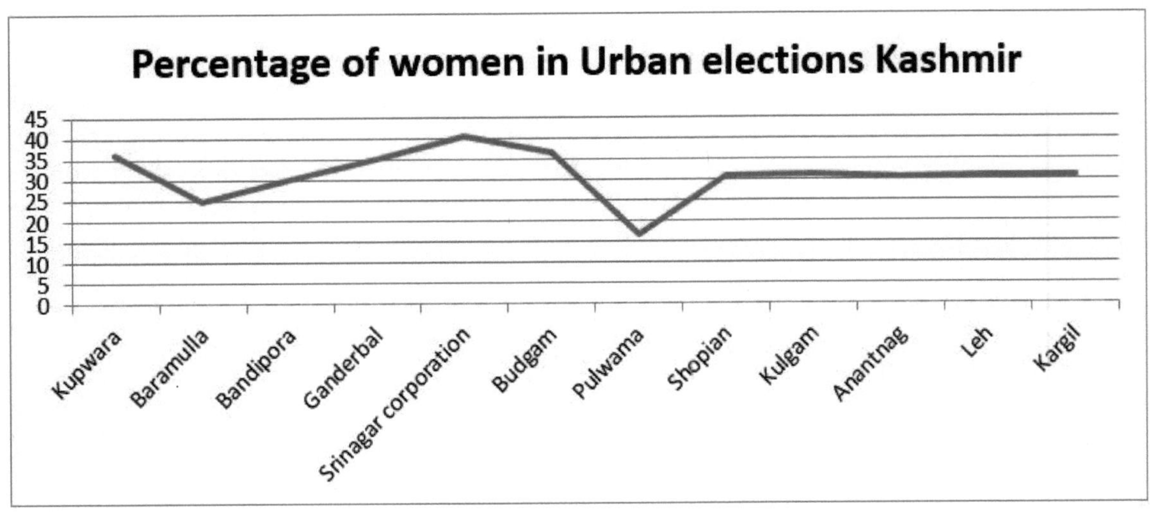


Fig. 2.3 Percentage of women in Urban Elections in Kashmir 2018

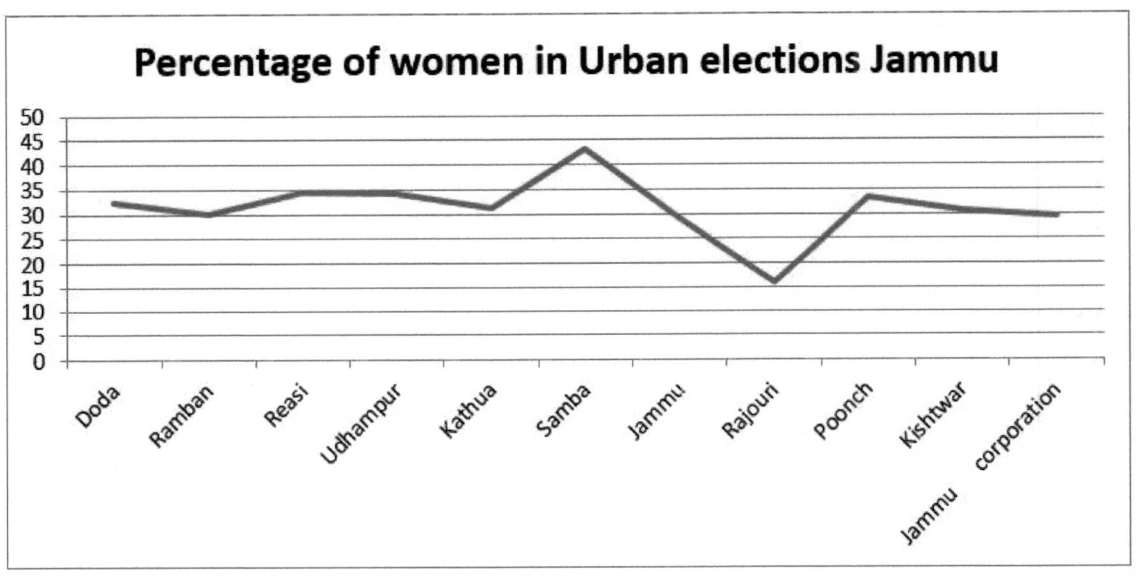


Fig. 2.4 Percentage of Women in Urban Elections Jammu 2018

| S.No. | Elections | Total contestants | Total women contestants | Percentage of total women contestants | Total number of women elected | Percentage of total women elected |
|---|---|---|---|---|---|---|
| 1 | 1971 | 32 | 0 | 0 | 0 | 0 |
| 2 | 1977 | 29 | 2 | 6.90 | 2 | 33.33 |
| 3 | 1980 | 25 | 0 | 0 | 0 | 0 |
| 4 | 1984 | 48 | 1 | 2.08 | 1 | 16.67 |
| 5 | 1989 | 63 | 1 | 1.59 | 0 | 0 |
| 6 | 1996 | 110 | 8 | 7.27 | 0 | 0 |
| 07 | 1998 | 86 | 2 | 2.33 | 0 | 0 |
| 8 | 1999 | 83 | 6 | 7.23 | 0 | 0 |
| 9 | 2004 | 83 | 4 | 4.82 | 1 | 16.67 |
| 10 | 2009 | 81 | 2 | 2.46 | 0 | 0 |
| 11 | 2014 | 83 | 3 | 3.61 | 1 | 16.67 |
| 12 | 2019 | 83 | 3 | 3.61 | 0 | 0 |

2.19 Table showing the performance of women in parliamentary elections in J&K, 1971-2014

Source: Statistical Data on Election, Election Department, Jammu and Kashmir Government, Jammu, and data culled from press clippings.

The empowerment is the slogan of every country of the world both developed and under developed countries. As we known various agencies of government and non-government organizations are working on it, in a day and night but were not successful in it. In the 20th century women were in very less number in the legislative assembly and local panchayats. These are the apex institutions that can help the women folk in the empowerment of women. In the state of Jammu and Kashmir, the women representation in the legislative assembly and in local self-government decreases as shown by data of 2008 elections, there were 67 women representatives as compared to 26 women representatives of the 2014. In local self-government the women representation was not satisfactory, it was a great opportunity for women to take part in decision making process but due to certain problems such as political disorder, patriarchal societies, less interest of political parties to give mandate to women, unawareness, poverty and illiteracy. Government of Jammu and Kashmir should take various steps for the increase of women participation in legislative assembly and local self-government even though some reservations have been given to women but are not sufficient. The state actors and non-state actors must jointly come forward to raise the issue of the rights of women and provide them equal opportunity and do not segregate them in any field.

Reference


1. Bhatia, N. (1990). *The Social Determinants of political participation among women and role of state.* PhD Thesis, submitted in the department of political science, university of Jammu, December, p.22.
2. Qureshi, Z. M. (1979). *Elections and state politics of india.* Sandeepa parkashan, Delhi.p.40.
3. Ibid, p.43
4. Anand, A. S. (1998). *The constitution of Jammu and Kashmir: it's Developments & Comments.* (Third Edition) Delhi: Universal Law Publishing Co. Pvt. Ltd., P. 30.
5. Proclamation cited in Anand, Ibid, p,110.
6. Tajuddin, M. and Mann, S. (2013-14). *politics of identities in Jammu and Kashmir, A contested terrain.* Jay Kay Book House, Jammu Tawi-180001 (J&K).
7. Chowdhary, R. Prashar, A. Vivek, P. (ed) (2007). *Elections in Jammu and Kashmir.* Kashmir Times, Publications, Residence Road, Jammu-180001.p.11.

8. Ibid p. 12.
9. Pre-Election atmosphere of terror was created so that no party candidate dared to come forth to contest elections.
10. As per the percentage of voters, Bakshi, National Conference did create a base for itself in the valley.
11. Chowdhary, R. Prashar, A. (2007). Elections in Jammu and Kashmir. Kashmir Times, Publications, Residency Road, Jammu-180001.p. 141.
12. Sharma, Y. R. (2002). *Political dynamics of Jammu and Kashmir.* Published by kuldeep Anand for Radh aKrishan& co., Jammu-180001 (J&K).
13. Sharma,Y. R. (2002). Political Dynamics of Jammu and Kashmir. Published by Kuldeep Anand for Radha Krishan Anand& co, Jammu-180001 (J&K) and Printed at Mehra Offset Press, Delhi.p.227.
14. INC and PDP both fielded 4 women contestants each. NC and Samajwadi Janta party (Rashtriya) SJP(R) gave tickets to 3 women candidates each. 2 Jammu and Kashmir National Panthers Party –(JKNPP) women candidates got the mandate of the party while Janta Dal (United)- JD(U), Bhartiya Janta party- BJP, Nationalist congress party-NCP, lok Jan Shakti party- LJNSP and Janta Dal Secular-JDS made bet on 1 women candidate each.
15. Aslam, M. (1996).*Local self-Government in India: Retrospect and prospect in Role of local self-Government in Rural Development*. AARRO, New Delhi.
16. Nisar, S.(2001). *Development of Local Self Government in J&K State (1846-1947).* Srinagar: Gulshan Publishers.

CHAPTER XXI

# Domestic Violence

Ramya Arvind
Asssistant professor
Department of Electronics and communication engineering,
Sengunthar Engineering college,
TamilNadu
rmyaarvind@gmail.com

## *Introduction*

House, Home, Sweet home, whatever we call it, the most loving place everyone wants to be in. The place where everything starts love, life, happiness. It also has a dark secret that everybody hides, everybody from the poorest to the wealthiest, happiest to the loneliest. No one could barely escape.

We can even compare it to the black hole in the space from which nothing can escape. It took centuries to confirm the existence of the black hole even with all these advanced technologies. Likewise how did we miss the black hole of our society that too in our vicinity? Did we missed it or hidden it from the limelight?

Shall we have a little talk about this black hole?

Yes, only we women can talk about this because we are the ones who are being engulfed by this giant black hole.

Shall we say the name of this forbidden?

Say it loudly at least now

*"DOMESTIC VIOLENCE".*

Now everyone can relate why this is compared with the black hole. As even light cannot escape the black hole, none of the women could have escaped this silent monster dwelling amongst us. Everyone reading this book has definitely come across this monster at least once in their life.

'Once in a life time' is a phrase suitable for only the rarest condition. Once in a day, once in a week, daily or on a regular basis is the apt term.

There arises a big question why particularly women? In a broad sense it seems to be related to both genders. But when you zoom in or create a Venn diagram, the majority will be women. A proud moment right? Is this the majority we dreamt? Shameful...

Domestic, the word that relates to a very close, habited place with our bonded ones. Just adding the word "violence" to it makes it the most painful crime against women.

Imagine how painful it will be for the women to be insulted, cheated, neglected and harassed by their own kith and kin. Violence doesn't mean you have to be actually physically hit by someone. A single word, a single negligible look will be enough to make someone feel inferior. As the victims of the domestic violence are overwhelmingly women, this often happens in the relationship either marital or living together.

Actually Domestic violence is often used as a synonym for intimate partner violence, which is committed by one of the people in the intimate relation against the other person.

In a broad sense, domestic violence involves violence against children, parents or elderly. But in any category when you notice, feminine gender is the most suffered, as though it is take it for granted category. Domestic violence happens widely to most women irrespective of caste, religion, social or economic status. Equally affecting everyone. At last we have achieved equality in one aspect.

## *CAUSES*

There should always be a cause for every effect. What do you think will be the cause? Each case will have a different cause and effect. But when you categorise the causes of domestic violence, mostly all causes fall under three categories and those are as follows

- Gender Inequality
- Economic Dependence
- Emotional Attachment

In a single view, we can see all pieces of the puzzle falls in the place and can instantly judge the victims are mostly women. From ancient times we are made to believe that men are stronger than women. Women means soft – hearted and psychologically weak. We have grown up hearing these words and are unknowingly inscribed our hearts. We are made weak by the society. Not all men are strong and all women are weak. Everyone has their own strength and weakness.

The above three main causes has one major root cause. Unbelievable. We have slowly and finally has reached the base which has given life to this monster and is keeping alive. What is it?

This basic idea is transmitted or inscribed in every individual's DNA since time unknown. But the idea is very clearly and cleverly transmitted to every human mind.

*"Chastity is only for women. It has nothing to do with men."*

How ridiculous it is? So automatically it implies that women should always be accompanied by men or should need the shelter of men. But who cares that the danger awaits in the shelter itself.

There is a famous saying,

*"The law maker should not be the law breaker".*

In this aspect, every men is a law breaker. In one or other way they are doing this to women whether intentionally or unknowingly. Yes we can accept the fact there are men who really treat women good but the number when compared to the majority is infinitesimal.

## *GENDER INEQUALITY*

Two genders are separately created by the God to care each other not to dominate one over other. Everything should be mutual. Respect, Love, Taking care everything should be mutual. But there is always an imbalance in this aspect. Men are always considered superior over women. This is socially induced and is inscribed in every man's DNA.

Researches shows that where there is a higher rate of gender inequality, the crime rate is higher. Yes, Domestic violence should be considered a crime, a serious crime .In countries where family setup prevails, there is a greater chance for this violence. This doesn't mean it is not happening outside marriage. But the percentage is higher. Due to this inequality, women are abused verbally, physically, sexually by men of their own family.

According to the World Economic forum's Global gender gap report 2021, India ranks 140$^{th}$ among 156 countries, becoming the third worst performer in South Asia. It slips 28 places as it was 112$^{th}$ place in 2020. This ranking is done based on the participation of women in various sectors like business, education and political. The survey further says that one-third of women are illiterate when compared to men.

In addition it says, one in four women has faced intimate violence in her lifetime. There comes our area of interest. Watch the term "INTIMATE VIOLENCE". What it means? Yes, Domestic violence. According to available statistics from around the world, about 33 per cent of the women have experienced violence in one form or the other in their intimate relationship at some point in their life (WHO, 1997).The crime rate is so high and unacceptable.

## *ECONOMIC DEPENDENCE*

Money is the base for many problems in the world. Even here it plays a vital role. Economic dependency of women is one of the key factor which defines her degree of freedom in private and public life. Another supporting factor is a culturally induced tradition in which men are the bread winner of the family and women are the caretaker. No worries in taking care of our blood and born but do women get the due respect?

For every small expenses, they have to depend on men of their family. In most cases even if she asks, it is denied. Even the basic needs like sanitary napkins are mere dream for many women even today. Mostly the needs of the women comes under the category of cost cutting while forming a family budget. The provider holds the monopoly and the dependent has to or made to oblige in order to make a living.

A happy family is a blessing. But nothing comes free of cost. Women are made to sacrifice their desires and yet live a happy and contented life. How ironic it is?

## *EMOTIONAL ATTACHMENT*

The phrase itself implies it is the barrier cum fence which every women puts around herself. Women think of it as a fence but does she know that the same fence is used as a barrier against her. Nature has given women a precious quality of giving a new life. She takes care of her children and family. Each and every women loves it but that was used as a main tool to emotionally make her oblige in all aspects. Even if the women has a difference of opinion in family decisions , her opinion is mostly neglected and what is more surprising is she is made to believe that her decision is wrong and also men has wider view of the society as they are prone to such situations.

Moreover, the culturally induced tradition that women should always oblige, adjust and adapt to their family members is a supportive factor for this emotional attachment. From the childhood, women are brought up with this idea inscribed in their mind. So even when they realise that they are being emotionally attacked, it becomes very difficult for them to come out of this circle. Their children's future and the family's social status are the two key reasons which make every women bound to their family's decisions. Even if the partner has an extra marital affair, women in the family are silenced due to these two reasons. Every second of a woman's life is spend for their family members. Yet the basic trust she keeps over her partner is mostly broken. How heart-breaking is it? It will be a life time deception for a woman. Yet many women are living with this scarred heart for the sake of their children.

But if the situation is vice-versa (there are always exceptions), the reaction of the men and the society is entirely different. Woman is openly accused of this conviction and mostly there will be divorce.

Domestic violence can also be learned through observation. If a male child sees his father abusing his mother, he might thought it as a usual male behaviour and might learn to do it in future which is very dangerous. (Anne.L.Ganley , Ph.D. , 1995)

Marriage and motherhood plays the behind the screen role for this emotional attachment. Like other causes, this one can't be categorized good or bad since the divider line is very delicate.

## *TYPES OF DOMESTIC VIOLENCE*

Violence and predation have been a part of human life for centuries. (Gavin de Becker,1997). Violence doesn't means one should be hit physically. Even playing with one's feelings, controlling one's activity or compelling oneself to do an action, everything is a form of violence.

Accordingly, the violence can be

- Verbal
- Physical
- Emotional
- Economic
- Sexual

So many ways women are abused! Even some women are not even aware that they are being abused in these ways and they are taking that as a part of their life

Marriage is an important thing in a women's life. It can also be considered a life changer. When married to a right person, it becomes an elixir of their life. But when married to a wrong person, it becomes their hell. Marital relationship is considered a key factor in the cases of domestic violence because all types above mentioned are likely to happen in the married life.

## *VERBAL ABUSE*

Verbal abuse is the most frequently occurring type of domestic violence. Everyone has been witnessing this type of abuse regularly in their life. We have seen our mothers and other women of our family undergoing this daily in their life. Verbal abuse cannot be taken easily because it is the most hurting one. Imagine insulted, neglected or scolded by our own life partner on a daily basis. Who can withstand that? Only a wife can.

By definition we can say verbal abuse is a range of words or behaviours used to manipulate, intimidate and maintain power and control over someone. These include insults, humiliation and ridicule, the silent treatment and attempts to scare, isolate and control.

Now it is easy to imagine the whole picture happening in every house. These behaviours are just as serious as other forms of abuse and may damage self-worth and well-being. This behaviours are not obvious from the beginning but as time passes you can differentiate these behaviours from the normal argument.

Constant humiliation in front of others is the first and foremost type of verbal abuse a woman experiences in the family. In any matter of discussion, women are denied chance to express their view and silenced as though she has no knowledge of anything. Even in the simple basic matters like dress selection or house interiors, she is not allowed to decide. When these arguments continues in front of the children, eventually in the due course, they will also start humiliating their mother. How painful for a women to be humiliated by her own family?

Even calling by name can tell you everything. The attitude will be clearly shown. They do it purposefully to show their power and control over her. Constant yelling and continuous sarcasm in front of others are done to belittle her. These things are done to make her feel inferior and to lower her self-confidence.

Continuous criticism and consent degradation for every action she performs is done in order to make her feel as though she is not even worth a penny without her partner. If she is a home maker alone, she is always criticized for not earning and also blamed for being idle in house. She transforms house into a home. She singlehandedly manages all household chores and saves so much of her family money. It should never be compared on the money basis.

For every mistake or a plan gone wrong, she is being blamed irrespective of the reason. In spite of accusation, she is not even allowed to give an explanation. Even the basis of our jurisdiction is that not even one innocent person should be punished. But in real life, daily thousands of innocent women are being punished.

Gas lighting or Circular arguments keep on emerging as a never ending cycle. It isn't unusual for two people to agree or argue about the same thing more than once until they found a common ground. But the abusers will reignite the old argument again and again just to push one's buttons, never intending to meet in the middle.

One cannot imagine how women are ill-treated inside their own home. But what is the end to all these abuses? Is it the fate of most women? There is no single answer but this depends on individual circumstances. How could one avoid these circumstances?

### *REMEDIES*

Reasoning and arguing with an abuser can be tempting but it is of no use. So somehow set your boundaries and avoid engaging in arguments. Get help and support from other family members. And also limit your exposure to the abuser as much as possible though it is very hard to get isolation inside the same house. Final step any women can think is to cut all ties with the abusive partner. But this is not easy if they have children. In those cases, one can find it helpful to seek counsellor's help. Sometimes an outsider's perspective can help you solve things.

## *PHYSICAL ABUSE*

Nature has given no one the right to assault the other living being. But Being a human, how could one do such an unhumanly act?

By definition, Physical abuse is an intentional act of causing any injury to a person. In most cases, children and women are the victims in the case of domestic violence. Physical abusement can be direct or indirect. In direct physical abusement, direct body to body contact occurs. Actions like slapping, hitting, punching, kicking, shaking, suffocating, pinching, biting, scratching etc., comes under this type. In indirect physical abuse, there is no direct body to body contact. Acts like spitting at someone, throwing things over are examples of indirect physical abuse.

## *CHILD PHYSICAL ABUSE*

Usually children are affected by this abusement as a result of parenting measure for keeping up the child's discipline. As an overview, this may seem acceptable but it should be avoided. Main causes for this child physical abusement are usually little exposure to positive parental approaches, stressful family environment etc.

### *EFFECTS*

Children who are victims of physical abuse faces many problems physically as well as psychologically. Physical problems include any injuries due to abusement. Psychological effects include aggressive behaviour, risk of substance use disorder (SUD), sometimes due to repeated abusement they will act as if they are immune to this act.

### *REMEDIES*

Parents should be learned to treat and handle children politely. Children should be taught disciplinary principles in a playful manner like through stories, games etc. The Parent – children together time should be managed to increase their bonding. Children are the future of every nation so they should be brought up with utmost care.

## *ADULT PHYSICAL ABUSE*

Adult physical abuse is seen as someone uses power or control over someone to cause harm or distress. The abuser could be in a closer proximity or in a close relationship with the victim. The abuser could be a partner, relative or a family member, neighbour etc. There are many factors that increase the risk of being physically abused such as age, specially-abled person, economically dependent persons etc. But sometimes circumstances also become the reason such as isolation, financial conditions etc.

In majority of adult physical cases, women are the victims. Men predominate women in all situations .In a closer conduct, wives are physically abused by their husbands. In the relationship, this will start as an argument then developed into a verbal abuse and finally results in physical abuse. Some men are aggressive by nature and short-tempered and they easily slap or hit their wife frequently. Women should not be considered as a property of men.

### *CAUSES*

There may be many causes for this typical physical abuse but the major reason here in India is Alcohol drinking. Many women has lost their entire life marrying a drunkard. Lakhs and lakhs of women in India are suffering because of this alcohol drinking. Those women are physically abused like slapped or hit daily by their husbands. No one cares for these poor human beings and are considered as though it is the duty of the wife to accept all things and should take care of the family as a bread winner of the family. She has to earn for her children's education also. Is she even can work and earn peacefully? No, even there she is being abused. But that should be considered a separate different unacceptable problem which shakes the basic morality of the society. Is it the fate of the women to accept all these and live a miserable life?

Another important reason for this type of violence in India is Dowry. Though the act of giving or receiving dowry is a crime, it is not fully eradicated. It is or should be given in the form of gift by the girl's parents. Due to the bride's endless desire, this continues over lifetime and if denied results in physical abuse sometimes death of the victim. In most cases, physical wounds, bruises, burns, cuts are seen and they are the signs that the person is being physically abused.

### *EFFECTS*

Physical abuse can cause long-term physical and mental problems not only for the victim but also their family. Physical injuries can be permanent and can make the victim paralysed for their lifetime and be dependent on others which makes the situation even worse. This may pave the way for another form of abuses. Mental problems include such that the victim feel inferior and fear everything and their confidence level drops. Fear and anxiety rises which causes many further health related problems.

*Case study example*

http://ssr-net.com/issues/Vol_4_No_1_June_2018/4.pdf

### *REMEDIES*

Women should seek the help of other family members. In the utmost conditions, they should be ready to cut all ties with the abuser. This will be difficult if they have children. They can deal it legally by filing a complaint in a police station. They can also make use of the Dowry prohibition act 1961. Women should be bold enough and nothing is more important than our life.

## *EMOTIONAL ABUSE*

Emotions are common for all living beings and they govern everything in the world. No one has ever mastered the art of handling emotions. Since emotions are the base for the family setup, they play an important role in daily life. In General it is said that men are materialistic and women are emotional beings. So women are more affected by this emotional abuse.

Mother, daughter, wife, sister mostly all forms of woman experiences this type of abuse. Women are made to believe that they are mentally weak and they are dependent on men in every situation of their life.

Emotional abuse is a type of abuse that make oneself feel inferior, fear or confused and mentally unstable. Emotional abuse can severely impact the mental health of the victim.

Constantly rejecting one's thought or ideas is a type of emotional abuse. Every woman faces this situation in her home. In the first hand, Women are not allowed to express their ideas or opinions freely. Even sometimes if they do so, their opinion is not even considered for discussion and she is humiliated in front of others. What do you think will be the cause of this action? Next time she never dares to give an opinion. It is a common type of emotional abuse every woman faces. It is a best way to destroy one's self-esteem.

Stonewalling is an extreme type of emotional abuse. Partner who stonewall may not overtly put anyone down. They punish by refusing even to think about their partner's perspective. At times even if they do so, they do it impatiently and in the last, as usual it is rejected.

Other form of emotional abuse comes from disengaging partners. They usually say "Do whatever you want and don't disturb me". They are generally workaholics or couch potatoes. They usually don't take responsibilities but wants the credit. In such cases wife has to take care of all household and family responsibilities but the credit alone goes to Mr. Husband. Wife has to act as everything is done perfectly with her husband's support and maintain her family and husband's status. No wife can or should outperform her husband. This is the base of a male chauvinistic society.

Isolation is other form of emotional abuse. Limiting your freedom of movement, stopping you from contacting others like friends are the emotional constraints every wife faces in her family. She is not allowed to talk freely with anyone and is stopped from doing normal social activities. Always doubting her and questioning about her whereabouts, calls, her conversation even in a family function these things won't be visible to others, only the victim will understand that she is under surveillance. For an outsider, she may look independent but actually every moment and movement of a wife is controlled by her husband. No one can deny this fact and is universal. Actually it is done under the label of love, protectiveness, possessiveness and social status. She accepts everything and yet live a happy life!

### *CAUSES*

Emotional war on women is not new to this society. In general, Men's supremacy over women is the main cause of emotional abuse. Other causes include social causes such as family status, an ideal woman image etc. Social ideology like men can have extra marital affair but women should not make a fuss about that and all these things are done under the cover of family welfare. A woman who knows how to handle all these emotional situations and run a smooth family will surely bag the title of an ideal woman.

### *REMEDIES*

Only the women holds the way out for this abuse. It is the women who have to differentiate the true emotions from the abusing and blackmailing ones. It is purely in the hands of women to decide whether it is a fence or barrier.

## ***ECONOMIC ABUSE***

Economy is the backbone for everything. No wonder it plays a vital role in domestic violence. Economic violence involves making or attempting to make someone financially dependent by maintaining total control over their financial resources, withholding access to money or forbidding employment or education.

Money becomes a way to control someone. Women are not allowed to go for the jobs in olden days. Their job is confined only in and around their home. They are not even exposed to day to day happenings of the world. Their way of getting money is controlled and they are prevented from buying things they need. This is where most women suffers. Nowadays women are allowed to study and work. At last change has come. Yes, women's entry into the labour force has given them a good degree of economic independence. Yet they can earn but not spend. In short we can say, women are always economic slaves.

There is another type of economic abuse where women are compelled to work. No matter whether she likes it or not, she has to earn for her family. This is a wide spreading culture now. As per the survey conducted by the world economic forum, the income of the women is only one-fifth of the men

Education is the basic right for every born individual whether male or female. But it is a sad reality that it is denied for most women. Poverty plays a vital role here. If a family has a male and a female child, in most cases the female child's education comes under the cost cutter.

The famous poet Mahakavi Bharathiyar clearly states the mentality of men of his times as

*"Aduppoothum pennukku padippetherku"*

which means anyway women are going to cook and what is the need for her to study.

Denial of basic education is clearly a form of domestic violence.

### *CAUSES*

Culturally induced tradition like women as always a dependent of men and socially induced view of men's supremacy are the two main causes for this economic violence. Countries like India, where family set-up prevails widely, this is most common and considered normal. Even educated women are made to oblige her partner's decisions particularly in banking and financial sector. Women's limited exposure to financial procedures and laws are also another reason.

### *REMEDIES*

Social and political commitment is required. Implementing laws and promoting gender equality should be done. Women should be knowledge about financial and banking sectors. They should be aware of taxation and other legal financial procedures. They should have a separate bank account and savings for their own safety. Women should safeguard their personal banking details like debit and credit card details.

## *SEXUAL ABUSE*

The worst form of domestic violence faced by most women today is this sexual abuse. All types of violence comes under this single type. The sexual abuse can be verbal, physical, emotional or economical. It is happening everywhere like in house, school, workplace etc. Even in a marital relationship, it is not advisable to have intimacy without the concern of both partners. Imagine when it is done outside the relationship. Irrespective of the age, all age groups of feminine gender are abused under this type of domestic violence. Even children, minor girls, no one escapes this trap. No place seems safer for females.

### *CAUSES*

Most important causes for this sexual abuse is the culture and value system and the relative power of men and women in our society. The way in which men and women are brought up in India strongly influences their behaviour in home or workplace. Women often lack self-confidence because of the way they are socialized and are customised to suffer in silence. Whereas men brought up with macho beliefs, who consider women as a mere toy to play with easily carry these values to anywhere. And also women often lack power and work in an insecure positions. Such patriarchal viewpoints give men the freedom of harassment while women remain vulnerable.

Development of mobile technology and reach of internet via mobile phones are also the important causes for this abuse. Media has been wrapped around technology and it not only entertains more or showers unlimited benefits but also was equally leaving negative impacts on the society. In the media, women are seen as an advertising tactic and a glamorous modelling object.

Nowadays women are becoming more economically independent and powerful. Due to this men are feeling insecure. Instead of competing, they take this sexual abuse as an easy, handy and final solution to overrule women.

### *EFFECTS*

The sexual abusement can cause serious physical and psychological effects in the victim and their family. It can cause depression, anxiety, sleeplessness, nightmares, shame and guilt, headaches, difficulty concentrating, alcoholism, feeling powerless, lack of self-confidence and self-esteem, loss of trust in people, suicidal thoughts etc. No words can explain how the victim will feel emotionally weak when they are abused by their own friends and relatives.

Globally , 1 in 3 women ae being subjected to physical or sexual partner violence.one in four adolescent girls aged 15 to 19 have experienced physical or sexual violence. Also a survey says a child goes missing every 8 minutes and only 50% of this number is recovered. Remaining children are verbally, physically and sexually abused and are never found. This figure doesn't reflect the effect of COVID-19 pandemic which has increased the risk factors of this violence.

## *REMEDIES*

Government has been taking various measures to prevent this cruelty. Government has enacted Protection of Children from Sexual Offence Act 2012 (POCSO) to handle child sexual abuse. For adult women abuse, Prevention, Prohibition and Redressal Act 2013(POSH act) has been passed. But there is not enough support from the public side. Social status is a main hindrance. Awareness should be created to make women mentally strong and act and stand against this shameful behaviour of men. Awareness should be created to change the view of the society over this type of offences. There are many law suits and articles that support women in these situations. Many government helplines are available and should be used by the victims on those situations. The most recent legislation is the Protection of Women from Domestic Violence Act (PWDVA). It is the civil law which protects women against verbal, physical, emotional, economic and sexual abuse.

## *CONCLUSION*

In a country like India, where there is a history of man dominating woman and mesogenic mind set of men has always turned out to be a hurdle in the life of women and women are not taken as a significant part of the society. This view has to be changed. This can only be achieved by proper education, powerful law against these crimes and equal social status for women. It is the right time to stand up against this injustice and to join hands with government to uproot this injustice and make a safe and better place for women to live.

*MAKE IT A BETTER PLACE TO LIVE.*

## *REFERENCE*

## *CASE STUDY EXAMPLES*

1. https://ecampusontario.pressbooks.pub/domesticviolenceinimmigrantcommunities/chapter/case-study-number-4-sonali-and-ravi/
2. https://www.flows.org.uk/search?q=sexual+abuse+Husna%27s+story
3. https://fb.watch/bBxH59vrVR/
4. https://fb.watch/bBxIi2xCwk/

**BIBLIOGRAPHY**

1. https://www.medicalnewstoday.com/articles/327346#ways-to-overcome-verbal-abuse
2. https://www.womenshealth.gov/relationships-and-safety/other-types/emotional-and-verbal-abuse
3. https://www.goodtherapy.org/learn-about-therapy/issues/physical-abuse
4. https://www.womenagainstabuse.org/education-resources/learn-about-abuse/types-of-domestic-violence
5. https://www.healthline.com/health/signs-of-mental-abuse#accusing-blaming-and-denial
6. https://www.nctsn.org/what-is-child-trauma/trauma-types/sexual-abuse
7. https://legislative.gov.in/sites/default/files/A2013-14.pdf
8. https://www.researchgate.net/publication/342233579_Women_Domestic_Violence_A_Study_in_India

Teaching the children to love and be kind can change the future

CHAPTER XXII

# The Obstacles confronted by a Female Bengali Multipotentialite and Sociologist of Kolkata

Gargi Saha
Research Collaborator
Institute of Social Sciences/Sociology
University of Minho, Gualtar Campus, Braga, Portugal
gargi.saha1408@gmail.com

**Introduction:**

We all have a tale to tell about our own lives that has ultimately shaped us into what we have become today. In this very context, I would like to mention Late Professor C. Wright Mills, a pre-eminent American Sociologist of the last century who claimed that, *"Neither the life of an individual nor the history of a society can be understood without understanding both"*, therefore; being a sociologist myself I truly believe that our lives as individuals revolve around the regulations and customs of that particular society to which we each belong. Just as we humans depend on the society for our survival similarly societies continue to prosper due to the existence of its members.

In the first place before I start elucidating about myself and the story of my life it is important to shed some light and understand the nature of the society where I come from and the situation and status of us women in that particular community.

Although India is a democratic country the very concept or idea of equality is hardly evident in daily life due to the existence of the patriarchal social structure of the Indian society in which men hold primary power and savour more privileges than women. So historically, patriarchy has embodied itself in the social, political, legal and economic confederation of the Indian culture and at its simplicity it means the absolute control of the father or the senior most male member over his family.

Like any other Indian community, Bengali community also has been consciously denying the opportunities for growth and development to women not only in the name of religion and socio-cultural practices but also by raising questions on their ability to perform, think and take ultimate decisions or hold prestigious positions in the society. The orthodox Brahmins of Bengal who held the most respectable position in the society formulated rules and regulations of their own to suppress and command over the women for the sake of protecting them from odds as according to them, unlike men, women were delicate and insecure and incapable of fighting the adversities of life. Thus, since then us women are being repressed not only in the society but also in our own homes.

Each one of us has a series of personal account of crucial moments, struggles and experiences of our own lives so do I.

**Challenges faced as the youngest female child in the family**:

My personal life story begins just like all the other girls born in an urban middle-class conservative as well as conventional joint family system. I belong to an extended family of grandparents, uncles and aunts, two cousin sisters, my parents and my own elder sister. Being one of the girl children that too the youngest of all the members in the family had no other way out but to submit to the dogmatic rules of the household. I have been raised in a very strict and rigid manner where my parents had high expectations regarding adhering to their adopted set of rules followed by disciplinary actions for undesired behaviour which in other words can be referred to as the 'authoritarian' style of parenting according to Diana Baumrind, who was internationally recognized as a pioneer of research in parenting styles.

My parents especially my father had been a martinet who demanded complete obedience and exercised constraints on my movements in and out of the house post-puberty. So since then it is always 'his way or the high way'. As the father of two daughters, at all times he has been concerned about our well-being and safety in the outside world and as a result someone or the other from home would always accompany us specifically in my case until I started attending college. However, the limitations continued even after becoming a full grown adult and were neither allowed to stay out of the house till late evening nor permitted to make new friends or rather socialise much with my schoolmates or batch mates from college to be precise with the opposite sex. As I grew up and started to understand and see things in a more matured way I came across some real facts surrounding me and felt that some things remain good when kept secret.

As another girl child of the family it became an obligation for my father to get me admitted in the same girl's school in which one of my elder cousin sisters and my own big sister took admission firstly because my father never preferred co-educational system of learning during those first crucial 18 years of a girl's all round development secondly, my sisters were there to watch over me as and when required and thirdly, on simple grounds of safeguarding my sister and me from mischievous and troublesome boys in general. So what I mean to say is that sometimes the father daughter relationship turns out to be a complicated one and it has also perhaps been explored less than the other familial relationships. For many years attention was mainly on the mothers as to how they affect their children's physical, emotional and spiritual wellbeing. Thus the parental role of a father was omitted from this equation for a long time since he has always been the bread winner and the giver. But in reality a father's influence in his daughter's life shapes her self-esteem, self-image, confidence and opinions about other men. Therefore the bond that a girl shares with her father can determine her ability to trust, her need for approval and her self-belief.

**Challenges encountered after I turned 20:**

When I was on the verge of starting my higher studies as a graduate student in spite of choosing a subject like Political Science and being in the merit lists of the prestigious institutions of Kolkata like Jadavpur University and Presidency college which was then under Calcutta University, I had to join Maulana Azad College (also under Calcutta University and an age-old reputed institution) as a student of Sociology in view of the fact that according to my father the college was just about 15 minutes of walkable distance from my home and the best for me since my own big sister also graduated from the same with flying colours. However, after few days I began to strongly connect myself to the discipline of Sociology thanks to my respected professors, seniors and batch mates in college. I was one of the youngest scholars to present papers in sociological issues in seminars and conferences held in Kolkata by the SAWB (Sociological Association of West Bengal) and also published abstracts for conferences outside West Bengal. Being a mediocre student in school as compared to my sisters and later on taking up humanities in +2 unlike my family members and trying to prove myself in every step of the way that even with humanities as a subject I can build a strong foothold for myself like those from science background has been a never ending struggle since then with my parents and myself which took a start in Calcutta (now Kolkata) 16 years ago. However, when women don't grow up affirmed and acknowledged by their parents specially fathers, they can suffer from low self-confidence and hesitate in taking important decisions in their lives so one should make sure that the emotional connection with the same is positive and strong enough.

**Challenges faced as a female artist/ingenious person:**

Being born in West Bengal a state which is the cultural centre or to be very specific the 'cultural capital' of India and getting introduced in traditional art forms from the very beginning as a child is a common thing in the Bengali households. Likewise, I was also initiated into singing firstly by my paternal grandmother and eventually other elders of the family also agreed since I developed a knack for the particular performing art as a minor. Seeing my interest in music and dance my parents thought to train me in both and thus my training started at a very tender age and I was privileged to receive the guidance of respected Gurus such as Shri Pradip Majumdar and Shrimati Susmita Goswami respectively from the esteemed musical establishment named Banichakra, from the musical stalwart himself Pandit Ajoy Chakraborty and his group of teaching staff at Shrutinandan, fortunate enough to be the 'shishya' of the Dhrupad maestro Pandit Falguni Mitra and his wife respected Guruma Shrimati Pratima Mitra, learnt some Bharatnatyam techniques as well from dance Guru Shrimati Thankamani Kutty and her students in Kalamandalam dance and research centre, Kolkata though not for long since my parents assumed that I won't be able to continue in both the art forms and devote equal amount of time in them as my studies would get hampered. During that period I also staged performances as a child artist in dance and music in various reputed halls in

Kolkata like Rabindra Sadan, Rabindra Bharati University, Madhusudan Mancha etc; and also auditioned and bagged a golden opportunity at the age of 10 to perform in a Bengali TV show for kids named 'Shobujer Deshe' organized by Etv Bangla. I have participated in musical championships in different genres of music and received awards as the best vocalist in Swar Prabhat talent search contest, 2001, came second in a competition held by Banichakra Cultural Association. I got a chance to showcase my skill as one of the youngest Hindusthani classical musicians in All India Radio competition in Kolkata as well and hence won accolades and appreciation in music from other eminent personalities in Kolkata. I was about to record for an album in a studio but was ultimately discouraged and immediately pulled down the ladder of success and like many other innocent simple and skilful girls I could not fight my way up as nobody stood beside me at that time. According to my mother I have always been innovative and experimental with things and my thought process has generally been out of the ordinary but although I was uniquely talented and was valued in my family, I was not expected to follow a career in the same just because there was no future for me in that field and I was incapable of establishing myself as a singer or dancer in Kolkata because of inner politics in the music industry.

**Challenges faced in the 2nd phase of life:**

Looking at the above scenario my family especially my father decided to get me married out of my birthplace just at the age of 21 as I neither could prove my worth as a musician nor as a good student in Sociology in Kolkata unlike my sisters. Nevertheless after marriage when I shifted to Hyderabad I remained firm in my decision to take up Sociology again as a post-graduation subject from Indira Gandhi National Open University as I was left with no other valuable option in spite of selecting and getting through the entrance exams conducted by the Osmania University and even after receiving my counselling letter for the same for joining the esteemed institution as a post-graduate student as riots were rampant in the city and university campus regarding the bifurcation of the two states Andhra and Telangana in the year 2009 and both my families including me got scared . Since then there was no looking back and I secured my Masters Degree with a **'First Class' Division** and this achievement was immense for me as I was mentally disturbed at that point of time being far away from my own home and my people in Kolkata, my comfort zone alongside managing the new role as a wife and being extremely ill concurrently. Nonetheless the day I met my better half, my husband 15 years ago in 2007 ,since then he has been taking care of me, supporting me, encouraging me in other words stood by me like a pillar of strength and now for our 4.6 year old son as well. I have been learning a lot from him over the years as to how to manage myself and stay focused and enjoy in whatever I do without bothering about the outside world because as according to him this is my life after all.

**Obstacles faced in the 3rd phase of life:**

However, being sick for a long time in India my ambitions in life and career almost took a backseat and I had to settle down as a house-worker post marriage and after completing my Masters degree. With the desire to become an assistant professor in Sociology I sat for the NET (National Eligibility Test) in 2019 for the first time and when I could not qualify in the first attempt I was disheartened and ashamed of my performance though I knew very well that I couldn't devote full time in my preparations as by then I was a mother to a 1 year old son. So the hunger within me to achieve something in life was still somewhere growing and as soon as we got the opportunity to come to Europe in April, 2019 on my husband's advice I applied for a temporary position in the University of Minho in Braga, Portugal in the department of Sociology in a SHARE (The Survey of Health, Ageing and Retirement in Europe) project as my husband got posted as a post doctoral research fellow there for 2 years. After reaching Braga I got selected through an online personal interview with the head of the project team and was offered the position of a research collaborator thereafter. Though it was not a paid position or a contract it was a respectable position in a foreign land and I felt proud representing my own country and gained invaluable experience from the same. Now again I am in search of a good paid position in Europe as due to the pandemic we had to leave Portugal in June 2021 and settle in France for the time being after my husband's contract ended there and we were no longer allowed to continue our stay and therefore my struggle continues.

Besides finding a good and stable career in Sociology I am still continuing to do things out of the box which gives me immeasurable happiness for example in October 2019 I was offered to host and anchor the official event regarding the 30th Constitution Day of India or the 'Samvidhan Divas 'on 26th November in Braga, Portugal on behalf of the Indian Embassy to Portugal by the then First Secretary to the Indian Embassy to Portugal, Shri Amararam Gurjar Sir. It was the first and one of the most memorable experiences for me and I was highly appreciated for the same by the then Ambassador to the Indian Embassy to Portugal Her Excellency Mrs. K. Nandini Singla, Sir Ricardo Rio, the Mayor of Braga and my fellow compatriots and other dignified people present that day. Even being away from my own country I have tried to stay connected to my roots and people through the social media and continued to follow my passion for music and creativity and participated and secured the 1st position in an online competition in the singing category organized by Milanti Society a facebook group in Kolkata even amidst the second wave of the ongoing pandemic and also represented India in the International Women's Day event 2021 organized by the association Bhoomi in Lisbon, Portugal in collaboration with the Indian Embassy to Portugal,Lisbon,India. Currently, I am the new creative head and group expert of a facebook group Impression headed by Soumi Chakraborty an astrologer, motivator and crystal healer from Kolkata, India residing in Manchester, United Kingdom. I love to write and have published 3 different kinds of chapters/articles till date on Indian women and Hindusthani classical music including a recipe for an International multi-cuisine book in Portugal.

I would like to end by saying that a woman can achieve anything in life and keep fighting her battle irrespective of caste, creed, colour and ethnicity and the challenges that comes her way if she believes in herself. As women we should all at once stop proving our worth to the society and start living for ourselves then only we can create a better tomorrow for other women at large.

CHAPTER XXIII

# Work-Life Balance of Women in the IT Industry: Issues and Challenges

Dr. Preeti Garg
Associate Professor
School of Business Studies
Shobhit Institute of Engineering & Technology
Deemed to be University, Meerut
preeti_garg25@yahoo.co.in

**Abstract:**

There is a drastic change in the role of men and women over the past 50 years. More women than ever before are now in the workforce reflecting the rise in educational levels and changing societal attitudes. They undergo a great amount of stress to balance their professional and personal life. Work Life Balance is the key issue bothering many corporate and employees in the Information Technology (IT) sector. Professional and personal life are the two sides of the same coin, the imbalance between these two leads to factors like stress, fatigue, poor performance, deteriorating quality of health, time management issues, lack of proper social support, elderly and childcare issues. The chapter studies the challenges and issues of work life balance amongst women in the IT industry.

**Keywords**: Work-Life Balance, Women, Challenges, IT Industry

**Introduction:**

Life is a set of things we pursue. No one can have a satisfying and fulfilling life without family, health, wealth, employment, social obligations, mental satisfaction, and spiritual enlightenment. To keep the wheel of life moving, hitting the balance is important. Work life balance means a harmonious and complete integration of work and non-work, so that people can acquire their skills in all the domains in which they live. The challenges of integrating work and family life are part of the daily reality for female employees.

An increasing number of working women are now playing a major role in the workplace which puts more pressure on the family, with the growing number of divorces and the rapid increase in the number of single-parent families, all of which puts more pressure on women professionals. The need for organizations to see their employees as responsible individuals who need time and energy outside of work. Finding the right balance between work and family life has become a major challenge in today's highly competitive global environment. Companies that support a healthy work ethic and encourage their employees to manage their energy effectively will excel. A few decades earlier, it was widely expected that new technologies would reduce working hours and bring relaxation and leisure to employees. But instead of bringing relief and leisure, advanced technology has left professionals, with little time left for paid work. In fact, technology has blurred the line between office and home, and employees are now expected to find office work, even when they are at home. These work pressures also have a direct impact on the health of employees.

**Work-life balance: Definitions**

Kofodimos(1993)

Work-life balance refers to the individual capability to properly manage personal and professional life.

Clark(2000)

Satisfaction and good functioning at work and at home with a minimum of role conflict.

Fisher (2001)

Range of work arrangements, both formal and informal, that exceed the statutory minimum and which assist employees to combine employment with their caring responsibilities and personal life outside the workplace.

Feldstead (2002)

Work-life balance as referring to the ability of individuals, regardless of age or gender, to find a rhythm that will allow them to combine their work with their non work responsibilities, activities and aspirations.

Clarke, Kock & Hill (2004)

Equilibrium between the amount of time and effort somebody devotes to work and personal activities, in order to maintain an overall sense of harmony in life.

**Work-Life Balance: Operational Definitions of Terms**

(i) IT: Information Technology (IT), according to the Information Technology Association of America (ITAA) is 'the study, design, development, implementation, support of management of computer based information systems, particularly software applications and computer hardware' (Wikipedia, 2015).

(ii) ITES: Information Technology Enabled Service is defined as outsourcing of processes that can be enabled with information technology and covers diverse areas like finance, human resource, administration, health care, telecommunication, manufacturing etc.

**Historical Background and Change in Work-Life Balance**

The term Work-Life Balance was first used in the United Kingdom in the late 1970s to describe the balance between work and personal life. In the United States, the term was introduced in 1986. The history of working life balance begins in the last half of the 19th century when revolutionaries successfully campaigned for long hours in the industry and were able to demonstrate that the reduction in working hours had no effect. on output levels. In the early 20th century, a campaign to reduce working hours continued with a series of pioneer studies that showed the relationship between time spent on work and productivity was complex. These studies also looked at the importance of motivation and behavior, fatigue, concentration, and attention to show that there were cases where a decrease in working hours led to an increase in productivity, and there was a full provision of working duration and intervals. rest, in some cases. During the 1960s and 1970s, although the term work-life balance was not yet established, a few factors could be identified that eventually led to the consolidation of current policy. These include:

1. Occupational health and safety;
2. International competition;
3. Equality; and
4. Flexible labor market.

In the 1960s the debate about the rate at which paid overtime was focused on organizing a group of informal workers and the joint management consultation of operational processes, within the framework of collective bargaining. This approach was at the heart of a report by the Royal Commission on Trades Unions and Employers Association in the late 1960's. The analysis is based on the experience of production negotiations of the past decade. Production negotiations realized that craft groups often use one side of the informal control in many aspects of their work processes. They pointed out that control includes the control of working hours where overtime is paid at premium rates. Many extra hours were usually unnecessary but were done to increase income. The result was a low productivity culture, coupled with a low wage rate for long working hours. The answer was to negotiate new -packages, which included major changes in job planning and operating procedures - including flexible work hours, work patterns - to increase basic wage rates and reduce overtime.

The 1970s were a period of change brought about by a variety of factors, increased international competition, technological changes, new organizational forms, increased participation of women, and the changing and more diverse needs of individuals. It was in the mid-1970s that the regime also began to recognize the importance of equality with the introduction of the Equal Payment Act in 1970 and the Discrimination Act in 1975. and obviously. It has been argued that many working hours among men in child-rearing years have deprived women of opportunities in two ways: they have made it difficult for men to participate in child care and home-building, leaving a burden on women to carry those responsibilities; have made it difficult for women to compete for higher-paying jobs.

In the 1980s politics focused on liberating the economy, including the labor market. At the heart of the labor market reform was the introduction of highly flexible work patterns commonly referred to as common types of employment (increased part-time employment / fixed term, etc.). This came at a time when there was a dramatic shift in the labor market in which the employment of people shifted from production to labor, which often favored the employment of women at that time. The introduction of flexible job types was an important factor in improving the supply of labor because it would allow groups of people who could not enter the labor market to have the opportunity to do so.

It was only in the 1990s, especially in the last decade that the Government began to play a role in intervening to give workers certain rights in terms of establishing the working life balance that they deserve.

**Factors influencing work and family spheres**

**Family and personal life influenced by:**

- Increasing participation of women in the workforce
- Increasing participation of childbearing women in the workforce
- Increasing participation of dual career couples in the workforce
- Increase in single-parent/single person households
- Increase in child care/elder care burden on employees
- Health and well-being considerations

**Work influenced by:**

- Long working hours/unpaid overtime
- Time squeeze
- Demand for shorter working hours
- Increase in part-time employees
- Work intensification and stress
- Changing work time

**Others factors:**

- Ageing population
- Rise of service sector industries
- Technology complexity of work
- Skill shortage
- Loss of social support network
- Globalisation and demographic shift of the workforce

Source: Naithani and Jha (2009)

**Growing number of female employees:**

Women are an important part of the global workforce today and there is growing awareness of creating more jobs for women in India. Today, many Indian women are no longer restricted to the roles of daughters, sisters, wives, and mothers. Now they feel responsible for their community and nation. Breaking the traditional glass ceiling; they come out and use their versatility, and their careful and multi-faceted management skills with full responsibility and gentle touch. This trend is evident in a variety of domains, including the Indian information and technology sector.

The balance of work life is most often seen as a women's issue, as they were considered primarily responsible for the smooth running of the family's daily affairs regardless of her work profile and legal obligations. Such inequalities have a detrimental effect on the health of the working woman as well as on social ills such as increased divorce rates, infertility due to high stress. The organization, which effectively addresses these issues, (provides a variety of services to measure employee health) leads to healthy interaction in the working environment of the company and its employees. Job demands are increasing, the burden and roles vary as well as the inequalities of working life at different stages of life. Ancient women were trapped in their kitchens while those employed were working in factories, farms, or shops. Very few women had access to higher education and were forced to depend on their fathers or husbands' mercy. Work life balance is one of the most challenging issues women employees face because of the type of role they play at home and at workplace. This ever-increasing pressure on working women leaves them with little time to spend with family. It, is important to note that the number of women who are ambitious, highly focused on jobs is also growing. Many women are absent from work as a means of supporting their families but instead are committed to continuously improving their careers and success in the workplace.

One of the most significant changes in the labor market in India over the past decade has been the influx of professional women. Women play a major role in economic growth. Over the years, Indian women have made great mark and have achieved success in fields across the country and overseas. The number of women working in the IT industry of 155 billion has risen to 34 percent, as companies seek to improve their level of gender diversity. The IT industry organization NASSCOM said about one third of the workforce in the sector is women working in various occupations. According to a report released in its tenth edition of the Diversity and Inclusion Summit, NASCOM revealed that the percentage of women working in the sector increased from 28 percent in the 2019 financial year to 34 percent in the 2020 financial year. In addition, the industry body expected the number of firms with more than 20 percent women at higher levels to rise to about 60 percent. India's IT sector employs 3.9 million people, according to NASSCOM. Additionally, approximately 51 percent of firms will have more than 20 percent women in the C-suite or higher management levels. Although the industry has been recruiting a large number of female employees at intervention levels since the last half of twelve years or more, most of them are not reaching the peak. They quit after giving birth or lacking support from their family.

NASSCOM in its report found that companies with at least 10 percent of women on board boards have a 2.5-5 percent higher profit per equity, firms where women at least 30 percent of C-suite have a 15 percent higher profit than others. .18 India's IT industry currently employs 3.9 million people, 34% of whom are women; the report brings forward, measures and policies that support the advancement of women in the workplace and the need for the whole industry to come together to provide the opportunities and support needed to successfully develop their work within the sector. This report is used by the IT industry as a scorecard to balance their gender-based policies and procedures. This gradual change but important social and cultural values should be noted and celebrated. The great potential within these incentives is still widely used and needs to be integrated, strengthened and empowered continuously for the benefit of the IT sector of India, our community and our nation. The aspects of India's information technology industry and work environment present some unique challenges for professionals in the industry. The challenges are exacerbated in the case of women specialists.

The information technology industry in India is characterized by a project-oriented organization and as the industry has grown, complex projects and strategies have been offered in India. Despite the glamor and the high salaries associated with the profession, women in the IT industry suffer from physical discomfort and stress, even in the splendid office environment. The high salaries and social status associated with the IT sector have enticed women to take up these jobs but many suffer from various causes such as late working hours.

Software experts are faced with the uncertainty and instability associated with long-term working pressures. This pressure is a result of two things. First, the time difference with the West, the US and Europe, makes it necessary for workers to work nights in India. In addition, the 24-hour information factory concept 24-7-365 support desk requires software engineers to conduct team meetings and visual work sessions, where team members need to use temporary flexibility, a more liquid way to set time or even hold calls of conferences without 8 to 6 normal working days or speeding up a software project with shifts. Secondly project-based work with unpredictable load and the requirement to deliver projects consistently over a set period of time and without critical interruptions, often involving extensive travel. The design of an industry project with rapid technological changes that make skills expire quickly requires software professionals to often re-train. Therefore, software professionals need to incorporate additional training and teaching hours to keep up with these changes. Women who wish to play a major role in technology need to maintain a high learning curve regularly. With the ongoing development taking place in this field, it is not enough to be a good worker in the IT industry; one has to keep updating the technical skills. No other industry sees such dramatic changes in technology from time to time.

However, it should be noted that in Indian society, where the role of a woman in relation to herself, her family and society is redefined, the new and expanded role of women with strong job ownership puts a lot of pressure on women's health. There are a variety of factors that cause stress in women's lives and thereafter are often exacerbated when both husband-and-wife work and have children growing up with parents. These ongoing worries can lead to disruption in women's mental well-being due to a lack of control over one's health and the hopeless perception that there is not enough time to have a reasonable balance in work and personal life.. Factors that lead to positive or negative perceptions of their work have a bearing on the balance of work life. This stress in women can lead to physical stress and lead to unhealthy health, headaches, gastritis, body aches, weakness, low morals etc, leading to chronic, high heart problems.

**Various techniques design for management of work & personal life for women:**

1. **Self-control:** Adequate self-control can be a challenge, especially when it comes to proper sleep, exercise, and proper nutrition. Self-control is recognizing that the proper use of spaces in our lives is important, and that the resources available, time, and health are limited.

2. **Time Management**: Effective time management involves making the best use of your day and the support resources you can call to keep up with the pace when your resources match your challenges.

3. **Managing Stress**: Today societies tend to get complicated over time. When confronted with increasing pressures, stress in a person is inevitable. More people, distractions, and noise require that each of us have the ability to keep peace and to work hard without stressful situations.

4. **Changing Management:** In our fast-paced world, change is important. Continuing to embrace new ways and re-adapt to others is essential for successful work and happy home life.

5. **Technology Management**: Managing technology effectively means making sure technology benefits the person, rather than the abuse.

6. **Recreation Management**: With the most neglected balance of working life supporting the sectors, leisure managers acknowledge the importance of rest and relaxation that one cannot change the short-term leisure, and that leisure time is an important part of one's experience.

**Challenges to Work-Life Balance in IT Industry**

1. Most organizations have policies on paper only. There is very little concern about the implementation of policies.

2. Lack of Communication about work-life programs. While an organization may offer a rich menu of work life benefits, a desirable outcome that brings positive business results - it is almost impossible if employees are unaware of the plans or do not understand them.

3. Implementing a work-life balance strategy takes time. Timescales for implementation need to be realistic.

4. Co-worker support: Employees who used work-life balance practices were perceived by co-workers as having lower levels of organisational commitment, which was thought to affect the subsequent allocation of rewards such as advancement opportunities and salary increases. Some staff that use flexible arrangements have reportedly experienced family friendly backlash or resentment from co-workers.

5. Managers play an important role in the success of work/life programs because they are in a position to encourage or discourage employees' efforts to balance their work and family lives. Where supervisors enthusiastically support the integration of paid work and other responsibilities, employees will be more likely to take up available work-life programs. On the other hand, it has been suggested that even in family-friendly organisations, managers may send negative signals indicating that the use of flexible benefits is a problem for them, their colleagues and the organisation as a whole.

**Conclusion:**

Women constitute an important part of work force. In today's time, corporate world is so demanding that work deadlines are getting tighter and due to this work pressure becomes exceedingly difficult to maintain a work-family balance for women employees. Nature of the sector and the changing aspirations and the roles of women in Indian society create a challenge for their work-family balance. Thus, achieving a good balance between work and family commitments is a growing concern for employees, organisation and government today, people are not only doing work for survival but also for personal satisfaction as well, beside salary employees prefer companies that offers attractive and exclusive work-life policies. If there is no balance between the persons working life and personal life, it will affect their performance and commitment towards the organisation. If the job is stressful, it will affect the personal life of people, leads to affect their concentration on work, level of commitment to the profession, the level of satisfaction, performance, productivity and the services provided to the society. In this chapter, an attempt is made to study issues affecting the work life balance of women employes in IT sector, problems and challenges towards work-life balance. For many working women, the work-life balance is one of life's greatest challenges. While men often feel conflicted between workplace and fatherhood demands as well, women usually suffer from more than their fair share of the burden of balancing family and work life.

**Reference:**


1. Ahuja, M. K. (2002). Women in information technology profession: A literature review, synthesis and research agenda. European Journal of Information Systems, 11, 20-34
2. Aiswarya, B. & Ramasundaramthe; G. (2011). Role of work-family conflict as a mediator between work-thought interference and job stress. International Management Review, 7(2), 25-34
3. Ajith, Madhu & Vidya, S. Patil. (2013). An empirical study on work-life balance for role prioritization of IT employees. RVIM Journal of Management Research, 5(1), 31-40
4. Amita Singh (2010). A study on the perception of work-life balance policies among software professionals. IUP Journal of Management Research, Hyderabad, 9(2) 51-29
5. Anuradha Jain (2017). Work-life balance for women professional, The Chartered Accountant Journal. 66(6) ,33-35
6. Anjana Vivek (2017). Scope and opportunities for women-chartered accountants in industry and practice, The Chartered Accountant Journal, 66(6), 23-28
7. Andy Field (2009), Discovering Statistics using SPSS, 3rd ed, Sage Publication Inc
8. Armstrong, D.J., Riemenschneider, C.K., Allen, M.J., & Reid, M. F. (2007). Advancement, voluntary turnover and women in IT: A cognitive study of workfamily conflict. Information & Management, 44, 142-153 180
9. Arfken, D. E., S. L. Bellar, M. M. Helms. (2004). The ultimate glass ceiling revisited: The presence of women on corporate boards, Journal of Business Ethics, 50 (2), 177-86
10. Aswini, S., & Kumaraswamy, M (2014). Work-life balance with special reference to public sector bank employees in Karnataka. GJRA- Global Journal for Research Analysis, 3(2), 37-41
11. Barbara Beham (2011). Work-family conflict and organisational citizenship behaviour: Empirical evidence from Spanish employees. Community, Work & Family, 14(1), 63-80
12. Barkha Gupta, Ankool & Manish Hyde (2016). Factors affecting quality of work-life among academicians, Anvesha Journal, 3(1), 21-24
13. Barbale & Gaur (2016). A study on work- life balance of employees at federal bank of India, Kothrud Pune, Indira Management Review,10 (2),45-54
14. Beauregard, Alexandra & Lesley C. Henry (2008). Making the link between work-life balance practices and organisational performance. Human Resource Management Review, 19(1)
15. · Bhatnagar & Rajadhyaksha (2001). Attitudes towards work and family roles and their implications for career growth of women: a report from India, Sex Roles, 45 (7/8), 549–565
16. Bird, J. (2006). Work-life balance: Doing it right and avoiding the pitfalls, Employment Relations Today, 33(3), 21-30 181
17. Blaug, Kenyon, & Lekhi, (2007). Stress at work: A report prepared for the work foundation's principal partners. Project Report. The work foundation, London
18. Brett, J. M., & Stroh, L. K. (1999). Women in management: How far have we come and what needs to be done as we approach 2000. Journal of Management Inquiry, 8(4), 392-398
19. Business Insider (2015). Mark-Zuckerberg just made face books paternal leave policy (assessed in August 2015)
20. Caroline Glynn & Claire Mc Cartney (2002). Work-life balance: The role of the manager. Rolley Park Institute
21. Castells, M. (1997), The Power of identity, 2 nd ed. MA: Blackwell Publishing, Cambridge.
22. Chawla, Deepak & Sondhi Neena (2011). Assessing work-life balance among Indian women professionals. The Indian Journal of Industrial Relations, 47(2), 341-351

23. Chandel K. & Kaur R. (2015). HR Intervention for work-life balance-A study of rail coach factory, Kapurthala (Punjab), Indian Management Studies Journal 19, 35-62
24. Deepa Chitnis & Sulabha Roorane (2015). Reflections of Indian judiciary on employers' responsibility for combating sexual harassment at workplace, SFIMAR Research Review, 10(1), 26-40
25. Devika, P.(2016). Work-life balance of women in IT sector. Anvesha International Journal of research in regional studies, law, social science, journalism and management practices,1(11),120-123 182
26. Delery, J.E. & Doty, D. H., (1996). Modes of theorizing in strategic human resource management. Academy of Management Journal, 39, 830-835
27. Donald R. Cooper & Pamela Schindler (2010). Business Research Methods, 12th ed. Tata McGraw Hill , New Delhi
28. Ezra, M., & Deckman, M. (1996). Balancing work and family responsibilities: flexi-time and childcare in the federal government. Public Administration Review, 56(2), 174-179
29. Foster L.B. (2002), Workplace Stress: Changing the pattern, Sales and Marketing Journal, 32–33

CHAPTER XXIV

# Influence of Mass Media in Women Empowerment: Challenges and Strategies

*Bidyut Pritom Gogoi,Khushboo Yadav, Nidhi Singh and Dipankar Saikia
*Corresponding Author
Department of Extension Education
Dr. Rajendra Prasad Central Agricultural University
Pusa, Samastipur, Bihar
bidyut.p98@gmail.com

**Abstract:**

Women are agents of human development, nurturers of humanity, catalysts in agriculture, economic development, natural resource management, protector of environment, etc. However, they suffer from lack of information, right to resources, control of assets, credits training and new technologies. Marginalized, subjugated and sitting on the edge, women in particular, rural women are disempowered and unable to contribute to development. Empowerment of rural women is a clarion call both for humanization and development perspective. Information is important resource and has power to transform human misery. Mass media has been found to have significant impact in raising issue of women, articulating grievances and molding opinion of people regarding rights of women. The power of mass media and community media in training, education and dissemination of relevant information has been verified. The chapter aims to critically analyze issues in use of mass media by rural women and suggest strategies to empower them.

**Keywords:** Mass Media, Empowerment, Rural Women, Development, Technologies

**Introduction**

"There is no chance of the welfare of the world unless the condition of women is improved. It is not possible for a bird to fly on one wing."

- *Swami Vivekananda*

I still remember when I used to spend my summer vacations at my maternal grandmother's home. Every morning she sat with the newspaper and tried to figure out the news from the pictures printed with the articles as she is an illiterate. The curiosity to know about the surrounding stimulated her enough to develop learning and reading skills. We cousins used to teach her alphabets, words, numbers, etc. Now she can recognize the words and figures and read out the headlines as well. The print media motived her for learning the basic skills.

Mass media plays a significant role in women's development and its empowerment. The plural nature of Indian culture and diverse role that women play is neither acknowledged nor communicated and is seen as marginal to national growth and development. Media having considerable influence over large audience should be an effective tool in the empowerment of women. Information is an important resource like any other resource. One of the most profound changes that contemporary Indian society has been witnessing during the nineties is transition from an industrial society to an information-based society. This ongoing transition has an embracing impact on several segments like the economy, living styles, entertainment industry, industrial production and agriculture. The rapid pace at which the media scenario is changing is the result of a convergence of telecommunication computing and microelectronics, which is termed as Information Technology. It is the increasing applications of Information Technology, as a determining factor in social and economic issues that is heralding the country rapidly towards an informative society. All these are sure signs that the informative society has eventually arrived in the country (Gupta and Aggarwal, 1996).

Media which is considered as the fourth pillar of the society and democratic medium of information has a significant role in shaping present day. Media can communicate information about and relevant to women powerfully.

Media can inform, educate and coordinate. Empowerment means freedom and power to control your life, it refers to consciousness about rights and responsibilities. Women can recognize their rights and take steps to decide responsible action. Women empowerment has become a significant topic of discussion in development and economics. Empowerment of women is a necessity for the very development of a society, since it enhances both the quality and the quantity of human resources available for development (Narayana and Ahmed, 2016). The social and economic empowerment could not be achieved without mass media in the era of technology.

**WOMEN AND MEDIA**

Do women have skills, knowledge and access to information technology? How are women portrayed in media? It is a common knowledge that allocation of space to women in print media is meagre. Even if it is there, the reasons are classic incidences to report rape, abuse or social perceptions of women. It is only now that more and more reports on women achievers and voices of dissent are being expressed (Kumar and Bhardwaj, 1988). Most women, especially in developing countries, are not able to access effectively the expanding electronic information highways and therefore cannot establish networks that will provide them with alternative sources of information. Inclusion of women in media will certainly decrease the negative portrayals of women internationally and to challenge instances of abuse of the power of an increasingly important industry. Self-regulatory mechanisms for the media need to be created and strengthened and approaches developed to eliminate gender-biased programming. Rural women are not too much media oriented. They haven't any kind of interest about news or the happenings. They have interest only in their surrounding and have their own world. The other media like audio-visual and mobile, these are used by them just for only entertaining purposes. Newspapers, radio, television and mobile, all have failed to create awareness among the rural women in respect of their demands, rights and condition as the media does not address serious issues about exploitation and in equal treatment to women in different spheres. Idealized beauty standards, irrelevant sexualization and domestication are only some of the ways that women in media are portrayed today (Indian journal of women and development, 2008). Thus, instead of highlighting the exploitation of woman, they end up becoming one of the reasons in increase of violence as their coverage more often than not tend to glorify the crime against women. The proper knowledge-based awareness can change the whole scenario of the rural society. Women are the pillar of success for any society. They are the backbone of any nation. So, the media should have to focus on those issues which are creating hindrance on the pathway of women development living in rural areas.

Acknowledged by my various teachers regarding the speaking skills, they suggested me to explore the journalism media as a career option. Fascinated with the journalism world I also started participating in inter school and regional debates and extempore competition conducted by my school and other schools. I also participated in an extempore competition organized by All India Radio, Akashvani, Bareilly Region. In the competition, I stopped speaking because I became blank at that time but the delegates cheered me for putting such a good story in front of them and I was awarded with a Consolation price. After that there was a time, I overcame my stage fear by regular practice and participation. But when there was a time to turn my dream into reality, my parents refused to allow for making a career in this field due to the gender discrimination, unsafe and uncertain nature of journalism media for women.

**RAISING WOMEN CONSCIOUSNESS**

There is an urgent need to involve women in decision making roles regarding the development of the new technologies. This is possible only when steps are taken to support women's education, training and employment to promote women's equal access to all areas and levels of the media. Women's full and equal participation in the media, including management, programming, education, training and research can mitigate the gap of gender imbalance. No doubt, research into all aspects of women and media can help in defining areas needing attention for integrating a gender perspective. Besides, we must also aim at gender balance in the appointment of women and men to all advisory, management, regulatory or monitoring bodies, including those connected to the private and State or public media. Encouragement is needed, to motivate freedom of expression of women. Increased the number of programmes for and by women can address to women's needs and concerns properly. Dissemination of information and the exchange of views need to be enhanced at all levels level, and support women's groups active in media work. Train women to make greater use of information technology for communication.

Non-governmental organizations, women's organizations and professional media organizations can recognize the specific needs of women and facilitate increased participation through use of appropriate languages, traditional, indigenous and other ethnic forms of media, such as story-telling, drama, poetry and song, reflecting their cultures, and utilize these forms of communication to disseminate information on development.

**STRATEGIES OF USING MEDIA FOR WOMEN EMPOWERMENT**

Communication is extremely important for women development and mass media play significant role. It is to be noted that growth of women's education and their entry into employment has contributed to the growth of media. In all spheres of life whether for controlling population growth, spread of literacy or improving quality of life for vast masses, women have crucial role to play. However, women can be expected to play this role when they become conscious of their strength and are not deliberately marginalized by male domination. In this context, media has an important role to play – to create awakening in women to achieve their potential as the prime movers of change in society. The television and radio had helped to promote the involvement of rural women in decisions that affect their livelihood. Perceptions and local knowledge play a key role in development, hence the need for a communication approach that ensures the problems to be resolved are perceived in the same way by the distinct groups concerned (women, men, elders, youth) as well as by the development communicators working with them. The individual participation of women in communication activities uses visual methods and group facilitation techniques for generating, analyzing and presenting information that helps to reveal the visions and voices of women. These development efforts were firmly rooted in women's realities and thus more responsive to their needs, aspirations, abilities and knowledge (Ganesamurthy, 2008). In today's world, print and electronic media play a vital role in effectively conveying message that needs to be conveyed.

The media should take into consideration the following points.

- The media must project the working women in the unorganized sector as worker and not merely as performing the duties of wife/daughter. They being major earners, they must be projected as producers and not merely consumers.
- The media should make deliberate attempts to not only project the problems of women in poverty, but should monitor in such a way that conflicting role models are not depicted, nor derogatory references to their work are made.
- To improve content and coverage, coordinated efforts for increased interaction between NGO's, women's social action group, research organizations, institutes of mass communication, and the media personnel should be developed.
- Developmental news should be aired through the medium of radio and television mainly on the following topics: Employment/ Job Prospects in India/ self-locality, inexpensive childcare and healthcare, educational facilities at their doorstep, dowry system, other legal rights like self-help, violence etc.

The media has the potential to make a far greater contribution to the advancement of women. Media, which wields immense power in a democracy - a power which is only expanding and not diminishing, needs carrying out a focused attention about women- related issues and the portrayal of women. According to Franklin (2009) in 'Using Traditional Drama Forms for Social Change', the impact of mainstream media on the attitude, behavior or decision-making of rural masses is superficial. It is necessary to use traditional media because they play a reinforcing role. The mainstream media quickly transmit information and news; the traditional media can supplement these effects by having a better impact on the motivational, behavioral or attitudinal aspects of the rural or illiterate people. It has been proved that traditional media have a greater role in affecting the attitude of illiterate masses. The message regarding family welfare, health and agricultural practices can be internalized by a competent resident practitioner of the folk media. Therefore, they are always participative and democratic.

**HEALTH AND MEDIA**

Health communication links the domains of communication and health and is increasingly recognized as a necessary element of efforts to improve personal and public health. Media with the technological advancement helped to link the human race and plays a dynamic role in multifaceted development. Multimedia penetrated the society in such an extent that most of the news and information are delivered through online platforms and other sources. There are many health programmes for developing awareness amongst the people of the society. Mass media considered as the best amongst them all when it comes to raise the consciousness and awareness of the problem. But when it comes to health problems, it can be seen that women are dealing with many problems as compared to men. As there is lack of accessibility of resources, illiteracy and financial dependency hampering the outreach of health-related issues among the particular gender can be seen more.

Women are a complex social animal as their body undergoes numerous physiological and psychological changes from birth to death. Considering, adolescence, maternal and old age period, the complex period of her life as most of the complications were associated from these periods. Other than that, female feticide, anemia, PCOS/PCOD, maternal mortality rate, unwanted pregnancy, AIDS, etc are some of the common problems prevalent now a days. The information regarding these issues is available on the internet but the accessibility is the problematic part mainly amongst the rural women. The urban women are able to access and reach to the information but end up to neglect the issues considering it as a cause of stress.

It has been two years since I was diagnosed with Poly Cystic Ovary Syndrome (PCOS). I refer online resources for developing my basic knowledge regarding this tremendously new topic which is quite a trend now a days as 1 out of 5 females are diagnosed with this problem. While digging deep into the articles, I got to know about my type of PCOS i.e., Insulin Resistance PCOS and also that this problem is a lifestyle disorder. But with this information, I also found out several misleading information regarding my health issues. That it cannot be cured and it is a lifelong disorder. But in reality, with the proper care and maintaining a healthy lifestyle we can eliminate this problem.

**Conclusion**

The role of Media is very important to accelerate social and economic empowerment of women. Media should create self-regulatory mechanisms so that misleading and improper gender-based programs are prevented. Media should focus success stories of established, successful and renowned women in spite of indecent representation of women. The media campaigns have potentials to disseminate the concept of gender equality. Mass Media could also make a strong contribution. Now with emerging alternate media, coming of Community media like Wall Newspapers, village information centers and community radio, there is hope for more dialogic communication for accelerating awareness. But with availability of so much information over the internet there are misleading information circulating around regarding health like "Reduction of weight in just 2 weeks" which will create a negative aspect of media on the people's lifestyle.

**REFERENCE:**


1. Gupta, V.S and Aggarwal, Vir Bala (1996). Media Policy and Nation Building – Select Issues and Themes. New Delhi: Concept Publishing Company.
2. Parkavi, K. (2016). Media and Women Health in India. *International Journal of Research–Granthaalayah*, **4** (4), 41-44.
3. Kumar, B., Gogoi, B.P., and Saikia, D. (2020). Role of Mass Media in Empowering Rural Women: Issues and Strategies, *National Conference on Women Empowerment through Entrepreneurship and Skill Development (NCWEES)*, ISBN: 978-93-89940-20-6, 38-42.
4. Malik, N., Bhardwaj, N., and Kumar, B., (2001). Village information centre: a strategy of using information technology for rural development. *Indian Association of Social Science Institutions quarterly* journal, **19**(3), 103-112.
5. Narayana, A., & Ahamad, T. (2016). Role of media in accelerating women empowerment. *International Journal of Advanced Education and Research*, **1**, 16-19.
6. Premlata and Jukariya, T. (2018). Role of Media in Empowering Women. *International Journal of Current Microbiology and Applied Sciences*. **7**(04): 1618-1623.

CHAPTER XXV

# Women's Participation in Workforce in India

Neelam Kumari
Research Scholar
University of Jammu, Jammu and Kashmir
Neelamjangral077@gmail.com

**Abstract:** Women must have all the opportunities to develop intellectually, socially and morally. There is a change in the society which is paying attention to women empowerment. Despite the fact that female literacy and education enrollment rates have been rising, India today has lower levels of women's workforce participation than many countries in Sub-Saharan Africa and the Middle East. India ranks 127th on the gender inequality index and 108th on the global gender gap index. Over the last decade, women's participation in the labor force has seen a dramatic decline. Latest government statistics suggest that women's labor participation rate fell from 29.4 percent in 2004-2005 to 22.5 percent in 2011-2012. The gender gap in the labor force is particularly stark when we consider that in the 15-59 age group, women's participation is only 32 percent in rural areas compared to 83 percent for men, and 21 percent in urban areas compared to 81 percent for men. The proportion of India's female population that is economically active is among the lowest in the world. While the female labor force participation rates vary considerably across developing countries, few countries in the world perform worse than India like Libya, Syria, and Yemen. Morocco, Samoa, Pakistan, Sudan, Egypt, Saudi Arabia, Somalia, Iraq, Iran, Jordan. These countries are largely spread across the Middle East, Africa and South East Asia where historically gender roles and stereotypes have continued to affect economic outcomes. The aim of the paper is to find out trends and occupational distribution of women's participation in workforce.

**KEY WORDS:** Women participation, Female literacy, Education Enrollment.

**Introduction**

The development of any nation is familiarly linked to its ability to develop and use of its human resource effectively. This is important for most developing countries like India. Women are an important part of the human resources plays a dominant role in the social, economic and political development of India. Female work participation rate is one of the important designates of female status in the economy. Women's participation in economic activities is important from the perspective of their personal development and their status in society. A country's progress and development depend on the participation rates of its women because they comprise around 50% of its human resources. Women employment is important for increasing their standard of living and well-being, where as economic welfare of women may not improve if they are engaged in low-paying distress driven work (Srivastva and srivastva, 2009).

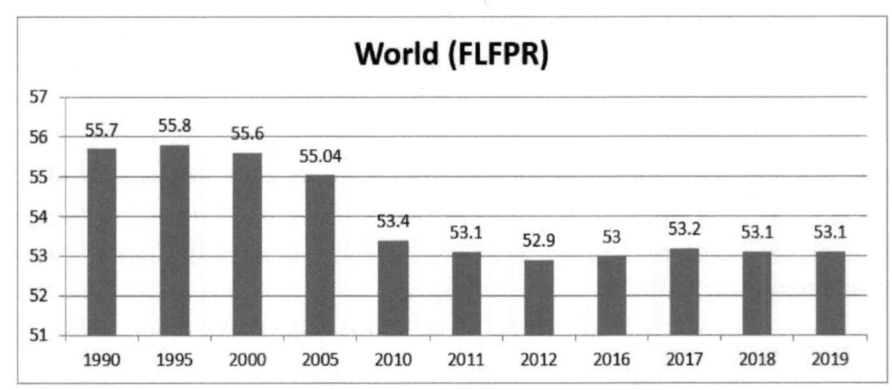


**Labor force participation Rate, female population ages 15-64 (modeled ILO estimates)**

**Source:** World Bank

FLFPR in World, it was 55.7% in the year 1990 and decreased by 2 percent in the year 2011 and then shows a declining trend and it was 53.13% in year 2019 and shows a stable trend then afterwards this figure is quite good then Indian (FLFPR figures) which shows a declining trend.

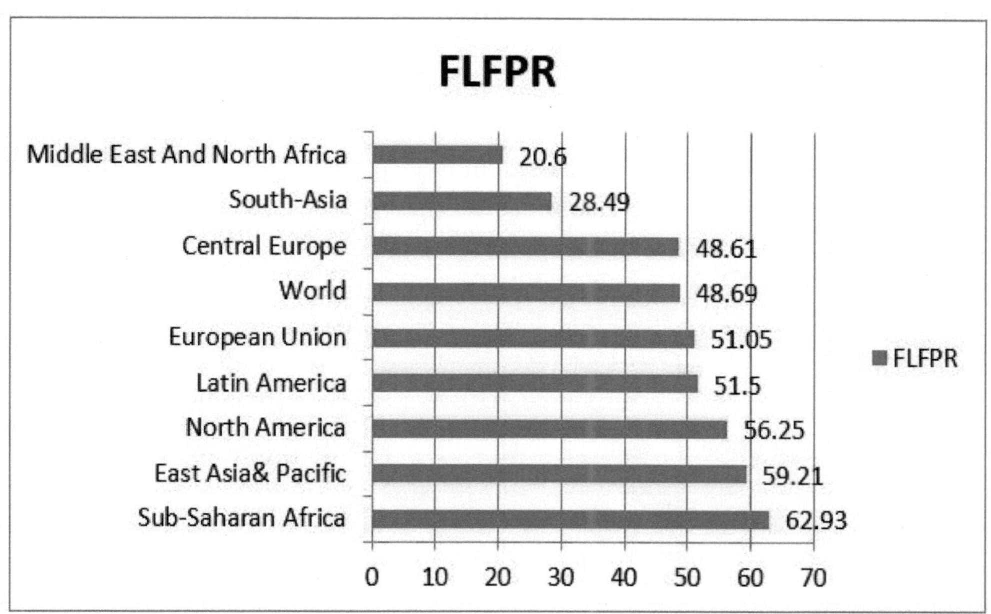


**Female labour force participation Rates, 2017**

**Source:** World Bank.

In middle East and North Africa, the FLFPR was 20.6% and the rate was also lower in South-Asia which was 28.49% and the rate was different in different regions of the world in Central Europe it was 48.61%, and the same rates in European Union and Latin America was 51.5% and quite higher in Sub-Saharan Africa where it was 62.93%.

**Female workforce participation varies in different countries of the world.**

While the participation rate has decreased in South Asia. In South Asia, female labour force participation rates range from 20% in Pakistan to almost 80% in Nepal due to social and economic factors. Women in Nepal are not affected by social norms they work mostly in subsistence agriculture they work by poverty rather than by choice. Bangladesh is one of the few countries of South Asia that has experienced an increase in employment due to growth in readymade garment Industry and an increase in livestock rearing. While in Srilanka with strong social indicators female labour force participation rates have remained only fairly stable of 33% in 2012 whereas Turkey has experienced declines in female participation rates from 36.1% in 1989 to 23.3% in 2005. This declining trend is due to rising urbanization as well as structural change in their country.

**International Comparatives**

The proportion of India's female population that is economically active is among the lowest in the world. While the female labor force participation rates vary considerably across developing countries, few countries in the world perform worse than India like Libya, Syria, and Yemen. Morocco, Samoa, Pakistan, Sudan, Egypt, Saudi Arabia, Somalia, Iraq, Iran, Jordan. These countries are largely spread across the Middle East, Africa and South East Asia where historically gender roles and stereotypes have continued to affect economic outcomes. In the South Asian regions only, Pakistan has a lower female labor force participation rate than India at 23.3 percent in 2015 (ILOSTAT). However, despite a higher fertility rate of 3.3 children per women and a lower female literacy rate of 46.3 % (Pakistan labor force survey 2010-11), the female labor force participation in Pakistan has continued to increase slowly over the past few years converging with the South Asian average. The Recently released Global Gender Gap Report 2017 by the world economic Forum which benchmarks 144 countries on their progress towards gender parity placed India the 108th position in 2017 a slip of 21 slots from 2016.The WEF measures gender gap across four pillars: Economic participation and opportunity, educational attainment, Health and survival and political empowerment. Across the economic participation and opportunities pillar, India is placed abysmally low at 139 out of 144 countries only better that Iran, Yemen, Saudi-Arabia, Pakistan, Syria. In country like India education and female labor force participation rate are not necessarily moving in the same direction. It is the Indian experience of a fall in female labor force participation rates despite robust economic growth, rising incomes, fall in fertility rates and improvement in female literacy that has risen in the international sphere.

India is an economic powerhouse on the global stage. It is the world's fastest-growing major economy in 2017 maintaining GDP growth above 7% since 2011-12. For India's women however, the year 2017 was significant for another reason – it was the year in which India's female labor force participation rates (FLFPR) fell to its lowest level since Independence. World Bank (2017) notes that India has amongst the lowest FLFLPRs globally with only parts of the Arab world being lesser.

The figure shows different years data:-

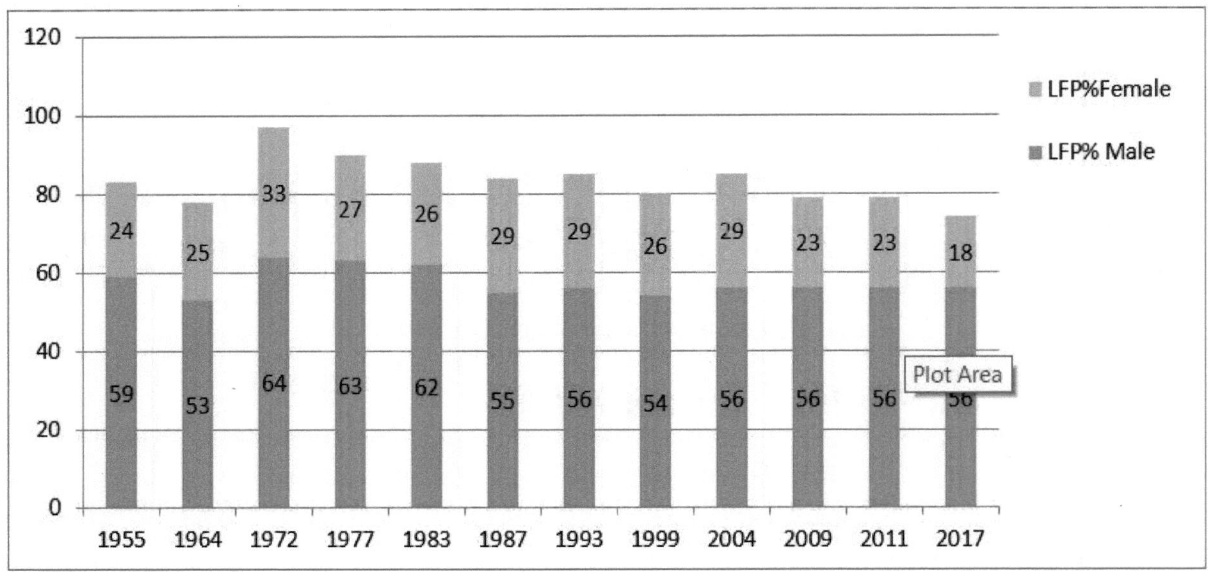


**Source:** NSSO Data

This is not sudden that women's participation in the labor force has shown a consistent decline over the last seven decades the figure shows this. The FLFPR peaked at 33% in 1972-73 and showed a decline till 1999-00, when it touched 26%. It is **17.5% in 2017-18 and it is at the lowest ever in Indian history.** This presents a queer conundrum – why is it that a country seeing considerable gains in female education, remarkable decreases in fertility rates, and increasing economic growth is not seeing a greater participation from women in the workforce?

Across the world India has very low female labor force participation rate. Low female labor force participation rates (FLFPRs) enact restraints on a country's development, the empowerment of its women, and the outcomes for its kids. Higher participation from women in the labor force has social and economic impact. In recent time period India is enjoying favorable demographic and economic conditions that would lead to increase in female labor-force participation rates. In India, economic growth rate has been increasing and high, substantial reduction in fertility rate; and significant increase in female education are noteworthy in India. India is passing through phase of 'demographic dividend', as the proportion of working-age people is quite high, this can boost per capita growth rates through labor force participation along with savings and investment effects. But if women largely are not participating actively in the labor force, this effect will be much weedier and India could run up labor shortages in key and leading sectors of the economy. Empirical evidences suggesting that employed women have greater negotiating power with positive repercussions on their own well-being along with their families. Increase in women's participation in the labor market is one of the key challenges of India's development (World Bank, 2001). An increase in female labor force participation rate and earning can lead to rapid growth and development, decrease poverty and enhance prosperity. It is evident that earning of women will have positive impact, not only on their own health but on the health and education of their children.

Comparatively female are investing more than men from their earning in the education and health of their children (Qian, 2008).

The Female Labor Force Participation rate for India remains abysmally low at around 27 % when the male labor force participation rate is 79.9%. The surprising part is that FLFP was 33.9 % in 2005 and has declined ever since. Clearly, the economic progress in India has not permeated to women, at least when you use FLFP as a proxy for women's economic progress. What is more astounding is that the FLFP for a country with similarly large population – China– is 64% and for the USA, a democracy like India, is 56.3% (World Bank, 2017).

**Objectives of the study**

1. To study the rate of participation of women in workforce, trends and occupational distribution.
2. To find out trends of female labor force participation in world.

**Review of Literature**

**Based on education**

Mammen and paxsun.(2000) study that how women's work participation rate changes with economic development of country. He also founds that women's education is the most important factor of female workforce participation rate. He further discussed that women's health status improves with development of mortality rate and education level. In a similar study, Edward .B.(2014) he examined in the study that Health survey 2006 to examine the relationship between female education and Women's labor force participation and fertility rates for Uganda. He examined further in his studies about results estimated from hypothesis shows that female education especially at the secondary and post-secondary school levels, reduced female fertility and increases the likelihood of females being engaged in the labor force. He also finds in his studies that reducing total fertility is expected to play an important role in achieving both the National development goals contained in the National development plan, and the Millennium Development goals. Also, Faridi and Rashid.(2014) they attempts to determine the factors that affect educated women's decision to participate in the labor force. They finds in their study that based on a field survey conducted in the district of Multan finds that there are some factors have a positive and effective impact on women's decision to work. In the same line of thought, Mishra and Gupta.(2011) they discussed in their study found that women education empowers the family and drives the economic growth of a nation. Also they examined in their study those development policies in women education like education and reservations. They also explored in their study that most recent National reports, in 2011, 45.9 percent of all enrolled undergraduates were women and 40.5 percent of all enrolled PHD scholars were women. They also showed in their studies that 61.25 percent among urban females with graduate degrees or higher were attending to domestic duties. They also explain in their study that the role of Social status and resident neighborhood as factor of women labor force participation. They further explained in their study that high social status which is calculated using social consumption as a proxy pushes women in salaried professions out of labor force and pulls women at waged labor levels into the labor force.

**Studies based on trends of labor force participation**

Arvind kumar.(2017) explains the trends and patterns of women's employment in agricultural sector in India. He used data from 1993-1994 to 2011-12 from national sample survey. He estimates from both usual principal and subsidiary status and analyzed from their study about the shifting of people from agriculture to non –agriculture sector in both rural and urban areas. Also he mentioned about the female's share is increasing more in secondary and tertiary sector. He also shares about structural change in the economy which leads to decline in agriculture sector of male and female participation. Lastly the author reveals about that female employment has shown a continues decline in all sectors than their male counterparts. Another study was done by, Aditi et al.(2013) examined from their study that women in India are over-represented in certain occupations and about 26% women were engaged in elementary occupations, 19% women were associated with craft and related trade works and 11% women were working in sales and service along with technicians. They further said that only 7% women workers were in administrative, executive and managerial occupations. There is a clear separation of women in sectors that are characterized by low wages, long hours and informal working engagements. Even within the sectors where women dominate, they rarely hold upper managerial posts and key positions. Similarly, Mansor et al.(2012) they discussed in their study that there is an increasing trend in macro data of the labor force participation rate of elderly aged 55-64 years. They also showed in their study that increase of household's expenditure from increasing living costs and inadequate old-age income. Their study updates the trend using micro-level data for 1989, 1999, 2009, and 2012 assess the trend in the labor force of the elderly over time & to determine the socio-demographic factors influencing a trend. They further examined in their study that four rounds of data of Malaysian household's Income found that age, marital status, gender are statistically significant in influencing elderly decisions to continue working in old age. Another study done by, Rahman et al.(2013) they reveal from the study that there exist a U-shaped relationship between economic growth and women's participation in the labor market but the study from Bangladesh does not support this argument. In fact in Bangladesh there has been an increase in female work force participation with the economic growth since the 1990s.They also highlighted in their study that Bangladesh has witnessed a substantial increase in female participation in intensive export-oriented industries in urban areas. The study also finds that the rapid expansion of micro-finance in rural areas has supported women's employment in poultry and livestock sector. They also shows in their study that the economy of Bangladesh as a whole and women's employment in urban areas seem to be too dependent on a single industry as other sectors are growing are either too small or are not employing women in large numbers in their industries.

**Methodology.**

The secondary data has taken from NSSO, World Bank, Annual Report, and PLFS 2017-18.

**Trends of women's workforce participation in India.**

India has experienced lowest women's labor force participation rates as the share of women that are engaged in economic activity in developing countries. India has 33 percent of female labor force participation in 2012, India's FLFP rate is below the global average of around 50% and 63% of East-Asia. India is the second most crowded country in the world with a population of 1.26 billion at end of the year 2014.Female work force participation rate of 33 percent indicates that only 125 million female are working out of 380 million working-ages Indian. Whereas the Gender Gap in participation among G-20 economies is highest in India at around 50 percent. The female labor force participation rate was in declining trend in India compared to other countries from 2004-05.When more female's women join the labor market that could enhance more jobs could be a source of growth and development of India. According to the 2014, Global Gender Gap Report founds a significant correlation between gender equality and GDP, the level of competitiveness human development indicators.

According to 2001census, the labor force participation rate for females aged 15-59 years was 40.02 percent in the 2011 census; this rate reduces to 37.4 percent. According to the NSSO (66$^{th}$ round), 2009-10 data shows that there is only 23 percent of women in workforce while comparing to 55.6 percent of men. The latest employment and unemployment survey data figures shows that in 2004-05 to 2009-10,female labor force participation declined from 33.3 percent to and around 26.5 percent in rural areas and from 17.8 percent to 4.6 percent in urban areas. Women's participation in rural areas and women's participation in rural areas reduce at a faster rate compared to urban areas. The rate of female labor force participation decreased from 49.0 percent to 37.8 percent in rural areas from 2004-05 and 2009-10, where as in urban areas there was a decline of only 5 percentages.

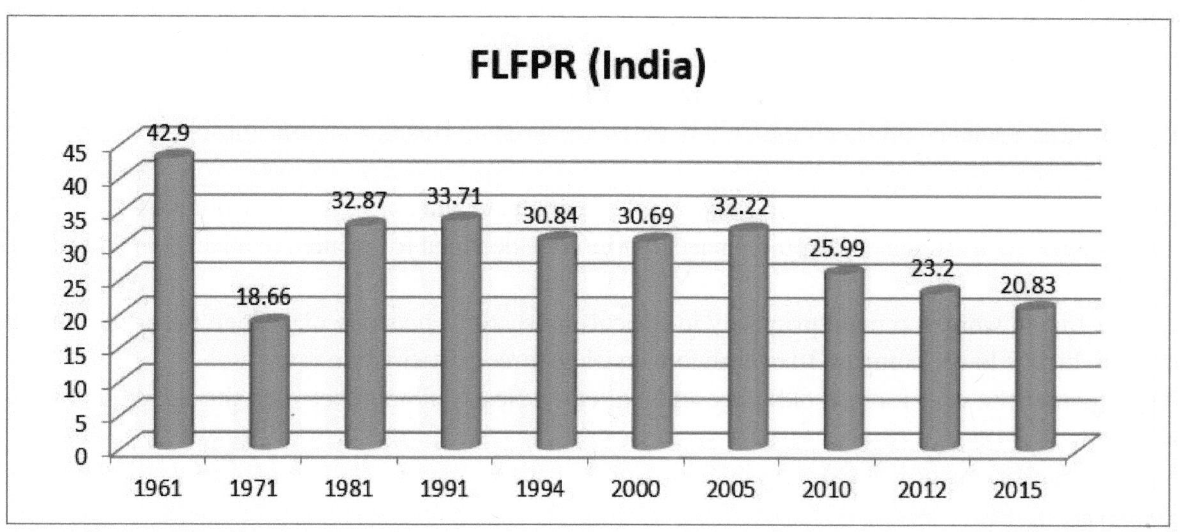


**Labour force participation rate, female (% of female population ages 15+) (national estimate) India**

**Source:** World Bank.

According to national estimates of FLFPR in India in 1961 were 42.9 which started declining and in year 2010 it was 25.99 and it remains 20.832 in 2015.

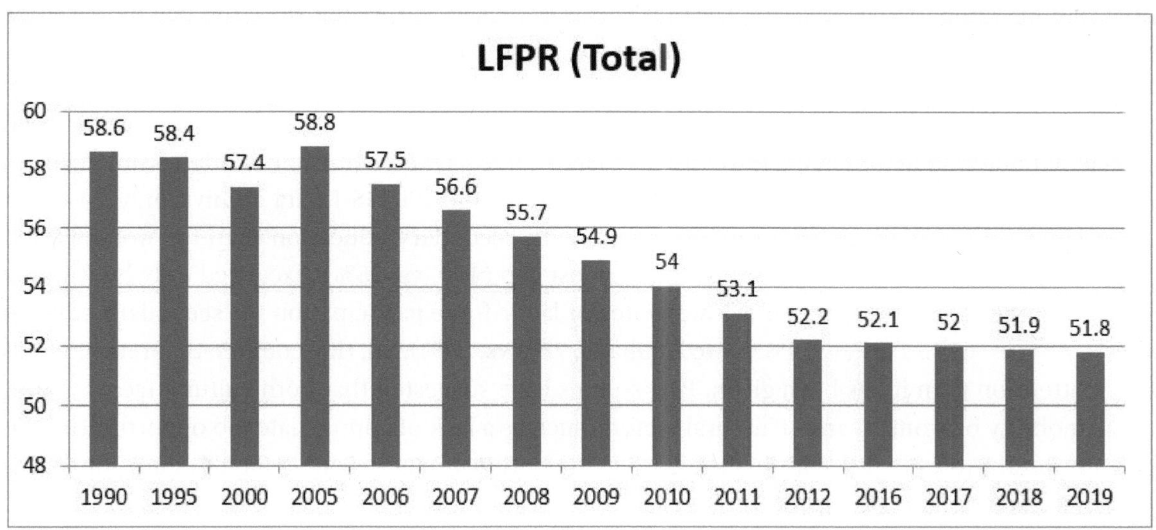


**Labour force participation rate, total (% of total population ages 15+) (modeled ILO estimate), India**

**Source:** World Bank

While looking on total labour force participation rates in India it comprised of Males and Females both, in the year 1990 it was 58.6(%), starts declining in the year 2008 it was 55.7(%) and in 2019 it was 51.8(%) it shows a declining trend in India.

**Reasons for Low and Declining Female Labor Force Participation Rate in India.**

World Banks has discussed and described various reasons for low and decaling female labor force participation rate in India in its publication entitled 'India Development Updates: Unlocking Women's Potential (World Bank, 2017). The reasons are as follows:

(1) Around 30% decline in female labor force participation in India is due to younger women staying in school longer as both secondary and tertiary enrolment rate increased substantially.

(2) Female labor force participation declines along the rural-urban gradation. It means as area become more urbanized, women who reside in those areas become less likely to work.

(3) 42% of India's science and technology graduates are women; this is a significant 'brain drain' from modern service sector.

(4) The female labor force participation rate for college graduate and above is only around 34%.

(5) During 2009-10, the female labor force participation rate declined for women of all level of education compare to 2004-05.

(6) Jobs for Indian women remain primarily in agriculture sector. The share of women in service and industry is less than 20% which is lower compare to overall female labor force participation rate.

(7) Women enter the workforce at older age and exit early. Nearly all men between the age group of 24-49 are in the labor force.

(8) Among the working age (15+), only 25% of working age women work, compare to nearly 80% working age men in 2011-12.

(9) During 2011-12, the female labor force participation rate declined for women of all ages compare to 2004-05.

**Education and women's participation in workforce.**

The low rates of Indian women's labor force participation have long been a magnet for academic inquiry.Most recent studies have noted the generally J-shaped or U-shaped relationship of women's education with their labor force participation. (Reddy, 1979, Sathar and Desai.2000). As national participation rates have continued to decline over the last few decades(Abraham 2013),cohort shifts out of low levels of education to intermediate and secondary education have been blamed for much of this decline. Most studies note the U-shaped relationship but usually fail to take the next step of trying to explain it empirically. This is especially surprising since the downward sloping part of the curve is so counter-theoretical. Neo-classical theory predicts that increases in women's education should usually lead to a rise in women's labor force participation rate. More education makes you more productive so your potential earnings rise, creating a greater incentive to join the labor force and substitute employment for leisure or home labor. India is unusual but not unique for having lower rates of labor force participation among adult women with secondary education. Among 71 countries with appropriate census data in the IPUMS-I data archive only 14 countries have lower rates of labor force participation for adult women with secondary education than for women with less than completed primary school. And India has the second largest gap (19% vs. 35%), exceeded only by Rwanda (72% vs. 92%). But several other countries also show lower rates of labor force participation for secondary educated women (e.g. Indonesia, 47% vs. 63%, Turkey, 34% vs. 46%, Ghana, 76% vs. 84%). So, this counter-theoretical result deserves more research attention than it has been given. Past studies have suggested that both cultural factors, such as norms restricting the mobility of women, and structural factors, such as a lack of appropriate job opportunities for educated women, play important roles in determining the U-shaped relationship between women's education and labor force participation in India (Das and Desai, 2003).

Theory also predicts that the relationship between education and employment is governed by both an income and a substitution effect. The substitution effect implies that educated women command higher wages that would encourage them to substitute participation in the labor force for leisure or home work. But the income effect on the other hand posits that educated women have higher incomes for the same amount of work encouraging them to devote more time to leisure or home work. In addition, and more importantly, educated women tend to marry educated men with higher incomes so the higher (unearned) family incomes would further discourage women's participation in the labor market. Combined with a cultural norm that confers higher status on women at home, other family income can act as a powerful deterrent to educated women's labor force participation. Where patriarchal norms are less dominant, the substitution effect should overshadow the income effect. But in India we would expect the income effect to be especially strong.

The negative relationships are likely because more educated women do not want to work in jobs that do not match their aspirations. The positive relationship with salaried positions is not sufficient to produce the expected overall positive relationship because there are not enough salaried positions open to women with moderate levels of education. The paper concludes by noting the possible importance of occupational sex segregation in excluding women from clerical and sales jobs that in most countries have been a major source of employment for moderately educated women.

| All India Labour Force Participation (in percent) | | | | | | | | | | | | |
|---|---|---|---|---|---|---|---|---|---|---|---|---|
| | Male | | | | | | Female | | | | | |
| Status | 1993-1994 | 1999-2000 | 2004-2005 | 2009-10 | 2011-12 | 2017-18 | 1993-1994 | 1999-2000 | 2004-2005 | 2009-2010 | 2011-2012 | 2017-2018 |
| Rural | | | | | | | | | | | | |
| Usual (ps+ss) | 56.1 | 54.0 | 55.5 | 55.6 | 55.3 | 54.9 | 33.0 | 30.2 | 33.3 | 26.5 | 25.3 | 18.2 |
| CWS | 54.7 | 53.1 | 54.5 | 54.8 | 54.5 | 54.4 | 27.6 | 26.3 | 28.7 | 23.1 | 21.5 | 16.1 |
| Urban | | | | | | | | | | | | |
| Usual (ps+ss) | 54.3 | 54.2 | 57.0 | 55.9 | 56.3 | 57.0 | 16.5 | 14.7 | 17.8 | 14.6 | 15.5 | 15.9 |
| CWS | 53.8 | 53.9 | 56.6 | 55.6 | 56.1 | 56.7 | 15.2 | 13.8 | 16.8 | 14.1 | 14.8 | 15.3 |

**Labor force participation rate (LFPR in per cent) according to usual status (ps+ss) and current weekly status (CWS) in NSS 50th (1993-94), 55th (1999-2000), 61st (2004-2005), 66th (2009-10),68th (2011-12) rounds and PLFS (2017-18)**

**Source:** Annual Report, PLFS, 2017-18.

LFPR for persons of all ages in usual status (ps+ss): Table shows that labor force participation rate is significantly lower for females than for males in both rural and urban areas. During 2017-18, according to usual status (ps+ss), about 54.9 per cent of rural males and 18.2 per cent of rural females were in the labor force. During this period, about 57 per cent of urban males and 15.9 per cent of urban females were in the labor force according to usual status (ps+ss). Between 2004-05 and 2011-12 as well as between 2011-12 and 2017-18, LFPR in usual status (ps+ss) for rural males remained almost at the same level. Between 2004-05 and 2011-12, for rural female, LFPR decreased by nearly 8 percentage points and between 2011-12 and 2017-18 it further decreased by around 7 percentage points. Between 2004-05 and 2011-12 as well as between 2011-12 and 2017-18 rounds, LFPR in usual status (ps+ss) for urban males remained at the same level. For urban females, between 2004-05 and 2011-12, LFPR decreased by about 2 percentage points and between 2011-12 and 2017-18, it remained almost at the same level.

LFPR for persons of all ages in current weekly status: From above table it is seen that during 2017-18, according to current weekly status, about 54.4 per cent of rural males and 16.1 per cent of rural females were in the labor force. During this period, about56.7 per cent of urban males and 15.3 per cent of urban females were in the labor force according to current weekly status. Between 2004-05 and 2011-12 as well as between 2011-12 and 2017-18, LFPR in current weekly status for rural males remained almost at the same level. Between 2004-05 and 2011-12, for rural female, LFPR decreased by nearly 7 percentage points and between 2011-12 and 2017-18 it further decreased by around 5 percentage points. Between 2004-05 and 2017-18, LFPR in current weekly status for urban males remained at the same level. For urban females, between 2004-05 and 2011-12, LFPR in current weekly status, decreased by about 2 percentage points and between 2011-12 and 2017-18, it increased by nearly 1 percentage point.

| All India | | | | | | | | | |
|---|---|---|---|---|---|---|---|---|---|
| | Rural | | | Urban | | | R+U | | |
| Age-group | Male | Female | Person | Male | Female | Persons | Male | Female | Person |
| PLFS (2017-18) | | | | | | | | | |
| 15-29 | 58.9 | 15.9 | 38.1 | 58.5 | 17.5 | 38.5 | 58.8 | 16.4 | 38.2 |
| 15 years and above | 76.4 | 24.6 | 50.7 | 74.5 | 20.4 | 47.6 | 75.8 | 23.3 | 49.8 |
| All ages | 54.9 | 18.2 | 37.0 | 57.0 | 15.9 | 36.8 | 55.5 | 17.5 | 36.9 |
| NSS 68th round (2011-2012) | | | | | | | | | |
| 15-29 | 64.9 | 27.1 | 46.4 | 60.7 | 18.1 | 40.5 | 63.6 | 24.4 | 44.6 |
| 15 years and above | 81.3 | 35.8 | 58.7 | 76.4 | 20.5 | 49.3 | 79.8 | 31.2 | 55.9 |
| All ages | 55.3 | 25.3 | 40.6 | 56.3 | 15.5 | 36.7 | 55.6 | 22.5 | 39.5 |
| NSS 66th round (2009-2010) | | | | | | | | | |
| 15-29 years | 68.0 | 30.2 | 49.6 | 61.0 | 16.8 | 40.1 | 65.9 | 26.3 | 46.8 |
| 15 years and above | 82.5 | 37.8 | 60.4 | 76.2 | 19.4 | 48.8 | 80.6 | 32.6 | 57.1 |
| All ages | 55.6 | 26.5 | 41.4 | 55. | 14.6 | 36.2 | 55.7 | 23.3 | 40.8 |
| NSS 61st round (2004-2005) | | | | | | | | | |
| 15-29 | 77.2 | 42.8 | 60.2 | 68.3 | 21.7 | 46.6 | 74.6 | 37.1 | 56.4 |
| 15 years and above | 85.9 | 49.7 | 67.7 | 7.2 | 24.4 | 53.0 | 84.0 | 42.7 | 63.7 |
| All ages | 55.5 | 33.3 | 44.6 | 57.0 | 17.8 | 38.2 | 55.9 | 29.4 | 43.0 |

**Labor force participation rates (in per cent) in usual status (ps+ss) during 61st (2004- 2005), 66th (2009-10), 68th (2011-12) rounds and PLFS (2017-18) for persons of age 15-29 years, 15 years & above and all persons**

**Source**: Annual Report, PLFS, 2017-2018.

LFPR for persons of age 15 to 29 years in usual status (ps+ss)

LFPR in usual status (ps+ss) for persons of age 15-29 years is presented. It is seen that during 2017-18, in India, LFPR for persons of age 15-29 years was 38.2 per cent: 38.1 per cent in rural areas and 38.5 per cent in urban areas. LFPR was around 59 per cent among males in both rural and urban areas. For female in rural areas, LFPR was nearly 15.9 per cent while for urban females, LFPR was nearly 17.5 per cent. For rural male, LFPR decreased by 12 percentage points between 2004-05 and 2011-12 which further decreased by 6 percentage points between 2011-12 and 2017-18. For rural female, LFPR decreased by 16 percentage points between 2004-05 and 2011-12 which further decreased by 11 percentage points between 2011-12 and 2017-18. For urban male, LFPR decreased by 8 percentage points between 2004-05 and 2011-12 which further decreased by 2 percentage points between 2011-12 2017-18. For urban female, LFPR decreased by 4 percentage points between 2004-05 and 2011-12 while it remained almost at the same level between 2011-12 and 2017-18. Thus, it is seen that during a period of 7 years between 2004-05 and 2011-12 and 6 years during a period of 2011-12 to 2017-18, among persons of age 15-29 years, the LFPR among males and females in rural areas and males in urban areas followed a decreasing pattern and the decrease (in terms of percentage points) during 2017-18 compared to 2011-12 was lower compared to the decrease in LFPR between 2004-05 and 2011-12. In urban areas, female LFPR though decreased between 2004-05 and 2011-12 did not further decrease between 2011-12 and 2017-18.

LFPR for persons of age 15 years and above in usual status (ps+ss)

LFPR in usual status (ps+ss) for persons of age 15 years and above is also presented. It is seen that during 2017-18, in India, LFPR for persons of age 15 years and above was nearly 49.8 per cent: 50.7 per cent in rural areas and 47.6 per cent in urban areas. Among rural male, LFPR was nearly 76.4 per cent and among urban male it was nearly 74.5 per cent. In rural areas nearly one-fourth of the females of age 15 years and above were in the labor force while in among urban females of age 15 years and above, nearly one-fifth were in the labor force. LFPR among rural male of age 15 years and above decreased by nearly 5 percentage points from 2004-05 to 2011-12 as well as from 2011-12 to 2017-18. LFPR among rural female of age 15 years and above, decreased by nearly 14 percentage points from 2004-05 to 2011-12 and it decreased further by 11 percentage points from 2011-12 to 2017-18. LFPR among urban male of age 15 years and above, decreased by nearly 3 percentage points between 2004-05 and 2011-12 and it further decreased by 2 percentage points between 2011-12 and 2017-18. LFPR among urban female of age 15 years and above decreased by nearly 4 percentage points between 2004-05 and 2011-12 and it remained at the same level between 2011-12 and 2017-18.

| All-India | | |
|---|---|---|
| **Category of persons** | **WPR in usual status (ps+ss)** | **CWS** |
| Rural | | |
| Male | 51.7 | 4.6 |
| Female | 17.5 | 14.8 |
| Person | 35.0 | 32.6 |
| Urban | | |
| Male | 53.0 | 51.7 |
| Female | 14.2 | 13.3 |
| Person | 33.9 | 32.9 |
| Rural+Urban | | |
| Male | 52.1 | 50.2 |
| Female | 16.5 | 14.4 |
| Person | 34.7 | 32.7 |

**WPR (in per cent) according to usual status (ps+ss) and CWS during 2017-18**

**Source**: Annual Report, PLFS, 2017-18

WPR in usual status (ps+ss)

In India, WPR according to usual status (ps+ss) was 34.7 per cent. WPR in rural areas was about 35 per cent and that in urban areas was about 33.9 per cent. In both rural and urban areas, WPRs for females were considerably lower than WPRs for males. In rural areas, WPRs for males and females were nearly 51.7 per cent and 17.5 per cent, respectively while in urban areas, WPRs for males and females were nearly 53 per cent and 14.2 per cent, respectively.

WPR in Current Weekly Status:It that the WPRs in is seen from above table that CWS were lower than the WPRs in usual status (ps+ss). In India, WPR in CWS was 32.7 per cent – 32.6 per cent in rural areas and 32.9 per cent in urban areas. The WPRs in CWS for males and females in rural areas were 49.6 per cent and 14.8 per cent, respectively. The corresponding figures for males and females in urban areas were 51.7 per cent and 13.3 per cent, respectively.

**Global trends of Women's participation.**

In 2018, the global working age population comprising women and men aged 15 years or older was 5.7 billion. Out of these 3.3 billion people or 58.4 percent were in employment and 172 million were unemployed. Both these groups taken together constitute the global labor force which therefore stood at 3.5 billion (38.6 percent) of working age were outside the labor force, including those engaged in education and unpaid care work and those in retirement. Within this group 140 million were in the potential labor force people who are looking for a job but are not available to take up employment. Around 61% of the world's working-age population participates in the labor market either by being actually employed or by searching for employment while being available for work. This participation rate has been declining on average by between 0.1 and 0.2 percentage points the year over the past 25 years with the steepest drop occurring in the aftermath of the global financial crisis of 2008.

**The Gender Gap in labor force participation is closing only marginally.**

The Global gap in labor force participation rates between women and men stood at 27 percentage points in 2018 less than half of all working age women (48 percent) were participating in the labor market in that year, compare with three-quarter of men (75 percent).The Gender Gap has been narrowing over the past 25 years because of the decline in the participation 1993-2003 was much smaller than that for men. In lower middle and upper middle Income countries male participation rates are quite similar ranging from 75 to 79 percent in 2018.By contrast the highest participation rate for women in the same year was 64 percent and was observed in low Income countries it a consequence of the economic as low as 35 %.The high female participation rates in low-Income countries are mainly a consequence of the economic necessity for women to contribute to the family income by engaging in market or subsistence activities.

On the other hand, the gender gap in labor force participation is closing rapidly in high-Income countries. Thus the participation rate for women in this country group rose by 3.5 percentage points from 1993 to 2018, while the participation rate for men fell by an equal amount over the same time span.

**Summary and Conclusion**

From the Vedic times, women have the highest place in society having all opportunities to develop intellectually, socially, morally. But now there more roles should be increased in economic activities day by day. Female work participation rate is one of the important designates of female status in the economy. Women's participation in economic activities is important from the perspective of their personal advancement, development and their status in the society. India has experienced lowest women's participation in the workforce as the share of women that are engaged in economic activities in developing countries when compared with different countries of the world.

**Reference:**

1. Annual Report, PLFS 2017-18.
2. Aditi, Nigam.(2013) Falling female labour force participation rate a puzzle, Retrieved from Economy.
3. Kumar, A. (2017) Emerging trends and pattern of women employment in India: Evidence from NSS data. IV (2):5,430-435.
4. Mammen and Paxson, C. (2000) Women's Work and Economic Development, *Journal of Economic perspectives*,14(4):141-164.
5. Muhammad, Z et.al. (2014)The correlates of Educated Women's labour force Participation in Pakistan: A micro study.
6. Mishra, A and Gupta, D. Social Status as a Driver of Female Labour force Participation in India.
7. Rahman and Rizwanul ,I et al.(2013) Female labour force participation in Bangladesh: trends, drivers and barriers, ILO.
8. Sharma, Punam. The Role and Position of Women Ancient Society in India.
9. Verick, S and Chaudhary, R. (2014) Female labour force participation in India and beyond:ILO Asia *–Pacific Working Paper Series.*
10. Verick, S and Rathi, A et al.(2014)India's urban work boom is leaving women behind.
11. Unni, J.(1998) Education and Women's Labour Market Outcomes in India: An analysis using NSS household Data
12. NSSO Data
13. World Bank

CHAPTER XXVI

# Child Marriages increased in India during Covid-19 Pandemic

*Sr. S. SAROJINI, AND **DINESH KARTHIK
*P.G.and **Research Scholar
Department of Chemistry
Shanmuga Industries Arts and Science College, Tamil Nadu
dineshkarthik2008@gmail.com

**ABSTRACT**

Marriage is a vital social institution and a means of forming a family, which allows society to continue to exist. This social process is expressed through rituals. In India, 45 percent of females under the age of 18 are married. The majority of females who marry before the age of 18 come from low-income or impoverished families. Domestic abuse, healthcare challenges, pregnancy problems, and mortality due to early pregnancy affect over 80% of girls. Feelings of hopelessness, helplessness, and severe depression are common symptoms of sexual abuse. In India, the COVID-19 pandemic has led to an increase in the number of child marriages.

**Keywords:** child marriage, COVID19, India, low-income.

## 1. INTRODUCTION

In India, child marriage has been practised for decades, with children being married off before reaching full physical and mental maturity. Religious traditions, societal standards, economic concerns, and deeply held prejudices all combine to create a toxic mix. There is a problem with child marriage in India. Regardless of its origins, child marriage is a serious human rights violation that causes long-term physical, psychological, and emotional harm. Sexual activity begins quickly after marriage, and pregnancy and childbirth at a young age can lead to the death of both the mother and the new born. Domestic abuse is more likely to occur in the homes of women who married while they were younger.

The COVID-19 pandemic has driven the social system into huge disarray. Attention has been drawn to COVID-19's direct effects on hospitalisation and deaths. However, the detrimental effect it has caused on the mental health of the younger generation has been highly underestimated.

The pandemic has had an indirect impact on the younger, and it is such oblique outcomes that constitute a serious threat to the generation's fate, particularly for the most vulnerable. The consequences are visible in all aspects of their lives, and they are significantly more intense for women and younger girls than for boys and younger men.

Due to limited connectivity and access to gadgets, many younger people were unaware of the change to online education. Limited access to basic services, including those that the young are most in need of, menstrual hygiene supplies, contraceptives, pregnancy-related and other reproductive care supplies.

A spike in early marriage is perhaps the least well documented result of the COVID-19 pandemic and associated lockdowns in India is a spurt in babies and early marriage. Drawing from insights from studies in preceding humanitarian disasters and crises in India and elsewhere, in addition to from reviews of cell phone and online surveys, and print and digital media reviews. I synthesise what is to be had and spotlight the probable effects on adolescents in India.

## 2. A SYSTEMATIC REVIEW

Child marriages exist in feudal societies where the Nagnika notion is widespread, according to Saraswat (2006). Parents have been told that they will go to hell if they do not marry their daughters before they reach puberty. The virtue of virginity prior to marriage is highly regarded in Indian culture. This is true for both women and certain men who have a lot of muscle. In a culture that values premarital virginity, getting the younger ladies of their childhood is one of the simplest ways to achieve it.

There are a lot of social, fitness, and financial downsides to marrying young. While there is no conclusive evidence that early marriage causes these negative outcomes, studies of the links between early marriages, poverty, low educational attainment, and other variables in various settings may have found that married women are more likely to engage in frequent unprotected sexual relationships. According to Miller and Lester (2003), marriage greatly increases the likelihood and demand of childbearing. In addition to the normal risks and responsibilities of child bearing, first-time mothers under the age of 16 have an increased risk of maternal and new-born mortality.

According to Haberland & Bracken (2004), married women have low levels of educational achievement, fewer or no social networks, limited mobility, and much less access to mainstream media such as television, radio, and newspapers than boys or unmarried women. In India, the average age at which women marry has increased little over time. Nonetheless, it is far lower than the prison age, and a large number of women remain married at a very early age, as reported by Rajan & Karkal (1989).

The issues include high birth rates, severe poverty and hunger, high illiteracy rates, and infant mortality. Mortality and low life expectancy, particularly amongst rural women, (Mr. Burns, 1998) The term "child marriage" refers to a wide range of socioeconomic settings. Tiny boys and women have been betrothed. Several of them are sound asleep, oblivious to what is going on. Then, if their unborn children appear to be of different sexes, households may agree to arrange a wedding for them. Then, there are marriages between young adults who marry their family members more than one year later, as opposed to marriages that may be consummated nearly a decade and a half later, according to Srivastava (1983).

Despite legal requirements to the contrary, it is obvious that early marriage is still the norm, and younger spouses may find it difficult to cope with a child once married. Sexually transmitted diseases (STDs), such as HIV/AIDS, are more common in children who participate in early sexual activity. Being married at a young age is a challenge. According to Yadav (2006), pregnancy is one of the top causes of maternal death in India.

As a result of toddler marriage, the reproductive and sexual fitness of female toddlers is the most harmed. increased mortality rates; a higher rate of obstetric complications; intrauterine growth retardation; pregnancy-induced hypertension; early births; increased mortality rates; a higher rate of RTIs and STIS; and foetal wastage (miscarriages or nonetheless births). The rates of neonatal and toddler death, as well as late transfer and low birth weight of the new child, Bhat, are all exceedingly high (2005). The dangers of early marriage harm not only the woman's toddler, but also the child she bears as a result of an early pregnancy. In India, one out of every 15 children dies before their first birthday, compared to at least one out of every 200 children in the developed world. (2004) (Agrawal &Mehra).

According to recent UNICEF research (2005), nearly half of Indian women between the ages of 20 and 24 marry before they reach the age of 18. When you consider the centuries and those who strictly enforced them, child marriages were nothing more than a game. Pre-adolescent and adolescent women, who account for a substantial share of India's population, are a vulnerable group. According to Verma, there is a higher risk of sickness and mortality as a result of early marriages (2004). Young brides, on the other hand, are under pressure to establish their fertility as soon as possible after the wedding and to produce children, particularly sons. A younger lady who rose to be meek and subservient, with little or no education, married to an older man, has a limited capability to negotiate sexual attraction. Khan, (1996). An early marriage, i.e., a toddler marriage, is linked to a high fertility price. The earlier a woman marries, the more likely she is to have a larger number of children, placing a greater demand on her fitness. Baht (2005)

Early marriages, according to studies, tend to leave the lady under male dominance, with no preference for initiating control, education, or fitness, leading to a life of domestic and financial servitude. It has been observed that children in most caste groups are forced to work at a young age, to the point that the monetary value of child labour has become a contributing factor to child marriages.

## 3. CASE STUDY OF CHID MARRIAGE

### 3.1 Case

TIRUVANNAMALAI: P Vidhya, 17, of Parvathy Agaram close to Polur, was a sufferer of early marriage. Tiruvannamalai district collector K S Kandasamy no longer intervened. The collector additionally ensured that she joined a nursing path. Her father, Pandurangan, died 12 years ago because of poor health, Vidhya's mom, Vijaya, 38, became the only breadwinner of the family. Vijaya laboured hard as a production labourer to train Vidhya and her more youthful brother. However, while Vidhya exceeded Class XII, her mom, spouse, and children began to wonder if instructing her had become a waste of money. The mom was determined to get her married to a 25-year-old antique tailor. But Vidhya turned towards the wedding as she desired to observe further. When her efforts to persuade her mom spouse, and children went in vain, Vidhya met the district collector, K S Kandasamy, 10 days earlier than her marriage, which had become scheduled for October 19, and filed a petition.

The collector instructed them that Vidhya may want to be a part of an undergraduate nursing programme. Kandasamy assured them that he could set up Rs.3 lakh for price and different expenses. *(Times of India, Chennai, November 28, 2018)*

**3.2 Case**

The Ganjam district administration in Odisha has foiled an attempt to marry off a 15-year-old woman to a man twice her age, according to officers. The marriage of the teenager, a pupil of Class VIII, became constant with a person of around 30 years of age in Patapur on Monday night. Acting on a tip-off, the kid improvement safety officer, police, and ChildLine activists rushed to the minor's residence in advance of her wedding. Childline activists rescued the minor and produced her earlier than the district baby welfare committee.

**3.3 Case**

New Delhi: Recently, the Union Cabinet made 21 years the minimum marriageable age for girls, in place of 18 earlier. What does this mean? It works in this way: while non-public legal guidelines that govern marriage and different non-public practises for groups prescribe certain standards for marriage — for example, Section 5(iii) of The Hindu Marriage Act, 1955 prescribes a minimum age of 18 for the bride and 21 for the groom — there is now an offer to amend the Child Marriage Prohibition Act.

The Indian Express recently reached out to three girls to learn about how their lives changed after they married at the age of 18. This is the tale of Bengaluru-primarily based totally Vimala, Mumbai-primarily based totally Saba (called modified) and Indrani from Kolkata. Vimala became compelled to marry her maternal uncle, her mom's brother. "I am now no longer inclined to get married." When I became 17, they gave me an engagement ring. We shouldn't get married to our uncles. I informed my mom that he or she could scold and hit me; she additionally burnt my palms sometimes, assuming I was in love with someone else, "she stated.

Indrani informed this outlet that she misplaced her father when she was young and had many siblings. "This is why I could not complete my education." After my marriage, I moved here to my in-legal guidelines location and it became a joint circle of relatives. I needed to be thoughtful of every person's needs. My focus shifted to how to make everyone else happy while I, in my opinion, desired to look at and work. She stated she became correct at embroidery, but became certain via means of marriage and couldn't pursue it.

Saba stated she was given married at the age of 17, after she became "sexually abused" by means of her "2nd cousin". "When I shared this with my dad and mom, they refused to accept it as true." It began after I turned six or seven years old, and while my dad and mom were given to know, they did no longer take it well. " She met a man at the age of 17, who claimed he desired to quit her formative years of suffering. But, after only a year of marriage, she realised she had made the wrong decision. *(The Indian Express, Wednesday, February 23, 2022)*

**3.4 Case**

A 14-year-old lady from Bihar's Purnea district was allegedly married off to a 40-year-old guy from Uttar Pradesh's Moradabad district on June 27. The police obtained the records of the alleged crime from a few villagers. According to the groom, a person from his village, who had a relative outside the minor's village, arranged this match.

On the constant date, the person arrived at Dimia Chhatarjan village in Purnea and the wedding took place in a mystery way in Dewanganj Kali Temple. However, after the wedding, while the bride refused to go along with the groom and cried, the nearby human beings came to recognise this alleged baby marriage. Soon, the information spreads throughout the whole village, and the locals object to it. The district Child Line additionally obtained the records concerning this, and shortly a crew reached the spot and rescued her.

According to the lady, she desired to take a look further, but her father, Girish Mandal, had forcefully married her off to a middle-aged guy. *(News Desk, June 29, 2021)*

**3.5 Case**

Haryana: A minor lady in Haryana's Hisar was bought for Rs 50,000 by her father and elder sister in exchange for her marriage. Fortunately, before the unlawful wedding ceremony should take place, the minor's mom informed the police, who subsequently stored the lady from the toddler marriage on Monday. The police raided the slums in the back of the New Auto Market in Hansi Place, wherein their own circle of relatives lives. However, the father-daughter duo, who bought the minor lady, fled the spot before the police could trap them. According to the information, the mom had informed the district safety officer that her husband and elder daughter were marrying off their minor youngsters for the change of Rs 50,000. As quickly as the police group reached the spot, each of the accused ran away.

The government then went to the in-laws' residence wherein the district girl and toddler improvement officer issued a note to the groom's own circle of relatives and requested them to be gift earlier than the police on Tuesday. This is the second case of a tried toddler marriage in Hansi inside 24 hours. On Sunday, a 14-year-old lady's marriage with a 39-year-old guy in Bogha Ram Colony was stopped by the district girls' and toddler welfare department. Notices for each aspect have been issued. The Hansi region has recently been in the news for witchcraft-related cases. Guys who are accused of witchcraft are allegedly crushed to death by every other guy and his sons. *(https://www.news18.com/news/india/haryana-police-rescues-minor-daughter-sold-for-rs-50000-by-family-3879233.html)*

**4. DISCUSSIONS AND FINDINGS**

**4.1 Factors Affecting Child Marriages**

As a result of financial advancement and human progress, women are at the crossroads of industry and reproduction, financial leisure, and human care. They are employees in each sphere. Women's discrimination, on the other hand, is pervasive. It all starts in the womb and ends in the tomb. Discrimination can be seen in schools, the workplace, one's close family, and in the socio-political realm. The toddler marriage machine is also a metaphor for gender discrimination. A lot of reasons can lead to a toddler's marriage.

**4.2 Spending less on women's education:** Human capital, also known as green human usable resources, plays a crucial role in economic development. Green human resources or human capital are required for the effective use of bodily capital. Someone's productive ability is determined by their level of education. Degrees in education determine academic achievement and human capital development and thus promote financial growth and improvement. The amount of money spent on a person's education impacts how capable he or she becomes.

In all developing countries, women have far fewer opportunities for education and career advancement than men. A country that invests more in education while also recognising the importance of increasing human capital. The same is true for individuals and families. In general, families discriminate between boys and girls (males and females) when it comes to school funding. Male children are treated as the destiny belongings and financial base of the family. Female children are treated as a burden on the family's financial base, whereas male children are treated as a few other assets as they are to be accepted to a person in marriage. are given significantly less or no importance as a result of this prejudice in expenditures on their education. People consider marriage as a cost-effective strategy to avoid spending money on a girl's education.

**4.3 Keeping Marriage Expenses to a Minimum:** A husband's reputation is often higher than a wife's inside one's own circle of kin. He is, of course, supposed to be more skilled than his wife. The spouse is believed to have a greater educational qualification than the wife when educational repute is considered. Many people like the experience of choosing a bridegroom who has the same educational qualifications as the bride, especially if higher-qualified bridegrooms require more dowry and other items. If the lady is educated, the groom must be educated even more than the bride, and further dowries must be supplied. The bigger the wedding costs, the more knowledgeable the bride is. This is one element of the opposing facet of the photograph because of triumph.

Because of the demonstrative effect, more educated women are directing marriage celebrations in accordance with their wishes and preferences, making them pricey and opulent. As a result, educating women increases the cost of marriage. As a result, many believe that it is far less difficult or burdensome for lessees to have a lady's marriage done as soon as she reaches puberty, or even before, at a younger age of thirteen or fourteen, or even younger, than to teach her.

**4.4 for Ancestral Property, without a percentage:** One of the variables that favours infant marriages to some extent is a woman's right to a share of her ancestors' property. If a woman marries at an early age, she may not need her proportion as an infant. Despite statutory requirements, female heirs are denied property rights in practise by resorting to early infant marriage for financial gain.

**4.5 Poverty Families: Women and children are frequently denied access to assets they do not own.** Female individuals, especially young girls, are victimised by the poverty of their own circle of relatives. A terrible own circle of relatives evidently jeopardises the woman's kids. Every chance is used to ward off the burden of a woman. So terrible households evidently motel to infant marriage to avoid any type of woman infant burden. Sometimes it is additionally perceived that terrible households are promoting ladies and the kid's marriage is a hidden form of promotion. Marrying infants to gods is a subculture that stems from their own circle of relative poverty.

**4.6 Socioeconomic Insecurity:** Social insecurity is one of the social elements that influence the infant marriage system. The fact that a married woman is less vulnerable to crime than a single woman is generally known. Married women are viewed differently by men (boys) than unmarried women. Unmarried women are thought to have nefarious motives. Ill-intentioned people commit crimes against lone females or males. Mothers and dads rush to marry off their daughters as soon as they reach puberty or earlier to prevent crimes, attacks, and mockery directed at single women.

**4.7 Single Parent Families:** Some families have just one parent, which forces them to lighten their load by marrying their under-18-year-old lady infant. It's just an excuse.

**5. PROBLEMS**

**5.1Asignificant burden in terms of in-legal guidelines inside one's own circle of relatives:** Women's domestic work encompasses a wide range of activities such as milling and pounding fresh grains, caring for livestock, cooking, and looking after children and the elderly. They must put in several hours of effort to obtain firewood and water from faraway locations. They also participate in family manufacturing to support their own circle of relatives‘ incomes, participate in expanding family claims by raising animals, and plant vegetables for family consumption. They are also very significant in agriculture. Women perform more arduous work in many households, but men manage property and money, giving women significantly less independence.

The trouble of a married infant in an in-legal residence is very burdensome. As a female family member, she has to play a couple of functions inside the legal guidelines of her own circle of relatives. They earn by supplementing their own and their relatives' earnings through productive sports. Maintenance of one's own circle of relatives and kids is another strenuous burden on the married infant. Being an infant, she has to play the function of a grown-up girl. Family duty is tough if she happens to be elderly in the in-legal guidelines‘ own circle of relatives. Family members expect more from her, but she is unable to meet their expectations. She has to attend to the wishes of aged people and different people inside her own circle of relatives as consistent with their exceptions that are regularly past her abilities.

**5.2 Early Pregnancy-Health Complications:** Child marriage evidently results in being pregnant early, resulting in many fitness complications. Without proper knowledge of her physiological condition, she will be unable to cope with changes in her frame throughout her pregnancy. Elderly girls, too, are no longer able to manage them properly. In the olden days, aged girls used to display the state of affairs perfectly all through being pregnant, all through transport, and put up transport times. However, today's adolescent girls lack both knowledge and the high-quality mindset required to be scientifically correct. This form of situation every now and then results in dependence upon neighbourhood quakes in an emergency.

**5.3 High Fertility Age Group:** When a woman is married under the age of sixteen, she typically tends to have extra kids, which makes being pregnant unwelcome. Girls are pressured to become pregnant and bear children.

**5.4 Inability to Plan or Manage Families:** Statistically, girls who marry early are likely to have extra kids. Among our respondents, the ones married below 15 averaged 4.96 kids; the ones married between 15 and 17 had 4.15; and people over the age of 18 averaged 3.12 kids. Young moms' workouts have much less affect and manage over their kids and feature much less capacity to make choices regarding their nutrition, fitness care, and family management.

**5.5 Preference for Male Child: Because of the preference for male infants, girls are pushed to conceive as frequently as they can until they give birth to a male infant.**

**5.6 Significant age difference between bride and groom: In general, there is a significant age difference between the bride and groom.** Most children in marriages, it is the bride who is an infant and no longer the bride groom. When the bride is an infant, she obviously does no longer have any freedom to specific her critiques on any of her own circle of relatives' lifestyles and she has to blindly obey the orders of the husband.

**5.7 Effect on female and female sexual fitness: Due to physiological immaturity in their sexual organs, young women may experience severe sex-related bodily aches.** Complications due to being pregnant at a younger age often consist of obstetric fistula (perforation of the bladder or bowel due to extended labour).

**5.8 Vulnerability to HIV Contamination:** A woman is physiologically more liable to contracting HIV than a man, as her vagina isn't always nicely covered with protecting cells and her cervix can be penetrated easily. In numerous instances, young girls are much more likely than younger guys to contract the sickness through heterosexual contact. Also, deeply entrenched socio-monetary inequalities compound their risk. Marriage can increase a woman's risk of contracting the virus, especially if her spouse is older and has had unprotected sexual relations with other partners. HIV infection affects the poorest and most disadvantaged in society, and married adolescent women may be more vulnerable to infection than unmarried women who aren't having sexual relations. Married adolescent women's incapability to barter more secure intercourse and different social pressures constitute an important channel of vulnerability.

1. **Suggestions and conclusions**

Eliminating early marriage is a good place to start. The findings of this investigation suggest the following solutions for dealing with this issue:

1. Look into the traditions surrounding early marriage. Inform your parents, friends, and children about the dangers of getting married young.

2. Establish a supportive network of (non-secular) leaders and instructors who can teach women how to bargain with their father and mother.

3. Increase fitness and networking people's awareness of the dangers of early marriage, prompting them to become champions and extrude marketing for their organisations and groups.

4. Build and strengthen networks with women's clubs, teachers, elders, local government officials, women's and children's organisations, network and non-sectarian leaders, and others.

5. Educate the court system, notably the police, judges, and prosecutors, on how to implement the legislation against early marriage.

6. Create strong support networks to keep women in education. Scholarships should be provided where possible, and instructors should be encouraged to help women.

7. Invite prominent professional women to speak to groups as role models and sources of inspiration for women.

8. Finally, given the reasons that contribute to infant weddings, all efforts should be focused on changing parents' and society's gender biases through effective teaching on the one hand, and poverty alleviation on the other.

**REFERENCE:**


1. R.S. Tripathi, R.P. Tiwari, Perspectives on Indian Women, (New Delhi,1999), P.161.
2. Simmi Jain, Encyclopaedia of Indian Women Through the Ages, (New Delhi, 2003), P.15
3. Acharya, R., Kalyanwala, S., and Jejeebhoy, S.J. 2009. *Broadening girls' horizons: Effects of a like skills education programme in rural Uttar Pradesh*, India New Delhi: Population Council.
4. Adukia, A. 2016. *Sanitation and Education*. Accessed on 24 May, 2017 at http://scholar. harvard.edu/files/adukia/files/adukia_sanitation_and_education.pdf.
5. Santhya, K.G., Ram, U., Acharya, R. et al. 2010. Associations between early marriage and young women's marital and reproductive health outcomes: Evidence from India. *International Perspectives on Sexual and Reproductive Health*, 36(3): 132-139.
6. Agarwal, Deepti & Mehra, Sunil. (2004). Adolescent Health Determinants for Pregnancy and Child Health Outcomes among the Urban Poor, Indian Pediatrics –Environmental Health Project, Special Article Services, Volume 41, New Delhi.
7. Bhatt, A. Sen and U. Pradhan (2005) "Child Marriage & the Law in India", Human Rights Law Network, New Delhi. P.259
8. Biswajit Ghosh, (2006): Trafficking in Women & Children, Child Marriage and Dowry: A Study for Action Plan in West Bengal, Dept of Women & Child Development & Social Welfare, Govt. of West Bengal & UNICEF.
9. Child and Law, Indian Council for Child Welfare, Chennai, Tamil Nadu, India, 1998, page 210
10. Miller S. & F. Lester (2003) „Improving the health and well being of married young first time mothers", W.H.O
11. UNICEF (2020) Early Marriage: A Harmful Traditional Practice: A Statistical Exploration.
12. Verma, A. (2004). Factors Influencing Anaemia among Girls of School Going Age (6-28 Years) from the slums of Ahmedabad City, Indian Journal of Community Medicine Jan-March, XXIX (1).
13. Malika Basu& Karoline Davis, The Unfortunate reality of Child Marriage in India, A World Vision India Publication, Chennai, 2015.
14. Nagi. B. S., Child Marriage in India: A Study of its differential patterns in Rajasthan, Mittal Publications, New Delhi, 1993.
15. Patricia Noller, Judith A. Feeney, "understanding Marriage – Developments in the Study of Couple Interaction", Cambridge University Press, New York, 2009
16. Prem Chowdhry, "Contentious Marriages, Eloping Couples – Gender, Caste, and Patriarchy in Northern India", Oxford University Press, New Delhi, 2009.

CHAPTER XXVII

# Dowry: The curse of the society

Ashok Kumar
Shri Ram College of Pharmacy, Banmore,
Morena (M.P.)

According to the National Crime Records Bureau (NCRB), 2019 data. A woman becomes a victim of dowry death roughly every 1 hour, becomes a victim of dowry cruelty every 4 minutes. on average, about 7500 women suffer from dowry death every year.

The word dowry is almost synonyms with Indian women. Dowry is considered as a Sacramental and Indispensable custom of marriage, especially in Hindu religion which turned into an illegal practice of the Society due to its Inhuman nature. According to Manu-Shastra, women were regarded as a lower class of people which denotes that they were undeclared slaves of such patriarchal society and such a society never lets women to observe equality in marital relationships. In Hindu marriage, it was considered as an important factor that determines their status and they never compromise in giving and receiving dowry.

Customs and rituals are part of the Indian culture until they don't cause any ill effects to society. But dowry practice disguised as a custom has victimized women in society in many ways and such practices endanger women's lives. In recent trends, literacy or government jobs are considered a tool for increasing their bargaining power in dowry negotiations instead of providing social awareness.

**The case: Chandra Singh V/S Kamlesh Singh**

On 28.2.1998, Mr. Chandra Singh filed complaint at police station Pisawan, District Sitapur, against Vishwaraj Singh and Kamlesh Singh under section 304B of IPC. Information was logged by the complainant that his sister was married to Kamlesh 4 years back. After marriage his sister was tortured by the accused. Kamlesh Singh used to beat her. When Janka devi (victim) came to her parent's house, she informed her family members about the accused.

One day, when Shivraj Singh (devi's second brother) went to meet his sister. Accused Vishwaraj Singh met him and told him that if he will not give **one buffalo and a bike** as a dowry then he has to face the dire consequences. Shivraj Singh stayed at his other sister's house for the night. The next day when he reached accused home, he was shocked to see that accused was preparing to take take the dead body of Janki Devi for cremation. Shivraj Singh asked what happened to Devi , Kamlesh got angry and didn't answer to him. Afterwards, Shivraj Singh sent Chandra Singh to complain. The complainant come to the house of his sister devi, thereafter he lodged FIR which was registered under 498A and 304B IPC and sec. ¾ D.P. act. Now, Kamlesh Singh, Vishwaraj Singh and Munshi Singh have been convicted for 10 years of imprisonment each under section 498A of IPC.

As we see in this case, the woman was tortured till her death for the dowry. The husband and in-laws play a central role in dowry death. As with any other form of domestic violence, a woman's ability to escape the abuse is largely dependent on the support systems and the resources available to her. This is especially true for victims of domestic violence because they are often subjected to years of abuse before the husband's family makes the ultimate decision to kill her. This section of chapter explores the legal instruments for the prohibition of dowry in India.

- Dowry prohibition act, 1961:

If any person, after the commencement of this act giving or taking of dowry, he shell be punishable with the fine which shell not be less than fifteen thousand rupees or (court decided value) impose a sentence of imprisonment for a terms of less than 5 years.

- Dowry death, section 304B IPC:

Punishable with a term of seven year of imprisonment.

- Cruelty on woman by husband or relative, section 498A IPC:

  Imprisonment up to three years and fine under section 498A.

- Other remedies:

  Intentional death of woman – section 302 IPC.
  Abetment of suicide of woman – section 306 IPC.
  Evidence act, 1872 section 113-B presumption as to dowry death.
  You might be thinking if these types of laws are exist than why is it still a problem?
  I think there are main four reasons behind these types of cases in this modern world.

**Suggestion:**

The concept of dowry never specific to any particular class of people, sections of people and it is more generalized in nature and study shows that there is no disparity between rich and poor in the issue of practicing dowry as a custom and studies revealed that more educated people consider as their literacy and job as a value added quality to demand more dowry . Advocating about awareness among high socio-economic group was ineffective in curbing these kind of practices because they are more prevalent in most enlightened part of our society and the only way prohibition is through stringent laws with effective implementation of by government machinery and active participation of judiciary in this issues whenever government machinery has failed.

**Conclusion:**

After interacting with victims of dowry, it was clear that 'everyone has a story to tell'. These women faced a lot of disgrace and dishonor. It was also clear that dowry is widely practiced. It has become a social malevolence and has created various economic, emotional and ethical problems in society. The dowry system is a constant financial stress on the woman's family. Women are ill-treated and beaten for the sake of dowry. Women face physical insecurity and mental anguish when they are not able to comply with the demands of their in-laws. The husband disparages the wife and treats her horribly without considering the effect on her health and feelings. Dowry degrades a woman's status and her parents are constantly worried about her well-being. The relationship of the husband and wife is ruined and conflict is created between family members. In many instances, the husband beats, abuses and fights with his wife for the sake of dowry. Shockingly, **even well-educated women were of the view that men have full authority over women.**

Such a situation is not only unfortunate but also deplorable, as marriage is meant to be a beautiful relation. It is also a social and legal bond between two persons that binds their lives together in all aspects. But as every coin has two faces, this blissful relation can sometimes turn into a nightmare. A girl who has dreamt of her marriage as a kind of fairy tale, who imagines her husband as a prince, can have her world turned upside down when she realizes what a horror it actually is. Dowry is one of the most horrendous and terrifying evils in our society which has taken deep roots. It has poisoned our social and familial environment. It is an utter nuisance to the girl's parents. Its prevalence has made people mentally distressed and financially insecure. It is high time that this evil be seen for what it is, rather than be justified with insidious excuses.

**REFERENCE**

1. Al-Turki, H.A., 2015. Effect of smoking on reproductive hormones and semen parameters of infertile Saudi Arabians. Urology annals, 7(1), pp.63–66.
2. Anon, Dowry. In SpringerReference
3. Basu, S., 2005. Dowry and inheritance,
4. Bradley, T., Tomalin, E. & Subramaniam, M., 2010. Dowry: Bridging the Gap Between Theory and Practice,
5. Chancey, L. & Dumais, S.A., 2009. Voluntary childlessness in marriage and family textbooks, 1950-2000. Journal of family history, 34(2), pp.206–223.
6. Cowan, A., 2010. Marriage and Dowry: Oxford Bibliographies Online Research Guide, Oxford University Press.
7. Goody, J. & Tambiah, S.J., 1973. Bridewealth and Dowry, CUP Archive.
8. Grossmann, I. & Varnum, M.E.W., 2015. Social structure, infectious diseases, disasters, secularism, and cultural change in America. Psychological science, 26(3), pp.311–324.
9. http://shodhganga.inflibnet.ac.in/bitstream/10603/52350/12/12_chapter%206.pdf
10. Hooja, S.L., 1969. Dowry System in India: A Case Study, Delhi] : Asia Press.
11. Katib, A.A. et al., 2014. Secondary infertility and the aging male, overview. Central European journal of urology, 67(2), pp.184–188.
12. Manning, W.D., Fettro, M.N. & Lamidi, E., 2014. Child Well-Being in Same-Sex Parent Families: Review of Research Prepared for American Sociological Association Amicus Brief. Population research and policy review, 33(4), pp.485–502.
13. Paul, M.C., 1986. Dowry and Position of Women in India: A Study of Delhi Metropolis,
14. https://indiankanoon.org/doc/123123670/
15. Sarda, M., 2011. The Concept of "Dowry" and "Dowry Death" - a Study in the Light of Supreme Court Decision in Ashok Kumar"s Case. SSRN Electronic Journal

CHAPTER XXVIII

# Reproductive Health of Women in India


*Pallavi Singh, **Vishakha Singh

*Research Scholar, Department of Family Resource Management & Consumer Science, Collage of Community Science, Acharaya Narendra Deva University of Agriculture & Technology Ayodhya, Uttar Pradesh

**Research Scholar, Department of Food Science & Nutrition, Collage of Community Science Assam Agriculture University Jorhat, Assam

singhpalu97@gmail.com



**Abstract**

Reproductive health of women remains a major development task in rural India. Educated women living in urban areas have less number of children as compared to illiterate women living in rural areas. The age-specific fertility rate was the highest (194.3) for women in the age-group 20-24 years followed by age-group 25-29 years (149.7) and 30-34 years (63.9). Infant Mortality

Rate (IMR) and Under 5 Mortality Rate also vary with the area they live. With social pressure of proving fertility, almost one third of young women in India give birth before they turn 18 and 53% by 20 years. Almost one-fifth of these pregnancies that resulted in live births are unplanned. Rural Indian women havelowlevelsofboth education and formallaborforceparticipation. Some major issues of women health are illiteracy, increasing demand of dowry, son preference, gender biasness, unhygienic conditions, less prenatal care, violent crimes against women etc. A woman'shealth affectsthehouseholdeconomic well-being,asawomanin poor health will be lessproductivein the labor force. Because ofthe wide variation in cultures,religions, and levels of developmentamong India. Women's health also variesgreatly from state to state.



Keywords: Reproductive health, Rural women, Illiteracy


**Introduction:**

Reproductive health of women remains a major development task in India. In India fertility rates among women greatly depend upon their education, age and living conditions. Educated women living in urban areas have less number of children as compared to illiterate women living in rural areas. The age-specific fertility rate was the highest (194.3) for women in the age-group 20-24 years, age-group 25-29 years (149.7) and 30-34 years (63.9). Infant Mortality Rate (IMR) and Under 5 Mortality Rate (U5MR) also vary with the area they live. Over the course of the 21$^{st}$ century, India has seen momentous and multi-dimensional changes in its population and sexual and reproductive health (SRH) situation. As of its 2011 census, India's population was 1.21 billion, and its decadal growth rate had declined more sharply over the 2001–2011 decade than in earlier. The total fertility rate is now 2.2 and has reached replacement level in 18 of its 29 states and its age structure places the country in the advantageous position of being able to reap the demographic dividend. The policy and program environment has shifted from a narrow focus on family planning to a broader orientation that stresses SRH and the exercise of reproductive rights. Yet, India may not meet several of the milestones set by Sustainable Development Goals (SDG). Reproductive health of a woman is maintained by reducing fertility rate and spacing among births. Women's health refers to the branch of medicine that focuses on the treatment and diagnosis of diseases and conditions that effect woman's physical and emotional well-being. Health status of women has ramification and impact on the human well-being and economic growth and on their families also. Woman with poor health is more likely to give birth to low weight infants and less care to their children. Moreover, Indian women have high mortality rates, particularly during childhood and in their reproductive years. Other problems in women in India are low level of education, son preference, pressure of dowry, lack of independence and decision making. All these factors also have impact on the health of women. In this way National Health Policy in India was formulated in 1983 with the motive to achieve an acceptable standard of good health amongst the general population of the country. Ministry of Women and Child Development developed a draft National Policy for Women in 2016, under which advancement, development and empowerment of women with appropriate strategies have been discussed.

Although, today's youth are relatively better educated and exposed to modern technologies of social communications than youth of the past, social vulnerabilities persist with marked influence of gender norms, early interruption of school education, early marriage, and pregnancy. Despite a strong policy on the minimum legal age at marriage, a sizeable proportion of Indian women get married before age 18 years and around 17 percent of women in the age group of 15-19 years have begun child-bearing. A recent study on 'Youth in India' found that 12 percent of young men and three percent of young women reported pre-marital sexual relations. For many youths, sexual and reproductive experiences were uninformed, unsafe, and for some, unwanted, primarily because of lack of awareness and skills in negotiating safe sex and discussing reproductive health matters with their parents and partners. The median age at first sexual exposure is 17.8 years, and even lower among women with no education and from the poorest economic strata (16.4 years). With lack of correct information on contraception and social pressure of proving fertility, 30 percent of women in India give birth before 18 years and 53 percent by age 20. Almost one-fifth of these pregnancies that result in live births are unplanned. Young women, often face social, economic, logistical, policy and health system barriers in accessing sexual and reproductive health (SRH) services, including safe abortion. Pregnancy and motherhood outside of marriage are stigmatized in many societies, which may cause unmarried pregnant women to seek abortion. As a result, young women often approach unskilled and illegal providers and face post abortion complications. young women (15-24 years) account for 45 percent of total maternal deaths in India. In addition, unsafe abortion alone accounts for 8-10 percent of maternal deaths in all women. This may be even higher among young women. Poor agency among youth which often influences young people's sexual and reproductive lives in terms of enabling them to exercise their choice and say in the timing of marriage and choice of partner, to make health-related decisions, to access health services, and to exercise informed choices about whether and when to engage in sexual relations and contraception. One way to address the gap between awareness of SRH issues and service availability and utilization is through youth-focused interventions. The rationale behind youth-focused interventions is to promote awareness and healthy behaviors; by creating a supportive environment, young women will be able to act on these health-promoting behaviors. Another aim of such interventions is to increase self-efficacy to engage in these health-promoting behaviors. Though behavior change communication (BCC) interventions have successfully been used in India to increase knowledge of contraceptive use, immunization, HIV/AIDS, and safe abortion among women of reproductive age.

**Key Issues of Women Health India:** Women and menhave nearly the same life expectancyat birth. Indian women have high mortalityrates, particularly during childhoodand in their reproductive years. The health of Indian women isintrinsically linked to their status insociety. Researches on women'sstatus has found that the contributionsIndian womenmaketofamiliesoften are overlooked,andinsteadtheyare viewedas economicburdens.Thereis a strongsonpreferencein India, as sonsareexpectedto care forparents astheyage. Thisson preference,alongwith high dowrycosts fordaughters,sometimes results in themistreatmentof daughters. Further,Indian women havelowlevelsofboth education and formallaborforceparticipation.Theytypicallyhavelittle autonomy,living underthecontrol of first their fathers,thentheirhusbands, and finally their sons. All of thesefactors exert a negative impact onthe health status of women.Poor health has repercussions notonly for women but also theirfamilies. Women in poor health aremore likely to give birth to low weightinfants. Theyalso are lesslikelyto be ableto providefoodandadequatecare fortheir children.Finally,a woman'shealth affectsthehouseholdeconomic well-being,asawomanin poor health will be lessproductivein the labor force. Because ofthe wide variation in cultures,religions, and levels of developmentamong India. Women's health also variesgreatly from state to state.

i. **Fertility Intertwined with Women's Health:** Many of the health problems of Indian women are related to or exacerbated by high levels of fertility. There are large differences in fertility levels by state, education, religion, caste and place of residence. Utter Pradesh, the most populous state in India, has a total fertility rate of over 5 children per woman. On the other hand, Kerala, which has relatively high levels of female education and autonomy, has a total fertility rate under 2.1 High levels of infant mortality combined with the strong son preference motivate women to bear high numbers of children in an attempt to have a son or to survive to adulthood. Numerous pregnancies and closely spaced births erode a mother's nutritional status, which can negatively affect the pregnancy outcome (e.g., premature births, low birth-weight babies) and also increase the health risk for mothers. Unwanted pregnancies terminated by unsafe abortions also have negative consequences for women's health. Reducing fertility is an important element in improving the overall health of Indian women. Increasing the use of contraceptives is one way to reduce fertility. While the knowledge of family planning is nearly universal in India, only 36 percent of married women aged 13 to 49 currently use modern Contraception.

v. **Over 100,000 IndianWomen Die Each Year fromPregnancy-Related Causes:** Maternal mortality and morbidity are two health concerns that are related to high levels of fertility. India has a high maternal mortality ratio approximately 453 deaths per 100,000 births. According to the report of the World Bank; the leading contributor to high maternal mortality ratios in India is lack of access to health care.

v. **Few Pregnant Women Receive Prenatal Care:** The most recent National Family Health Survey (NFHS) found that the pregnant women in India received less prenatal care during their pregnancies. The proportion receiving no care varied greatly by educational level and place of residence. Nearly half of illiterate women received no care compared to just 13 percent of literate women. Women in rural areas were much less likely to receive prenatal care than women in urban areas. Thus, there is a definite need to educate women about the importance of health care for ensuring healthy pregnancies and safe childbirths. Another reason for the low levels of prenatal care is lack of adequate health care centers. 16 percent of the population in rural areas lives more than 10 kilometers away from any medical facility.

v. **Majority of Births in India Take Place at Home:** Place of birth and type of assistance during birth have an impact on maternal health and mortality. Births that take place in non-hygienic conditions or births that are not attended by trained medical personnel are more likely to have negative outcomes for both the mother and the child. The NFHS survey found that nearly three quarters of all births took place at home and two-thirds of all births were not attended by trained medical personnel. While health care is important, there are several other factors that influence maternal mortality and health.

v. **One in Five Maternal Deaths Related to Easily Treated Problem:** Anemia, which can be treatedrelatively simply and inexpensivelywith iron tablets, is another factorrelated to maternal health and mortality. Between 50 and 90 percent of allpregnant women in India sufferfrom anemia. Severe anemiaalso increases the chance of dyingfrom a hemorrhage during labor.

v. **Violent Crime against Woman:** Violence against women is a health problem that is often ignored by authorities who view such behavior as beyond their purview. In certain societies, violence, such as wife beating, is perceived as "normal" or as a husband's right. Violence against women is detrimental to economic development because it deprives women of the ability to participate fully in the economy by depleting both their emotional and physical strength. Violence against women also can have negative consequences for the children of the victims. Many of the victims are young women; 30 percent of all reported rapes happened to girls who were age 16 or younger (National Crime Records Bureau (NCRB). Often women are tortured by other women such as a mother-in-law.

v. **Dowry Deaths Increasing:** The most media-sensationalized type of violence against women in India is dowry death. When a woman marries, her family provides the husband's family with gifts (e.g., clothes, household goods, and cash). In many instances, the demand for these gifts does not end with the marriage but continues, as the husband's family persists in making additional dowry demands for years after the wedding. A dowry death is defined as the unnatural death of a woman caused by burns or bodily injury occurring within the first 7 years of marriage, if it can be shown that the woman was subjected to cruelty by her husband or her husband's relatives shortly before death in connection with a demand for dowry. The rates of dowry deaths are higher among the poor and the lower castes. Alcoholism is also associated with increases in violence against women.

v. **Nowhere to Turn:** Unfortunately, because many crimes against women are domestic, women have limited recourse. Many women who suffer from domestic violence have little or no education, are not likely to be able to support themselves, and are unlikely to be able to turn to their parents if they leave their husbands because their parents either will not (because of the social stigma) or cannot (because of economics) take them in.

v. **More than Half of Indian Children Are Malnourished:** Malnutrition is another serious health concerns that Indian woman face. The negative effects of malnutrition among women are compounded by heavy work demands, by poverty, by childbearing and rearing, and by special nutritional needs of women, resulting in increased susceptibility to illness and consequent higher mortality. While malnutrition in India is prevalent among all segments of the population, poor nutrition among women begins in infancy and continues throughout their lifetimes. Women and girls are typically the last to eat in a family; thus, if there is not enough food, they are the ones to suffer most. According to the NFHS; Indian children have among the highest proportions of malnourishment in the world. More than half (53 percent) of all girls and boys under 4 years of age were malnourished, many women never achieve full physical development. This incomplete physical development poses a considerable risk for women by increasing the danger of obstructed deliveries.

v. **Mother's Education Strongly Related to Children's Malnutrition:** Mother's education, is highly correlated with the level of malnutrition among children. Children of illiterate mothers are three times as likely to be severely undernourished as children of educated mothers. Nutritional status of children also differs by state. Bihar and Uttar Pradesh have the highest proportion of undernourished children and Kerala has the lowest, consistent with the different levels of socio-economic development in these states.

v. **Excess Female Deaths:** One of the reasons for the poor health of Indian women is the discriminatory treatment girls and women receive compared to boys and men. This deficit of females is due to higher female than male mortality rates for every age group up to age 30.

v. **HIV/AIDS in India Is a Little Understood Epidemic:** The HIV/AIDS epidemic in India is spreading rapidly and increasingly will affect women's health in coming years. The highest rates of infection are found in population groups with certain high-risk behaviors (i.e., sex workers, intravenous drug users, and sexually transmitted disease patients). However, infection also is increasing in the general population. The epidemic is fueled by both married and unmarried men visiting sex workers who have high rates of infection. Despite the alarming growth of the epidemic, most women in India have very little knowledge of AIDS. The NFHS found that a large majority of Indian women had never heard about AIDS. Even among those who had heard of the disease, there were many misconceptions about modes of transmission. Indian women could benefit from a strengthened national HIV/AIDS education program and intervention programs targeting groups most susceptible to HIV infection.

**Opportunities to improve access to maternal health care of the women in India:** In an ideal maternal health system, all women would have access to comprehensive, seamless medical care with links to behavioral, economic, and social supports as needed, and they would be engaged in this system before, during, and after pregnancy. Lack of access to maternal health care is a result of many factors and creating the ideal maternal health system requires multiple steps. The pillars of the ideal system are: Accessible, Affordable, Risk-appropriate, High quality, Patient centered, Innovative, Coordinated, Equitable.

- **Accessible;Delivers Care via a Multidisciplinary Workforce:** Maternal health care is delivered by a range of providers, including specialty providers (e.g., obstetricians and gynecologists), family physicians and other primary care physicians, and advanced practice nurses (e.g., midwives, community health workers, and doulas). Each of these health care professionals plays a critical role in delivering maternal health care before, during, and after pregnancy.

- **Affordable;Reduces Financial Barriers for Mothers and Families:** Affordability is a primary barrier to accessing health care for those who are uninsured and those who have insurance plans with high premiums or high deductibles. Although laws and regulations have expanded access to health insurance and coverage of maternal health and family planning-related services. In addition, uninsured rates for people living in rural areas were higher than the rates for people living in urban areas, and, and women living below 100% of the Federal Poverty Level had higher uninsured rates compared to other groups. While uninsured women are less likely to seek needed health care overall, 38% of all women do not seek health-related services (e.g., receive recommended preventive care or follow up care, fill a prescription) due to cost.

- **Risk-Appropriate;Exemplifies a High-Functioning Maternal Health System:** Access to risk-appropriate, quality care is an indicator of a high-functioning maternal health system. Studies comparing quality of care and maternal health outcomes among rural versus urban hospitals have shown differing results. While access to risk-appropriate care during labor and delivery is critical, access to risk-appropriate care during and after pregnancy is also essential in monitoring and managing high-risk conditions such as diabetes or hypertension. The variability in quality and preparedness among rural maternal health services highlights the need for policies and programs to ensure that rural women have access to risk-appropriate care. Lack of access to risk appropriate health care is also attributable, in part, to availability of hospital and obstetric units in rural areas, particularly given that nearly half of all rural areas have no hospital-based services.

- **High Quality; Provides Safe, Timely, Efficient, and Effective Care and Services:** There are numerous frameworks that outline what constitutes high-quality care. The Institute of Medicine (now the Health and Medicine Division of the National Academies of Sciences, Engineering, and Medicine) identified safety, timeliness, efficiency, and effectiveness as a few key elements. Safety entails avoiding harm to patients from the care that is intended to help. Timeliness pertains to reducing waits and the occasional harmful delays in receiving or delivering care. Efficiency calls for organizations and practices to minimize waste of resources such as equipment, supplies, ideas, and energy. Effectiveness means that the services being provided are evidence-based, while avoiding underuse, misuse, or the provision of services for those not likely to benefit. In 2016, the World Health Organization released, Standards for Improving Quality of Maternal and Newborn Care in Health Facilities, that includes guidelines to help, "end preventable maternal and newborn morbidity and mortality," and to ensure that, "every pregnant woman and newborn should have skilled care at birth with evidence-based practices".

- **Innovative; Leverages Telehealth and Related Technology:** Telehealth is the use of electronic information and telecommunication technologies to support long-distance clinical health care, as well as, patient and professional health-related education, public health, and health administration. Telemedicine is the application of telehealth solely as it relates to clinical services. Opportunities exist to utilize telehealth and telemedicine, to expand access to maternal health care among women living in rural areas. There are many forms of telehealth, including live video (synchronous telehealth), store-and-forward (asynchronous telehealth), remote patient monitoring, mobile health (mHealth), and electronic consults (e-consults), that can meet many different needs for women and providers in rural areas before, during, and after pregnancy. Structural and legislative opportunities to expand use of telemedicine include improving access to broadband, ensuring the cost of technologies and devices are reasonable and establishing policies that promote use of telemedicine among providers to expand access to maternal health services.

- **Coordinated; Connects Women to Behavioral and Social Supports:** Access to behavioral and social services (e.g., family support, financial services, violence prevention, and nutrition support) are critical to the overall health and wellness of women before, during, and after pregnancy. Access to these services, particularly among women in rural communities, is inadequate. Rural communities often have limited access to social services such as housing support, employment services, childcare, and home visiting programs, all of which impact health outcomes for rural populations. For some women who otherwise do not have access to health care, or who do not actively seek health care regularly, pregnancy offers an opportunity to connect with a medical home that is coordinated and integrated with behavioral, economic, and social supports. However, for women covered by Medicaid that opportunity may be time-limited.

- **Equitable; Provides High-Quality, Patient-Centered Care to All Women:** Access to quality maternal health care is just one factor among many that influence maternal health outcomes. Research has shown that, while there have been improvements in quality of care broadly; these efforts have not reduced health disparities for women of color. A number of person- and system-level factors contribute to the perpetuation of health disparities, including institutional bias. Given that causes are multi factorial, solutions are far more complex than just improving quality of care. The interplay of structural determinants (e.g., socioeconomic position, race/ethnicity), maternal circumstances (e.g., living and working conditions, transportation), and behavioral, psychological, and biological factors help to explain disparities in health outcomes in rural areas. Access to transportation, stable housing, child care, healthy foods, and health insurance are central to ensuring that women, particularly women living in rural areas, are able to access the maternal health care they need before, during, and after pregnancy. Addressing these needs may not be sufficient to eliminate racial and ethnic disparities experienced by women of color living in rural communities. As demonstrated by the National Healthcare Quality and Disparities Report, issued annually by the Agency for Healthcare Research and Quality, improvements in health care quality do not always result in reductions of racial and ethnic disparities. Achieving health equity requires a specific focus on closing the gap.

**Conclusion:**Reproductive health of women is directly linked with the adequate health and development of her children. The sustainable Development Goals (SDGs) of World Health Organization addresses key challenges among women like reproductive health, poverty, inequality, violence against women, which, otherwise also is necessary for the global success. In India, many reproductive health problems go untreated and taken as “Normal”. Even in many cases woman herself thinks that her illness related to reproductive issues do not require medical attention. Many National policies are functioning towards the improvement, enhancement and development of woman reproductive health.

**References:**

1. Sushanta K. Banerjee Janardan Warvadekar Kathryn L. Amit Rawat (2012); Are Young Women in India Prepared to Deal with Sexual and Reproductive Health Issues? A Case Study of Jharkhand, India.
2. Linda Sanneving,Nadja Trygg,Deepak Saxena, Dileep Mavalankar, and Sarah Thomsen (2013); Inequity in India: the case of maternal and reproductive health.
3. Ijyaa Singh, Ankita Shukla, Jissa Vinoda Thulaseedharan & Gurpreet Singh(2021); Contraception for married adolescents (15–19 years) in India: insights from the National Family Health Survey-4 (NFHS-4).
4. Dr. Mamta Bansal. (2017); Status of Reproductive Health of Women in India: A Review, ISSN: 2320-5407, Int. J. Adv. Res. 5(10), 1397-1403.
5. Jitendra Kumar Meena , Anjana Verma , Jugal Kishore , and Gopal Krishan Ingle-(2015);Sexual and Reproductive Health: Knowledge, Attitude, and Perceptions among Young Unmarried Male Residents of Delhi.
6. Sushanta K. Banerjee, Kathryn L. Andersen, Janardan Warvadekar, Paramita Aich, Amit Rawat & Bimla Upadhyay (2015); How prepared are young, rural women in India to address their sexual and reproductive health needs? A cross-sectional assessment of youth in Jharkhand.

7. Sharad D. Iyengar, Kirti Iyengar, and Vikram Gupta 2009; Maternal Health: A Case Study of Rajasthan, 27(2): 271–292.
8. Reproductive Health of Women Living In Slum: A Case Study of Gopanpally Slum, Hyderabad (2020);Volume -10 | Issue - 5 | ISSN No. 2249 - 555X.
9. Kranti S. Vora , Dileep V. Mavalankar , K.V. Ramani , Mudita Upadhyaya (2009); Maternal Health Situation in India: A Case Study.
10. Improving Access to Maternal Health Care in Rural Communities

# Solution ?

Photo credit: Shraddha

CHAPTER XXIX

# Problems Faced by Women in Modern India

Sumera Yaseen
Research Scholar
Institute of Home Science, University of Kashmir
Sumiyaseen9858@gmail.com

**Introduction**

Women plays a vital role in the overall development of any society. Women has a much stronger role than man because she has to take care not only of herself but of the whole family like daughter, grand-daughter, sister, daughter-in-law, wife, mother, mother-in-law, grand-mother etc. Earlier in India, women faced issues like child marriage, Sati Pratha, ban on widow marriage, exploitation of widows, devadasi system, etc. However, almost all such old practices have almost vanished. But that doesn't mean an end to the challenges women face. Violence against women is caused by ineffective legal justice system, weak legal principles and male dominated social and political structures. Research have shown that violence against women begins at home in the early age especially in the rural areas by the family members, relatives, neighbors, and friends. On the other hand, they have found themselves oppressed and subjugated by the men in patriarchal society. Violence against women can be domestic or public, physical, emotional or mental. Women have a fear of violence that prevents them from full participation in many areas of life (Wani, 2020). Another common problem for women is gender based discrimination which they face from birth and continues till death. Illiteracy, lack of proper education, responsibility for household chores, rape, sexual harassment at workplace, etc. are some of the major problems for women in India. However, there have been many positive changes in the status of women as the number of educated people in the country is increasing.

**Methodology**

The present study is based on secondary source of data. The data is gathered from different journals, reports and other sources wherever found necessary.

In Indian society, women generally face various issues and problems (Agnihotri and Malipatil, 2018). Some of the problems are mentioned below:

**Domestic violence:**

Women are being subjected to various forms of violence almost every day which is disrupting the society. Due to increasing crimes against women, women are being subjected to massive violence on daily basis. According to the women and child development official, it is like a local and widespread disease that affects about 70% of Indian women. This is done by the husband's relative or other family member. Women may experience violence within the family (dowry related harassment, death, marital rape, wife-battering, sexual abuse, deprivation of healthy food, female genital mutilation, etc.) or outside the family (kidnapping, rape, murder, etc.) (Khanam, 2016).

**Dowry deaths:**

On an average, one women dies every hour in the country due to dowry. The burning death of Indian women have often been attributed to dowry disputes. In dowry-related deaths, the groom's family commits murder or suicide. The Dowry Prohibition Act, passed in India in 1961, prohibits the application, payment or acceptance of dowry, "as a consideration for marriage", where "dowry" is defined as a gift demanded or given as a precondition for a marriage (Bhawana, 2014).

**Sexual harassment at the workplace:**

Today, almost all working women are sexually harassed, regardless of their status, personal characteristics or job type. When they go to file complaint, they face sexual harassment in transport, at work places, in educational institutes and hospitals, at home and even in police stations. It is shocking that the law protectors are violating and outraging modesty of women. Most women focus on poor service jobs while men are in apposition of immediate surveillance, which allows them to exploit their female subordinates (Bharati, et.al,).

**Women trafficking:**

Indian constitution prohibits all forms of trafficking under Article 23. It has been observed that poor families and tribal societies have become the biggest targets of smugglers. Trafficking has become a major humanitarian problem throughout human society. Trafficking in its broadest sense involves the exploitation of girls by pushing them into practices such as prostitution, forced labor or services, or slavery and the trade in human organs. In the case of children who have been trafficked or have been victims of child marriage, it violates the right to education, employment and self-determination (Kumar, 2016).

**Conclusion**

Violence against women in its various forms is a violation of human rights, the nature of which deprives women of their ability to enjoy fundamental freedoms. Violence against women is hidden in a culture of silence. It is suggested that violence against women, regardless of discrimination should be a matter of serious concern in itself, and be addressed directly as violation of human rights. The legislature has enacted various laws in the interest of women. Women are the present and future of India. But today in the world of 21st century, women have gained an incredible position in every field and their life style has improved, they are not inferior to men in any way. Despite the formation of various effective rules and regulations by the Government of India to curb and control crimes against women, the number and frequency of crimes against women are increasing day by day. The status of women in the country has been more aggressive and alarming in the last few years.

**Reference:**

1. Wani, I. (2020). Women in India: Issues and challenges. *Kashmir observer.*
2. Agnihotri, R.R and Malipatil, (2018). A brief study on women problems in India. *International journal of development research.* 8 (8), 22583-22587.
3. Khanam, K. (2016). Problems of women in modern India. *International journal of* Interdisciplinary *research in Science Society and Culture.* 2 (1), 310-322.
4. Bhawana, D., and Neetu, S. (2014). Crime against women and societal ills: An overview. *International Journal of Advanced Scientific and Technical Research.* 4 (3), 44-56.
5. Barati, A., Arab, R.O. Masoumi, S.S., (). Challenges and Problems faced by Women workers in India. *Chronicle of the Neville Wadia Institute of Management Studies and Research.* 76-82.
6. Kumar, V.V. (2016). Violation of Human Rights in India – A Review. *International Journal of Commerce and Law.* 3 (1), 20-31.

CHAPTER XXX

# Empowerment of Women for buying Packaged Food

*Madhu Chauhan and **Dr. Garima Babel
*Ph.D. Scholar Faculty of Home Science, MLSU
**Associate professor Department of Home Science P. G. Girls College, B.N University, Udaipur
rathoremadhu2@rediffmail.com

**Abstract**

In the present era consumer is the king when the predominance of people in a particular group feels one way or another about a product, service, entity, person, product or entity in positive or negative ways. Urban women are most powerful consumers in the world as they control almost 80 percent of the household spending. This chapter is the study of how women consumer buys, what they buy, when they buy and why they buy "Packaged food". The Packaged food is trending area where buying is significantly visible, targeting the consumers and thus influencing their purchasing behavior. The women consumer purchase various packaged food for their basic needs in order to sustain life.The aim of this paper was to explore and understand women consumer empowerment of perceptions for buying behavior and awareness of packaged food. Keywords: Consumer, Awareness, Packaged food, Occupation, Buying.

**Introduction**

A healthy lifestyle is an important trend shaping business actions today, while packaged food on the other hand influences the purchase behavior of consumers. Following trends is imperative in today's competitive business environment. One trend that companies are increasingly interested in is a healthy lifestyle. Packaged food is an everyday necessity, very often purchased instinctively, without too much thought and processing. The Indian packaged food market registered double-digit constant value growth in 2016, in line with its performance over 2011-2016 as a whole. Rice, pasta and noodles was the only category to register faster constant value growth during the year, as it recovered from the impact of the controversy surrounding the discovery of MSG and lead in Nestlé's market-leading noodles brand, Maggi in 2015. The purchase decision is made directly, in front of the shelf, when the customer is in contact with the product. Marketing literature (Kotler & Keller, 2006) recognizes packaging and the information available on the packaging as an important element of products. Generally, food is prepared depending on the habits, tastes, social status, economic factor, availability, traditions, habitats, etc., of the people of that region. They are very popular in the Western Region of the world. Even India is being influenced by these packaged foods. This chapter is useful to create empowerment of women consumers about the packaged food. It's essential for consumers' attitude towards packaged food and their knowledge about health problems arising due to use of packaged food. It also gives information about knowledge and attitude towards use and buying information regarding packaged food. It's helpful in obtaining consumer information about the practices and the services which empower them and make them aware of their rights and responsibilities and help to ensure their welfare. I hope that this content is helpful for the awareness of the consumer and will influence a sense of rightness and responsibility towards buying packaged food. It is necessary for protection and empowerment of innocent consumers and educating them for safeguarding themselves from unscrupulous and frequent practices of the buying packaged food.

**MAIN REASON FOR POPULARITY OF PACKAGED FOOD:**

1. Emergence of Industrial society (i.e., metropolitan cities) – Development of the metropolitanCities due to increase in population, emergence of industries, evolution of various new factors, time factor, etc., created the need for instant foods in the market.

2. Reduced domestic servants – Due to industrialization, the labour category is getting attracted to it because of better emoluments and hence there is a shortage of home maids-servants. Due to this, the housewives in order to save time started using instant foods.

**3.** Women folk taking to job- As the literacy rate is increasing among women, a large number of them in our country are taking up jobs to setup their own status in the society and to use the extra income generated. These are creating the need for ready-to-eat foods.

**4.** Emergence of nuclear families- Earlier times, a single family consisted of many people i.e., a group of several nuclear families were living in a single place. Hence larger quantities of the food used to be prepared together. But as joint families started disappearing due to various reasons, each single family started using these instant foods in order to save time and energy.

**5.** Prices of raw materials- These forms one of the major factors for the use of instant foods in the present world. As the prices of some of the raw materials are continuously increasing, the purchases of these foods are more economical.

**6.** New products- As there are different new products coming up in the markets daily that are very cheap and easy for using and preparing, the popularity of instant foods is increasing.

**7.** Drudgery of work- In order to award the heavy laborious work like grinding manually and other drudging works, people opt for instant foods, which are easy to prepare and eat.

**8.** Convenience- Instant foods are convenient to prepare and are economical. This increased its usage by the people as it saves the time, energy and money.

**9.** Increasing income- Due to establishments of multi-national companies in India, the lady of the house also started working, because of which there is no time to prepare food at home. Hence this created the need to opt for instant foods.

**10.** Standard of living- The standard of living is also changing due to raise in income level, influence of western countries, more global trade, traveling etc., Hence, people are changing their taste to instant foods more compared to the old traditionally prepared foods.

**11.** Media- In the modern era, the media, particularly electronic and print media, are playing an important role in creating awareness of the products manufactured and released in the market.

The above factors are responsible for the popularity of instant food products in Indian market. The marketer should see to it that the instant food is available to the consumers without any difficulty at competitive rates. The products should be provided to consumers by keeping in mind as when they want, where they want and the manner in which they want. These methods help in increasing the sales of the product with good feedback from the Customers and creating a niche for instant foods in the market. Though there are so many instant foods available in the market, their popularity is increasing in a slow pace, especially in the rural markets, due to lack of awareness compared to larger cities where they are widely available and also more popular.

**CONSUMER GUIDANCE AND PROTECTION**

**Which is needed to protect from**

- Illiteracy
- Poverty
- Unfamiliarity with product features
- Inadequate supply of goods and services
- Monopoly and monopolistic competition
- Cheating by sellers
- Misleading advertisements
- Weak law enforcing network

**CONSUMER PROTECTION ACT 1986**

It is an important landmark in the history of consumer protection legislation in India. This act was passed to provide for better protection to consumers. It applies to all goods and extends to the whole India except Jammu and Kashmir. It applies not only to the private sector but also to the public sector and government agencies.

**OBJECTIVE OF THIS ACT**

- To provide for better protection to the interest of the consumers.
- To promote and protect consumers right.
- To promote for the establishment of a machinery for the speedy settlement of consumer disputes. Consumer protection council and consumer dispute Redressed Agencies have been set up under this act to safeguard the interest of the consumer

**IMPORTANT CONSUMER LEGISLATIONS IN INDIA:**

**CONSUMER PROTECTION ACT** -1986: this act was passed to provide for better protection to consumer.

**AGRICULTURE PRODUCES (grading and marking act, 1937):** This was set up by the Directorate of marketing and Inspection of the Government of India to cover various quality levels of agricultural commodities. The quality of cereals, spices, oils, butter, ghee, pulses, eggs, honey, etc. are defined in this act. It also provides for categorization of commodities into various grades depending on the degree of purity in each case.

**STANDARD WEIGHTS AND MEASURES (Packed commodities) Rules 1977:** this rule is applicable to the whole of India and to commodities packed for sale /distribution / delivery.

**DRUG CONTROL ACT:** It is related to the consumption; of intoxicating drinks and drug s except for medical purposes the drug includes all medicines for internal and external use in the diagnosis, treatment, mitigation or prevention of disease in human beings or animals.

**THE PREVENTION OF FOOD ADULTERATION ACT, 1954:** The P.F.A. lays down minimum standard requirements for all categories of food. According to the P.F.A. the term adulteration is the art of mixing something impure with something pure or genuine or one. All kinds of adulteration whether prohibited. The P.F.A. protects the consumers and ensures that punishments are given to offenders

**ESSENTIAL COMMODITIES ACT-1955:** This act is related to control and check inflationary trends and to ensure equitable distribution of essential commodities. To have an effective check and control over false trade mark, false trade descriptions and misleading advertisement, the Trade and Merchandise marks act, 1958 was exacted.

**THE HOUSEHOLD ELECTRICAL APPLIENCES:** (Quality control order, 1976) - To protect the consumer and ensure that the appliances in the market are safe, the government introduced the H.E.A. The specified standard is "I.S.I. STANDARD" for the H.E.A. I.S.I. standards serve as a guide for production of goods. I.S.I gives licenses to manufactures, which produce goods according to Indian standards and I.S.I mark is put on their goods.

**THE MONOPOLIES AND RESTRICTIVE TRADE PRACTICES COMMISSION:** The M.R.T.P. Act was passed in 1969. Any consumer organization having a membership of at least 25 consumers or individual may make trade practice now the jurisdiction of the commission is so widened as to include the following trade practices are false representation with regard to quality of goods. Misleading advertisement and. offering of gift prizes and other items not with the intention of promoting sales. Hoarding or refused to sell goods.

**CONSUMER PROTECTION AGAINST WHOM**

- Restoring the high pricing
- Adulteration
- Businessmen selling substandard goods.
- Black marketing
- Short weighing.

**GOVERNMENT AND CONSUMER PROTECTION**

The government adopts several measures some indirect to protect the consumer for example:

- Fixing of pricing.
- Ensuring people distribution and control of goods in the market.
- Educating people and making necessary information available.
- During emergency enforcing the rationing and price control.

- Banning certain commodities that are detrimental to the physical and moral health of the people.
- Ensuring labels on various packed commodities
- Encouraging research and development.

## GUIDELINES TO WOMEN CONSUMER FOR WISE BUYING TOWARDS PACKAGED FOOD

- Buying is an art; we should spend our hard, earned money very carefully.
- These days the manufacturers and dealers have learnt the art of sailing. They sell sub standard good by befouling the consumers.
- They spend a lot on advertisement beautiful packing the same thing is made available in different designs and colors.
- The shop keepers and agents are given lucrative commission to influence the consumers in various ways. The consumer in this way is made to buy the substandard commodities that they do not there by endangering their family economy.
- One should pre-decide the quantity and number of goods to be purchased. Only necessary items should be included in the list of shopping.
- Things should not be bought in a hurry, because it does not give an opportunity of comparing different commodities. Buying at leisure provide satisfaction and save money too.
- A consumer should ask about the quality, price etc. fearlessly before buying. Things should be purchased from price or cooperative stores.
- Things should not be purchased for their beautiful and attractive packing. One should listen to the shopkeeper but should not be influenced by his rhetoric.
- One should examine the brand, label, standard mark and date of Expiry before buying all these shows the worthiness of the goods.
- At the time of purchasing due attention be given to W.M.Consumer should always take the bill. The bill should show the name of items, measurement, weights, date, price, code no., if any. This is the consumer for legal redress.
- They should not be misguided by deceptive advertisement. The expenditure on advertisement is also added to the price. Attractive advertisement does not always signify the worthiness of the commodity shown.

## CONCLUSION

The present paper is an effort to evaluate the consumer awareness and buying behavior of consumer empowerment of women towards packaged food. In the modern days, where the life is at fast pace time has become very valuable to every person & hence "Packaged Foods" play an important role in everyone's day-to-day life. Also, the food habits in India have changed due to the Western influence and the usage of these foods is on the rise. A number of laws and regulations encourage and enforce the protection of consumer rights - to information, choice, safety, to be heard, to consumer education, and to services for empowering of women consumer. The aim of this paper was to explore and understand women consumer empowerment perceptions for buying behavior and awareness of packaged food.

**Reference:**

**1.** Usha V.& Vijaykumar H.S. 2007, A study on buying behavior of consumers towards Instant Food Products in Kolar District M.BA. (In Agriculture Management) Thesis, Univ. Agri. Sci. Dharwad.

**2.** Kotler, P. & Keller, K. L. (2006). *Marketing management, 12th edition*. New Jersey: Pearson Higher Education.

**3.** www. Article.mercola.com

**4.** www.shodhganga.inflibnet.ac.in

CHAPTER XXXI

# Domestic Violence: A Public Issue

Tejvendra Singh Yadav
ShriRam college of pharmacy,
Banmore, Morena (M.P.)

यत्र नार्यस्तु पूज्यन्ते रमन्ते तत्र दवेताः |
यत्रैतास्तु न पूज्यन्ते सर्वास्तत्राफलाः क्रियाः ||

*(मनुस्मृता अध्याय 3, श्लोक 56)*

India is a country where women are considered as goddess but still, they are suffering from several women related issue like domestic violence, rape, dowry, harassment etc. Women are still not safe in our society.

The nature of domestic violence, its cause and its prevalence must be fully understood in order to plan effective prevention and intervention strategies. We should examine not only the determinants and consequences of violence but also relevant economics, social and culture factors. Most of the current Indian literature focuses primarily on the linkage between the socialization of women into subordinate position, male patriarchal and domestic violence. However, these explanations do not provide an understanding of how violence seeps into certain relationship or why husbands abuse their wife's perpetuation of physical crime, verbal abuse and mental torture of women pervade in every society whether developed, undeveloped or urban. Several legal provision have been made by government to contain this socio- psycho problem of domestic violence. Domestic violence act, 2005 (PWDV ACT, 2005) has been made. As per the data of national crime records bureau (NCRB), about 84% of women had experienced physical violence in one form or the other like beating, slapping, pushing and kicking, burning with rod and hurling injurious objects, assaulted with weapons.

Let's, understand the nature of domestic violence with the true story from a small village Antroli of Kheda district, Gujarat. A woman got victim of domestic violence due to child marriage and orthodox mentality of society.

**The case:**

The survivor belongs to a middle-class family who likes to visit different places and spent time with her friends. She has friendly nature and easily mixes with people. She was also talkative and cooperative. She used to help other in their work. Her family's main source of income is farming. They have a small house and a little land from which they earn their livelihood. She has one younger brother. She belongs to a joint family in which she lives with parents, grandparents, siblings. She also belongs to a Brahmins community. In her (survivor) in laws house, husband works as a labour in private sector and her father-in-law work as a farmer. Her husband has only one younger brother and he belongs to nuclear family. Her marital relation is not working properly because her husband is in habit of drinking. Her husband drinks on regular basis and if she or his family tries to stop him than he threatened to commit suicide. He used to beat, slap and push his wife after drinking. He doses physical abuse (hitting, slapping, pushing and beating with objects), emotional abuse (verbal abuse, threatening to commit suicide) and economical abuse (not providing money for basic needs also). He shows disagreement in all her interests and desires. Survivor tolerated this for two years and later she decided to leave her husband's house and want an independent life. Now she become self-cantered and doesn't like to interact and communicate others without any work. Most of the time she wants to be left alone and if someone asks about her husband, tears come into her eyes. The survivor did not file any complain against her husband due to the society. In beginning, she hasn't taken any initiative to solve her problem but after she got counselling and advise from a CRP member of kaira social service society (KSSS) Ahmedabad, Gujarat her decision changed. In starting, she was not ready to meet counsellor and haven't discuss anything. As she got isolated and thought that her life will be like this only and she can't do anything about it. She almost lost social interactions, after certain iteration with counsellor, she told her story to him. During interview, when counsellor asked about the human rights and especially about women's rights to survivor, she said that she don't have any ideas about these rights. She simply told that the girls of this society have to obey their parents and the society. The survivor was not aware about domestic violence act, 2005. But she knows the term "*gharelu hinsa*" i.e., she knows that if husband or in laws harass any married girl than it can we called as domestic violence but she was not aware about the types and its details. Now after counselling, she is overcoming from depression and isolation.

In this case the survivor has faced domestic violence for two years because she thought that the so-called reputation of her parents in the society will be destroyed and she was not aware about her rights. Most of women lost their identity and some women also lost their lives after suffering from these problems and same happen in this case also. And there are many women who don't file complain against their husband for sake of children, who are still studying in school, and they are vulnerable to abuse from abusive husband/in-laws. They are forced to submit to the conditions of violence.

**The causes of domestic violence:**

In this case the main cause of domestic violence is the alcoholism. But this is not the only reason for domestic violence. The major factor behind the violent behaviour of men is the patriarchal attitude which perceives women as an object and gives her a low status in the society. There are also other reasons which are included. Dowry system (indicating dangers of domestic violence, if falling short on dowry expectation) orthodox society is another reason which prevents women from walking out of the violent relationship e.g. '*pativrata nari*' is considered ideal in Indian society. Other reasons may include lack of support, lack of awareness, poverty, alcoholism, unemployment etc.

**Legal remedies to prevent domestic violence:**

There are two main government measures which can help in prevention of domestic violence.

1. Criminal offence: In 1983, domestic violence was recognised as a specific criminal offence by the introduction of section 498A into the Indian penal code (IPC). This section deals with cruelty by a husband or his family towards a married woman.
2. Protection of women from domestic violence Act, 2005: protection of women from domestic violence Act, 2005 ensures that reporting of case of domestic violence against women to a protection officer. The Act was to make justice available to women who may not always want criminal proceedings.

**The conclusion:**

The cases of domestic violence are increasing day by day even after the enactment of several laws for the protection of women. Global research indicates that one in every three women has been the victim of emotional, physical or sexual violence in their homes. In this case the survivor has faced domestic violence for two years because she thought that the reputation of her parents in the society will destroy. And even though justice has been served but the question remains, where is a woman really safe, if she's not safe even at times inside her own home. We as a society has to change because it is society that breaks the laws. There has to be a cultural change, a change in mind-set across all demographic of society. Because it is not an indivisible problem. It is a human right issue and we all are human beings. And nobody has the right to treat a human being different than they would like to be treated "themselves".

**REFERENCE:**


1. http://en.wikipedia.org/wiki/Protection_of_Women_from_DomesticViolence_Act 2005
2. http://www.youthkiawaaz.com/2010/02/ddomestic-violen and in-india-causes-consequences-and-remedies-2/
3. Laws against domestic violence :Underused or Abused? By Madhu Kishwar
4. http://www.dvmen.org/dv.htm
5. http://www.pcvconline.org/
6. Violence Against Women in India: Evidence from Rural Gujarat" by Leela Visaria. Gujarat Institute of Development Studies. P. 14-25. In Domestic Violence in India: A Summary Report of Three Studies. International Center for Research on Women: Washington, DC, September, 1999.
7. Flavia, Agnes. 1990. "Violence in the family: Wife beating." In Rehana Ghadially, ed., Women in Indian Society: A Reader. Sage Publications.

8. Heise, L, J. Pitanguy, and A. Germaine. 1994. "Violence against Women--The Hidden Health Burden." World Bank Discussion Paper 255. Washington, D.C.: World Bank.
9. Jejeebhoy, Shireen. 1998. "Wife beating in rural India: A husband's right? Evidence from survey data." Economic and Political Weekly 33(15): 855-862.
10. Krishnaraj, Maithreyi, ed. 1991. Women and Violence--A Country Report: A Study Sponsored by UNESCO. Bombay : Research Center for Women's Studies, SNDT Women's University.
11. Mahajan, A. 1990. "Instigators of wife battering." In Sushama Sood, ed., Violence against Women. Jaipur: Arihant Publishers.
12. Miller, Barbara D. 1992. "Wife-beating in India: variations on a theme." In D. A. Counts, J. .K. Brown, and J.C. Campbell, Sanctions and Sanctuary: Cultural Perspectives on the Beating of Wives. Boulder: Westview Press.
13. Rao, Vijayendra. 1997. "Wife-beating in rural south India: A qualitative and econometric analysis." Social Science and Medicine 44(8): 1169-1180.

CHAPTER XXXII

# Work Force Participation: A Challenge

M K Ganeshan
Ph.D Research Scholar, Alagappa Institute of Management, School of Management
Dr. C. Vethirajan
Professor & Head, Department of Corporate Secretaryship, School of Management,
Alagappa University, Tamil Nadu
mkganeshanmba@gmail.com

**Introduction**

Change is a fact of human life. The importance of studying women's work force participation role in the day's society is more pertinent than ever because of the changing attitude in the society towards the same. Important among them are the changing value systems with the increase in literacy, in increase participation of women in politics, economy and popular movements. The prominent change in women's participation, which was previously restricted to the West, is now equally visible in India and other third-world countries.

Till recently women were treated on a different footing or pedestal, depriving them of their rights but with the changing times, the role of women has changed from child bearing and rearing to bread earner. Thus the new cultural milieu is making it inevitable for than to face the emerging reality in the contemporary Indian society.

The labour strength is made up of both working and without a job people. Work force participation rate is represents the number of people in the labor force as a percentage of the civilian non institutional population. In other words, the participation rate is the proportion of the population that is either employed or actively seeking employment. Increasing the number of working women has the potential to provide significant social and economic benefits around the world, but political and social norms, as well as actual laws, remain women out of the employees in various developing countries. Access to education, finance, and transportation can help increase their independence and labor-force participation. Female executives may also increase firm productivity. Cultural and social norms make it difficult for women to realize their full economic potential, and safety concerns limit their physical and economic mobility. Furthermore, gender inequities and a lack of enabling workplace conditions make it more difficult for women to actively participate in the labour market. The female labour force participation rate is the percentage of women aged 15 and up who are economically active. This includes both employed and unemployed individuals.

**The Role of Women in the Workforce**

Today, the median female workforce share in the world is 45.4 percent. (https://globalvolunteers.org/global-role-of-women). Women's formal and informal labour has the potential to transform a community from a relatively autonomous society to a participant in the national economy. Despite significant challenges, women's small businesses in rural developing communities can not only provide a lifeline for an extended family, but also form a networked economic foundation for future generations. In recent decades, the role of women in the urban and rural labour markets has grown exponentially. The theme for International Women's Day 2019 was chosen to identify innovative ways to advance gender equality and women's empowerment, accelerating the 2030 Agenda, and building momentum for the effective implementation of the new United Nations Sustainable Development Goals. Of fact, women's opportunities in the world still fall behind men's. However, women's historical and current roles are undeniable.

**Addressing the problem:** Girls and women might feel more autonomous and seek career and business opportunities if they have access to soft skills training and financing. Furthermore, transportation that reduces mobility constraints can enable girls and women to continue their education and work. It's also suggested that removing fundamental barriers to women being promoted to management roles could boost efficiency in garment companies.

**Increasing women's mobility encourages them to continue their education and participate in the labour force:** Three IGC studies have thoroughly evaluated the Bihar government's bicycle programme, which pays money to girls in grade 9 to purchase bicycles. According to studies, the programme reduced the gender gap in age-appropriate secondary school enrolment by 40%, resulting in a 32 percent rise in girls' secondary school enrollment and a dropout rate for females of less than 5%. According to another study, the programme appears to change both the girls' and their families' goals. Furthermore, despite the fact that existing female-only bus routes benefit their users significantly, they serve few women due to their relatively limited geographic coverage, limited schedules, and lack of advertising; the problems experienced by women when using public transportation were discovered.

**Soft skills can improve girls' and women's educational and health outcomes:** It is suggested that programmes that teach females communication and negotiation skills are well received by participants and may help them feel more in control of their lives and gain access to resources. Girls who received the negotiating treatment reported feeling less hungry, having more control over their futures, and having more pleasant interactions with others.

**Access to microfinance increases female participation in the labour market in the long run:** Greater access to microfinance loans resulted in a considerable increase in female labour force participation in India, with the effect being driven by self-employment rather than salaried jobs. While participating women were more likely to have the last say on household spending, this was not linked to a boost in their empowerment. The findings also show that higher access to microfinance reduces fertility in the long run as a result of increased labour force participation.

**Female managers could improve productivity in garment firms:** To provided training to female employees in garment factories and found female trainees to be as or more effective than the male trainees. Despite this finding, the promotion rate for the female trainees (55%) is significantly lower than that for male trainees (85%). There is a few evidence that female managers increase efficiency and reduce worker absenteeism, while male managers have lower rates of excellence defects.

## CHALLENGES OF WOMEN'S WORK FORCE PARTICIPATION

### Responsibility of Household Care

The most important of the women are already working as "household care providers". This degree may vary depending on one's economic, cultural, and social status, as well as the presence of familial support. As a result, whether women start a job or start their own business, their family responsibilities put them at a disadvantage compared to males. According to the Unpaid Care Work Paper (2014) by the Organization for Economic Cooperation and Development (OECD), Indian men spend only 36 minutes per day on unpaid care obligations, while women spend 360 minutes. Gender inequality in unpaid care work is also a missing link in the examination of gender differences in labour outcomes such as labour force participation, income, and job quality, according to the paper. Skilling work placing married women in hyper local jobs in cities (in the retail sector), found that despite matching other expectations like the quality of job, safety at workplace, near to home, salary expectation, the married women still prioritized domestic duties and were willing to work only on "specific hours" that do not hinder their daily routines. These household duties, which include various kinds of care and household work, cannot be unnoticed by the preponderance of women in Indian patriarchal society. According to the Economic Survey 2018-19, the share of women attending domestic responsibilities climbed from 46% in 2005 to 65% in 2018, in the age group of 30-59 years, when the majority of women are out of school and married.

Women's Labor Force Participation is a critical concept for women and Women Labour Force Participation Rate ( LFPR). Between 2005 and 2018, the LFPR fell by 20 percentage points.

Many studies present opposing views for this fall. The first viewpoint is upbeat, with the major reason being "increasing household income" as a result of more women seeking higher education. The second point of view is pessimistic, claiming that "a lack of quality occupations or self-employment prospects," in combination with low earnings, long commuting hours, work scheduling, migrations, and safety concerns, limit women's mobility and freedom, resulting in this drop. Why women's LFPR is declining is a difficult puzzle to solve, especially when opinions differ. It cannot, without a doubt, be linked to only one or two distinct causes. Using various economic, cultural, and social lenses to develop a holistic understanding of this multi-layered problem could aid in the development of better solutions and the implementation of necessary policy reforms. From 2005 to 2021, India's labour force participation rate averaged 50.60 percent, with a peak of 63.70 percent in the fourth quarter of 2005 and a low of 45.90 percent in the second quarter of 2020.

**Unable to Work "Extra" Hours**

For the first time, information on hours worked in various categories of paid work was collected in the Periodic Labour Force Survey (PLFS) 2017-18. In both urban and rural areas, men worked 7-8 hours more per week than women in the regular wage or salaried employee category. In the case of self-employment or casual work, the difference was greater than 11-12 hours. Employers or contractors may interpret this as a loss of "productivity" (despite the fact that women spend 10 times more time than men on a daily basis in unpaid care responsibilities at home), and they prefer hiring men over women if there is no relevant need that only women can do that task.

**Same Reasons, Different Impact**

In the last two decades of our skilling work, which focused on preparing youngsters for entry-level occupations, primarily in the service and healthcare sectors, we've discovered that the primary reasons for women quitting their jobs fall into two categories:

i. Personal: marriage, lack of family support, health issues, higher education, domestic duties
v. Job Related: office distance, work timing, difficulties in getting leaves etc. Though males have equal motivations for quitting (other than household chores), women have a greater impact on quitting than men due to their susceptible economic, cultural, and social status in society.

**Absence of Segmented Approach**

As we have several categories under self-employed and wage-employed, issues are varied for different segments of the female workforce. According to the Economic Survey 2019-20, women employers who hire workers (0.5%), own-account workers who do not hire workers on a regular basis (20%), and contributing unpaid family labourers (32%), fall under the self-employed category; regular wage & salaried workers (21%) and casual workers (32%) fall under the wage employed category (27 per cent). Aside from that, the third category is dependent contract workers, who work on a contract basis to produce or provide services (e.g. those who generally work on piece-rate basis). When it comes to raising women's LFPR, any one remedy or policy reform may not be sufficient. Rather than taking a blanket approach, we should think about each of these categories, understand their major concerns, and develop solutions that solve issues specific to that segment.

**Good Intention, Unintended Consequence**

As issues are different for different segments, even the two key recent reforms- one is Sexual Harassment of Women at Workplace Act-2013 and, another is Changes in Maternity Benefit Act-2017, brought with very good intention are not very effective and creating unintended consequences. Employers, for example, may view women as an additional cost if they opt for 24 weeks of maternity leave. Hiring men is preferred, especially in smaller organizations and for entry-level positions. Similarly, if the Sexual Harassment of Women at Workplace Act is not well disseminated within enterprises and implemented as a checklist agenda, it acts as a deterrent to integrating diversity into teams, and most managers are content to form an all-male team. In our working lives, most of us must have encountered similar biases.

**Lack of Major Reforms**

In India's case, enacting a Domestic Workers Act could be low-hanging fruit. which could have a direct impact on more than 4.5 million such workers (of which 65 per cent are women). According to the International Labour Organization (ILO), the number of domestic workers in India is underreported. Actual figures could range from 20 million to 80 million.

**Vocational and STEM Careers**

The notion that India's dropping women's participation rate is due to a growing number of women partaking in education, including higher education in Science, Technology, Engineering, and Math (STEM). According to the LFPR, the majority of these women want to attain good careers. However, India's Technical and Vocational Education and Training (TVET) system currently provides little possibilities for women to develop demand-driven skills. For example, women account for less than a quarter of total enrolments in ITIs, and their training completion rate is less than 5%. Women participants encounter additional problems, such as a lack of suitable hostel infrastructure, toilet facilities, the availability of female trainers, and the lack of women-friendly trades, in addition to the poor quality and outdated curriculum that impacts participants in these programmes. Although there are provisions for women-only ITIs (WITIs), the number of WITIs is quite small.

While India produces 43% of STEM graduates, just 14% of them work in scientific, engineering, and technology research institutes. "Gender stereotypes concerning STEM are widespread throughout the socialization process, during which girls learn and adopt gender roles," according to UNESCO's groundbreaking report, Cracking the Code: Girls' and Women's Education in STEM. Women's STEM schooling achievements and aspirations for STEM careers are influenced by a lack of self-efficacy (confidence in one's competence).

**Caste, Class and Religion**

Which highlights the findings of a unique longitudinal research conducted in Palanpur Local (Uttar Pradesh) for the past eight decades and sheds new light on women's role in the village economy? "With the exception of men leaving agriculture, which is a random factor." Due to the scarcity of suitable jobs, most women who enter the labour force fall into one of three categories:

- widowed women,
- suitable opportunities for women with some education, and
- Cases where the household's economic status changed."

The various pathways for women's engagement in the workforce are influenced by caste-based livelihood activities. Working is only permitted for women from higher castes if the jobs are "respectable." According to several researches, Muslim women have the lowest LFPR, and Hindu women from the advanced castes have the lowest LFPR. The widely cited obstacle to women entering the labour force is the increasing household income effect, or a shift in class.

**When Jobs are Scarce**

According to a Pew Research Centre survey conducted in India in 2012, 84 percent of respondents agreed that "when employment is limited, men should have more right to a job than women." According to the National Sample Survey Office (NSSO), the CODVID-19 shutdown has had an impact on India's unemployment rate, which has reached a four-decade high of 6.1 percent. This is certain to have a severe impact on women LFPR.

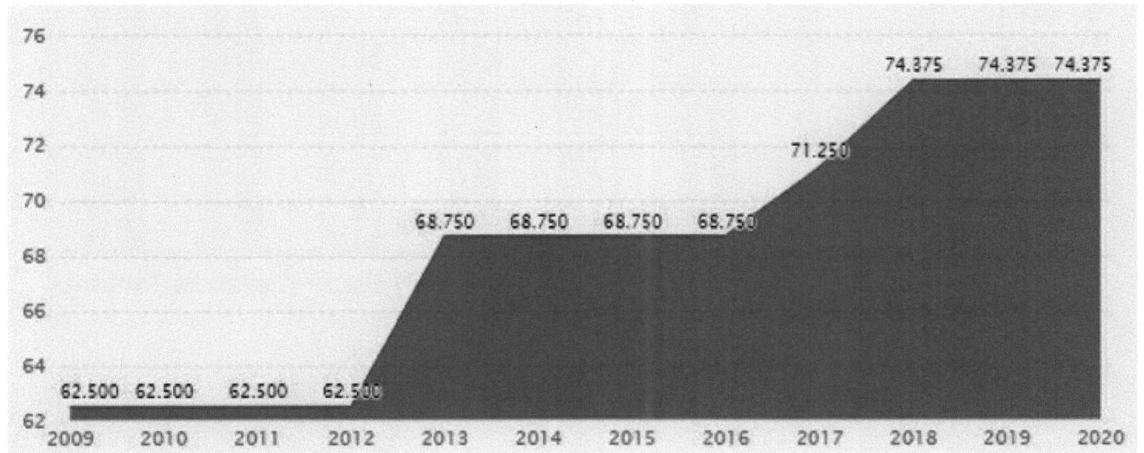


**Figure 1: Women Business and the Law Index Score: scale 1-100 from 1970 to 2020**

Source:www.ceicdata.com- world Bank

| LAST | PREVIOUS | MIN | MAX | UNIT | FREQUENCY | RANGE |
|---|---|---|---|---|---|---|
| 74.375<br>2020 | 74.375<br>2019 | 51.875<br>1987 | 74.375<br>2020 | NA | yearly | 1970 - 2020 |

**Figure 2: Women Business and the Law Index Score: scale 1-100 from 1970 to 2020**

Source: www.ceicdata.com- World Bank

In 2020, India's Women Business and Law Index Score were 74.375 on a scale of 1-100. This remained unchanged from the previous year's figure of 74.375. India in: Women Business and the Law Index Score: scale 1-100 data is updated yearly, with 51 observations averaging 60.000 from December 1970 to 2020. The data peaked at 74.375 in 2020 and peaked at 51.875 in 1987, with a high of 74.375 in 2020 and a low of 51.875 in 1987. The data for India IN: Women Business and the Law Index Score: scale 1-100 is still active in CEIC and is reported by the World Bank. The information is classed as India - Table IN the Global Database. The World Bank is a global financial institution. WDI stands for "Policy and Institutions." The index assesses the impact of laws and regulations on women's economic prospects. The average score of each of the eight sections (going places, starting a job, getting paid, getting married, having children, running a business, managing assets, and getting a Pension) is used to generate the overall score, with 100 being the greatest attainable score. Women, Business, and the Law (World Bank). Instead of using the reporting years used by WBL (https://wbl.worldbank.org/), the WDI and Gender Databases use the data coverage years for the reference period. For example, WBL data for YR2020 (report year) correlates to WDI and Gender Databases data for YR2019.

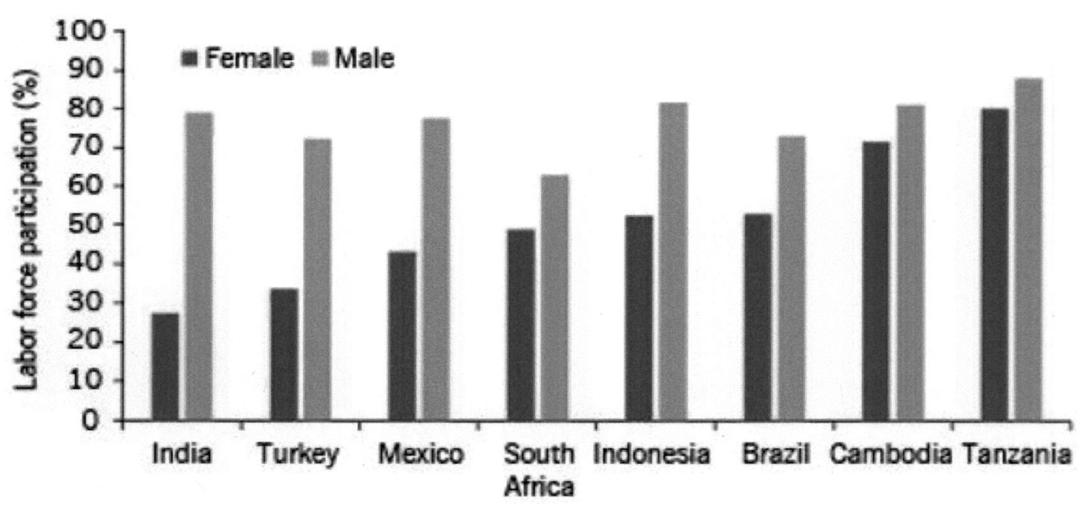


**Figure 3: Gender disparities in work force Participation**

Source: ILO statistical database

**Pros:**

- Female labour force participation is a critical driver (and result) of growth and development.
- Women work in developing countries to alleviate poverty and as a coping mechanism in the face of adversity.

- Women's participation is the result of a variety of economic and social factors. Access to high-quality education (beyond secondary school) is critical to improving women's employment outcomes.

**Cons:**

- Even when gender disparities in participation rates are small, women earn less than men and are more likely to work in low-wage jobs, such as domestic labour.
- Education raises the reservation wage and women's expectations, but it must be matched by job creation.
- Due to the prevalence of underreporting, data on women's participation rates do not accurately reflect women's work.

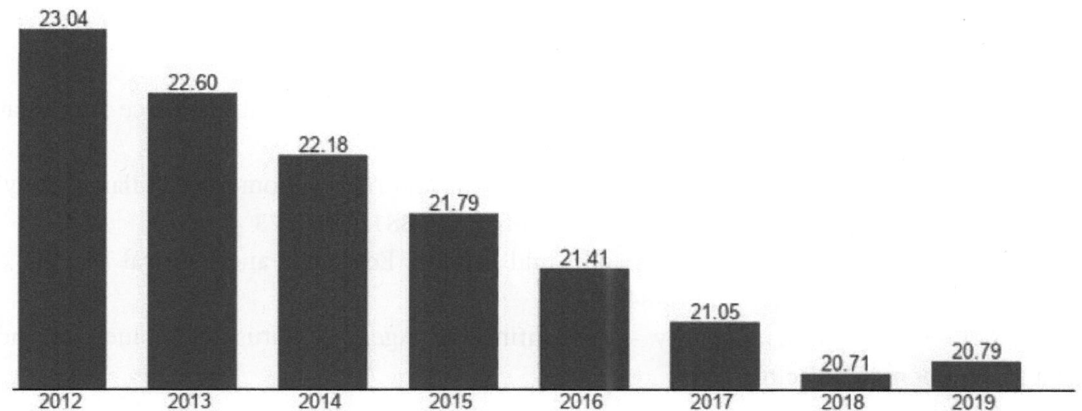


**Figure 4: Female labor force participation rate, 2012 - 2019**

Source: www.theglobaleconomy.com/India/Female_labor_force_participation

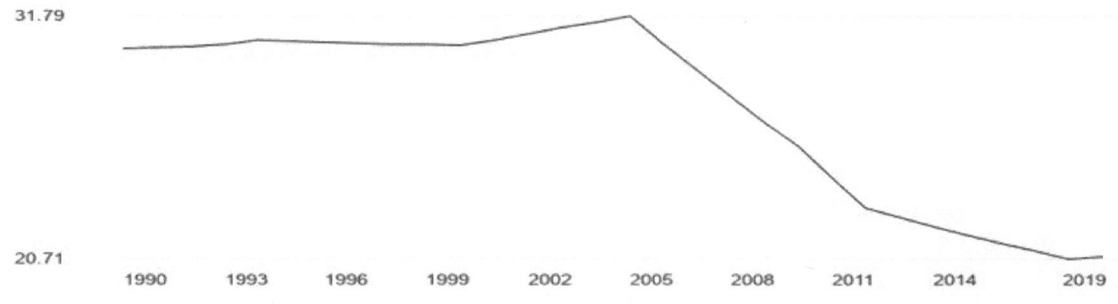


**Figure 5: Female labor force participation rate, 1990 - 2019**

Source: www.theglobaleconomy.com/India/Female_labor_force_participation

India: Female labor force participation rate, 1990 - 2019: For that indicator, we provide data for India from 1990 to 2019. During that time, India's average value was 27.66 percent, with a low of 20.71 percent in 2018. In 2005, the highest percentage was 31.79 percent. The latest value from 2019 is 20.79 percent.

**Impact of COVID-19**

The recent UN policy brief: According to the Impact of COVID-19 on Women, "the impacts of COVID-19 have exacerbated for women and girls simply by virtue of their dender". The key takeaway was that women were always identified as the most vulnerable group, including single mothers, widows, and disabled women. Subarna, a working mother from Mumbai, has started an online petition called #ChoresHaveNoGender, which highlights how unequal distribution of unpaid household work was a harsh blow to women across India during the lockdown. The strain on existing supply and demand for various paid jobs, primarily as a result of reverse migration, is also clearly visible.

**Conclusion**

Today we see women in all walks of life but there are several more that are very far away from the forces of modernization. They are cut off from the rest of society. Because of religious constraints that they blindly accept as a result of ignorance. How much longer can this continue? A citizen of a free India cannot rely solely on government funds. No national perspective plan can help women unless they themselves decide to take their life in their hands. A small but steady start would be to become aware of societal processes. Electronic media has taken up the role of disseminating knowledge in today's world where skills and information are obtained via the internet from the comfort of one's own home or office. The key to women's development is with women themselves, when all women's endeavors to walk the path of development the nation will progress in no time at all.

**Reference:**

1. Bloom, D.E., Canning, D., Fink, G. and Finlay, J.E. (2007). 'Fertility, Female Labour Force Participation, and the Demographic Dividend' NBER Working Paper – 13583.
2. Chakrapani, C., and Vijaya Kumar, S. (1994). 'Changing status and role of women in Indian society'. 1st Edition, Publisher: M.D. Publications, ISBN 10: 8185880271 / ISBN 13: 9788185880273
3. Dev, S.M. (2004). 'Female Work Participation and Child Labour'. Economic and Political Weekly. 39(07), ISSN (Print) - 0012-9976 | ISSN (Online) - 2349-8846
4. Gopalan, Sarala. (2002). Towards Equality - the Unfinished Agenda. Status of Women in India. National Commission for Women: New Delhi.
5. Kewal, Krishan. (2019).Changing role of women in Indian Society. Scholarly Research Journal for Humanity Science & English Language, 7(36), 9561-9565, (O) ISSN 2348-3083
6. Mazumdar, S. and Guruswamy, M. (2006). 'Female Labour Force Participation in Kerala: Problems and Prospects' International Institute for Population Sciences (IIPS), Mumbai – India
7. Neera Desai and Maithreyi Krishna Raj (1987). 'Women and Society in India'. Ajanta Books: New Delhi
8. Sher, Verick. and Ruchika, Chaudhary. (2014). Women's labour force participation in India: Why is it so low? ILO Decent Work Team for South Asia-Snapshot of women's labour market trends in India and South Asia. ILO Asia-Pacific working paper series, ISSN 2227-4391; 2227-4405
9. Sethi, Raj Mohini. (1976). Modernization of working women in developing societies. New Delhi: National Pub. House
10. Shivani, Sehgal. (2012), Status of a woman in Indian society, International Journal of Research Review in Engineering Science and Technology (IJRREST), 1(1), 74-76 ISSN 2278- 6643.
11. Srivastava, N. and Srivastava, R. (2010). 'Women, Work and Employment Outcomes in Rural India', Economic and Political Weekly 45(28), 49-63
12. https://tradingeconomics.com.
13. https://www.ceicdata.com/en/indicator/india/labour-force-participation-rate
14. https://data.worldbank.org/indicator/SL.TLF.CACT.FE.ZS?locations=IN
15. https://globalvolunteers.org/global-role-of-women/

CHAPTER XXXIII

# Challenges in Women Entrepreneurship: A Study based on Rural Area of Punjab

Rajwinder Kaur
Research Scholar, University School of Business
Chandigarh University, Punjab
bimbrarajwinder@gmail.com

**Abstract**

Entrepreneurship is an important aspect for the growth and development of the country. It is important for implementing skills and knowledge and getting output. Entrepreneurship helps in increasing production in the country and contributes to the economic activities of the country. Women entrepreneurship is one of the essential aspects in entrepreneurship as in women entrepreneurship women put in effort and operate the enterprise. It also helps to reduce gender gap from society and encourage women empowerment. Though women entrepreneurship is very much beneficial for the economy, women face several challenges in it. So, this paper is an attempt to explore entrepreneurship and challenges faced by rural women. The study uses primary and secondary data to generate results. It also highlights various suggestions to overcome the challenges in women entrepreneurship.

Keywords: Challenges, Economic, Entrepreneurship, Rural, Women.

## 1. INTRODUCTION

Entrepreneurship is an important economic activity not only for individuals but for providing employment opportunities to others also. Among youth it is becoming a more interesting opportunity for their career and employment. Apart from this, entrepreneurship also plays a great role in the development of economy and economic growth. In recent times this topic has gained attention and people are more attracted towards this phenomenon. Moreover, for developing countries like India it is a need of the hour, to make India self-reliant and strong from an economic point of view. Entrepreneurship should be encouraged as much as possible.

With all such important considerations it is also necessary that entrepreneurs should have required knowledge and skills to build a strong foundation so that others and the economy can be benefited from this. Passion, creativity, vision, dedication, ability and self confidence etc are the qualities of entrepreneurs. Without passion and vision no one can get success in this field because this aspect needs a lot of hard work and dedication. But after success it provides fruitful results for individuals as well as for society.

In the main highlights of the self-reliant movement it is specifically mentioned that the government has plans to privatize public sector enterprises. This is a big opportunity in front of the coming entrepreneurs to show their passion and contribute to the economy in terms of making India self-reliant. To support entrepreneurship in India, the government also provides assistance to young entrepreneurs for their support and success. Various schemes are established by the Indian government and state governments to support entrepreneurs. For the assistance of students as entrepreneurs, educational institutions also provide financial and other help so that people can benefit and contribute to the economy. For the growth and development of the entrepreneurs in India apart from the government, banks also provide financial assistance to people. RBI provides many loans and other schemes for the benefit of entrepreneurs. Risk taking is an integral part of any entrepreneurial activity which can never be fully removed and repaired so it directly or indirectly affects the self-efficiency of people.

Women entrepreneurship is one where women come forward and operate entrepreneurship businesses. In rural India women are not encouraged to come forward so it is a good way to prove that women are not lacking behind. Indian women have a long path to go to take their rights as Indian women do not have rights as the men have. Still Indian society is male dominated and all the important decisions of life are taken by men only. Thus, women entrepreneurship is a good way for women to come forward and break all evil traditions of society where women are considered less than men.

## 2. LITERATURE REVIEW

In today's world women entrepreneurship is essential for the social and economic growth of the country. It not only contributes to the economic activities of the country but is also helpful to raise the standard of living and helpful in removing gender inequality from the society (Mehta, 2013; Johar, 2015). Despite many social and economic difficulties Indian women come a long way and still have a very long journey. There are many reasons for women to opt for entrepreneurship in India. But the progress of women entrepreneurship is very slow as compared to other countries (Goyal and Parkash, 2011).

Women entrepreneurship is key for the development in the economy (Vasan, 2016).Many researchers explored that there are many skills required for women entrepreneurship. Women entrepreneurship also plays a great role in women empowerment (Mantok, 2016). Factors which are responsible for women empowerment in women entrepreneurship are economic status, confidence and worth etc. Self help groups are a very good option for empowering women and making them capable of standing for their rights (Nachimuthu and Gunatharan, 2012).

Many factors influence women entrepreneurship like fund support, social support and financial support. These factors are important for establishing a business as well (Guled and Kaplan, 2018). Although women entrepreneurship is good for the economy and society but there are many challenges which are faced by women in operating any kind of business. There is need to implement policies and procedures with honesty so that barriers from this field can be removed (Rani and Sinha, 2016; Veena and Nagaraja, 2014). Many researchers feel that women entrepreneurship contribute majorly to the economy of any region. Study of Morocco shows that access to the market-place is the big challenge for women entrepreneurship (Bouzekraoui and Ferhane, 2017).

There are many examples where women entrepreneurship is performing better in every term. There are some examples from Gujarat where women entrepreneurship and innovation are developing in a better way (Bulsara, Chandwani and Gandhi, 2014). Under globalization women entrepreneurship faced many other challenges as the political system of every country is different and it affects each and every activity in the country (Kumari, 2012).

### 2.1 Gaps in the Study:

The study is based on exploring the women entrepreneurship challenges. Most of the past studies are done on the basis of secondary data taken from secondary sources. The present study is based on exploring women entrepreneurship challenges faced by rural women by personally meeting them. Extensive challenges are explored based on the opinion of rural women in the selected area of Punjab. Earlier studies are limited only for a few challenges but the present study presents all the possible challenges faced by rural women entrepreneurship.

## 3. OBJECTIVES OF THE STUDY

The present study fulfills following objectives:

- To extensively explore the challenges faced by rural women entrepreneurship.
- To suggest ways and means through which the challenges faced by rural women entrepreneurship can be reduced to some extent.

## 4. RESEARCH METHODOLOGY

The present study is based on primary and secondary data sources. Primary data includes interviews of 30 women involved in entrepreneurship business of any kind. Interviews were conducted face to face by meeting rural women and through telephone. All 30 samples are randomly selected for collection of data. The area for sample selection was rural areas of Punjab and different districts of Punjab. Data was collected from 3 districts; namely Ropar, Mohali and Ludhiana. 10 individuals were selected from each district.

Primary data for the study is collected in interview form. Following are some of the questions asked during interview:

1. Are you involved in entrepreneurship business?
2. What are the prime challenges faced by you as a woman while doing this business?

3. What are your suggestions to overcome these challenges?

The study also used secondary data. Many secondary sources were explored like research papers, articles on women entrepreneurship, websites and internet etc. for the purpose of this study. Some databases were also used for the study, which includes Google Scholar, ResearchGate and EBSCO Host etc.

**5. ANALYSIS AND INTERPRETATION**

Following are the various challenges in rural women entrepreneurship:

**Lack of Financial Resources:** The big and foremost challenge faced by rural women entrepreneurs is lack of financial resources. Due to scarcity of financial resources women entrepreneurs are not able to meet their daily expenses and their production gets affected. The lack of funds and their availability becomes a big challenge for them and they are even not able to bring essential things which are required for the production.

**Lack of Support from Family:** In India still women are considered less as compared to men. So when any woman starts any kind of entrepreneurial business then she needs a lot of support from family. But sometimes due to traditional value systems women are not supported by their families and they lack behind. For establishment of any work family support is essential so that women get encouraged and feel motivated.

**Lack of Infrastructure Facilities:** In rural areas due to lack of available funds women entrepreneurs face the challenge of lack of infrastructural facilities. Proper infrastructure facilities are very essential to keep raw material and finish products safe. But poor storage space and lack of infrastructure facilities creates big problems for them.

**Lack of Knowledge and Skills:** For doing any type of business, skills and knowledge are extremely important things. Without skill and knowledge of the particular field no one can run a business smoothly. So when it comes to women entrepreneurs then it is clear that due to lack of skill and knowledge women are not able to make the entrepreneurship business to a certain reach. They are not aware about the current trends of the market.

**Fear of Investing Money in Business:** As due to uncertainty and risk in every type of business rural women entrepreneurs have fear of investing money in business. First they are lacking in appropriate funds and then they have fear of investing those funds in the business. Due to lack of funds in the business they face more challenges to maintain the business.

**Lack of Marketing Facilities:** Proper marketing of products is the most important thing to earn profits from any business. But in the business of rural women entrepreneurship there are a lack of marketing channels to sell the product to appropriate consumers. Due to this, rural women entrepreneurs are not able to generate much profit.

**Lack of Skilled Laborers:** Skilled labor is one which is specialized in making products. But skilled labor is very hard to find. If they have skill then they demand more money but entrepreneurs are not able to pay huge amounts to skilled labor. Lack of skilled labor is also a cause of low quality of products and not being able to maintain standard of products.

**Unable to Maintain Quality of Products:** Every time a customer wants high quality products at minimal cost. But rural entrepreneurial businesses are not able to make quality products at cheaper cost. This becomes a big challenge for them when quality of product is not maintained at reasonable costs.

**Power Failure:** Another big challenge is frequent power failure in rural areas and they have no backup plan for that. In today's time electricity is used everywhere and without the help of power no activity is possible. Power delays are also a big cause of work delays due to which extra cost is borne by entrepreneurs and they are not able to maintain business expenses.

**Negative Attitude of Society:** In Indian society today also working women in rural areas have a negative image. When it comes to owning a business then the Indian society is not able to accept that and this becomes a huge hurdle in the path of their success. Negative attitude of society demotivates and distracts women from their real goals.

**High Cost of Operations:** As rural areas are established far from the places where all the essential things are available. So reaching urban areas and collecting raw material and then selling finished products in the urban areas becomes too expensive for a rural women entrepreneur. High cost of operations is not able to generate appropriate returns to the entrepreneur.

**Mobility Constraints:** As rural women always have mobility constraints and they have to take care of family and children etc. Even they have no helper for household work so each and every activity is managed by themselves only. With all these activities and responsibility they have challenges in moving from one place to another.

## 6. WAYS AND MEANS THROUGH WHICH THE CHALLENGES FACED BY RURAL WOMEN ENTREPRENEURSHIP CAN BE REDUCED TO SOME EXTENT

All the rural women entrepreneurial challenges can be reduced by adopting some of the following measures:

**Creation of Finance Pools:** By creating finance pools or pools of funds by rural women can help them at the time of scarcity of funds. Women can also make a few savings every month and start a scheme where they can invest and get return back whenever they require. Women of rural areas can also invest in self-help groups so that timely funds can be generated at the time of requirement.

**Help from Cooperative Societies:** Cooperative societies are made for the help of rural area people and they provide money to people at the time of requirement. The cooperative societies also provide funds to needy people at very cheaper interest rates. These societies themselves work for no profit and no loss aspect.

**Training Programs:** Training and development programs are helpful for providing business related knowledge to the people. Through training programs people listen to each other and share their problems and trainers also provide solutions to their problems. They also teach ways and means to establish business and run a business smoothly.

**Assistance from Government:** Through the positive initiatives of government rural women entrepreneurship can perform better and contribute to the economy. Government needs to make such plans so that more and more women take initiatives to produce on their own.

**Establishment of Women Help Centers:** Women help centers are for helping women and they are also established by women themselves to help each other. Like women help centers, other initiatives can also be beneficial for women to establish their own business.

**Need to make Balance between Personal & Professional Life:** The most important thing is to make balance in every part of life. It is always essential to have balance in the personal and professional life of women otherwise things deteriorate more and more. It is also helpful to maintain business activities smoothly, without any hurdles.

## 7. CONCLUSION

Women entrepreneurship is a good initiative from each and every point like social and economic. Rural women entrepreneurship is one of the ways to generate and earn income by involving in economic activity. But rural women entrepreneurship is not as easy as it seems. Women face many challenges and hurdles in the entrepreneurial journey. Many social, financial and personal challenges are there which restricts women to move forward. But if a woman is passionate and ready to accept all the challenges then she can get big success in this journey. Many challenges and hurdles can be removed just by taking a few positive steps to move forward towards the successful journey.

## REFERENCE:


1. Bouzekraoui, H., & Ferhane, D. (2017). An Exploratory Study of Women's Entrepreneurship in Morocco. *Journal of Entrepreneurship: Research & Practice,* 2017, 1-19.
2. Bulsara, H. P., & Chandwani, J., & Gandhi, S. (2003). Women Entrepreneurship and Innovation in India: An Exploratory Study. *International Journal of Innovation, 2(1),* 32-44.
3. Goyal, M., & Parkash, J. (2011). Women Entrepreneurship in India-Problems and Prospects. *International Journal of Multidisciplinary Research,* 1(5), 195-207.
4. Guled, N. S., & Kaplan, B. (2018). Factors Influencing Women Entrepreneurs' Business Success in Somalia. *Research in Business and Management,* 5(1), 13-24.
5. Johar, S. (2015). A study on the Development of Women Entrepreneurship in Ghaziabad, UP, India. *International Journal of Applied and Pure Science and Agriculture,* 1(12), 75-80.
6. Kumari, S. (2012). Challenges and Opportunities for Women Entrepreneurship in India under Globalization. *IOSR Journal of Business and Management,* 5(2), 29-35.
7. Mantok, S. (2016). Role of Women Entrepreneurship in Promoting Women Empowerment. *International Journal of Management and Applied Science,* 2(10), 48-51.

8. Mehta, P. (2013). Women Entrepreneurship: Purpose, Problems & Prospects: A Study of Udaipur District. *Pacific Business Review International,* 5(11), 8-16.
9. Nachimuthu, G. S., & Gunatharan, B. (2012). Empowering Women through Entrepreneurship: A study in Tamil Nadu, India. *International Journal of Trade, Economics and Finance,* 3(2), 143-147.
10. Rani, J., & Sinha, S. K. (2016). Barriers Facing Women Entrepreneurs in Rural India: A Study in Haryana. *Amity Journal of Entrepreneurship,* 1(1), 86-100.
11. Vasan, M. (2016). Problems and Prospects of Women Entrepreneurs in India. *Shanlax International Journal of Management,* 3(1), 312-315.
12. Veena, M., & Nagaraja, N. (2014). A Study on Problems Faced by Women Entrepreneurs in Mysore District. *International Journal of Engineering and Management Research,* 4(1), 45-50.

CHAPTER XXXIV

# Education

Aditi Bhardwaj[1], Vinay Jain[2], Abhishek Jain[3],
Pankaj Sharma[4], Bhavna Sharma[5]
[1]Department of Computer Science [2]Department of Pharmacognosy [3]Department of Mechanical Engineering
[4]Department of Pharmaceutics [5]Department of Engineering Chemistry
ShriRam Institute of Information Technology, Morena, (M.P.), India
aditibhardwaj026@gmail.com

**Abstract:**

In Indian society, women still have to face a lot of problems, it is often seen that if a man is educated then he can educate himself but if a woman is educated then her whole family is educated. We have seen that women play an important role not only in the development of their families but also in the development of the country through education. In Indian society, women have to face a lot of problems, which are as follows: child marriage, Violence, Poverty and many more. If a woman is educated then she will use her right against all these troubles and can easily overcome all these things. If a woman is educated then she is able to decide what is right and what is wrong on her basis, she can take her own decision. Not only does she develop herself, but she also develops her family, her society, her country. In the field of education, we should pay attention to some such points by which we can increase the education of girls. We can make the people around us aware about the education of girls and we can explain all these things to the people by campaigning, by explaining to the people of different types of advertisements. Girls can walk shoulder to shoulder with boys and there can be a sense of equality among them and this effect is possible only on the basis of education.

**Introduction:**

There are so many problems which is faced by women in Indian society like physical and mental health problems, lack of education, improper health facilities, gender discrimination, unequal rights, dowry related problems [1]. All of us need to understand that an educated women play an important role in our society. With the help of education women achieve their goal at top positions in each and every field. If we look into the history so many discussions and debates are related to the issue of women education. Education and employment as a means of income generation became indicators of women's involvement in the development process, but again under this phase a large chunk of rural women were left behind. Education is the key point of women empowerment when women is educated and earn money she invests in their children, household etc. thus, enhancing family wealth. In so many rural area women are uneducated due to which they lag behind in many ways [2]. The parameters of women empowerment are:

- Building a positive self-image and self-confidence.
- Developing the ability to think critically.
- Building group connection and encouraging decision making.
- Provide all means for economic independence.
- Verifying equal participation in the process of bringing about social changes [3].

Research by the World Bank and other organizations shows that by increasing the education in girl increase the wages and leads to quick economic growth than educating only boys.

**What is the current ratio of women's education in the world?**

In the United States in 2020, around 91.3 percent of women had passed high school or had obtained a higher educational degree. The Indian government has committed regarding education for all; however, India still has a very low female literacy rate in Asia. In 1991, less than 40 percent of the 330 million women aged 7 years and above were literate, which means that there are over 200 million illiterate women in India today [4].

**The Challenges faced by the women:** - According to UNESCO estimates, around the world, 129 million girls are out of school, including 32 million of primary school age, and 97 million of secondary school age. Globally, primary, and secondary school enrollment rates are getting closer to equal for girls and boys (90% male, 89% female). But while enrollment rates are similar – in fact, two-thirds of all countries have reached gender parity in primary enrollment– completion rates for girls are lower in low-income countries where 63% of female primary school students complete primary school, compared to 67% of male primary school students. In low-income countries, secondary school completion rates for girls also continue to lag, with only 36% of girls completing lower secondary school compared to 44% of boys. Similarly, if we look at the high secondary completion rate in low-income countries, a very disproportionate ratio was found, which is 26% of young men and 21% of young women [5].

**Poverty:** - Poverty is the most important factor that decided whether a girl can complete her education or not. Studies consistently confirm that girls who faced many disadvantages such as low family income, living in poor or under-served places or who have disability or belong to a minority ethnic-linguistic group are at the forefront of access and completion of education [5].

**Child Marriage:** - Child marriage is also a very big problem in our society. In India about 40% of girls have child marriage. Girls who marry at young age are more likely to drop out of school while those girls who marry at the right age are capable of their own. They are more likely to have children at a young age and have faced high level of violence by their partner. It affects their children's education, lifecycle and health as well as their ability to earn. Eliminating this practice will increase the expected educational achievement of women and also increase their potential income. The report estimates that ending child marriage could result in at least more than US$500 billion a year [6].

**Violence:** -Violence in today's time is a huge negative point that prevents girls from moving forward; Family members prevent girls from accessing and completing education, often girls are forced to travel long distances to go to school. They are prone to the risk of violence which can be experienced in many schools. Recent statics estimate that every year around 60 million girls are harassed while attending school, often with serious consequences on their mental or physical health. This results in low attendance of girls and high dropout rate.

**Covid 19:** - Covid-19 is having a huge negative impact on the education of today's children, especially Covid19 has had a negative impact on the health and well-being of girls and many are getting threatened that they can't return to school even after reopening. As girls stay at home due to the closure of schools, their household chores and household responsibilities increases, as a result of which girls spend more time helping at home rather than studying. In the time of pandemic, the prevalence of domestic violence against women and girls has also increased significantly endangering their health security and overall well-being [7].

There are some points which if we apply, then there will be a great impact on the education of girls and their education will increase.

1. **Removal of difficulties and obstacles in studies and schooling:** -We have to make girls understand the importance of education. Explain the facilities available to girls such as scholarships, stipends etc. as well as eliminate the long distance and lack of security by building schools. Teaching self-defense to girls telling how they can fight themselves. To make girls understand the importance of education, to understand how much difference they can bring in their lives and in the society. For this we can run community awareness campaigns involving social workers, local community leaders so that girls understand the importance of education and complete their education to make themselves capable [8].

1. **Promoting Safe Schools:**- To make school safe, we have to create a safe and inclusive learning environment for which we need to rebuild schools. To help girls with sanitation facilities and menstrual hygiene management, for which we have to make girls aware of how can they maintain hygiene? [9].

We should observe our school classroom and ourselves and also we have to find ways to let everyone in the school community know that school is a safe place and a safe place for girls to pursue their schooling. Harassment often occurs in schools wherein students often maintain silence, they do not tell anyone about the prejudice, harassment or bullying that they experience and often believe that nobody will help them and it may make things worse. We must make sure that the society and we all stand for all students or we stand for those who suffer from this kind of harassment. We must make sure that we will fight for them against them we should do some such propaganda so that the children can open up about every small and big thing happening against them, their parents, their teachers or any adult. We have to inculcate openness in children so that adults can be open to share their problems [10].

3. **Improve Education Quality:** -Women have an important role in the development of society, along with taking care of their family, women also take the society forward a lot. I firmly believe that education is a major factor for their development. To increase the quality of education, we should invest in the professional development of teachers, at the same time we should select those teachers who give proper education to the children, apart from this we should provide the learning and teaching material to every school so they can give a good education to the students.[11]

**Some young female entrepreneurs in India who are making a mark:**

1. **Kiran Mazumdar Shaw:** - She was born on 23rd March 1953 in Bengaluru, Karnataka, India. She started her journey in 1978 from his garage in India. Indian business woman, Chairman and Managing Director of Biocon India Group since 1978. Kiran Mazumdar Shaw has many degrees to her name [12].

2. **Falguni Nayar:**- Falguni Nayar belong to Gujrati family. She is born on 19th February 1963. She has done her Bachelor and Master degree in management. She has a command on Hindi, Gujrati, English and also French language. She started her professional career in Kotak Mahindra group and she work around 19 years in that group. In her professional experience Falguni Nayar not only worked in India in fact she has an experience of work out of India also. In 2012 Falguni Nayar established her business which is famous all over India which is known by the Brand name "Nykaa". It provides all its products in online and offline mode both all over the India and as well as outside the country [12].

3. **Shahnaz Husain:** - Shahnaz Husain was educated at St. Mary's Convent inter college, Prayagraj, India. She is the chairwoman of The Shahnaz Husain Group. She is the first Muslim women entrepreneur in India who started her journey in the field of Indian skincare brand. She has franchise all over India, she has grown up her business and also with that she provided employment to many people. She was awarded the "World's Greatest Woman Entrepreneur" by Success Magazine in 1996 and she was awarded "Padma Shri" by the Indian Government in 2006. Today, Shahnaz Husain is also known as the 'Queen of Herbal Beauty Care' and a beauty icon internationally [13].

4. **Vandana Luthra:** - Vandana Luthra the owner of VLCC. In the area of cosmetics field VLCC is the famous and unique brand. Vandana Luthra has completed her studies in nutrition and cosmetology from Germany and she established her company name as VLCC in 1989 with her first VLCC center in Safdarjung Enclave in New Delhi. Vandana Luthra's mother was an Ayurvedic doctor. She got inspiration from her mother, She received "Padma Shri" by Government of India. Vandana Luthra went on to define the country's wellness industry with VLCC's tremendous success. One of the top women entrepreneurs in India, she is a recipient of several awards and accolades such as Padma Shri (2013) by the Government of India, Women Entrepreneur of the Year Award (2010) by The Enterprise Asia, etc. [14].

5. **Aditi Gupta:** -Aditi Guptais an engineering graduate and completed her graduation from National Institute of Design. She was born in Garhwa, Jharkhand, India. Their aim is to educate and make people aware about menstruation. The story began when Aditi herself attained puberty. There are many misconceptions about

menstruation in the society or in the minds of many people. When girls enter in their puberty, at that time they do not have any information about menstruation. How can they handle that thing, how can they take care of their hygiene? To solve all these problems, Aditi Gupta invented Menstrupedia Comic so that girls can read it and know everything about Menstruation. She wanted to educate people about these things. Aditi Gupta is an emerging face, a prominent face not only in her area but in all over India on the strength of her education. In 2014 she was included in the list of Forbes India under 30 [15].

6. **Radhika Ghai Aggarwal:** -Radhika Ghai Aggarwal had done her post-graduation degree in the field of advertising and public relation and also, have MBA from Washington University in St. Louis USA. She founded the online marketplace, shopclues.com with her partners Mr. Sanjay Sethi and Mr. Sandeep Agarwal in 2011. She is the first woman from India to have entered in the Unicorn Club. In 2016, she won the woman entrepreneur of the year award in Entrepreneur India Awards and CEO of the year award in CEO India awards. Radhika has made her name not only within the country but also around the world won so many awards [15].

**Education is a very good tool to end violence against women: -**

Lack of education leads to negative consequences throughout the life of women. An uneducated girl cannot take decision of her family on her own. A child bride has to face health related problems and psychological distress. An educated girl is more capable in managing assets and her finances and also, she has chances to access credits. An educated girl is not educated in herself, but she educates her family, her society, and the people around her as well. [16]

**Conclusion:** Education is the basic right of every individual, so we should provide education to every girl so that not only she become capable in herself but will also be able to illuminate the name of her society. There are many problems for girls such as Domestic Violence, Illiteracy, Child bride, Discrimination between boys and girls in society and so on. In the era of education, girls have not only gone all over the world but today's girl has also gone to space and in today's era, girls are not less than boys, we should make sure that we should provide education to every girl.

**Reference:**

1. Malhotra S, Shah R. Women and mental health in India: An overview. Indian journal of psychiatry. 2015 Jul;57 (Suppl 2): S 205.

2. Bhat RA. Role of Education in the Empowement of Women in India. Journal of Education and Practice. 2015;6(10):188-91.

3. Leary MR. Interpersonal aspects of optimal self-esteem and the authentic self. Psychological Inquiry. 2003 Jan 1;14(1):52-4.

4. Educational Statistics at a Glance: 2014 (http://mhrd.gov.in/sites/upload_files/mhrd/files/statistics/EAG2014_0.pdf). Last access March 15, 2022.

5. Girls education overview. https://www.worldbank.org/en/topic/girlseducation#1. Last access March 15, 2022.

6. Malhotra A, Elnakib S. 20 years of the evidence base on what works to prevent child marriage: A systematic review. Journal of Adolescent Health. 2021 May 1;68(5):847-62.

7. C.L. Forte, M. Plesons, M. Branson, V. Chandra-Mouli

What can the global movement to end child marriage learn from the implementation of other multi-sectoral initiatives? BMJ Glob Health, 4 (2019), p. e001739

8. S. Lee-Rife, A. Malhotra, A. Warner, A.M. Glinski **What works to prevent child marriage: A review of the evidence** Stud Fam Plann, 43 (2012), pp. 287-303

9. M. Steinhaus, L. Hinson, A.T. Rizzo, A. Gregowski **Measuring social norms related to child marriage among adult decision-makers of young girls in Phalombe and Thyolo, Malawi** J Adolesc Health, 64 (2019), pp. S37-S44

10. L. Stark, I. Seff, K. Asghar, *et al.* **Building caregivers' emotional, parental and social support skills to prevent violence against adolescent girls: Findings from a cluster randomised controlled trial in Democratic Republic of Congo** BMJ Glob Health, 3 (2018), p. e000824.

11. Pande R, Kurz K, Walia S, MacQuarrie K, Jain S, Eckman A, Jain A, Kambou SD, Bartel D, Crownover J (2011). Improving the reproductive health of married and unmarried youth in India.

12. R. Jensen. Do labor market opportunities affect young women's work and family decisions? Experimental evidence from India Q J Econ, 127 (2012), pp. 753-792.

13. D.D. Hallfors, H. Cho, S. Rusakaniko, *et al.* The impact of school subsidies on HIV-related outcomes among adolescent female orphans J Adolesc Health, 56 (2015), pp. 79-84

14. P. Nanda, N. Datta, P. Das, *et al.* Making change with cash? Impact of a conditional cash transfer program on age of marriage in India (2016)

15. S. Baird, E. Chirwa, C. McIntosh, B. Özler. The short-term impacts of a schooling conditional cash transfer program on the sexual behavior of young women. Health Econ, 19 (2010), pp. 55-68

16. A. Raj, L. McDougal, J.G. Silverman, M.L.A. Rusch. Cross-Sectional time series analysis of associations between education and girl child marriage in Bangladesh, India, Nepal and Pakistan, 1991-2011 PLoS One [Internet], 9 (2014), p. e106210

# Where there's a Will there's a Way

Photo credit: Shraddha

# The End !

***Hope you enjoyed reading this book. You can contact us and share your valuable suggestions at yochalenz@gmail.com***

**Thanks for supporting us !**

Printed by Libri Plureos GmbH in Hamburg,
Germany

9 798887 725666